History of the
19th Army Corps

History of the 19th Army Corps
of the Union Army During the American Civil War

Richard B. Irwin

History of the 19th Army Corps of the Union Army During the American Civil War
by Richard B. Irwin

First published in 1892 under the title
History of the Nineteenth Army Corps

Leonaur is an imprint of Oakpast Ltd

Material original to this edition and
presentation of text in this form
copyright © 2009 Oakpast Ltd

ISBN: 978-1-84677-894-0 (hardcover)
ISBN: 978-1-84677-893-3 (softcover)

http://www.leonaur.com

Publisher's Notes

The views expressed in this book are not necessarily
those of the publisher.

Contents

Introductory	9
New Orleans	11
The First Attempt on Vicksburg	21
Baton Rouge	34
La Fourche	44
Banks in Command	51
Organizing the Corps	61
More Ways Than One	65
Farragut Passes Port Hudson	69
The Teche	77
Bisland	84
Irish Bend	92
Opelousas	106
Banks and Grant	116
Alexandria	122
Back to Port Hudson	129
The Twenty-Seventh of May	137
The Fourteenth of June	153
Unvexed to the Sea	170
Harrowing La Fourche	189
In Summer Quarters	204
A Foothold in Texas	210
Winter Quarters	219
The Red River	223
Sabine Cross-Roads	237
Pleasant Hill	248

Grand Ecore	256
The Crossing of Cane River	260
The Dam	268
Last Days in Louisiana	274
On the Potomac	282
In the Shenandoah	292
The Opequon	300
Fisher's Hill	315
Cedar Creek	328
Victory and Home	349
Appendices	355

In loving remembrance of their late commander
Major-General William Hemsley Emory
and of the many comrades who laid down their lives in the service of their country, this history is inscribed by the surviving members of the Society of the Nineteenth Army Corps

Introductory

The history of the Nineteenth Army Corps, like that of by far the greater number of the organizations of like character, in which were arrayed the great armies of volunteers that took up arms to maintain the Union, is properly the history of all the troops that at any time belonged to the corps or served within its geographical limits.

To be complete, then, the narrative my comrades have asked me to write must go back to the earliest service of these troops, at a period before the corps itself was formally established, and must continue on past the time when the earlier territorial organization became merged or lost and the main body of the corps was sent into the Shenandoah, down to the peace, and the final muster of the last regiment.

If hitherto less known and thus less considered than the proud record of those great corps of the Armies of the Potomac, of the Tennessee, and of the Cumberland, on whom in the fortune of war fell the heat and burthen of so many pitched battles, whose colours bear the names of so many decisive victories, yet the story of the Nineteenth Army Corps is one whose simple facts suffice for all that need to told or claimed of valour, of achievement, of sacrifice, or of patient endurance. I shall, therefore, attempt neither eulogy nor apology, nor shall I feel called upon to undertake to criticise the actions or the failures of the living or the dead, save where such criticism may prove to be an essential part of the narrative. From the brows of other soldiers, no one of us could ever wish to pluck the wreaths so dearly won, so honourably worn; yet, since the laurel grows wild on every hill-side in this favoured land, we may without trespass be permitted to gather a single spray or two to decorate the sacred places where beneath the cypresses and the magnolias of the lowlands of Louisiana, or under the green turf among the mountains of Virginia, reposes all that was mortal of so many thousands of our brave and beloved comrades.

CHAPTER 1

New Orleans

The opening of the Mississippi and the capture of New Orleans formed important parts of the first comprehensive plan of campaign, conceived and proposed by Lieutenant-General Scott soon after the outbreak of the war. When McClellan was called to Washington to command the Army of the Potomac, one of his earliest communications to the President set forth in general terms his plans for the suppression of the Rebellion. Of these plans, also, the capture of New Orleans formed an integral and important part. Both Scott and McClellan contemplated a movement down the river by a strong column. However nothing had been done by either toward carrying out this project, when, in September, 1861, the Navy Department took up the idea of an attack on New Orleans from the sea.

At the time of the secession of Louisiana, New Orleans was not only the first city in wealth, population, and importance in the seceded States, but the sixth in all the Union. With a population of nearly 170,000 souls, she carried on an export trade larger than that of any other port in the country, and enjoyed a commerce in magnitude and profit second only to that of New York. The year just ended had witnessed the production of the largest crop of cotton ever grown in America, fully two fifths of which passed through the presses and paid toll to the factors of New Orleans. The receipts of cotton at this port for the year 1860-1861 were but little less than 2,000,000 bales, valued at nearly $100,000,000. Of sugar, mainly the production of the State of Louisiana, the receipts considerably exceeded 250,000 tons, valued at more than $25,000,000; the total receipts of products of all kinds amounted to nearly $200,000,000.

The exports were valued at nearly $110,000,000; the imports at nearly $23,000,000. It is doubtful if any other crop in any part of the world then paid profits at once so large and so uniform to all persons interested as the cotton and sugar of Louisiana. If cotton were not exactly king, as it was in those days the fashion to assert, there could be no doubt that cotton was a banker, and a generous banker for New Orleans. The factors of Carondelet Street grew rich upon the great profits that the planters of the "coast," as the shores of the river are called, paid them, almost without feeling it, while the planters came, nearly every winter, to New Orleans to pass the season and to spend, in a round of pleasure, at least a portion of the net proceeds of the account sales. In the transport of these products nearly two thousand sailing ships and steamers were engaged, and in the town itself or its suburb of Algiers, on the opposite bank, were to be found all the appliances and facilities necessary for the conduct of so extensive a commerce. These, especially the work-shops and factories, and the innumerable river and bayou steamers that thronged the levee, were destined to prove of the greatest military value, at first to the Confederacy, and later to the forces of the Union. For food and fuel, however, New Orleans was largely dependent upon the North and West. Finally, beside her importance as the guardian of the gates of the Mississippi, New Orleans had a direct military value as the basis of any operations destined for the control or defence of the Mississippi River.

About the middle of November the plan took definite shape, and on the 23rd of December Farragut received preparatory orders to take command of the West Gulf Squadron and the naval portion of the expedition destined for the reduction of New Orleans. Farragut received his final orders on the 20th of January, 1862, and immediately afterward hoisted his flag on the sloop-of-war *Hartford*.

The land portion of the expedition was placed under the command of Major-General Benjamin F. Butler. On the 10th and 12th of September, 1861, Butler had been authorized by the War Department to raise, organize, arm, uniform, and equip, in the New England States, such troops as he might judge fit for the purpose, to make an expedition along the eastern shore of Maryland and Virginia to Cape Charles; but early in November, before Butler's forces were quite ready, these objects were accomplished by a brigade under Lockwood, sent from Baltimore by Dix. On the 23rd of November the advance of Butler's expedition sailed from Portland, Maine, for Ship Island, in the steamer *Constitution*, and on the 2nd of December, in reporting the sailing, Butler submitted to the War Department his plan for invading the coast of Texas and the ultimate capture of New Orleans.

On the 24th of January, 1862, McClellan, then commanding all the armies of the United States, was called on by the Secretary of War to report whether the expedition proposed by General Butler should be prosecuted, abandoned, or modified, and in what manner. McClellan at once urged that the expedition be suspended. In his opinion, "not less than 30,000 men, and it is believed 50,000, would be required to insure success against New Orleans in a blow to be struck from the Gulf." This suggestion did not meet the approval of the government, now fully determined on the enterprise.

Brigadier-General J. G. Barnard, the chief engineer of the Army of the Potomac, an engineer also of more than common ability, energy, and experience, was now called into consultation. On the 28th of January, 1862, he submitted to the Navy Department a memorandum describing fully the defences of Forts Jackson and St. Philip and outlining a plan for a combined attempt on these works by the army and navy. The military force required for the purpose he estimated at 20,000 men.

Meanwhile the work of transferring Butler's forces by sea to Ship Island had been going on with vigour. He had raised thirteen regiments of infantry, ten batteries of light artillery, and three troops of cavalry, numbering in all about 13,600 men. To these were now added from the garrison of Baltimore three regiments, the 21st Indiana, 4th Wisconsin, and 6th Michigan, and the 2nd Massachusetts battery, thus increasing his force to 14,400 infantry, 275 cavalry, and 580 artillerists; in all, 15,255 officers and men.

On the 23rd of February, 1862, Butler received his final orders: "The object of your expedition," said McClellan—

> . . . . is one of vital importance—the capture of New Orleans. The route selected is up the Mississippi River, and the first obstacle to be encountered (perhaps the only one) is in the resistance offered by Forts St. Philip and Jackson. It is

expected that the navy can reduce these works. Should the navy fail to reduce the works, you will land your forces and siege-train, and endeavour to breach the works, silence their guns, and carry them by assault.

The next resistance will be near the English bend, where there are some earthen batteries. Here it may be necessary for you to land your troops to co-operate with the naval attack, although it is more than probable that the navy, unassisted, can accomplish the result. If these works are taken, the city of New Orleans necessarily falls.

After obtaining possession of New Orleans, the instructions went on to say, Butler was to reduce all the works guarding the approaches, to join with the navy in occupying Baton Rouge, and then to endeavour to open communication with the northern column by the Mississippi, always bearing in mind the necessity of occupying Jackson, as soon as this could safely be done. Mobile was to follow, then Pensacola and Galveston. By the time New Orleans should have fallen the government would probably reinforce his army sufficiently to accomplish all these objects.

On the same day a new military department was created called the Department of the Gulf, and Butler was assigned to the command. Its limits were to comprise all the coast of the Gulf of Mexico west of Pensacola harbour, and so much of the Gulf States as might be occupied by Butler's forces. Since the middle of October he had commanded the expeditionary forces, under the name of the Department of New England.

Arriving at Ship Island on the 20th of March, he formally assumed the command of the Department of the Gulf, announcing Major George C. Strong as Assistant Adjutant-General and Chief of Staff, Lieutenant Godfrey Weitzel as Chief Engineer, and Surgeon Thomas Hewson Bache as Medical Director. To these were afterward added Colonel John Wilson Shaffer as Chief Quartermaster, Colonel John W. Turner as Chief Commissary, and Captain George A. Kensel as Acting Assistant Inspector-General and Chief of Artillery.

By the end of March all the troops destined for the expedition had landed at Ship Island, with the exception of the 13th

Connecticut, 15th Maine, 7th and 8th Vermont regiments, 1st Vermont and 2nd Massachusetts batteries. Within the next fortnight all these troops joined the force except the 2nd Massachusetts battery, which being detained more than seven weeks at Fortress Monroe, and being nearly five weeks at sea, did not reach New Orleans until the 21st of May. Meanwhile, of the six Maine batteries, all except the 1st had been diverted to other fields of service.

While awaiting at Ship Island the completion of the preparations of the navy for the final attempt on the river forts, Butler proceeded to organize his command and to discipline and drill the troops composing it. Many of these were entirely without instruction in any of the details of service. On the 22nd of March, he divided his forces into three brigades of five or six regiments each, attaching to each brigade one or more batteries of artillery and a troop of cavalry. These brigades were commanded by Brigadier-Generals John W. Phelps and Thomas Williams, and Colonel George F. Shepley of the 12th Maine. When finally assembled the whole force reported about 13,500 officers and men for duty, and from that moment its strength was destined to undergo a steady diminution by the natural attrition of service, augmented, in this case, by climatic influences.

The fleet under Farragut consisted of seventeen vessels, mounting 154 guns. Four were screw-sloops, one a side-wheel steamer, three screw corvettes, and nine screw gunboats. Each of the gunboats carried one 11-inch smooth-bore gun, and one 30-pounder rifle; but neither of these could be used to fire at an enemy directly ahead, and, in the operations awaiting the fleet, it is within bounds to say that not more than one gun in four could be brought to bear at any given moment. With this fleet were twenty mortar-boats, under Porter, each carrying one 13-inch mortar, and six gunboats, assigned for the service of the mortar-boats and armed like the gunboats of the river fleet. Farragut, with the *Hartford*, had reached Ship Island on the 20th of February; the rest of the vessels assigned to his fleet soon followed. Then entering the delta, from that time he conducted the blockade of the river from the head of the passes.

The Confederacy was now being so closely pressed in every quarter as to make it impossible, with the forces at its command, to defend effectively and at the same moment every point menaced by the troops and fleets of the Union. Thus the force that might otherwise have been employed in defending New Orleans was, under the pressure of the emergency, so heavily drawn from to strengthen the army at Corinth, then engaged in resisting the southward advance of the combined armies of the Union under Halleck, as to leave New Orleans, and indeed all Louisiana, at the mercy of any enemy that should succeed in passing the river forts. At this time the entire land-force, under Major-General Mansfield Lovell, hardly exceeded 5,000 men. Of these, 1,100 occupied Forts Jackson and St. Philip, under the command of General Duncan; 1,200 held the Chalmette line, under General Martin L. Smith, and about 3,000, chiefly new levies, badly armed, were in New Orleans. Besides this small land-force, the floating defences consisted of four improvised vessels of the Confederate navy, two belonging to the State of Louisiana, and six others of what was called the Montgomery fleet. These were boats specially constructed for the defence of the river, but most of them had been sent up the river to Memphis to hold off Foote and Davis. The twelve vessels carried in all thirty-eight guns. Each of the boats of the river-fleet defence had its bows shod with iron and its engines protected with cotton. This was also the case with the two sea-going steamers belonging to the State. Of this flotilla the most powerful was the iron-clad *Louisiana*, whose armour was found strong enough to turn an 11-inch shell at short range, and, as her armament consisted of two 7-inch rifles, three 9-inch shell guns, four 18-inch shell guns, and seven 6-inch rifles, she might have proved a formidable foe had her engines been equal to their work.

At the Plaquemine Bend, twenty miles above the head of the passes and ninety below New Orleans, the engineers of the United States had constructed two permanent fortifications, designed to defend the entrance of the river against the foreign enemies of the Union. These formidable works had now to be passed or taken before New Orleans could be occupied. Fort St. Philip, on the left or north bank, was a work of brick and earth, flanked on either hand by a water battery. In the main work were mounted, in barbette, four 8-inch columbiads and one 24-pounder gun; the upper water battery carried sixteen 24-pounders, the lower one one 8-inch columbiad, one 7-inch rifle, six 42-pounders, nine 32-pounders, and four 24-pounders. Besides these, there were seven mortars, one of 13-inch calibre, five of 10-inch, and one of 8-inch. Forty-two of the guns could be brought to bear upon the fleet ascending the river.

Fort Jackson, on the south or left bank of the river, was a casemated pentagon of brick, mounting in the casemates fourteen 24-pounder guns, and ten 24-pounder howitzers, and in barbette in the upper tier two 10-inch columbiads, three 8-inch columbiads, one 7-inch rifle, six 42-pounders, fifteen 32-pounders, and eleven 24-pounders, in all sixty-two guns. The water battery below the main work was armed with one 10-inch columbiad, two 8-inch columbiads, and two rifled 32-pounders. Fifty of these pieces were available against the fleet, but of the whole armament of one hundred and nine guns, fifty-six were old 24-pounder smooth-bores.

The passage of the forts had been obstructed by a raft or chain anchored between them. The forts once overcome, no other defence remained to be encountered until English Turn was reached, where earthworks had been thrown up on both banks. Here at Chalmette, on the left bank, it was that, in 1815, Jackson, with his handful of raw levies, so signally defeated Wellington's veterans of the Peninsula, under the leadership of the fearless Pakenham.

Fort St. Philip stands about 700 yards higher up the river than Fort Jackson; the river at this point is about 800 yards wide, and the distance between the nearest salients of the main works is about 1,000 yards. A vessel attempting to run the gauntlet of the batteries would be under fire while passing over a distance of three and a half miles. The river was now high, and the banks, everywhere below the river level, and only protected from inundation by the levees, were overflowed. There was no standing room for an investing army; the lower guns were under water, and in the very forts the platforms were awash.

When the fleet was ready, Butler embarked eight regiments and three batteries under Phelps and Williams on transports, and, going to the head of the passes, held his troops in readiness to co-operate with the navy. On the 16th of April the fleet took up its position. The mortar-boats, or "bombers," as they began to be called, were anchored between 3,000 and 4,000 yards below Fort Jackson, upon which the attack was mainly to be directed. From the view of those in the fort, the boats that lay under the right bank were covered by trees. Those on the opposite side of the river were screened, after a fashion, by covering their hulls with reeds and willows, cut for the purpose.

On the 18th of April the bombardment began. It soon became evident that success was not to be attained in this way, and Farragut determined upon passing the forts with his fleet. Should he fail in reducing them by this movement, Butler was to land in the rear of Fort St. Philip, near Quarantine, and carry the works by storm. Accordingly, he remained with his transports below the forts, and waited for the hour. Shepley occupied Ship Island with the rest of the force.

Early in March the raft, formed of great cypress trees, forty feet long and fifty inches through, laid lengthwise in the river about three feet apart, anchored by heavy chains and strengthened by massive cross-timbers, had been partly carried away by the flood. To make good the damage, a number of large schooners had then been anchored in the gap. On the morning of the 21st of April this formidable obstruction was cleverly and in a most gallant manner broken through by the fleet.

On the night of the 23rd of April, Farragut moved to the attack. His fleet, organized in three divisions of eight, three, and six vessels respectively, was formed in line ahead. The first division was led by Captain Bailey, in the *Cayuga*, followed by the *Pensacola*, *Mississippi*, *Oneida*, *Varuna*, *Katahdin*, *Kineo*, and *Wissahickon*; the second division followed, composed of Farragut's flag-ship, the *Hartford*, Commander Richard Wainwright, the *Brooklyn*, and the *Richmond*; while the third division, forming the rear of the column, was led by Captain Bell, in the *Sciota*, followed by the *Iroquois*, *Kennebec*, *Pinola*, *Itasca*, and *Winona*.

At half-past two o'clock on the morning of the 24th of April the whole fleet was under way; a quarter of an hour later the batteries of Forts Jackson and St. Philip opened simultaneously upon the *Cayuga*. It was some time before the navy could reply, but soon every gun was in action. Beset by perils on every hand, the fleet pressed steadily up the river. The Confederate boats were destroyed, the fire-rafts were overcome, the gunners of the forts were driven from their guns, and when the sun rose Farragut was above the forts with the whole of his fleet, except the *Itasca*, *Winona*, and *Kennebec*, which put back disabled, and the *Varuna*, sunk by the Confederate gunboats. The next afternoon, having made short work of Chalmette, Farragut anchored off New Orleans, and held the town at his mercy.

The casualties were 37 killed and 147 wounded, in all 184. The Confederate loss was 50, 11 killed and 39 wounded. The *Louisiana*, *McCrea*, and *Defiance*, sole survivors of the Confederate fleet, escaping comparatively unhurt, took refuge under the walls of Fort St. Philip.

Leaving Phelps, with the 30th Massachusetts and 12th Connecticut and Manning's 4th Massachusetts battery, at the head of the passes, in order to be prepared to occupy the works immediately on their surrender, Butler hastened with the rest of his force to Sable Island in the rear of Fort St. Philip. When the transports came to anchor on the morning of the 26th, the Confederate flags on Forts St. Philip and Jackson were plainly visible to the men on board, while these, in their turn, were seen from the forts. Here the troops received the news of Farragut's arrival at New Orleans. On the morning of the 28th they saw the Confederate ram *Louisiana* blown up while floating past the forts, and on the same day Jones landed with the 26th Massachusetts and Paine with two companies of the 4th Wisconsin and a detachment of the 21st Indiana, to work their way through a small canal to Quarantine, six miles above Fort St. Philip, for the purpose of seizing the narrow strip by which the garrison must escape, if at all. This was only accomplished by a long and tiresome transport in boats, and finally by wading. However, at half-past two on the afternoon of the 28th April, the Confederate flags over Forts Jackson and St. Philip were observed to disappear; the national ensign floated in their stead; and soon it became known that Duncan had surrendered to Porter.

Porter immediately took possession and held it until Phelps came up the river to relieve him. Then Major Whittemore, of the 30th Massachusetts, with about two hundred men of his regiment, landed and took command at Fort St. Philip, while Manning occupied Fort Jackson. Almost simultaneously the frigate *Mississippi* came down the river, bringing Jones with the news that his regiment was at Quarantine, holding both banks of the river, and thus effectually sealing the last avenue of escape; for at this time the levee formed the only pathway. On the 29th Phelps put Deming in command of Fort Jackson, intending to leave his regiment, the 12th Connecticut, in garrison there, and to place Dudley, with the 30th Massachusetts, at Fort St. Philip; but before this arrangement could be carried out, orders came from Butler, designating the 26th Massachusetts as the garrison of the two forts, with Jones in command. Phelps, with his force, was directed to New Orleans.

On the 1st of May Butler landed at New Orleans and took military possession of the city. Simultaneously, at five o'clock in the afternoon, the 31st Massachusetts with a section of Everett's 6th Massachusetts battery, and six companies of the 4th Wisconsin, under Paine, disembarked and marched up the broad levee to the familiar airs that announced the joint coming of "Yankee Doodle" and of "Picayune Butler."

The outlying defences on both banks of the river and on the lakes were abandoned by the Confederates without a struggle. Forts Pike and Wood, on Lake Pontchartrain, were garrisoned by detachments from the 7th Vermont and 8th New Hampshire regiments. The 21st Indiana landed at Algiers, and marching to Brashear, eighty miles distant on Berwick Bay, took possession of the New Orleans and Opelousas railway. New Orleans itself was occupied by the 30th and 31st Massachusetts, the 4th Wisconsin and 6th Michigan, 9th and 12th Connecticut, 4th and 6th Massachusetts batteries, 2nd Vermont battery, and Troops A and B of the Massachusetts cavalry. At Farragut's approach Lovell, seeing that further resistance was useless, abandoned New Orleans to its fate and withdrew to Camp Moore, distant seventy-eight miles, on the line of the Jackson railway.

Chapter 2

The First Attempt on Vicksburg

With the capture of New Orleans the first and vital object of the expedition had been accomplished. The occupation of Baton Rouge by a combined land and naval force was the next point indicated in McClellan's orders to Butler. Then he was to endeavour to open communication with the northern column coming down the Mississippi. McClellan was no longer General-in-chief; but this part of his plan represented the settled views of the government.

On the 2nd of May, therefore, Farragut sent Craven with the *Brooklyn* and six other vessels of the fleet up the river. On the 8th, as early as the river transports could be secured, Butler sent Williams with the 4th Wisconsin and the 6th Michigan regiments, and two sections of Everett's 6th Massachusetts battery, to follow and accompany the fleet. The next day Williams landed his force at Bonnet Carré, on the east bank of the river, about thirty-five miles above the town. After wading about five miles through a swamp, where the water and mud were about three feet deep, the troops halted at night at Frenier, a station of the Jackson railway, situated on the shore of Lake Pontchartrain, about ten miles above Kenner. A detachment of the 4th Wisconsin, under Major Boardman, was sent to Pass Manchac. The Confederates made a slight but ineffective resistance with artillery, resulting in trivial losses on either side. The bridges at Pass Manchac and Frenier being then destroyed, on the following morning, the 10th, the troops marched back the weary ten miles along the uneven trestle-work of the railway from Frenier to Kenner and there took transport. After their long confinement on shipboard, with scant rations, without exercise or even freedom of movement, the excessive heat of the day caused the troops to

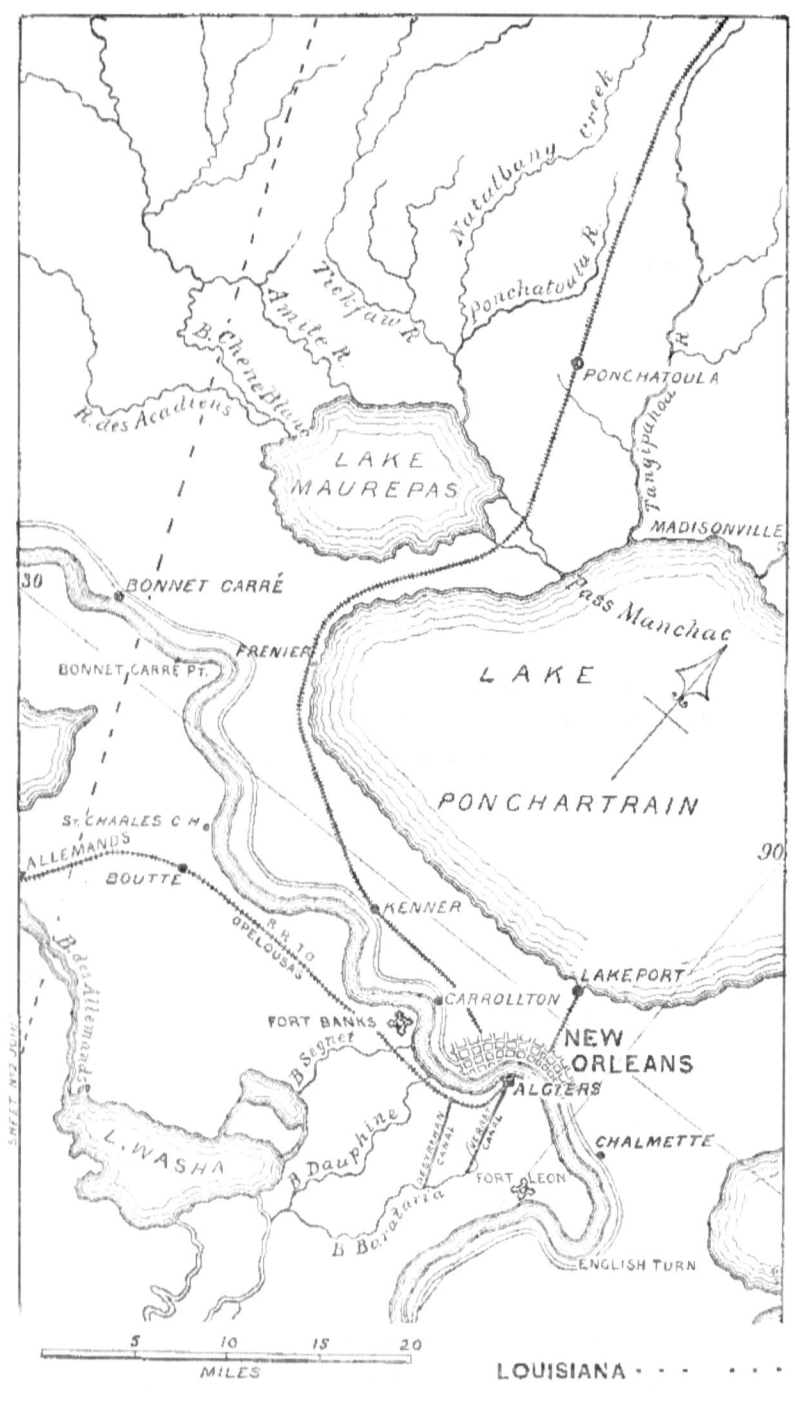

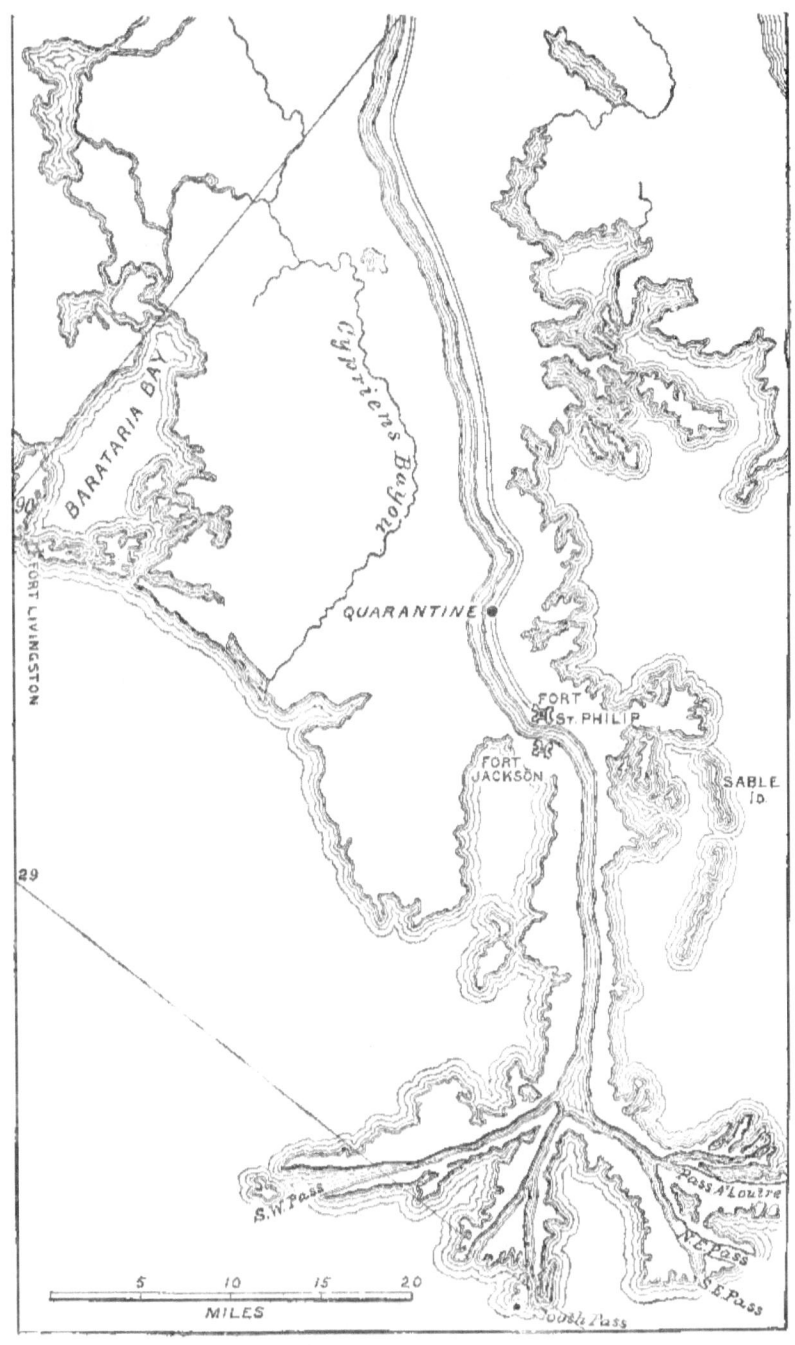

· · · · · · · SHEET I.

suffer severely. The embarkation completed, the transports, under convoy of the navy, set out for Baton Rouge. There on the morning of the 12th of May the troops landed, the capitol was occupied by the 4th Wisconsin, and the national colours were hoisted over the building. The troops then re-embarked for Vicksburg.

Natchez surrendered on the 12th of May to Commander S. Phillips Lee, of the *Oneida*, the advance of Farragut's fleet. On the 18th of May the *Oneida* and her consorts arrived off Vicksburg, and the same day Williams and Lee summoned "the authorities" to surrender the town and "its defences to the lawful authority of the United States." To this Brigadier-General Martin L. Smith, commander of the defences, promptly replied: "Having been ordered here to hold these defences, my intention is to do so as long as it is in my power."

On the 19th the transports stopped for wood at Warrenton, about ten miles below Vicksburg, and here a detachment of the 4th Wisconsin, sent to guard the working party, became involved in a skirmish with the Confederates, in which Sergeant-Major N. H. Chittenden and Private C. E. Perry, of A Company, suffered the first wounds received in battle by the troops of the United States in the Department of the Gulf. The Confederates were easily repulsed, with small loss.

Almost at the instant when Farragut was decided to run the gauntlet of the forts, Beauregard had begun to fortify Vicksburg. Up to this time he had trusted the defence of the river above New Orleans to Fort Pillow, Helena, and Memphis.

When Smith took command at Vicksburg on the 12th of May, in accordance with the orders of Lovell, the department commander, three of the ten batteries laid out for the defence of the position had been nearly completed and a fourth had been begun. These batteries were intended for forty-eight guns from field rifles to 10-inch columbiads. The garrison was to be 3,000 strong, but at this time the only troops present were parts of two Louisiana regiments. When the fleet arrived, on the 18th, six of the ten batteries had been completed, and two days later twenty-three heavy guns were in place and the defenders numbered more than 2,600.

The guns of the navy could not be elevated sufficiently for their projectiles to reach the Confederate batteries on the bluff, and the entire land-force, under Williams, was less than 1,100 effectives. Even had it been possible by a sudden attack to surprise and overcome the garrison and seize the bluffs, the whole available force of the Department of the Gulf would have been insufficient to hold the position for a week, as things then stood.

The truth is that the northern column with which, following their orders, Butler and Farragut were now trying to co-operate had ceased to exist; Jackson meant Beauregard's rear; and, as for any co-operation between Halleck and Williams, Beauregard stood solidly between them. On the 17th of April, the day before Porter's mortars first opened upon Forts Jackson and St. Philip, the whole land force of this northern column, under Pope, at that moment preparing for the attack on Fort Pillow, had been withdrawn by imperative orders from Halleck, and, on the very evening before the attack on Fort Pillow was to have been made, had gone to swell the great army assembled under Halleck at Corinth; but as yet neither Butler nor Farragut knew anything of all this. Save by the tedious roundabout of Washington, New York, the Atlantic, and the Gulf, there was at this time no regular or trustworthy means of communication between the forces descending the Mississippi and those that had just achieved the conquest of New Orleans and were now ascending the river to co-operate with the northern column. Thus it was that a single word, daubed in a rude scrawl upon the walls of the custom-house, meeting the eyes of Paine's men after they had made a way into the building with their axes, gave to Butler the first intelligence of the desperate battle of the 6th and 7th of April, on which the fate of the whole Union campaign in the West had been staked, if not imperilled, and which in its result was destined to change materially the whole course of operations in the Gulf Department. That word was Shiloh.

By the 26th of May the *Oneida* had been joined by the rest of the fleet, under the personal command of the restless and energetic flag-officer. On the afternoon of this day the fleet opened fire. The Confederates replied sparingly, as much to economize their ammunition and to keep the men fresh, as to avoid giving the Union commanders information regarding the range and effect of their fire.

The river was now falling. The *Hartford* in coming up had already grounded hard, and so remained helpless for fifty hours, and had only been got off by incredible exertions. Provisions of all kinds were running very low. On the 25th of May, after a thorough reconnaissance, Farragut and Williams decided to give up the attempt on Vicksburg as evidently impracticable. Farragut left Palmer with the *Iroquois* and six gunboats to blockade the river and to amuse the garrison at Vicksburg by an occasional bombardment in order to prevent Smith from sending reinforcements to Corinth.

While Williams was descending the river on the 26th, the transports were fired into by the Confederate battery on the bluff at Grand Gulf, sixty miles below Vicksburg. About sixty rounds were fired in all, many of which passed completely through the transport *Laurel Hill*, bearing the 4th Wisconsin, part of the 6th Michigan, and the 6th Massachusetts battery. One private of the 6th Michigan was killed and Captain Chauncey J. Bassett, of the same regiment, wounded. The *Ceres*, bearing the remainder of the 6th Michigan and the 6th Massachusetts battery, was following the *Laurel Hill* and was similarly treated. After a stern chase of about twenty miles, the convoy was overhauled, and the gunboat *Kineo*, returning, shelled the town and caused the withdrawal of the battery. During the evening Williams sent four companies of the 4th Wisconsin, under Major Boardman, to overtake the enemy's battery and break up the camp, about one mile and a half in the rear of the town. Boardman came upon the Confederates as they were retiring, and shots were exchanged. The casualties were few, but Lieutenant George DeKay, a gallant and attractive young officer, serving as *aide-de-camp* to General Williams, received a mortal wound.

On the 29th the troops under Williams once more landed and took post at Baton Rouge. During their absence of seventeen days, the Confederates had improved the opportunity to remove much valuable property that had been found stored in the arsenal on the occasion of the first landing of the Union forces.

On his return to New Orleans Farragut received pressing orders from the Navy Department to take Vicksburg. He therefore returned with his fleet, reinforced by a detachment of the mortar flotilla, and Butler once more despatched Williams, this time with an increased force, to co-operate. Williams left Baton Rouge on the morning of the 20th of June with a force composed of the 30th Massachusetts, 9th Connecticut, 7th Vermont, and 4th Wisconsin regiments, Nims's 2nd Massachusetts battery and two sections of Everett's 6th Massachusetts battery. This time a garrison was left to hold Baton Rouge, consisting of the 21st Indiana and 6th Michigan regiments, the remaining section of Everett's battery and Magee's Troop C of the Massachusetts cavalry battalion. On the 22nd of June the transports arrived off Ellis's Cliffs, twelve miles below Natchez, where Williams found three gunboats waiting to convoy him past the high ground. Here he landed a detachment consisting of the 30th Massachusetts regiment and two guns of Nims's battery to turn the supposed position of two field-pieces said to have been planted by the Confederates on the bluffs, while a second force, composed of the 4th Wisconsin, 9th Connecticut, the other two sections of Nims's battery, and the four guns of Everett's, marched directly forward up the cliff road. An abandoned caisson or limber was all that the troops found.

On the 24th, anticipating more serious resistance from the guns said to be in position on the bluffs at Grand Gulf, Williams entered Bayou Pierre with his whole force in the early morning, intending to strike the crossing, about seventeen miles up the stream, of the railway from Port Gibson to Grand Gulf, and thence to move directly on the rear of the town. Half-way up the bayou the boats were stopped by obstructions and had to back down again. Toward noon the troops landed and marched on Grand Gulf in two detachments, one under Paine, consisting of the 4th Wisconsin and 9th Connecticut regiments and a section of Nims's battery; the other, under Dudley, embracing the remainder of the force. Paine had a short skirmish with the enemy near Grand Gulf, and captured eight prisoners, but their camp, a small one, was found abandoned. The same evening the troops re-embarked, and on the 25th arrived before Vicksburg.

The orders from Butler, under which Williams was now acting, required him to take or burn Vicksburg at all hazards. Here, too, we catch the first glimpse of the famous canal upon which so much labour was to be expended during the next year with so little result. "You will send up a regiment or two at once," Butler said, "and cut off the neck of land beyond Vicksburg by means of a trench, making a gap about four feet deep and five feet wide."

To accomplish this purpose Williams had with him four regiments and ten guns, making an effective force in all less than three thousand, rapidly diminished by hard work, close quarters, meagre rations, and a bad climate nearly at its worst.

On the 24th of June the *Monarch*, commanded by Lieutenant-Colonel Alfred W. Ellet, arrived in the reach above Vicksburg. This was one of the nondescript fleet of rams, planned, built, equipped, and manned, under the orders of the War Department, by Ellet's elder brother, Colonel Charles Ellet, Jr., but now acting under the orders of the Commander of the Mississippi fleet. Ellet promptly sent a party of four volunteers, led by his young nephew, Medical Cadet Charles R. Ellet, to communicate with Farragut across the narrow neck of land opposite Vicksburg. This was the first direct communication between the northern and southern columns. By it Farragut learned of the abandonment of Fort Pillow by the Confederates on the 4th of June, and the capture of Memphis on the 6th, after a hard naval fight, in which nearly the whole Confederate fleet was taken or destroyed. There Charles Ellet was mortally wounded. When the *Monarch* party went back to their vessel, they bore with them a letter from Farragut, the contents of which being promptly made known by Ellet to Davis, brought that officer, with his fleet, at once to Vicksburg. On the following day, June 25th, a detachment of the 4th Wisconsin, sent up the river overland by Colonel Paine, succeeded in establishing a second communication with the *Monarch*, believing it to be the first.

Farragut's fleet, now anchored below Vicksburg, comprised the flagship *Hartford*, the sloops-of-war *Brooklyn* and *Richmond*, the corvettes *Iroquois* and *Oneida*, and six gunboats. Porter had joined with the *Octorara*, *Miami*, six other steamers, and seventeen of the mortar schooners. The orders of the government were peremptory that the Mississippi should be cleared. The Confederates held the river by a single thread. The fall of Memphis and the ruin of the famous river-defence fleet left between St. Louis and the Gulf but a solitary obstruction. This was Vicksburg.

Vicksburg stand at an abrupt turn, where within ten miles the winding river doubles upon itself, forming on the low ground opposite a long finger of land, barely three quarters of a mile wide. Opposite the extreme end of this peninsula, known as De Soto, the bluff reaches the highest point attained along the whole course of the river, the crest standing about 250 feet above the mean stage of water. Sloping slowly toward the river, the bluff follows it with a diminished altitude for two miles. Here stands the town of Vicksburg, then a place of about ten thousand inhabitants. Below the town the bluffs draw away from the river until, about four miles beyond the bend, their height diminishes to about 150 feet. For the defence of this line, as has been already seen, a formidable series of batteries had been constructed, extending from the bluff at the mouth of Chickasaw Bayou on the north to Warrenton on the south. These batteries now mounted twenty-six heavy guns, served by gunners comparatively well trained and instructed, and supported against an attack by land by about 6,000 infantry under Lovell. Almost simultaneously with the arrival of Farragut and Williams, came Breckinridge with his division, augmenting the effective force of the defenders to not less than 10,000. On the 30th of May Beauregard evacuated Corinth and drew back to Tupelo; Halleck did not follow; and so 35,000 Confederates were now set free to strengthen Vicksburg. Thus defended and supported Vicksburg was obviously impregnable to any attack by the combined forces of Farragut and Williams. On the 28th of June, Van Dorn arrived and took command of the Confederate forces.

After some preliminary bombarding and reconnoitring Farragut, who was well informed as to the condition of the defences, determined upon repeating before Vicksburg his exploit below New Orleans. Accordingly, on the 28th of July, in the darkness of the early morning, under cover of the fire of Porter's mortar flotilla, Farragut got under way with his fleet to pass the batteries of Vicksburg. The fleet was formed in two columns, with wide intervals, the starboard column led by the *Hartford*, the port column by the *Iroquois*. The battle was opened by the mortars at four o'clock, the enemy replying instantly. By six o'clock the *Hartford* and six of her consorts had successfully run the gauntlet, and lay safely anchored above the bend, while the rest of the fleet, through some confusion of events or misapprehension of orders, had resumed its former position below the bend. The losses of the navy in this engagement were fifteen killed and thirty wounded, including many scalded by the effect of a single shot that pierced the boiler of the *Clifton*. The eight rifled guns of Nims's and Everett's batteries having been landed, were placed in position behind the levee at Barney's Point, and replied effectively to the fire of the heavy guns on the high bluff, at a range of about fourteen hundred yards. This slight service was the only form of active co-operation by the army that the circumstances admitted; yet all the troops stood to arms, ready to do any thing that might be required.

On the 1st of July Davis joined Farragut with four gunboats and six mortar-boats of the Mississippi fleet. On the 9th Farragut received orders from the Navy Department, dated on the 5th, and forwarded by way of Cairo, to send Porter with the *Octorara* and twelve mortar-boats at once to Hampton Roads. Porter steamed down the river on the 10th. This was obviously one of the first-fruits of the campaign of the Peninsula just ended by the withdrawal of the Army of the Potomac to the James. Indeed, at this crisis, all occasions seemed to be informing against the Union plan of campaign, and the same events that drew the Confederate armies together served to draw the Union armies apart. Just as we have seen Pope called away from Fort Pillow on the eve of an attack that must have resulted in its capture, and taken in haste to swell the slow march of Halleck's army before Corinth, so now, when for a full month Corinth had been abandoned by the Confederates, Halleck's forces were being broken up and dispersed to all four of the winds, save that which might have blown them to the south. Halleck declared himself unable to respond to Farragut's urgent appeal for help. "I cannot," he said, when urged by Stanton; "I am sending reinforcements to General Curtis, in Arkansas, and to General Buell, in Tennessee and Kentucky." Not only this, but he was being called upon by Lincoln himself for 25,000 troops to reinforce the Army of the Potomac before Richmond. "Probably I shall be able to do so," Halleck told Farragut, "as soon as I can get my troops more concentrated. This may delay the clearing of the river, but its accomplishment will be certain in a few weeks."

Meanwhile Williams was hard at work on the canal. In addition to such details as could be furnished by the troops without wholly neglecting the absolutely necessary portions of their military duties, Williams had employed a force of about 1,200 negroes, rather poorly provided with tools. The work was not confined to excavation, but involved the cutting down of the large cottonwoods and the clearing away of the dense masses of willows that covered the low ground and matted the heavy soil with their tangled roots. By the 4th of July the excavation had reached a depth in the hard clay of nearly seven feet. The length of the canal was about one and a half miles. By the 11th of July the cut, originally intended to be four feet deep and five feet wide, with a profile of twenty square feet, had been excavated through this stiff clay to a depth of thirteen feet and a width of eighteen feet, presenting a profile of 234 feet. The river, which, up to this time, had been falling more rapidly than the utmost exertions had been able to sink the bottom of the canal, had now begun to fall more slowly, so that at last the grade was about eighteen inches below the river level. In a few hours the water was to have been let in. Suddenly the banks began to cave, and before any thing could be done to remedy this, the river, still falling, was once more below the bottom of the cut. Although with this scanty and overworked force he had already performed nearly twelve times the amount of labour originally contemplated, Williams does not seem to have been discouraged at this; his orders were to make the cut, and his purpose clearly was to make it, even if it should take, as he thought it would, the whole of the next three months. He set to work with vigour to collect labourers, wheelbarrows, shovels, axes, carts, and scrapers, and "to make a real canal," to use his own words, "to the depth of the greatest fall of the river at this point, say some thirty-five to forty feet." But this was not to be.

Until toward the end of June, the *Polk* and *Livingston*, the last vestiges of the Confederate navy on the Mississippi spared from the general wreck at Memphis, lay far up the Yazoo River, with a barrier above them, designed to cover the building of the ram *Arkansas*. This formidable craft was approaching completion at Yazoo City. The Ellets, uncle and nephew, with the *Monarch* and *Lancaster*, steamed up the Yazoo River to reconnoitre. The rams carried no armament whatever, but this the Confederate naval commander in the Yazoo did not know; so, unable to pass the barrier, he set fire to his three gunboats immediately on perceiving Ellet's approach. On the 14th of July, Flag-Officers Farragut and Davis sent the gunboats *Carondelet* and *Tyler*, and the ram *Queen of the West*, on a second expedition up the Yazoo to gain information of the *Arkansas*. This object was greatly facilitated by the fact that the *Arkansas* had at this very moment just got under way for the first time, and was coming down the Yazoo to gather information of the Federal fleet. The *Arkansas*, which had been constructed and was now commanded by Captain Isaac N. Brown, formerly of the United States Navy, was, for defensive purposes, probably the most effective of all the gunboats ever set afloat by the Confederacy upon the western waters. Her deck was covered by a single casemate protected by three inches of railroad iron, set aslant like a gable roof, and heavily backed up with timber and cotton bales. Her whole bow formed a powerful ram; the shield, flat on the top, was pierced for ten guns of heavy calibre, three in each broadside, two forward, and two aft. Had her means of propulsion proved equal to her power of attack and defence, it is doubtful if the whole Union navy on the Mississippi could have stood against her single-handed. The situation thus strangely recalls that presented by the *Merrimac*, or *Virginia*, in Hampton Roads before the opportune arrival of the *Monitor*. On board the *Tyler* was a detachment of twenty sharpshooters of the 4th Wisconsin regiment, under Captain J. W. Lynn, and on the *Carondelet* were twenty men of the 30th Massachusetts regiment, under Lieutenant E. A. Fiske. About six miles above the Yazoo the Union gunboats encountered the *Arkansas*. The unarmed ram *Queen of the West* promptly fled. After a hard fight the *Carondelet* was disabled and run ashore, and the *Tyler* was forced to retire, with the *Arkansas* in pursuit. The sharpshooters of the 4th Wisconsin suffered more severely than if they had been engaged in an ordinary pitched battle, Captain Lynn and six of his men being killed and six others wounded.

The *Queen of the West*, flying out of the mouth of the Yazoo under a full head of steam, gave to the fleet at anchor the first intimation, though perhaps a feeble one, of what was to follow. Not one vessel of either squadron had steam. The ram *Bragg*, which might have been expected to do something, did nothing. The *Arkansas*, so seriously injured by the guns of the *Carondelet* and *Tyler* that the steam pressure had gone from 120 pounds to the square inch down to 20 pounds, kept on her course, and proceeded to run the gauntlet of the Union fleet, giving and taking blows as she went. Battered, but safe, she soon lay under the guns of Vicksburg.

This decided the fate of the campaign, and extinguished in the breast of Farragut the last vestige of the ardent hope he had expressed to the government a few days earlier that he might soon have the pleasure of recording the combined attack of the army and navy, for which all so ardently longed. The river was falling; the canal was a failure. Of the officers and men of the army, two fifths, and of the effective force of the army nearly three fourths, were on the sick-list. There was no longer any thing to hope for or to wait on. The night that followed the exploit of the *Arkansas* saw Farragut's fleet descending the river and once more running the gauntlet of the batteries of Vicksburg. A flying attempt was made by each vessel in succession, but by all unsuccessfully, to destroy the offending *Arkansas*.

On the 24th of July, Williams, with his small force, under convoy of Farragut's fleet, sailed down the river. So ended the second attempt on Vicksburg, usually called the first, when remembered. Its sudden collapse gave the Confederates the river for another year.

CHAPTER 3

Baton Rouge

On the 26th of July, the troops landed at Baton Rouge. In the five weeks that had elapsed since their departure their effective strength had been diminished, by privations, by severe labour, and by the effects of a deadly climate, from 3,200 to about 800. For more than three months, ever since their re-embarkation at Ship Island on the 10th of April, they had undergone hardships such as have seldom fallen to the lot of soldiers, in a campaign whose existence is scarcely known and whose name has been well-nigh forgotten; but their time for rest and recreation had not yet come.

No sooner did Van Dorn see the allied fleets of Davis and Farragut turning their backs on one another and steaming one to the north and the other to the south, than he determined to take the initiative. His preparations had been already made in anticipation of this event. He now ordered Breckinridge to hasten with his division to the attack of Baton Rouge, and even as the fleet got under way, the train bearing Breckinridge's troops was also in motion.

Breckinridge received his orders on the 26th, and arrived at Camp Moore by the railway on the 28th. At Jackson he had been told that he would receive rations sufficient for ten days, but he could get no more than half the quantity. Van Dorn had estimated the Union force to be met at Baton Rouge as about 5,000, and had calculated that Breckinridge would find himself strong enough to dislodge the Union army and drive it away. In fact, Van Dorn estimated Breckinridge's division, including 1,000 men under Brigadier-General Ruggles that were to meet him at Camp Moore, at 6,000 men. The *Arkansas* was to join in the attack, and she was justly considered a full offset to any naval force the Union commander would be likely to have stationed at Baton Rouge. Breckinridge left Vicksburg with less than 4,000. On the 30th of July he reports his total effective force, including Ruggles, at 3,600. The same day he marched on Baton Rouge, and on the 4th of August encamped at the crossing of the Comite, distant about ten miles from his objective. His morning report of that day shows but 3,000 effectives, according to the methods by which effective strength was commonly counted by the Confederates.

The distance from Camp Moore to Baton Rouge is about sixty miles, and the march had been thus retarded to await the co-operation of the *Arkansas*. This Breckinridge was finally assured he might expect at daylight on the morning of the 5th of August. The *Arkansas* had in fact left Vicksburg on the 3rd. Van Dorn's object obviously was by crushing Williams to regain control of the Mississippi from Vicksburg to Baton Rouge, to break the blockade of Red River and to open the way for the recapture of New Orleans. Williams was expecting the attack and awaited the result with calmness.

At Baton Rouge the Mississippi washes for the last time the base of the high and steep bluffs that for so many hundreds of miles have followed the coasts of the great river and formed the contour of its left bank, overlooking its swift yellow waters and the vast lowlands of the western shore. The bluff is lower at Baton Rouge than it is above and slopes more gently to the water's edge; and here the highland draws back from the river and gradually fades away in a south-easterly direction toward the Gulf, while the surface of the country becomes more open and less broken. The stiff post-tertiary clays that compose the soil of these bluffs were in many places covered with a rich growth of timber, great magnolias and beautiful live oaks replacing the rank cottonwood and tangled willows of the lowlands, as well as the giant cypresses of the impenetrable swamps, with their mournful hangings of Spanish moss, and the wild grape binding them fast in a deadly embrace.

Six roads led out of the town in various directions. Of these the most northerly was the road from Bayou Sara. Passing behind the town its course continued toward the south along the river. Between these outstretched arms ran the road to Clinton, the Greenwell Springs road, by which the Confederates had come, the Perkins road, and the Clay Cut road.

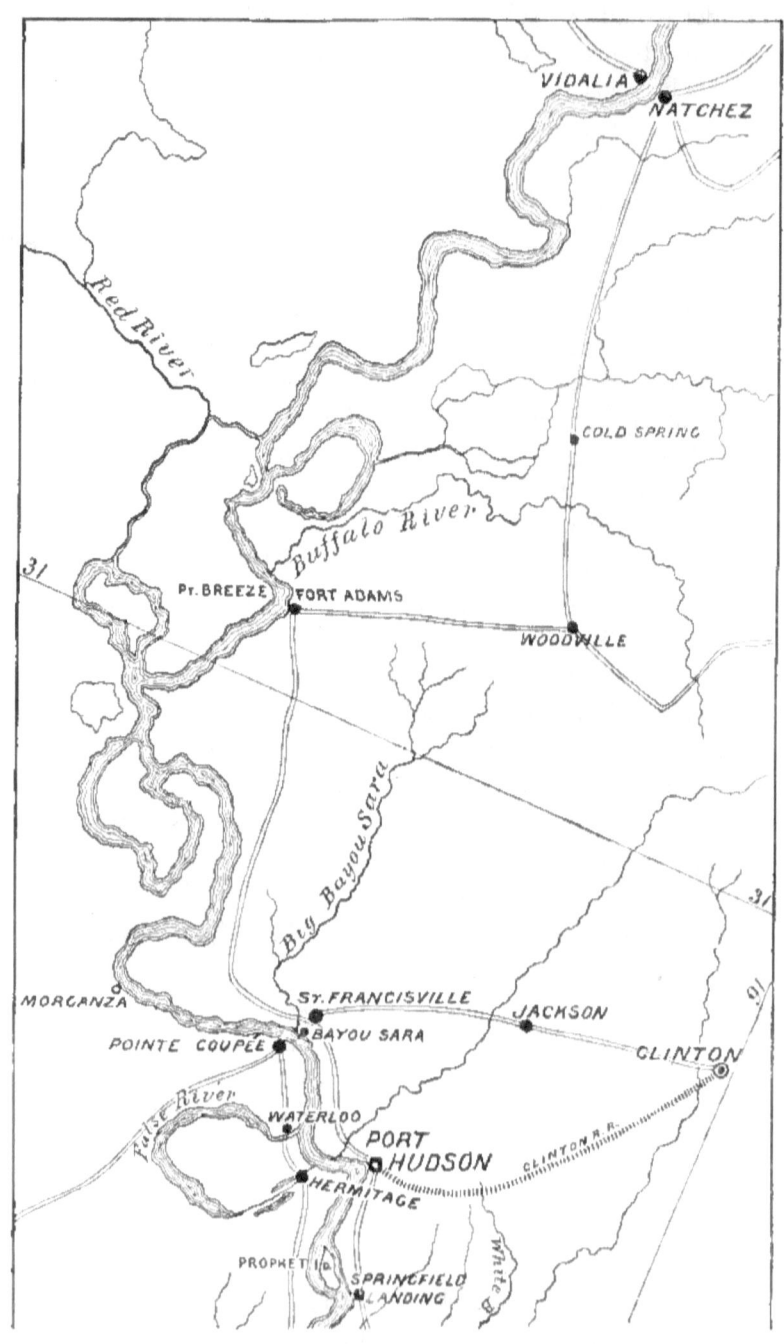

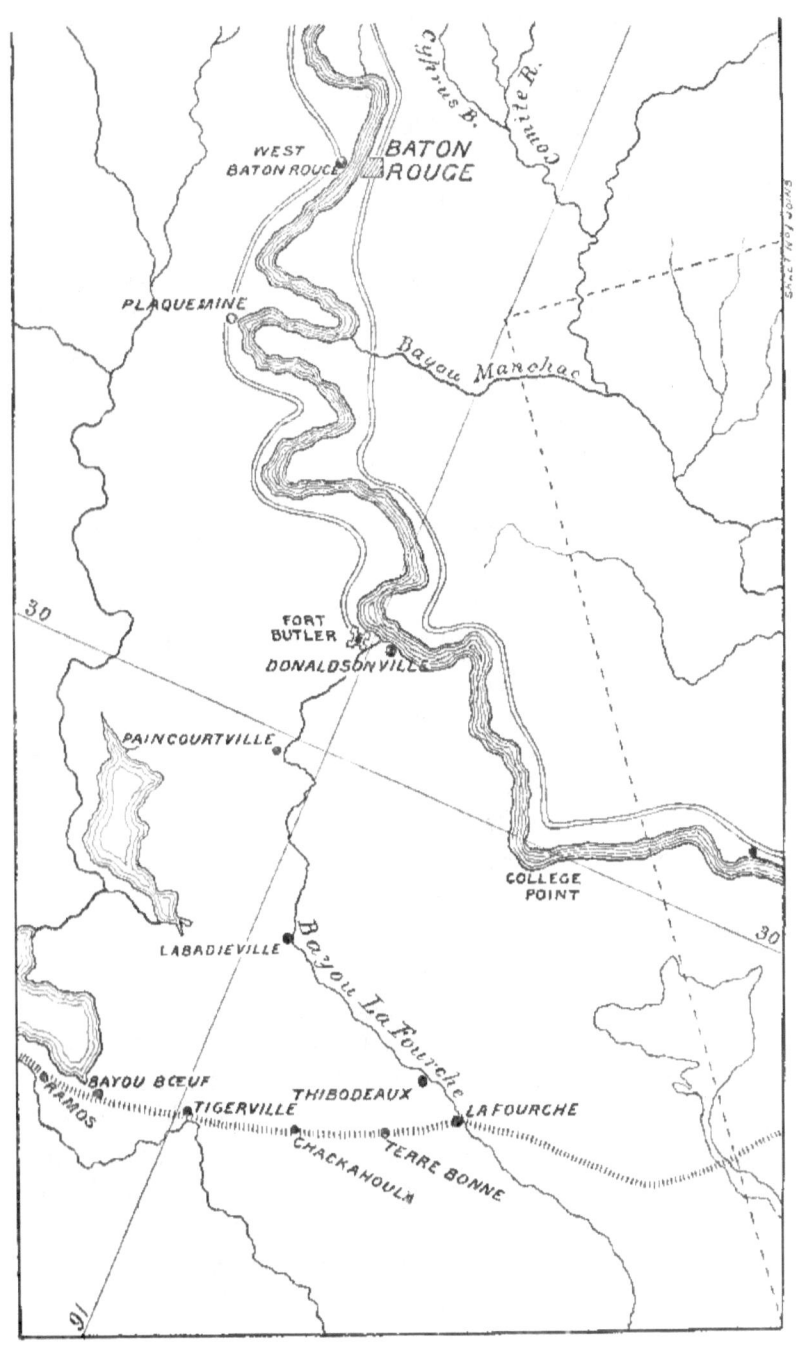

SHEET II.

In numbers the opposing forces were nearly equal. The Confederates went into action with about 2,600, without counting the partisan rangers and militia, numbering 400 or 500 more. Williams had about 2,500 fighting men. He had eighteen guns, the Confederates eleven. On both sides the men were enfeebled by malaria and exposure; yet the Confederates had left their sick behind, while the Union force included convalescents that came out of the hospital to take part in the battle. "There were not 1,200," said Weitzel after the battle, "who could have marched five miles. None of our men had been in battle; very few had been under fire." Among the Confederates were many of the veterans of Shiloh and more of the triumphant defenders of Vicksburg. The advantages of position was slight on either side. On the one hand Williams was forced to post his left with regard to the expected attack of the *Arkansas*, so that in the centre his line fell behind the camps. To offset this his right rested securely on the gunboats. As it turned out the *Arkansas* was not encountered, and the gunboats told off to meet her were therefore able to render material assistance on the left by their oblique fire across Williams' front.

Breckinridge commanded four picked brigades, three selected from his own division and one of Martin L. Smith's Vicksburg brigades, the whole organized in two divisions, under Brigadier-Generals Charles Clark and Daniel Ruggles. Clark had the brigades of Brigadier-General Bernard H. Helm and Colonel Thomas B. Smith, of the 20th Tennessee, with the Hudson battery and Cobb's battery. Ruggles had the brigades of Colonel A. P. Thompson, of the 3rd Kentucky, and Colonel Henry W. Allen, of the 4th Louisiana, with Semmes's battery. From right to left the order of attack ran, Helm, Smith, Thompson, Allen. Clark moved on the right of the Greenwell Springs road, and Ruggles on the left. Scott's cavalry was posted on the extreme left, four guns of Semmes's battery occupied the centre of Ruggles's division, while in Clark's centre were the four guns of the Hudson battery and one of Cobb's; the other two having been disabled in a panic during the night march before the battle. On the extreme right the Clinton road was picketed and held by a detachment of infantry and rangers and the remaining section of Semmes's battery.

To meet the expected attack, Williams had posted his troops in rear of the arsenal and of the town, occupying an irregular line, generally parallel to the Bayou Sara road, and extending from the Bayou Grosse, on the left, to and beyond the intersection of the Perkins and Clay Cut roads, on the right. On the extreme left, behind the Bayou Grosse, was the 4th Wisconsin, commanded by Lieutenant-Colonel Bean. Next, but on the left bank of the bayou, stood the 9th Connecticut. Next, and on the left of the Greenwell Springs road, the 14th Maine. On the right of that road was posted the 21st Indiana, under Lieutenant-Colonel Keith, with three guns attached to the regiment, under Lieutenant J. H. Brown. Across the Perkins and Clay Cut roads the 6th Michigan was formed, under command of Captain Charles E. Clarke, while in the rear of the interval between the 6th Michigan and the 21st Indiana stood the 7th Vermont. The extreme right and rear were covered by the 30th Massachusetts in column, supporting Nims's battery, under Lieutenant Trull. On the centre and left were planted the guns of Everett's battery, under Carruth, and of Manning's 4th Massachusetts battery.

The left flank was supported by the *Essex*, Commander William D. Porter; the *Cayuga*, Lieutenant Harrison; and the *Sumter*, Lieutenant Erben; the right flank by the *Kineo*, Lieutenant-Commander Ransom, and *Katahdin*, Lieutenant Roe.

These dispositions were planned expressly to meet the expected attack by the ram *Arkansas*, and in that view the arrangement was probably the best that the formation of the ground permitted. But the fighting line was very far advanced; the camps still farther; the reserve on the right was posted quite a mile and a half behind the capitol, and, as at Shiloh, no portion of the line was fortified or protected in any way, though the field was an open plain and the converging roads gave to the attacking party a wide choice of position.

About daylight Breckinridge moved to the attack in a summer fog so dense that those engaged could at first distinguish neither friend nor enemy. The blow fell first, and heavily, upon the centre and right, held by the 14th Maine, 21st Indiana, and 6th Michigan. As our troops were pressed back by the vigour of the first onset, the exposed camps of the 14th Maine, 7th Vermont, and 21st Indiana fell into the hands of the Confederates. The 9th Connecticut, with Manning's battery, moved to the support of the 14th Maine and 21st Indiana, on the right of the former, and the 4th Wisconsin formed on the left of the 14th. Further to the right, the 30th Massachusetts advanced to the support of the 21st Indiana and 6th Michigan, covering the interval between the two battalions to replace the 7th Vermont. In the first fighting in the darkness and the fog this regiment had been roughly handled; its colonel fell, a momentary confusion followed, and the regiment drifted back into a convenient position, where it was soon reformed, under Captain Porter. Nims brought his guns into battery on the right of the 6th Michigan.

The battle was short, but the fighting was severe; both sides suffered heavily, and each fell into some disorder. At different moments both wings of the Confederate force were broken, and fell back in something not very unlike panic. The colours of the 4th Louisiana were captured by the 6th Michigan. As the fog lifted, under the influence of the increasing heat, it became clear to both sides that the attack had failed. The force of the fierce Confederate outset was quite spent. The Union lines, however thinned and shattered, remained in possession of the prize. "It was now ten o'clock," says Breckinridge. "We had listened in vain for the guns of the *Arkansas*: I saw around me not more than 1,000 exhausted men." The battle was over. Indeed it had been over for some hours; these words probably indicate the period when the Confederate commander gave up his last hope.

The *Arkansas*, disabled within sight of the goal by an accident to her machinery, was run ashore and destroyed by her commander to save her from capture. The Confederate losses were about 84 killed, 313 wounded, and 56 missing; total, 453. Clark was severely wounded and made prisoner. Allen was killed, and two other brigade commanders wounded. Helm, Hunt, and Thompson had been previously disabled by an accident during the night panic.

The Union losses were 84 killed, 266 wounded, and 33 missing; total, 383. The heaviest loss fell upon the 21st Indiana, which suffered 126 casualties, and upon the 14th Maine, which reported 118. Of the killed, 36, or nearly one half, belonged to the 14th Maine, while more than two thirds of the killed and nearly two thirds of the total belonged to that regiment and the 21st Indiana. The 4th Wisconsin, being posted quite to the left of the point of attack, was not engaged.

Colonel G. T. Roberts, of the 7th Vermont, fell early in the action, and near its close Williams was instantly killed while urging his men to the attack. In him his little brigade lost the only commander present of experience in war; the country, a brave and accomplished soldier. If he was, as must be confessed, arbitrary, at times unreasonable, and often harsh, in his treatment of his untrained volunteers, yet many who then thought his discipline too severe to be endured, lived to know, and by their conduct vindicate, the value of his training.

The Confederates appear to have suffered to some extent during the last attack, until the lines drew too near together, from the fire of the *Essex* and her consorts. Ransom also speaks of having shelled the enemy with great effect during the afternoon from the *Kineo* and *Katahdin*, accurately directed by signals from the capitol; but no other account even mentions any firing at that period of the day; the effect cannot, therefore, have been severe, and it seems probable that the troops against whom it was directed may have been some outlying party.

Cahill's seniority entitled him to the command after Williams fell, yet during the remainder of the battle Dudley seems to have commanded the troops actually engaged. Shortly after the close of the action Cahill assumed the command and sent word to Butler of the state of affairs.

The Confederates were still to be seen upon the field of battle. Their force was naturally enough over-estimated. Another attack was expected during the afternoon, and reinforcements were urgently called for. Butler had none to give without putting New Orleans itself in peril. However, during the evening he determined to release from arrest a number of officers who had been deprived of their swords by Williams at various times, and for various causes, mainly growing out of the confused and as yet rather unsettled policy of the government in reference to the treatment of the negroes, and to send all these officers to Baton Rouge. Among them were Colonel Paine of the 4th Wisconsin and Colonel Clark of the 6th Michigan. Since the 11th of June Paine had been in arrest; an arrest of a character peculiar and perhaps unprecedented in the history of armies. Whenever danger was to be faced, or unusual duty to be performed, he might wear his sword and command his men, but the moment the duty or the danger was at an end he must go back into arrest. Paine, who was an extremely conscientious officer, as well as a man of high character and firmness of purpose, had from the first taken strong ground against the use of any portion of his force in aid of the claims of the master to the service of the slave. Williams, strict in his idea of obedience due his superiors, not less than in his notions of obedience due to him by his own inferiors in rank, stood upon his construction of the law and the orders of the War Department, as they then existed; hence in the natural course of events inevitably arose more than one irreconcilable difference of opinion. Paine was now ordered to go at once to Baton Rouge and take command. He was told by Butler to burn the town and the capitol. The library, the paintings, the statuary, and the relics were to be spared, as well as the charitable institutions of the town. The books, the paintings, and the statue of Washington, he was to send to New Orleans; he was then to evacuate Baton Rouge and retire with his whole force to New Orleans.

At midnight on the 6th of August Paine arrived at Baton Rouge. There he found every thing quiet, with the troops in camp on an interior and shorter line, but expecting another attack. There was in fact an alarm before morning came, but nothing happened. On the 7th Paine took command and set about putting the town in complete condition for an effective defence. With his accustomed care and energy he soon rectified the lines and entrenched them with twenty-four guns in position, and, in co-operation with the navy, concerted every measure for an effective defence, even against large numbers.

Breckinridge, however, after continuing to menace Baton Rouge for some days, had, by Van Dorn's orders, retired to Port Hudson, and was now engaged in fortifying that position. Ruggles was sent there on the 12th of August. The next day Breckinridge received orders from Van Dorn, then at Jackson, to follow with his whole force. "Port Hudson," Van Dorn said, "must be held if possible." "Port Hudson," remarks Breckinridge, in his report of the battle of Baton Rouge, "is one of the strongest points on the Mississippi, which Baton Rouge is not, and batteries there will command the river more completely than at Vicksburg."

Meanwhile Butler had changed his mind with regard to the evacuation of Baton Rouge, and had directed Paine to hold the place for the present. With an accuracy unusual at this period, Butler estimated Breckinridge's entire force at 5,000 men and fourteen guns. On the 13th the defences were complete, the entrenchments forming two sides of a triangle of which the river was the base and the cemetery mound the apex. The troops stood to arms at three o'clock every morning; one fourth of the force was constantly under arms, day and night, at its station. At two points on each face of the entrenchment flags were planted by day and lights by night, to indicate to the gunboats their line of fire.

On the 16th of August Butler renewed his orders to burn and evacuate Baton Rouge. Its retention up to this time he had avowedly regarded as having political rather than military importance. Now he wrote to Paine:

> I am constrained to come to the conclusion that it is necessary to evacuate Baton Rouge. . . . Begin the movement quietly and rapidly; get every thing off except your men, and then see to it that the town is destroyed. After mature deliberation I deem this a military necessity of the highest order.

Against these orders Paine made an earnest appeal, based upon considerations partly humane, partly military. He was so far successful that Butler was induced to countermand the order to burn. The movement was not to be delayed on account of the statue of Washington. However, the statue had been already packed. It is now in the Patent Office at the national capital. All the books and paintings were brought off, "except," to quote from Paine's diary, "the portrait of James Buchanan, which we left hanging in the State House for his friends." Finally, on the 20th, Paine evacuated Baton Rouge, and on the following day reached the lines of Carrollton, known as Camp Parapet, and turned over his command to Phelps.

CHAPTER 4

La Fourche

On the 2nd of August Paine was assigned to the command of what was called the "reserve brigade" of a division under Phelps. The brigade was composed of the 4th Wisconsin, 21st Indiana, and 14th Maine, with Brown's battery attached to the Indiana regiment. But this was not to last, for the tension that had long existed between Phelps and the department commander, on the subject of the treatment of the negroes, as well as on the question of arming and employing them, finally resulted in Phelps's resignation on the 21st of August. On the 13th of September he was succeeded by Brigadier-General Thomas W. Sherman, himself recently relieved from command of the Department of the South, partly, perhaps, in consequence of differences of opinion of a like character.

On the 29th of September the division, then known as Sherman's, was reorganized, and Paine took command of the 1st brigade, composed of the 4th Wisconsin, 21st Indiana, and 8th New Hampshire regiments with the 1st and 2nd Vermont batteries and Brown's guns of the 21st Indiana. Paine's command also included Camp Parapet. These lines had been originally laid out by the Confederates for the defence of New Orleans against an attack by land from the north; as, for example, by a force approaching through Lake Pontchartrain and Pass Manchac. They were now put in thorough order, and the Indianans, who had received some artillery instruction during their term of service at Fort McHenry, completed the foundation for the future service as heavy artillerists by going back to the big guns. In October and November the 8th New Hampshire and 21st Indiana were transferred to Weitzel's brigade and were replaced in Paine's by the 2nd Louisiana and temporarily by the 12th Maine.

The official reports covering this period afford several strong hints of a Confederate plan for the recapture of New Orleans. With this object, apparently, Richard Taylor, a prominent and wealthy Louisianan, closely allied to Jefferson Davis by his first marriage with the daughter of Zachary Taylor, was made a major-general in the Confederate army, and on the 1st of August was assigned to command the Confederate forces in Western Louisiana. It seems likely that the troops of Van Dorn's department, as well as those at Mobile, were expected to take part.

On the 8th of August orders were issued by the War Department transferring the district of West Florida to the Department of the Gulf. West Florida meant Pensacola. Fort Pickens, on the sands of Santa Rosa, commanding the entrance to the splendid harbour, owed to the loyalty of a few staunch officers of the army and the navy the proud distinction of being the one spot between the Chesapeake and the Rio Grande over which, in spite of all hostile attempts, the ensign of the nation had never ceased to float; for the works at Key West and the Dry Tortugas, though likewise held, were never menaced. Though Bragg early gathered a large force for the capture of the fort, the only serious attempt, made in the dawn of the 9th of October, 1861, was repulsed with a loss to the Confederates of 87, to the Union troops of 61. Of these, the 6th New York had 9 killed, 7 wounded, 11 missing—in all, 27. In December the 75th New York came down from the North to reinforce the defenders. Finally, after learning the fate of New Orleans, Bragg evacuated Pensacola, and burned his surplus stores, and on the 10th of May, 1862, Porter, seeing from the passes the glare of the flames, ran over and anchored in the bay. The advantage thus gained was held to the end.

This transfer gave Butler two strong infantry regiments, as well as several fine batteries and companies of the regular artillery, but at the same time correspondingly increased the territory he had to guard, already far too extensive and too widely scattered for the small force at his disposal.

Toward the end of September Lieutenant Godfrey Weitzel, of the engineers, having been made a brigadier-general on Butler's recommendation, a promotion more than usually justified by service and talent, a brigade was formed for him called the Reserve Brigade, and consisting of the 12th and 13th Connecticut, 75th New York, and 8th New Hampshire, Carruth's 6th Massachusetts battery, Thompson's 1st Maine battery, Perkins's Troop C of the Massachusetts cavalry, and three troops of Louisiana cavalry under Williamson. From that time, through all the changes, which were many and frequent, Weitzel's brigade changed less than any thing else, and its history may almost be said to be the military history of the Department.

Taylor, with his accustomed energy and enthusiasm, had collected and organized a force, primarily for the defence of the La Fourche country and the Teche, ultimately for the offensive operations already planned. Butler at once committed to Weitzel the preparations for dislodging Taylor and occupying La Fourche. This object was important, not only to secure the defence of New Orleans, but because the territory to be occupied comprised or controlled the fertile region between the Mississippi and the Atchafalaya. The country lies low and flat, and is intersected by numerous navigable bayous, with but narrow roadways along their banks and elsewhere none. Without naval assistance, the operation would have been difficult, if not impossible; and the navy had in Louisiana no gunboats of a draught light enough for the service. With the funds of the army Butler caused four light gunboats, the *Estrella*, *Calhoun*, *Kinsman*, and *Diana*, to be quietly built and equipped, the navy furnishing the officers and the crews. Under Commander McKean Buchanan they were then sent by the gulf to Berwick Bay.

When he was ready, Weitzel took transports, under convoy of the *Kineo*, *Sciota*, *Katahdin*, and *Itasca*, landed below Donaldsonville, entered the town, and on the 27th of October moved on Thibodeaux, the heart of the district. At Georgia Landing, about two miles above Labadieville, he encountered the Confederates under Mouton, consisting of the 18th and 33rd Louisiana, the Crescent and Terre Bonne regiments, with Ralston's and Semmes's batteries and the 2nd Louisiana cavalry, in all reported by Mouton as 1,392 strong. They had taken up a defensive position on both sides of the bayou. Along these bayous the standing room is for the most part narrow; and as the land, although low, is in general heavily wooded and crossed by many ditches of considerable depth, the country affords defensive positions at once stronger and more numerous than are to be found in most flat regions. Small bodies of troops, familiar with the topography, have also this further advantage, that there are few points from which their position and numbers can be easily made out.

After a short but spirited engagement Mouton's force was compelled to retreat. Weitzel pursued for about four miles.

Mouton then called in his outlying detachments, including the La Fourche regiment, 500 strong, 300 men of the 33rd Louisiana, and the regiments of Saint Charles and St. John Baptist, burned the railway station of Terre Bonne and the bridges at Thibodeaux, La Fourche Crossing, Terre Bonne, Des Allemands, and Bayou Boeuf, and evacuated the district. By the 30th, every thing was safely across Berwick Bay. For this escape, he was indebted to an opportune gale that compelled Buchanan's gunboats to lie to in Caillou Bay on their way to Berwick Bay, to cut off the retreat. Mouton's report accounts for 5 killed, 8 wounded, and 186 missing; in all 199. Among the killed was Colonel G. P. McPheeters of the Crescent regiment.

Weitzel followed to Thibodeaux, and went into camp beyond the town. He claims to have taken 208 prisoners and one gun, and states his own losses as 18 killed, and 74 wounded, agreeing with the nominal lists, which also contain the names of 5 missing, thus bringing the total casualties to 97.

Arriving off Brashear a day too late, Buchanan was partly consoled by capturing the Confederate gunboat *Seger*. On the 4th and 5th of November he made a reconnaissance fourteen miles up the Teche with his own boat, the *Calhoun*, and the *Estrella, Kinsman, Saint Mary's*, and *Diana*, and meeting a portion of Mouton's forces and the Confederate gunboat *J. A. Cotton*, received and inflicted some damage and slight losses, yet with no material result.

Simultaneously with Weitzel's movement on La Fourche, Butler pushed the 8th Vermont and the newly organized 1st Louisiana Native Guards forward from Algiers along the Opelousas Railway, to act in conjunction with Weitzel and to open the railway as they advanced. Weitzel had already turned the enemy out of his position, but the task committed to Thomas was slow and hard, for all the bridges and many culverts had to be rebuilt, and from long disuse of the line the rank grass, that in Louisiana springs up so freely in every untrodden spot above water, had grown so tall and thick and strongly matted that the troops had to pull it up by the roots before the locomotive could pass.

So ended operations in Louisiana for the year. Until the following spring, Taylor continued to occupy the Teche region, while Weitzel rested quietly in La Fourche, with his headquarters at Thibodeaux and his troops so disposed as to cover and hold the country without losing touch. On the 9th of November, the whole of Louisiana lying west of the Mississippi, except the delta parishes of Plaquemine and Terre Bonne, was constituted a military district to be known as the District of La Fourche, and Weitzel was assigned to the command.

Meanwhile General Butler, with the consent of the War Department, had raised, organized, and equipped, in the neighbourhood of New Orleans, two good regiments of Louisianans, the 1st Louisiana, Colonel Richard E. Holcomb, and the 2nd Louisiana, Colonel Charles J. Paine, both regiments admirably commanded and well officered; three excellent troops of Louisiana cavalry, under fine leaders, Captains Henry F. Williamson, Richard Barrett, and J. F. Godfrey; and beside these white troops, three regiments of negroes, designated as the 1st, 2nd, and 3rd Louisiana Native Guards. This was the name originally employed by Governor Moore early in 1861, to describe an organization of the free men of colour of New Orleans enrolled for the defence of the city against the expected attack by the forces of the Union.

This action was taken by Butler of his own motion. It was never formally approved by the government, but it was not interfered with. These three regiments were the first negro troops mustered into the service of the United States. At least one of them, the 1st, was largely made up of men of that peculiar and exclusive caste known to the laws of slavery as the free men of colour of Louisiana. All the field and staff officers were white men, mainly taken from the rolls of the troops already in service; but at first all the company officers were negroes. As this was the first experiment, it was perhaps, in the state of feeling then prevailing, inevitable, yet not the less to be regretted, that the white officers were, with some notable exceptions, inferior men. Fortunately, however, courts-martial and examining boards made their career for the most part a short one. As for the coloured officers of the line, early in 1863 they were nearly all disqualified on the most rudimentary examination, and then the rest resigned. After that, the government having determined to raise a large force of negro troops, it became the settled policy to grant commissions as officers to none but white men.

The 1st and 2nd regiments were sent into the district of La Fourche to guard the railway.

Then, between Butler and Weitzel, in spite of confidence on the one hand and respect and affection on the other, began the usual controversy about arming the negro. To one unacquainted with the history of this question and of those times it must seem strange indeed to read the emphatic words in which a soldier so loyal and, in the best sense, so subordinate as Weitzel, declared his unwillingness to command these troops, and to reflect that in a little more than two years he was destined to accept with alacrity the command of a whole army corps of black men, and at last to ride in triumph at their head into the very capital of the Confederacy.

With the exception of the levies raised by its commander, the Department of the Gulf had so far received no access of strength from any quarter. From the North had come hardly a recruit. In the intense heat and among the poisonous swamps the effective strength melted away day by day. Thus the numbers present fell 3,795 during the month of July; in October, when the sickly season had done its worst, the wastage reached a total of 5,390. At the time of the battle of Baton Rouge, Butler's effective force can hardly have exceeded 7,000. When his strength was the greatest it probably did not exceed, if indeed it reached, the number of 13,000 effective. The condition of affairs was therefore such that Butler found himself with an army barely sufficient for the secure defence of the vast territory committed to his care, and for any offensive operation absolutely powerless. To hold what had been gained it was practically necessary to sit still; and to sit still then, as always in all wars, was to invite attack.

These things Butler did not fail to represent to the government, and to repeat. At last, about the middle of November, he received a few encouraging words from Halleck, dated the 3rd of that month, in which he was assured that the—

.... delay in sending reinforcements has not been the fault of the War Department. It is hoped that some will be ready to start as soon as the November elections are over. Brigadier-generals will be sent with these reinforcements.

With them was to be a major-general, the new commander of the department; but this Halleck did not say.

CHAPTER 5

Banks in Command

When the campaigns of 1862 were drawing to an end, the government changed all the commanders and turned to the consideration of new plans. With President Lincoln, as we have seen, the opening of the Mississippi had long been a favoured scheme. His early experience had rendered him familiar with the waters, the shores, and the vast traffic of the great river, and had brought home to him the common interests and the mutual dependence of the farmers, the traders, the miners, and the manufacturers of the States bordering upon the upper Mississippi and the Ohio on the one hand, and of the merchants and planters of the Gulf on the other. Thus he was fully prepared to enter warmly into the idea that had taken possession of the minds and hearts of the people of the Northwest. From a vague longing this idea had now grown into a deep and settled sentiment. Indeed in all the West the opening of the Mississippi played a part that can only be realized by comparing it with the prevailing sentiment of the East, so early, so long, so loudly expressed in the cry, "On to Richmond!"

That the President should have been in complete accord with the popular impulse is hardly to be wondered at by any one that has followed, with the least attention, the details of his remarkable career. Moreover, the popular impulse was right. Wars take their character from the causes that produce them and the people or the nations by whom they are waged. This was not a contest upon some petty question involving the fate of a ministry, a dynasty, or even a monarchy, to be fought out between regular armies upon well-known plans at the convergence of the roads between two opposing capitals. The struggle was virtually one between two peoples hitherto united as one,—between the people of the North, who had taken up arms for the maintenance and the restoration of the Union, and the people of the South, who had taken up arms to destroy the Union. Of such an issue there could be no compromise; to such a contest there could be no end short of exhaustion. For four long years it was destined to go on, and at times to rage with a fury almost unexampled along lines whose length was measured by the thousand miles and over a battle-ground nearly as large as the continent of Europe. Looked at merely from the standpoint of strategy, and discarding all considerations not directly concerning the movements of armies, true policy might, perhaps, have dictated the concentration of all available resources in men and material upon the great central lines of operations, roughly indicated by the mention of Chattanooga and Atlanta,—the road eventually followed by Sherman in his triumphant march to the sea. Apart, however, from considerations strictly tactical, the importance of cutting off the trans-Mississippi region as a source of supply for the main Confederate armies was obvious; while from the governments of Europe, of England and France above all, the pressure was great for cotton, partly, indeed, as a pretext for interfering in our domestic struggle to their own advantage, but largely, also, to enable those governments to quiet the cry of the starving millions of their people.

Instructed, as well as warned, by the events of the previous summer, the President now resolved on a combined attempt by two strong columns. On the 21st of October he sent Major-General John A. McClernand to Indiana, Illinois, and Iowa, with confidential orders, authorizing him to raise troops for an expedition, under his command, to move against Vicksburg from Cairo or Memphis as a place of rendezvous, and "to clear the Mississippi River and open navigation to New Orleans." Perhaps because of the confidence still felt in Grant by the President himself, although within narrowing limits, Grant was not to share the fate of McClellan, of Buell, and of so many others. The secret orders were not made known to him, yet it was settled that he was to retain the command of his department, while the principal active operations of the army within its limits were to be conducted by another. Even for this consideration it is rather more than likely he was indebted in a great degree to the exceptional advantage he enjoyed in having at all times at the seat of government, in the person of Washburne, a strong and devoted party of one, upon whose assistance the government daily found it convenient to lean.

A few days later, on the 31st of October, Major-General Nathaniel P. Banks was sent to New York and Boston, with similar orders, to collect in New England and New York a force for the co-operating column from New Orleans. On the 8th of November this was followed by the formal order of the President assigning Banks to the command of the Department of the Gulf, including the State of Texas.

This assignment was wholly unexpected by Banks. It was, indeed, unsought and unsolicited, and the first offer, from the President himself, came as a surprise. At the close of Pope's campaign, when the reorganized Army of the Potomac, once more under McClellan, was in march to meet Lee in Maryland, Banks had been forced, by injuries received at Cedar Mountain, to give up the command of the Twelfth Army Corps to the senior division commander, Brigadier-General A. S. Williams. As soon as this was reported at headquarters, McClellan created a new organization under the name of the "Defences of Washington," and placed Banks in command.

For some time after this Banks was unable to leave his room; yet, within forty-eight hours, a mob of thirty thousand wounded men and convalescents, who knew not where to go, and of stragglers, who meant not to go where they were wanted, was cleared out of the streets of Washington, and pandemonium was at an end. Order was rather created than restored, since none had existed in any direction. The Fifth Corps was sent to join the army in the field; within a fortnight, a full army corps of able-bodied stragglers followed; the fortifications were completed; ample garrisons of instructed artillerists were provided. These became "the Heavies" of Grant's campaigns. Almost another full army corps was organized from the new regiments. Finally the whole force of the defences, about equal in numbers to Lee's army, was so disposed that Washington was absolutely secure. The dispositions for the defence of the capital and the daily operations of the command were clearly and constantly made known to the President and Secretary of War as well as to the General-in-chief. Thus it was that, less than two months later, in the closing days of October, President Lincoln sent for Banks and said: "You have let me sleep in peace for the first time since I came here. I want you to go to Louisiana and do the same thing there."

On the 9th of November Halleck communicated to Banks the orders of the President to proceed immediately to New Orleans with the troops from Baltimore and elsewhere, under Emory, already assembling in transports at Fort Monroe. An additional force of ten thousand men, he was told, would be sent to him from Boston and New York as soon as possible. Though this order was never formally revoked or modified, yet in fact it was from the first a dead letter, and Banks, who received it in New York, remained there to complete the organization and to look after the collection and transport of the additional force mentioned in Halleck's instructions. Including the eight regiments of Emory, but not counting four regiments of infantry and five battalions of cavalry diverted to other fields, the reinforcements for the Department of the Gulf finally included thirty-nine regiments of infantry, six batteries of artillery, and one battalion of cavalry. Of the infantry twenty-one regiments were composed of officers and men enlisted to serve for nine months. Even of this brief period many weeks had, in some cases, already elapsed. To command the brigades and divisions, when organized, Major-General Christopher C. Auger, and Brigadier-Generals Cuvier Grover, William Dwight, George L. Andrews, and James Bowen were ordered to report to Banks.

The work of chartering the immense fleet required to transport this force, with its material of all kinds, was confided by the government to Cornelius Vanderbilt, possibly in recognition of his recent princely gift to the nation of the finest steamship of his fleet, bearing his own name. This service Vanderbilt performed with his usual vigour, "laying hands," as he said, "upon every thing that could float or steam," including, it must be added, more than one vessel to which it would have been rash to ascribe either of these qualities.

Before the embarkation each vessel was carefully inspected by a board of officers, usually composed of the inspector-general or an officer of his department, an experienced quartermaster, and an officer of rank and intelligence, who was himself to sail on the vessel.

This last was a new, but, as soon appeared, a very necessary precaution. When every thing was nearly ready the embarkation began at New York, and as each vessel was loaded she was sent to sea with sealed orders directing her master and the commanding officer of the troops to make the best of their way to Ship Island, and there await the further instructions of the general commanding. Ship Island was chosen for the place of meeting because of the great draught of water of some of the vessels. At the same time Emory's force, embarking at Hampton Roads, set out under convoy of the man-of-war *Augusta*, Commander E. G. Parrott, for the same destination with similar orders.

For three months the *Florida* had lain at anchor in the harbour at Mobile, only waiting for a good opportunity to enter upon her historic career of destruction. Since the 20th of August the *Alabama* was known to have been scourging our commerce in the North Atlantic from the Azores to the Antilles. On the 5th of December she took a prize off the northern coast of San Domingo. Relying on the information with which he was freely furnished, Semmes expected to find the expedition off Galveston about the middle of January. In the dead of night, "after the midwatch was set and all was quiet," he meant, in the words of his executive officer,[1] slowly to approach the transports, "steam among them with both batteries in action, pouring in a continuous discharge of shell, and sink them as we went." Fortunately Semmes's information, though profuse and precise, was not quite accurate, for it brought him off Galveston on the 13th of January: the wrong port, a month too late. What might have happened is shown by the ease with which he then destroyed the *Hatteras*.

To guard against these dangers, it had been the wish of the government, and was a part of the original plan, that the transports sailing from New York should be formed in a single fleet and proceed, under strong convoy, to its destination. However, it soon became evident that as the rate of sailing of a fleet is governed by that of its slowest ship, the expedition, thus organized, would be forced to crawl along the coast at a speed hardly greater than five miles an hour. This would not only have exposed three

---

1. "Cruise and Combats of the *Alabama*," by her Executive Officer, John Mackintosh Kell.—*Century War Book*, vol. iv., p. 603.

ships out of five, and five regiments out of six, for at least twice the necessary time to the perils of the sea, increased by having to follow an inshore track at this inclement season; it would not only have introduced chances of detention and risks of collision and of separation, but the peril from the *Alabama* would have been augmented in far greater degree than the security afforded by any naval force the government could just then spare. Therefore, the slow ships were loaded and sent off first and the faster ones kept back to the last; then, each making the best of its way to Ship Island, nearly all came in together. Thus, when the *North Star*, bearing the flag of the commanding general and sailing from New York on the 4th of December, arrived in the early morning of the 13th at Ship Island, nearly the whole fleet lay at anchor or in the offing; and as soon as a hasty inspection could be completed and fresh orders given, the expedition got under way for New Orleans. The larger vessels, however, like the *Atlantic*, *Baltic*, and *Ericsson* being unable to cross the bar, lay at anchor at Ship Island until they could be lightened.

Truly grand as was the spectacle afforded by the black hulls and white sails of this great concourse of ships at anchor, in the broad roadstead, yet a grander sight still was reserved for the next day, a lovely Sunday, as all these steamers in line ahead, the *North Star* leading, flags flying, bands playing, the decks blue with the soldiers of the Union, majestically made their way up the Mississippi. Most of those on board looked for the first time, with mingled emotions, over the pleasant lowlands of Louisiana, and all were amused at the mad antics of the pageant-loving negroes, crowding and capering on the levee as plantation after plantation was passed. So closely had the secret been kept that, until the transports got under way from Ship Island for the purpose, probably not more than three or four officers, if so many, of all the force really knew its destination. Nor was it until the two generals met at New Orleans that Butler learned that Banks was to relieve him.

On the 15th of December Banks took the command of the Department of the Gulf, although the formal orders were not issued until the 17th. The officers of the department, as well as of the personal staff of General Butler, were relieved from duty and permitted to accompany him to the North. The new staff of the department included Lieutenant-Colonel Richard B. Irwin, Assistant Adjutant-General; Lieutenant-Colonel William S. Abert, Assistant Inspector-General; Major G. Norman Lieber, Judge-Advocate; Colonel Samuel B. Holabird, Chief Quartermaster; Colonel Edward G. Beckwith, Chief Commissary of Subsistence; Surgeon Richard H. Alexander, Medical Director; Major David C. Houston, Chief Engineer; Captain Henry L. Abbot, Chief of Topographical Engineers; First-Lieutenant Richard M. Hill, Chief of Ordnance; Captain Richard Arnold, Chief of Artillery; Captain William W. Rowley, Chief Signal Officer.

Banks's orders from the government were to go up the Mississippi and open the river, in co-operation with McClernand's expedition against Vicksburg. "As the ranking general of the Southwest," Halleck's orders proceeded—

> .... you are authorized to assume control of any military forces from the upper Mississippi which may come within your command. The line of the division between your department and that of Major-General Grant is, therefore, left undecided for the present, and you will exercise superior authority as far north as you may ascend the river. The President regards the opening of the Mississippi river as the first and most important of all our military and naval operations, and it is hoped that you will not lose a moment in accomplishing it.

Immediately on assuming command Banks ordered Grover to take all the troops that were in condition for service at once to Baton Rouge, under the protection of the fleet, and there disembark and go into camp. Augur was specially charged with the arrangements for the despatch of the troops from New Orleans. Before starting they were carefully inspected, and all that were found to be affected with disease of a contagious or infectious character were sent ashore and isolated.

On the morning of the 16th the advance of Grover's expedition got under way, under convoy of a detachment of Farragut's fleet, led by Alden in the *Richmond*. Grover took with him about 4,500 men, but when all were assembled at Baton Rouge there were twelve regiments, three batteries, and two troops of cavalry. The Confederates, who were in very small force, promptly evacuated Baton Rouge, and Grover landed and occupied the place on the 17th of December. After sending off the last of the troops, Augur went up and took command. The lines constructed by Paine in August were occupied and strengthened, and all arrangements promptly made for the defence in view of an attack, such as might not unnaturally be looked for from Port Hudson, whose garrison then numbered more than 12,000 effectives. The two places are but a long day's march apart. Since the occupation in August, the Confederate forces at Port Hudson had been commanded by Brigadier-General William N. R. Beall. On the 28th of December, however, he was relieved by Major-General Frank Gardner, who retained the command thenceforward until the end. While the war lasted, Baton Rouge continued to be held by the Union forces without opposition or even serious menace.

An attempt to occupy Galveston was less fortunate. This movement was ordered by Banks a few days after his arrival at New Orleans, apparently under the pressure of continued importunity from Andrew J. Hamilton, and in furtherance of the policy that had led the government to send him with the expedition, nominally as a brigadier-general, but under a special commission from the President that named him as military governor of Texas. On the 21st of December, three companies, D, G, and I, of the 42nd Massachusetts, under Colonel Isaac S. Burrell, were sent from New Orleans without disembarking from the little *Saxon*, on which they had made the journey from New York. With them went Holcomb's 2nd Vermont battery, leaving their horses to follow ten days later on the *Cambria*, with the horses and men of troops A and B of the Texas cavalry. Protected by the flotilla under Commander W. B. Renshaw, comprising his own vessel, the *Westfield*, the gunboats *Harriet Lane*, Commander J. M. Wainwright; *Clifton*, Commander Richard L. Law; *Owasco*, Lieutenant Henry Wilson; and *Sachem*, Acting-Master Amos Johnson; and the schooner *Corypheus*, Acting-Master Spears, Burrell landed unopposed at Kuhn's Wharf on the 24th, and took nominal possession of the town in accordance with his instructions. These were indeed rather vague, as befitted the shadowy nature of the objects to be accomplished. General Banks wrote:

The situation of the people of Galveston makes it expedient to send a small force there for the purpose of their protection, and also to afford such facilities as may be possible for recruiting soldiers for the military service of the United States.

Burrell was cautioned not to involve himself in such difficulty as to endanger the safety of his command, and it was rather broadly hinted that he was not to take orders from General Hamilton. In reality, Burrell's small force occupied only the long wharf, protected by barricades at the shore end, and seaward by the thirty-two guns of the fleet, lying at anchor within 300 yards.

Magruder, who had been barely a month in command of the Confederate forces in Texas, had given his first attention to the defenceless condition of the coast, menaced as it was by the blockading fleet, and thus it happened that Burrell's three companies, performing their maiden service on picket between wind and water, found themselves confronted by the two brigades of Scurry and Sibley, Cook's regiment of heavy artillery, and Wilson's light battery, with twenty-eight guns, and two armed steamboats, having their vulnerable parts protected by cotton bales.

Long before dawn on the 1st of January, 1863, under cover of a heavy artillery fire, the position of the 42nd Massachusetts was assaulted by two storming parties of 300 and 500 men respectively, led by Colonels Green, Bagby, and Cook, the remainder of the troops being formed under Scurry in support. A brisk fight followed, but the defenders had the concentrated fire of the fleet to protect them; the scaling ladders proved too short to reach the wharf, and as day began to break, the baffled assailants were about to draw off, when, suddenly, the Confederate gunboats appeared on the scene and in a few moments turned the defeat into a signal victory. The *Neptune* was disabled and sunk by the *Harriet Lane*, the *Harriet Lane* was boarded and captured by the *Bayou City*, the *Westfield* ran aground and was blown up by her gallant commander, and soon the white flag floated from the masts of all the Union fleet. Wainwright and Wilson had been killed; Renshaw, with his executive officer, Zimmermann, and his chief engineer, Green, had perished with the ship. The survivors were given three hours to consider terms.

When Burrell saw the flag of truce from the fleet, he too showed the white flag and surrendered to the commander of the Confederate troops. The Confederates ceased firing on him as soon as they perceived his signal, but the navy, observing that the fire on shore went on for some time, notwithstanding the naval truce, thought it had been violated; accordingly the *Clifton*, *Owasco*, *Sachem*, and *Corypheus* put out to sea, preceded by the army transport steamers *Saxon* and *Mary A. Boardman*. On the latter vessel were the military governor of Texas, with his staff, and the men and guns of Holcomb's battery.

The Confederates lost 26 killed and 117 wounded; the Union troops 5 killed and 15 wounded, and all the survivors (probably about 250 in number) were made prisoners save the adjutant, Lieutenant Charles A. Davis, who had been sent off to communicate with the fleet. The navy lost 29 killed, 31 wounded, and 92 captured. So ended this inauspicious New Year's day.

The transports made the best of their way to New Orleans with the news. The *Cambria*, with the Texas cavalry and the horses of the 2nd Vermont battery, arrived in the offing on the evening of the 2nd of January. For two days a strong wind and high sea rendered fruitless all efforts to communicate with the shore; then learning the truth, the troops at once returned to New Orleans.

Orders had been left with the guard ship at Pilot Town to send the transport steamers, *Charles Osgood* and *Shetucket*, with the remainder of the 42nd, directly to Galveston. It was now necessary to change these orders, and to do it promptly. The bad news reached headquarters early in the afternoon of the 3rd January: "Stop every thing going to Galveston," was at once telegraphed to the Pass.

Chapter 6

Organizing the Corps

Meanwhile the new troops continued to come from New York, although it was not until the 11th of February that the last detachments landed. The work of organizing the whole available force of the department for the task before it was pursued with vigour. In order to form the moving column, as well as for the purposes of administration, so that the one might not interfere with the other, the main body of troops was composed of four divisions of three brigades each. The garrisons of the defences and the permanent details for guard and provost duty were kept separate. While this was in progress orders came from the War Office dated the 5th of January, 1863, by which all the forces in the Department of the Gulf were designated as the Nineteenth Army Corps, to take effect December 14, 1862, and Banks was named by the President as the corps commander.

To Augur was assigned the First division, to Sherman the Second, to Emory the Third, and to Grover the Fourth. Weitzel, retaining his old brigade, became the second in command in Augur's division. In making up the brigades the regiments were so selected and combined as to mingle the veterans with the raw levies, and to furnish, in right of seniority, the more capable and experienced of the colonels as brigade commanders. Andrews, who had been left in New York to bring up the rear of the expedition, became Chief-of-Staff on the 6th of March, and Bowen was made Provost-Marshal General.

To each division three batteries of artillery were given, including at least one battery belonging to the regular army, thus furnishing, except for the second division, an experienced regular officer as chief of artillery of the division. The cavalry was kept, for the most part, unattached, mainly serving in La Fourche, at Baton Rouge, and with the moving column. The 21st Indiana, changed into the 1st Indiana heavy artillery, was told off to man the siege train, for which duty it was admirably suited. When all had joined, the whole force available for active operations that should not uncover New Orleans was about 25,000. Two thirds, however, were new levies, and of these half were nine months' men. Some were armed with guns that refused to go off. Others did not know the simplest evolutions. In one instance, afterwards handsomely redeemed, the colonel, having to disembark his men, could think of no way save by the novel command, "Break ranks, boys, and get ashore the best way you can." The cavalry, except the six old companies, was poor and quite insufficient in numbers. Of land and water transportation, both indispensable to any possible operation, there was barely enough for the movement of a single division. In Washington, Banks had been led to expect that he might count on the depots or the country for all the material required for moving his army; yet Butler found New Orleans on the brink of starvation; the people had now to be fed, as well as the army, and the provisions that formerly came from the West by the great river had now to find their way from the North by the Atlantic and the Gulf. The depots were calculated, and barely sufficed, for the old force of the department, while the country could furnish very little at best, and nothing at all until it should be occupied.

Again, until he reached his post, Banks was not informed that the Confederates were in force anywhere on the river save Vicksburg, yet, in fact, Port Hudson, 250 miles below Vicksburg and 135 miles above New Orleans, was found strongly entrenched with twenty-nine heavy guns in position and garrisoned by 12,000 men. Long before Banks could have assembled and set in motion a force sufficient to cope with this enemy behind earthworks, the 12,000 became 16,000. Moreover, Banks was not in communication either with Grant or with McClernand; he knew next to nothing of the operations, the movements, or the plans of either; he had not the least idea when the expedition would be ready to move from Memphis; he was even uncertain who the commander of the Northern column was to be. On their part, not only were

Grant, the department commander; McClernand, the designated commander of the Vicksburg expedition; and Sherman, its actual commander, alike ignorant of every thing pertaining to the movements of the column from the Gulf, but, at the most critical period of the campaign, not one of the three was in communication with either of the others. Under these conditions, all concert between the co-operating forces was rendered impossible from the start, and the expectations of the government that Banks would go against Vicksburg immediately on landing in Louisiana were doomed to sharp and sudden, yet inevitable, disappointment.

Grant, believing himself free to dispose of McClernand's new levies, had projected a combined movement by his own forces, marching by Grand Junction, and Sherman's, moving by water from Memphis, on the front and rear of Vicksburg.

Sherman set out from Memphis on the 20th of December in complete ignorance of Halleck's telegram of the 18th, conveying the President's positive order that McClernand was to command the expedition. Forrest cut the wires on the morning of the 19th just in time to intercept this telegram, as well as its counterpart, addressed to McClernand at Springfield, Illinois. On the 29th of December, Sherman met with the bloody repulse of Chickasaw Bluffs. On the 2nd of January he returned to the mouth of the Yazoo, and there found McClernand armed with the bowstring and the baton.

Where was Grant? While his main body was still at Oxford, in march to the Yallabusha, Forrest, the ubiquitous, irrepressible Forrest, struck his line of communications, and, on the 20th of December, at the instant when Sherman was giving the signal to get under way from Memphis, Van Dorn was receiving the surrender of Holly Springs and the keys of Grant's depots. There seemed nothing for it but to fall back on Memphis or starve. Of this state of affairs Grant sent word to Sherman on the 20th. Eleven days later the despatch was telegraphed to Sherman by McClernand; nor was it until the 8th of January that Grant, at Holly Springs, learned from Washington the bad news from Sherman, then ten days old. As if to complete a very cat's-cradle of cross-purposes, Washington had heard of it only through the Richmond newspapers.

The collapse of the northern column, coupled with the Confederate occupation of Port Hudson, had completely changed the nature of the problem confided to Banks for solution. If he was to execute the letter of his instructions at all, he had now to choose between three courses, each involving an impossibility: to carry by assault a strong line of works, three miles long, defended by 16,000 good troops; to lay siege to the place, with the certainty that it would be relieved from Mississippi, and with the reasonable prospect of losing at least his siege train in the venture; to leave Port Hudson in his rear and go against Vicksburg, upon the supposition, in the last degree improbable, that he might find Grant, or McClernand, or Sherman there to meet him and furnish him with food and ammunition. This last alternative appears to have been the one towards which the government leaned, as far as its intentions can be gathered, yet Banks could only have accepted it by sacrificing his communications, putting New Orleans in imminent peril, and creating irreparable and almost inevitable disaster as a price of a remote chance of achieving a great success. In point of fact, in the early days of January, McClernand, accompanied by Sherman as a corps commander, was moving toward the White River and the brilliant adventure of Arkansas Post. After capturing this place on the 11th, McClernand meant to go straight to Little Rock, but Grant rose to the occasion and peremptorily recalled the troops to Milliken's Bend. "This wild-goose chase," as Grant not inaptly termed it, cost McClernand his new-fledged honours as commander of "The Army of the Mississippi," and brought him to Sherman's side as a commander of one of his own corps; a bitter draught of the same medicine he had so recently administered to Sherman.

Had Banks marched against Vicksburg at the same time that McClernand was moving on Little Rock, with Grant cut off somewhere in northern Mississippi, the Confederate commanders must have been dull and slow indeed had they failed to seize with promptitude so rare an opportunity for resuming, at a sweep, the complete mastery of the river, ruining their adversary's campaign, and eliminating 100,000 of his soldiers.

Thus, almost at the first step, the two great expeditions were brought to a standstill. They could neither act together nor advance separately. The generals began to look about them for a new way.

CHAPTER 7

More Ways Than One

Since Port Hudson could neither be successfully attacked nor safely disregarded, the problem now presented to Banks was to find a way around the obstacle without sacrificing or putting in peril his communications. The Atchafalaya was the key to the puzzle, and to that quarter attention was early directed, yet for a long time the difficulties encountered in finding a way to the Atchafalaya seemed well-nigh insuperable. The rising waters were expected to render the largest of the bayous that connect the Atchafalaya and the Mississippi navigable for steamboats of small size and light draught. Of these there were, indeed, but few, so that the work of transporting troops from the one line to the other must have been, at the best, slow and tedious, yet, once accomplished, the army would have found itself, with the help of the navy, above and beyond Port Hudson, with a sufficient line of communications open to the rear, and the Mississippi and the Red River closed against the enemy.

The Confederates had in Western Louisiana, near the mouth of the Teche, a small division of Taylor's troops, about 4,500 strong, with one gunboat. At first Banks thought to leave a brigade, with two or three light-draught gunboats, on Berwick Bay to observe Taylor's force, and then to disregard it as a factor in the subsequent movements. This, while the Atchafalaya was high and the eastern lowlands of the Attakapas widely overflowed, might have been safely done, but all these plans were destined to be essentially modified by a series of unexpected events in widely different quarters.

In the second week of January, Weitzel heard that Taylor meditated an attack on the outlying force at Berwick Bay, and that with this view the armament of the gunboat *Cotton* was being largely augmented. Weitzel resolved to strike the first blow. For this purpose he concentrated his whole force of seven regiments, including four of his own brigade, besides the 21st Indiana, 6th Michigan, and 23rd Connecticut, with Carruth's and Thompson's batteries, four pieces of Bainbridge's battery, Barrett's Troop B of the Louisiana cavalry, and Company B of the 8th New Hampshire, commanded by Lieutenant Charles H. Camp. The 1st Louisiana held Donaldsonville and the 114th New York guarded the railway. To open the way, as well as to meet the fire of the *Cotton*, there were four gunboats of the light-draught flotilla under Buchanan—the flagship *Calhoun*, *Estrella*, *Kinsman*, and *Diana*.

At three o'clock on the morning of the 13th of January the crossing of Berwick Bay began; by half-past ten the gunboats had completed the ferriage of the cavalry and artillery; the infantry following landed at Pattersonville; then the whole force formed in line and, moving forward in the afternoon to the junction of the Teche with the Atchafalaya, went into bivouac. The next morning began the ascent of the Teche. The 8th Vermont was thrown over to the east or left bank of the bayou, while the main line moved forward on the west bank to attack the *Cotton*, now in plain sight. The gunboats led the movement, necessarily in line ahead, owing to the narrowness of the bayou. On either bank Weitzel's line of battle, with skirmishers thrown well forward, was preceded by sixty volunteers from the 8th Vermont and the same number from the 75th New York, whose orders were to move directly up to the *Cotton* and pick off her gunners. The line of battle moved forward steadily with the column of gunboats. Between the Union gunboats and the *Cotton* the bayou had been obstructed so as to prevent any hostile vessel from ascending the stream beyond that point. A brisk fight followed. Under cover of the guns of the navy and of the raking and broadside fire of the batteries, the 8th Vermont and 75th New York first drove off the land supports and then moving swiftly on the *Cotton* silenced her. In this advance the Vermonters captured one lieutenant and forty-one men. The *Cotton* retreated out of range. That night her crew applied the match and let her swing across the bayou to serve as an additional obstruction. In a few moments she was completely destroyed.

Then, having thus easily gained his object, Weitzel returned to

La Fourche. His losses in the movement were 1 officer and 5 men killed, and 2 officers and 25 men wounded. Lieutenant James E. Whiteside, of the 75th New York, who had volunteered to lead the sharpshooters on the right bank, was killed close to the *Cotton*, in the act of ordering the crew to haul down her flag. Among the killed, also, was the gallant Buchanan—a serious loss, not less to the army than to the navy.

During a lull in the naval operations above Vicksburg, occasioned by the want of coal, eleven steamboats that had been in use by the Confederates on the Mississippi between Vicksburg and Port Hudson, took advantage of Porter's absence to slip up the Yazoo for supplies. There Porter's return caught them as in a trap.

Toward the end of January Grant landed on the long neck opposite Vicksburg, and once more set to work on the canal. Porter now determined to let a detachment of his fleet run the gauntlet of the batteries of Vicksburg for the purpose of destroying every thing the Confederates had afloat below the town. The ran *Queen of the West*, Colonel Charles R. Ellet, protected by two tiers of cotton bales, was told off to lead the adventure. On the 2nd of February she performed the feat; then passing on down the river, on the 3rd, ran fifteen miles below the mouth of the Red River, and the same distance up that stream, took and burned three Confederate supply steamboats, and got safely back to Vicksburg on the 5th. Porter was naturally jubilant, for, as it seemed, the mastery of the great river had been the swift reward of his enterprise.

A week later Ellet again ran down the Mississippi and up the Red, burning and destroying until, pushing his success too far, he found himself under the guns of Fort De Russy. A few shots sufficed to disable the *Queen of the West*, which fell into the hands of the Confederates, while Ellet and his men escaped in one of their captures.

Below Natchez they met the *Indianola* coming down the river, after safely passing Vicksburg. On the 24th the Confederate gunboat *Webb*, and the ram *Queen of the West*, now also flying the Confederate colours, came after the *Indianola*, attacked her off Palmyra Island, and sank her. Thus, as suddenly as it had gone from them, the control of the long reach of the Mississippi once more passed over to the Confederates.

At this news Farragut took fire. Between him and the impudent little Confederate flotilla, whose easy triumph had suddenly laid low the hopes and plans of his brother admiral, there stood nothing save the guns of Port Hudson. These batteries he would pass, and for the fourth time, yet not the last, would look the miles of Confederate cannon in the mouth. Banks, whose movements were retarded and to some extent held in abeyance, from the causes already mentioned, promptly fell in with the Admiral's plans, and both commanders conferring freely, the details were soon arranged.

CHAPTER 8

Farragut Passes Port Hudson

While Farragut was putting his fleet in thorough order for this adventure, looking after all needful arrangements with minute personal care, Banks concentrated all his disposable force at Baton Rouge. By the 7th of March, leaving T. W. Sherman to cover New Orleans and Weitzel to hold strongly La Fourche, Banks had a marching column, composed of Augur's, Emory's, and Grover's divisions, 15,000 strong. On the 9th of March tents were struck, to be pitched no more for five hard months, and the next morning the troops were ready, but repairs delayed the fleet, the last vessels of which did not reach Baton Rouge until about the 12th. On that day, for the first time, Banks reviewed his army, on the old battle-ground, in the presence of the admiral, his staff, and many officers of the fleet. The new regiments, with some exceptions, showed plainly the progress already attained under the energetic training and constant work of their officers. The degree of instruction and care then apparent forecast the value of their actual service. The 38th Massachusetts and 116th New York were specially commended in orders.

To hold Baton Rouge about 3,000 men were detached, under Chickering, including the 41st Massachusetts, 173rd New York, 175th New York, 1st Indiana heavy artillery, 3rd Louisiana native guards, Mack's battery, and Troop F of the Rhode Island cavalry.

All arrangements being concerted for the passage of the batteries on the evening of the 14th of March, Grover set out on the afternoon of the 13th, followed, at daybreak the next morning, by Emory, with Augur bringing up the rear. In the afternoon Grover went into camp, covering the intersection of the Bayou Sara road and the road that leads from it toward the river. Emory formed on his left, covering the branches of this road that lead to Springfield Landing and to Ross Landing, his main body supporting the centre at Alexander's plantation. Augur, on the right, held the cross-road that leads from the Bayou Sara road by Alexander's to the Clinton road at Vallandigham's. At two o'clock in the afternoon the signal officers opened communication from Springfield Landing with the fleet at anchor near the head of Prophet Island, and a strong detachment was posted near the landing to maintain the connection.

As the Confederates were known to have a force of about 1,200 cavalry somewhere between Clinton and Baton Rouge, strong detachments became necessary to observe all the approaches and to hold the roads and bridges in the rear in order to secure the withdrawal of the army when the demonstration should be completed, as well as to guard the operation from being inopportunely interrupted. These dispositions reduced the force for battle to about 12,000.

It had been intended to concentrate nearly all the artillery near the river in the vicinity of Ross Landing in such a manner as to engage, or at least divide, the attention of the lower batteries of Port Hudson; but the maps were even more imperfect than usual, and when a reconnaissance, naturally retarded by the enemy's advance guard, showed that the road by which the guns were to have gone into position did not exist, the daylight was already waning. A broken bridge also caused some delay.

At five o'clock in the afternoon Banks received a despatch from Farragut announcing an important change in the hour fixed for the movement of the fleet. Instead of making the attempt "in the gray of the morning," as had been the admiral's first plan, he now meant to get under way at eight o'clock in the evening. When darkness fell, therefore, it found the troops substantially in the positions already described, yet with their outposts well thrown forward.

About ten o'clock the fleet weighed anchor and moved up the river. The flagship *Hartford* took the lead, with the *Albatross* lashed to her port side, next the *Richmond* with the *Genesee*, the *Monongahela* with the *Kineo*, and last the side-wheeler *Mississippi* alone. The *Essex* and *Sachem* remained at anchor below, with the mortar boats, to cover the advance. An hour later a rocket shot up from the bluff and instantly the Confederate batteries opened fire. They were soon joined by long lines of sharpshooters. To avoid the shoal that makes out widely from the western bank, as well as to escape the worst of the enemy's fire, both of musketry and artillery, the ships hugged closely the eastern bluff; so closely, indeed, that the yards brushed the leaves from the overhanging trees and the voices of men on shore could be distinctly heard by those on board. Watch-fires were lighted by the Confederates to show as well the ships as the range; yet this did more harm than good, since the smoke united with that of the guns ashore and afloat to render the fleet invisible. On the other hand, the pilots were soon unable to see.

The *Hartford*, meeting the swift eddy at the bend, where the current describes nearly a right angle, narrowly escaped being driven ashore. The *Richmond*, following, was disabled by a shot through her engine-room when abreast of the upper battery at the turn. The *Monongahela*'s consort, the *Kineo*, lost the use of her rudder, and the *Monongahela* herself ran aground on the spit; presently the *Kineo*, drifting clear, also grounded, but was soon afloat again, and, with her assistance, the *Monongahela* too swung free, after nearly a half hour of imminent peril. Then the *Kineo*, cast loose by her consort, drifted helplessly down the stream, while the *Monongahela* passed up until a heated bearing brought her engines to a stop and she too drifted with the current.

Last of the fleet, the *Mississippi*, unseen in the smoke, and therefore safe enough from the Confederate guns, yet equally unable to see either friend, foe, or landmark, was carried by the current hard on the spit; then, after a half hour of ineffectual exertion, lying alone and helpless under the concentrated aim of the Confederate batteries, she was abandoned and set on fire by her captain. About three in the morning, becoming lighter, as the fire did its work, she floated free and drifted down the stream one mass of flames, in plain view, not merely of the fleet, but also of the army, condemned to stand to arms in sight and sound of the distant battle and now to look on idly as, with a mighty flash and roar, the *Mississippi* cast to the heavens her blazing timbers, amid a myriad of bursting shells, in one mountain of flame: then black silence.

Thus, when at last the gray of the morning came, the *Hartford*

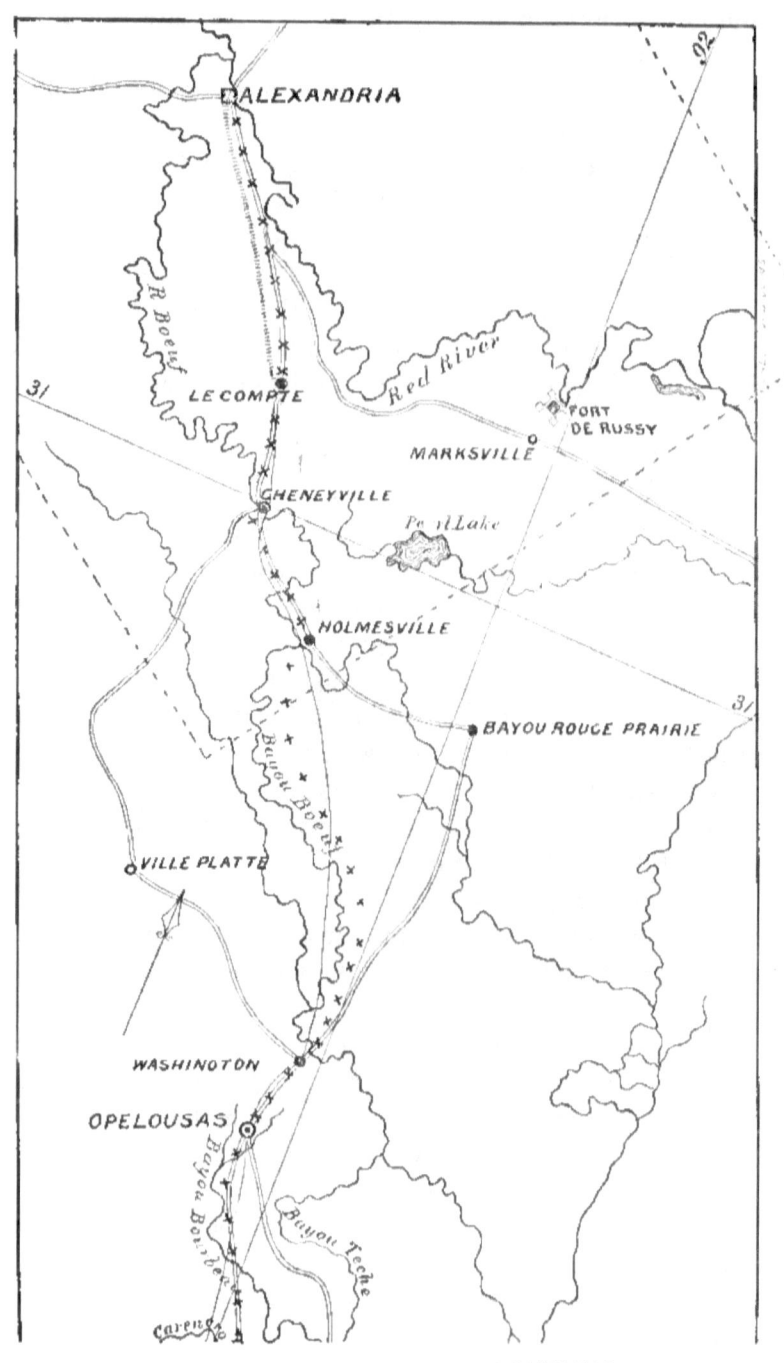

LOUISIANA

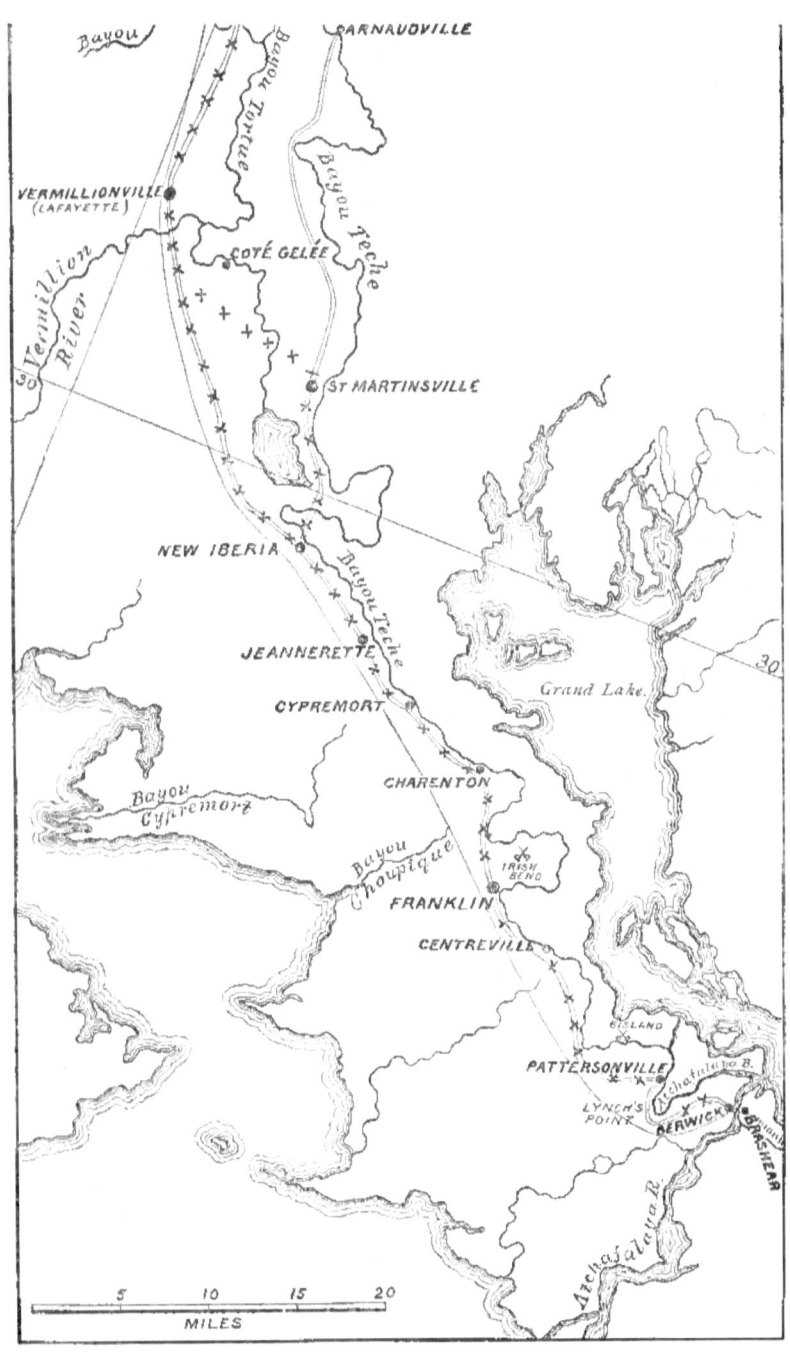

SHEET III.

and *Albatross* rode in safety above Port Hudson, while the *Richmond*, *Monongahela*, *Genesee*, and *Kineo*, all battered and more or less injured, lay at anchor once more near Prophet Island, and the *Mississippi* had perished in a blaze of glory.

Narrowly escaping the total failure of his plans and the destruction of his fleet, Farragut had so far succeeded in his objects that henceforth the Confederates practically lost the control of the Mississippi above Port Hudson, as well as the use of the Red River as their base of supplies. Save in skiff-loads, beef, corn, and salt could no longer be safely carried across the Mississippi, and the high road from Galveston and Matamoras was closed against the valuable and sorely needed cargoes brought from Europe by the blockade runners.

As for the army, it had gained some facility of movement, some knowledge of its deficiencies, and some information of great future value as to the topography of the unknown country about Port Hudson; more than this could hardly have been expected. Indeed, the sole object of the presence of the army was defeated by the movement of the fleet so many hours before the time agreed upon. This object was to make a diversion that might attract the enemy's attention and thus tend to reduce the fire of musketry on the exposed decks of the fleet, and to draw off or hold off the fire of the field-pieces that might otherwise be massed on the river front. The disparity between the relative strength of Banks's army and that of the garrison was too well known to justify the thought of an actual attack upon the works.

Such, however, was not the opinion of the government, which to the last seems to have taken for granted that all that was needed to insure the surrender of Port Hudson was a desire to attack it. Even after the surrender, Halleck, in his annual report for 1863, speaking of the position of affairs in March, said: "Had our land forces invested Port Hudson at this time, it could have been easily reduced, as its garrison was weak . . . but the strength of the place was not then known." In truth, the place was never so strong, before or after, as at this time; nor is it often in war that the information tallies so nearly with the fact. The effective strength of the garrison was more than 16,000. Gardner's monthly report accounts for 1,366 officers and 14,921 men present for duty, together 16,287 out of a total present of 20,388. Besides the twenty-two heavy guns in position, he had thirteen light batteries.

Morning found the army alone and in a bad position, either for attack or defence. Nothing was to be gained by staying there, and much was to be risked. As soon, therefore, as word came through the ever-active and adventurous signal-officers that all was well with what remained of the fleet, Banks once more took up the line of march for Baton Rouge, and went into bivouac in great discomfort on the soggy borders of the Bayou Montesanto, about eight miles north of the town.

Meanwhile, what had become of Farragut? The last seen of the *Hartford* and *Albatross* was on the morning of the 15th by the signal officers at Springfield Landing. The two vessels then lay at anchor beyond the bend above Port Hudson. Several attempts were made to communicate with the Admiral across the intervening neck of lowland. The first was on the 16th, by Parmele, with the 174th New York and a squadron of the 2nd Rhode Island cavalry. Next, on the 18th, Banks, eager to advance the effort, took Dudley's brigade, two sections of Rails's battery, and Magen's troop, and joined Parmele. But for a time these efforts accomplished nothing, since it was impossible to see far over the flat and wooded country; and the Confederates having cut the great levee at Morganza, the whole neighbourhood was under water and the bridges gone. Finally, on the 19th, Colonel Charles J. Paine went out with the 2nd Louisiana, the 174th New York, and a small squad of cavalry, and leaving first the infantry and then most of the troopers behind, and riding on almost alone, succeeded in crossing the bend and gained the levee at the head of the old channel known as Fausse River, about three miles above Port Hudson. There he had a good view of the river, yet nothing was to be seen of the *Hartford* and *Albatross*. Again, on the 24th, Dudley sent Magen with his troop to Hermitage Landing. Pushing on with a few men, Magen got a full view of the reach above Waterloo for five miles, but he too learned nothing of the fleet. Farragut had in fact gone up the river on the 15th, after vainly attempting to exchange signals with his ships below and with the army, and was now near Vicksburg in communication with Admiral Porter, engaged in concerting plans for the future. Before getting under way he had caused three guns to be fired from the

Hartford. This was the signal agreed upon with Banks, but for some reason it was either not heard or not reported.

Just before separating at Baton Rouge, Banks had handed to Farragut a letter addressed to Grant, to be delivered by the Admiral in the event of success. This letter, the first direct communication between the two generals, Grant received on the 20th of March, and from it derived his first information of the actual state of affairs in the Department of the Gulf. After stating his position and force Banks wound up by saying: "Should the Admiral succeed in his attempt, I shall try to open communication with him on the other side of the river, and, in that event, trust I shall hear from you as to your position and movements, and especially as to your views as to the most efficient mode of co-operation upon the part of the forces we respectively command."

With the *Hartford* and *Albatross* controlling the reach between Port Hudson and Vicksburg, as well as the mouth of the Red River and the head of the Atchafalaya, Banks might now safely disregard the movements of the Confederate gunboats. Accordingly, while waiting for Grant's answer, he turned to the execution of his former plan.

Chapter 9

The Teche

In effect, this plan was to turn Port Hudson by way of the Atchafalaya. For the original conception, the credit must be given to Weitzel, who seems indeed to have formed a very similar scheme when he first occupied La Fourche. However, his force was, at that time, barely sufficient for the defence of the territory confided to his care. Not only was there then no particular object in moving beyond the Atchafalaya, but any advance in that direction would have exposed his little corps to disaster on account of the great facilities afforded by the numberless streams for a movement by detachments of the enemy into his rear. It was largely to prepare for an advance into Western Louisiana, as well as to defend his occupancy of La Fourche, that Butler, upon Weitzel's suggestion, had created the gunboat flotilla.

Soon after Banks took the command, Weitzel, who had opinions and the courage to enforce them, laid his ideas before his new chief. On the 18th of January, disturbed by hearing that Admiral Farragut meant to take one of the army gunboats, recently transferred to the navy, away from Berwick Bay, instead of sending more, Weitzel expressed himself strongly in a despatch to headquarters.

> With such a naval force in that bay, in co-operation with a suitable land force, the only true campaign in this section could be made. Look at the map. Berwick Bay leads into Grand Lake, Grand Lake into the Atchafalaya, the Atchafalaya into Red River. Boats drawing not more than four or five feet and in the force I mention [10 or 12], with a proper land force, could clear out the Atchafalaya, Red River, and

Black River. All communications from Vicksburg and Port Hudson cross this line indicated by me. By taking it in the manner I propose, Vicksburg and Port Hudson would be a cipher to the rebels. It would be a campaign that 100,000 men could not so easily fight, and so successfully. It is an operation to which the taking of Galveston Island is a cipher and the capture of the Mobile Bay forts a nonentity.

With these views Banks was himself in accord, yet not in their entirety. The pressure of time led him to desire to avoid divergences into the Teche country. If it were possible, he wished to gain the Atchafalaya by some route at once speedier and more direct. While the explorations were in progress to discover such a route, Weitzel once more took occasion to urge his original plan. On the 15th of February, he wrote to Augur, his division commander:

> I feel it a duty which I owe you and my country to address you at this late hour in the night on the present proposed movement on Butte à la Rose and the Teche country. . . . In all honesty and candour, I do not believe the present plan to be a proper one. . . . Sibley's Texas brigade is somewhere in the Opelousas country. . . . Mouton's main body is in rear of entrenchments on Madame Meade's plantation, six miles below Centreville. If we defeat these two commands we form a junction with our forces near Vicksburg. By pursuing our success to Alexandria, we may capture General Mouton's force, and with little loss, unless it form a junction with Sibley. If it forms a junction, we will meet them near Iberia and engage them in open field, and with a proper force can defeat them. General Emory's whole division (moved to Brashear City) and my brigade can do this work. Let the light transportation, now with General Emory, and all destined for and collected by me be collected at Brashear City. Let two of the brigades be moved to and landed at Indian Bend, while the other two are crossed and attack in front. If Mouton escapes (which I think, if properly conducted, will be doubtful) we form a junction at Indian Bend. We proceed to attack and with much superior force, because I do not believe Mouton and Sibley united will exceed 6,000 men.

We can defeat them, pursue our success to Alexandria and of course get Butte à la Rose; our gunboats to facilitate its fall, attacking it as they cannot accompany us farther up than Saint Martinville. I believe this to be the true and only correct plan of the campaign.

These views were unquestionably sound; they were such as might have been expected of an officer of Weitzel's skill and experience and special knowledge of the theatre of operations. Supported by the strong current of events, they were now to be carried into effect.

At the date of this despatch, Emory's division had been for several weeks near the head of the Bayou Plaquemine, with headquarters at Indian Village, endeavouring to find or force a waterway to the Atchafalaya, while Weitzel was holding his brigade in readiness to co-operate by a simultaneous movement against Taylor on the Teche. Many attempts were made by Emory to carry out the object confided to him, yet all proved failures. Bayou Sorrel, Lake Chicot, Grand River, and the Plaquemine itself, from both ends of the stream, were thoroughly explored, but only to find the bayous choked with driftwood impossible to remove, and until removed rendering the streams impassable. Two of these drifts in Bayou Sorrel were carefully examined by Captain Henry Cochen, of the 173rd New York. The first he reported to be about a mile in length, "composed of one mass of logs, roots, big and small trees, etc., jammed tightly for thirty feet, the whole length of my pole." The second drift, just beyond, was found nearly as bad, and farther on lay another even worse. Moreover, a thorough reconnaissance showed the whole country, between the Mississippi and the Atchafalaya above the Plaquemine, to be impracticable at that season for all arms. After more than a month of this sort of work, Emory was called across the river to Baton Rouge to take part in the events narrated in the last chapter.

Banks returned to New Orleans on the 24th of March, and the next day ordered Grover to embark and move down the river to Donaldsonville, and thence march down the Bayou La Fourche to Thibodeaux. At the same time Emory was ordered, as soon as Grover's river transports should be released, to embark his command for Algiers, and thence move by the railway to Brashear.

Meanwhile, on the 18th of March, Weitzel learned of the presence of the *Queen of the West* and *Webb* in the Atchafalaya, and as this seemed to indicate an intention to attack him, and the navy had no more light-draught gunboats to spare for his further security, to avoid having his hand forced and the game spoiled, he discreetly fell back on the 21st to the railway bridge over Bayou Boeuf, and took up a position where he was not exposed, as at Brashear, to the risk of being cut off by any sudden movement of the enemy.

On the 28th of March the *Diana* was sent to reconnoitre the Confederate position and strength on the lower Teche; but continuing on down the Atchafalaya, instead of returning by Grand Lake as intended, and thus running into the arms of the enemy, she fell an easy prey. The *Calhoun* went to her relief, but ran aground, and the *Estrella* had to go to the assistance of the *Calhoun*. Acting-Master James L. Peterson, commanding the *Diana*, was killed, and Lieutenant Pickering D. Allen, aide-de-camp to General Weitzel, was wounded. With the *Diana* there fell into the enemy's hands nearly one hundred and fifty prisoners. This gave the Confederates three rather formidable boats in the Atchafalaya and the Teche.

The movement of the troops was necessarily slow, as well by reason of the extremely limited facilities for transportation, as because of the state of the roads, but by the 8th of April every thing was well advanced, and on that day Banks moved his headquarters to Brashear. Weitzel, who had been reinforced by the siege-train, manned by the 1st Indiana heavy artillery, had already re-occupied his former front on Berwick Bay. Emory was in bivouac at Bayou Ramos, about five miles in the rear of Weitzel, and Grover at Bayou Boeuf, about four miles behind Emory. Thus the whole movement was almost completely masked from the Confederates, who from their side of the bay saw only Weitzel, and knew little or nothing of the gathering forces in his rear. So little, indeed, that Taylor, with his usual enterprise, seems to have thought this a favourable moment for attempting upon Weitzel the same operation that Weitzel had been so long meditating for the discomfiture of Taylor.

Emory marched early in the morning of the 9th of April and closed up on Weitzel, who, an hour later, about ten o'clock, began to cross. No enemy was seen save a small outpost, engaged in observing the movement. This detachment retired before Weitzel's advance, without coming to blows. Weitzel at once sent his Assistant Adjutant-General, Captain John B. Hubbard, with Perkins's and Williamson's troops of cavalry and one section of Bainbridge's battery to discover the enemy's position. The Confederates were found to be in some force in front of Pattersonville, with their cavalry pickets advanced to within a mile of Weitzel's front.

As soon as Weitzel had completed his crossing, and released the boats, Emory followed him. The four brigades bivouacked in front of the landing-place that night. The gunboats, having done the greater share of the ferriage, went back to the east bank for Grover.

Grover, who had marched from Bayou Boeuf at nine o'clock, just as Emory was arriving at Brashear, came there, in his turn, early in the afternoon. The plan had been that Grover should embark immediately, and, having his whole force on board by an early hour in the night, the boats should set out at daylight, so as to place Grover by nine o'clock on the morning of the 11th in position for the work cut out for him. With few pilots, and the shores unlighted, it was out of the question to attempt the navigation of the waters of the Grand Lake during the night. However, it was not until the night of the 11th that Grover was able to complete the embarkation of his division. To understand this it is necessary to observe that Emory and Weitzel, in making the passage of Berwick Bay, were merely crossing a short ferry, so that the boats engaged in the transfer could be loaded rapidly to almost any extent, so long as they remained afloat, and being unloaded with equal facility, were in a few minutes ready to repeat the operation. In Grover's case, however, the infantry, artillery, cavalry, and stores had all to be taken care of at once, with every provision for fighting a battle. For this the artillery was considered indispensable, and it was not without great trouble and long delay that the guns and horses were got afloat. Fate seemed to be against Grover, for after all had been accomplished by the greatest exertion on his part, as well as on the part of his officers and the corps quartermasters, a fog set in so dense that the pilots were unable to see their way. This continued until nine o'clock on the morning of the 12th; then at last the movement began.

About noon, on the 11th of April, Weitzel, leading the advance of the main column, moved forward. At once his skirmishers felt the skirmishers of the enemy, who retired slowly, without attempting any serious opposition. In the evening, Weitzel rested in line of battle a short distance above Pattersonville. Emory followed closely, and went into bivouac on Weitzel's left. The march had not been begun earlier, and the enemy was not pressed, because it was desired to keep him amused until Grover should have gained his rear, and Grover had not yet started.

After the early morning of Sunday, the 12th of April, had been spent in light skirmishing and in demonstrations of the cavalry, designed to observe the enemy, and at the same time to attract and hold his attention, word came that Grover was under way. Banks knew that the passing fleet must soon be in plain sight of the Confederates. Therefore, it was now necessary to move promptly, and to feel the enemy strongly, yet not too strongly, lest he should abandon his position too soon and suddenly spoil all. From this moment it is important to remember that, save in the event of complete success, no word could come from Grover for nearly two days. The first news from him was expected to be the sound of his guns in the enemy's rear.

At eleven o'clock the bugle again sounded the advance. The whole line moved forward, continually skirmishing, until, about four o'clock in the afternoon, the infantry came under fire of the Confederate guns in position on the lines known as Camp Bisland. The line of march led up the right bank of the Atchafalaya until the mouth of the Teche was reached, thence up the Teche, partly astride the stream, yet mainly by the right bank. At first Weitzel formed on the right, Emory on the left, but as the great bend of the Teche was reached, about four miles below Bisland, and by the nature of the ground the front became narrowed at the same time that in following the change of direction of the bayou the line was brought to a wheel, Weitzel took ground to the left in two lines, while Emory advanced Paine's brigade into the front line on Weitzel's right, placed Ingraham in his second line, and made a third line with Godfrey.

Then finding the enemy beyond the Teche too strong for the cavalry to manage single-handed, Banks called on Emory to reinforce the right bank. Emory sent Bryan across with the 175th New York and a section of the 1st Maine battery, commanded by Lieutenant Eben D. Haley. They were to push the enemy back, and to conform to the advance of the main line.

The day was hot, the air close, and the march over the fields of young cane, across or aslant the heavy furrows and into and over the deep ditches, was trying to the men, as yet but little accustomed to marches. Fortunately, however, there was no need of pressing the advance until Grover's guns should be heard. About half-past five in the afternoon a brisk artillery fire began, and was kept up until night fell; then Emory moved the 4th Wisconsin forward to hold a grove in front of a sugar-house, near the bayou, well in advance of his right, in order to prevent the Confederates from occupying it, to the annoyance of the whole line.

After dark all the pickets were thrown well forward in touch with those of the enemy, but the main lines were drawn back out of range, for the sake of a good night's sleep before a hard day's work.

Chapter 10

Bisland

The works behind which the Confederates now stood to battle were named Camp Bisland or Fort Bisland, in honour of the planter whose fields were thus given over to war. The defences consisted of little more than a line of simple breastworks, of rather low relief, thrown completely across the neck of dry land on either bank of the Teche, the flanks resting securely on the swamps that border Grand Lake on the left and on the right extend to the Gulf. The position was well chosen, for five miles below Centreville, where the plantation of Mrs. Meade adjoins the Bethel Place, the neck is at its narrowest. The Teche, passing a little to the left of the centre of the works, enabled the guns of the *Diana*, moving freely around the bends, to contribute to the defence, while the obstructions placed below the works hindered the ascent of the bayou by the Union gunboats. The Confederate right was also somewhat strengthened by the embankment of the unfinished railroad to Opelousas. On the other hand, from the nature of the ground, low and flat as it was, the works were in part rather commanded than commanding; yet the difference of level was inconsiderable, and for a force as small as Taylor's, outnumbered as his was, any slight disadvantage in this way was more than compensated by the shortness of the line.

Along the banks of the bayou were a few live oaks; on either flank the swamp was densely wooded, mainly with cypress, cottonwood, and willow, with an outlying and almost impenetrable canebrake, while between the attacking columns and the Confederate position, on either bank of the bayou, stretched a field where the young shoots of the sugar-cane stood knee-high. This was crossed at right angles with the bayou, by many of those wide and deep ditches by which the planters of Louisiana are accustomed to drain their tilled lowlands.

Such was the scene of the action now about to be fought, known to the Union army as the battle of Bisland or Fort Bisland; to the Confederates, as the battle of Bethel Place or Bayou Teche.

During the whole of the night of the 12th a dense fog prevailed, but this lifting about eight o'clock on the morning of Monday, the 13th of April, disclosed a day as bright and beautiful as the scene was fair. At an early hour the whole line advanced to within short musketry range, in substantially the same order as on the previous day. An attack by a detachment of Confederate cavalry upon the skirmishers of the 4th Wisconsin, in advance of the sugar-house, was easily thrown off, and a later demonstration by the Confederate infantry upon Paine's position in the grove shared the same fortune. Emory moved first the 8th New Hampshire, and afterwards the 133rd and 173rd New York, to the support of the 4th Wisconsin. At the same time Banks ordered Emory to send the other four regiments of Gooding's brigade and the two remaining sections of the 1st Maine battery to reinforce Bryan with the 175th New York on the left bank of the Teche, in order to be prepared, not only to meet a flank movement of the Confederates from that direction, but also to carry to works on that side, should this be thought best. After these dispositions had been completed the advance was steady and continuous, yet not rapid, until toward noon the last of the Confederates retired behind their breastworks and opened fire with musketry. The ditches already spoken of hindered the progress of the Union artillery, yet not seriously, while they afforded an excellent protection for the supports of the batteries and enabled the lines of infantry to rest at intervals: no small gain, for the sun grew very hot, and the march over the heavy windrows and across the deep ditches was exhausting.

The Confederate gunboat *Diana* took position well in front of the works, so as to command completely the right flank of Emory and Weitzel as they approached by a fire that, had it not been checked, must have enfiladed the whole line. Just as this fire was beginning to be disturbing it was silenced by a fortunate shot from one of the two 30-pounder Parrott guns, served by the 1st Indiana,

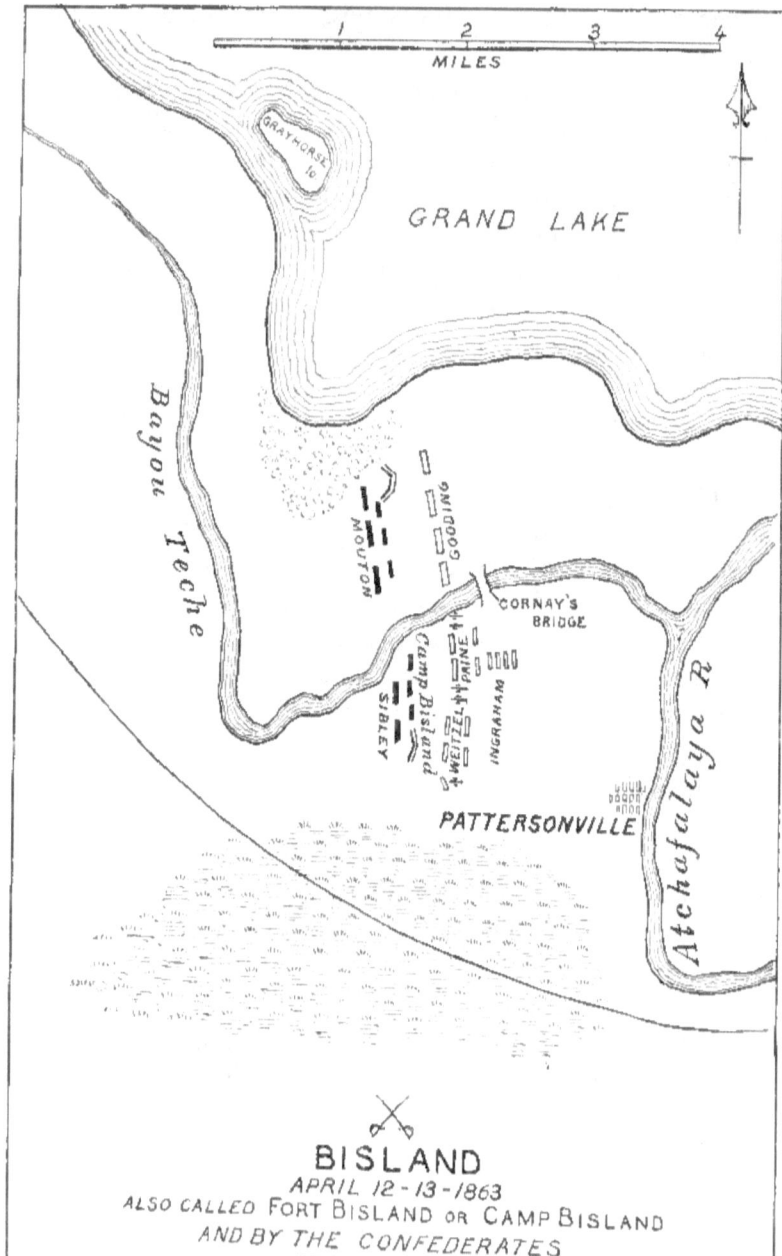

posted in rear of Weitzel's left and trained upon the *Diana*, under the personal supervision of Arnold. The third shot from this battery, aimed at the flash of the *Diana's* guns, exploded in her engine room; then above the trees, whose leafage full and low hid the vessel, was seen a flash like a puff of vapour; a rousing cheer was heard from the sharpshooters of the 4th Wisconsin and 8th New Hampshire, who had been told off to keep down the fire of the gunboat; and the *Diana* was seen to pass up the bayou and out of the fight.

All risk of an enfilade file being thus removed, the whole Union line quickly closed with the Confederates, and the engagement became general with artillery and musketry. On both sides of the bayou the firing was brisk, at times even severe. Save where the view was broken here and there by the trees or became lightly clouded by the smoke of battle, the whole field lay in plain sight. As the course of the Teche in ascending turned toward the left, Gooding, on the east bank, had the wheeling flank, while Weitzel formed the pivot.

Gooding went forward in gallant style, his men quickening their pace at times to a run, in order to keep the alignment with the main body on the west bank. Perceiving on his extreme right, toward the lake, a fine grove or copse, Gooding threw out Sharpe with the 156th New York to examine the wood with a view of attempting to turn the left flank of the Confederate lines. These, as it proved, did not extend beyond the grove, but there ended in an unfinished redoubt. Indeed, nearly the whole of the Confederate works on the east side of the bayou, although laid out long since, had been but recently and hastily thrown up, after it became known to Taylor that Banks was crossing to attack him. In the wood, about five hundred yards in advance of the breastworks, Mouton had posted Bagby's 3rd Texas regiment. The Texans held their ground so stiffly that Gooding found it necessary to send his own regiment, the 31st Massachusetts, to the support of Sharpe. Mouton supported Bagby with the left wing of the 18th Louisiana and part of Fournet's and Waller's battalions. Gooding's men carried the rifle-pits in the wood by a spirited charge, in which they took two officers and eighty-four men prisoners. His main line in the open ground between the wood and the bayou was formed by the 38th Massachusetts, deployed as skirmishers, covering the front and followed, at a distance of about one hundred and fifty yards, by the 53rd Massachusetts, in like order. Behind the 53rd, two sections of the 1st Maine battery were posted to command two parallel plantation roads leading up the bayou, while the third section was held in reserve. After the 31st Massachusetts had gone to the support of the right, the main line here was composed of the 175th New York. Shortly after five o'clock the 53rd Massachusetts relieved the 38th, which had expended its ammunition, and was falling back under orders to replenish. When this was done, the 38th once more advanced and formed in support of the skirmish line.

Meanwhile on the left of the Teche the main body moved forward in two lines of battalions deployed, Paine on the right and Weitzel on the left, while Ingraham, in column of companies, formed the reserve for both. Paine's first line on the right, nearest the bayou, was composed of the 4th Wisconsin and 8th New Hampshire, his second line of the 133rd New York and the 173rd New York. Mack's 20-pounders commanded the bayou road, and Duryea went into battery in advance of the centre, between Paine and Weitzel.

Weitzel's front line was composed of the 8th Vermont and 114th New York, with the 12th Connecticut, 160th New York, and 75th New York in the second line. The guns of Bainbridge and Carruth went into battery near the left flank, and working slowly kept down the fire of the Confederate artillery in their front. When the fire of musketry became hot, Weitzel sent the 75th New York to try to gain the canebrake on the left, in advance of the enemy's works, with a view of turning that flank. Of this movement Taylor says in his report that it was twice repulsed by the 5th Texas and Waller's battalion, under Green, and the 28th Louisiana, Colonel Gray, aided by the guns of Semmes's battery and the Valverde battery. However, the counter-movement on the part of the Confederates, being begun in plain view, was instantly seen, and Banks sent word to Weitzel to check it. With this object, Weitzel ordered the 114th New York to go to the support of the 75th. A brisk fight followed, without material advantage to either side. In truth, the canebrake formed an impenetrable obstacle to the combatants, who, when once they had passed within the outer edge of the tangle, were unable either to see or approach one another, although the struggle was plainly visible from the front of both armies.

The reserve of Parrott guns, manned by the 1st Indiana and composed of four 30-pounders and four 20-pounders, was posted under McMillan to cover the left flank and the broken centre where it was pierced by the bayou, as well as to watch for the return of the *Diana* to activity. Toward evening the remaining guns of the 1st Indiana, two 12-pounder rifles under Cox, after being posted in support of the centre, were sent to the left to assist Bainbridge and Carruth, whose ammunition was giving out.

Banks, after gaining advanced positions in contact with the enemy, forbore to press them hard because, as has been seen, his whole purpose was to hold the Confederates where they stood until he could hear of Grover or from Grover. As the day advanced without news or the long-expected sound of Grover's guns, Banks began to grow impatient and to fear that the adventure from which so much had been hoped had somehow miscarried. He therefore became even more anxious than before lest the Confederates should move off under cover of the coming night. Accordingly, during the afternoon, although it had been his previous purpose not to deliver an assault until certain that Grover held the Confederate line of retreat, Banks gave discretionary orders to Emory and Weitzel to form for an attack and move upon the Confederate works if a favourable opportunity should present itself. The exercise of this discretion in turn devolved upon the commanders of the front line, that is, upon Weitzel and Paine, for Gooding, being out of communication, except by signal, with the troops on the west bank, was occupied in conforming to their movements. Paine and Weitzel, after conferring, resolved to attack, and having made every preparation, only waited for the word from the commanding general.

The day was waning; it was already past four o'clock; and Banks was still somewhat anxiously weighing the approach of night and the cost of the assault against the chance of news from Grover, when suddenly, straight up the bayou, and high above the heads of Banks and his men, a 9-inch shell came hurtling, and as it was seen to burst over the lines of Bisland, from far in the rear broke the deep roar of the *Clifton's* bow-gun. Soon from below the obstructions that barred her progress came a messenger bearing the long-expected tidings of Grover. At last he was on land and in march toward his position. With a sense of relief Banks recalled the orders for the assault and drew his front line back out of fire of the Confederate musketry so that the men might rest. To relieve the exhausted skirmish line, the 4th Massachusetts and the 162nd New York of Ingraham's brigade were sent forward from the reserve, leaving him only the 110th New York.

By dawn the next morning, at all events, Banks calculated, the turning column would be in place; accordingly during the night he gave orders to assault along the whole front as soon as it should be light enough to see. However, shortly after midnight, sounds were heard on the picket line, indicating some unusual movement behind the Confederate works. When, at daybreak, the various skirmishers moved forward in eager rivalry, they found the Confederates gone. Captain Allaire, leading his company of the 133rd New York, was the first to enter the works; the regiment itself and the 8th New Hampshire followed closely, and the colours of the 8th were the first to mount the parapet, where they were planted by Paine. On the left bank, this honour fell to the 53rd Massachusetts. But in truth the surge was so nearly simultaneous that the whole line of entrenchments on both sides of the bayou, from right to left, was crossed almost at the same instant.

It was nine o'clock on Monday night when Taylor learned of Grover's movements and position, as narrated in the next chapter. Taylor at once began to move out of the lines of Bisland and to direct his attention to Grover in order to secure a retreat. Just before daylight Green, to whom, with his 5th Texas, Waller's battalion, and West's section of Semmes's battery, Taylor had given the more than usually delicate task of covering the rear, marched off the ground, leaving nothing behind save one 24-pounder siege gun and a disabled howitzer of Cornay's battery. Without losing an instant the pursuit of the retreating Confederates was begun, Weitzel leading the way, and was conducted with vigour and with scarcely a halt, notwithstanding the energetic opposition of the Confederate rear-guard, until early in the afternoon, just beyond Franklin, Emory's advance guard, under Paine, following the bayou road, ran into Grover's under Dwight, approaching from the opposite direction. Weitzel, having entered Franklin without opposition, kept the left-hand or cut-off road until he came to the burnt bridge over the Choupique, by which, as will presently be seen, the Confederates had escaped.

Gooding, after occupying the works in his front, crossed the Teche by a bridge to the west bank and fell into Emory's column behind Ingraham. The *Clifton*, as soon as the obstructions could be removed, got under way and moved up the bayou abreast with the advance of the army.

The losses of the Nineteenth Army Corps in this its first battle were 3 officers and 37 men killed, 8 officers and 176 men wounded; in all 224. The 38th Massachusetts headed the list with 6 killed and 29 wounded, and Gooding's brigade, to which this regiment belonged, reported 87 casualties, or 38 per cent. of the whole. In the six light batteries 15 horses were killed and 12 wounded, and one caisson of the 1st Maine was upset and lost in crossing the Teche to go into action.

The losses of the Confederates have never been reported and no means are known to exist for estimating them.

The disparity of the forces engaged was more than enough to overcome the Confederate advantage of position, for Banks had 10,000 men with 38 guns, while Taylor reports but 4,000 men with four batteries, estimated at 24 or 25 guns. To these must be added the *Diana*, until disabled on Monday morning, and to the Union strength the *Clifton*, after she arrived and opened fire at long range on Monday afternoon.

At Bisland the new headquarters flags were for the first time carried under fire. These distinguishing colours, as prescribed in General Orders on the 18th of February, were guidons four feet square attached to a lance twelve feet long, made for convenience in two joints. In camp or garrison they served to indicate the quarters of the general commanding the corps, division, or brigade, while on the march they were borne near his person by a mounted orderly, commonly a trusty sergeant. The flag of the Nineteenth Army Corps was blue with a white four-pointed star in the middle, and on the star the figures 19 in red. From this the division flags differed only in having a red ground and the number of the division in black. The brigade flags had blue, white, and blue horizontal stripes of equal width, with the number of the brigade in black in the white stripe. Thenceforward these colours were borne through every engagement in which the corps took part. Not one of them was ever abandoned by its bearer or taken by the enemy.

CHAPTER 11

Irish Bend

Grover's instructions were to gain a landing on the shore of Grand Lake, and then marching on Franklin, to cut off Taylor's retreat or to attack him in the rear, as circumstances might suggest.

We have seen how, instead of being ready to move from Berwick Bay on the morning of the 10th of April, Grover found his departure delayed by the various causes already mentioned until the morning of the 12th was well advanced.

The flotilla, under Lieutenant-Commander Cooke, composed of the flag-ships *Estrella*, *Arizona*, *Clifton*, and *Calhoun*, having completed the ferriage of Emory and Weitzel over Berwick Bay, was now occupied in assisting the army transports to convey Grover to his destination, besides standing ready to protect his movement and his landing with its guns.

About noon, when off Cypress Island, the *Arizona* ran hard and fast aground, and four precious hours were lost in a vain attempt to get her afloat. If, in the light of after events, this may seem like time wasted, it should always be remembered that all four of the gunboats were crowded with troops, while an attack from the *Queen of the West* and her consorts was to be looked for at any moment. Finally, rather than to put the adventure in peril by a longer delay, Cooke determined to leave the *Arizona* to take care of herself, and once more steaming ahead, at half-past seven o'clock, the gunboats and transports came to anchor below Miller's Point, off Madame Porter's plantation. At this place, known as Oak Lawn, Grover in the orders under which he was acting had been told he might expect to find a good shell road leading straight to the Teche, and crossing the bayou about the middle of the bow called Irish Bend.

Grover at once sent Fiske with two companies of the 1st Louisiana ashore in the *Clifton*'s boats to reconnoitre. It was midnight when, after carefully examining the ground, Fiske returned to the gunboat and reported the road under water, and quite impracticable for all arms. The fleet then got under way, and proceeding about six miles farther up the lake, anchored beyond Magee's Point.

Before daylight Dwight sent two of his staff officers, Captain Denslow and Lieutenant Matthews, ashore, with a small detachment from the 6th New York, to examine the plantation road leading from this point to the Teche. The road being found practicable for all arms, the debarkation began at daybreak.

Dwight landed first. As soon as his leading regiment, the 1st Louisiana, reached the shore, Holcomb threw forward two companies, under Lieutenant-Colonel Fiske, as skirmishers, and formed the battalion in line to cover the landing.

Taylor, when he first learned that the gunboats and transports had passed up Grand Lake, had sent Vincent, with the 2nd Louisiana cavalry and a section of Cornay's battery, to Verdun landing, about four miles behind Camp Bisland, to observe and oppose the movement. This was about noon on Sunday, the 12th. In the evening, hearing of the progress of the fleet, Taylor sent a second section of Cornay's battery to the lake, and going himself to Vincent ordered him to follow the movement and try to prevent a landing. The next morning Taylor sent Reily with the 4th Texas, to join Vincent and aid him in retarding Grover's progress.

Taylor seems to have censured Vincent for letting Grover land, yet in truth Vincent was not to blame. The line he had to watch was too long for his numbers, and the Union flotilla could and did move more rapidly on the lake than the Confederate troops by the roads. When he had stationed his pickets at the probable landing-places, and taken up a central position to support them, he had done all that lay in his power. The range and weight of the 9-inch shells of the navy were alone enough to put a serious opposition to the landing out of the question, but as soon as Vincent found where the attempt was to be made, he disposed his men and guns to retard it. Two of Cornay's guns even tried, ineffectually of course, to destroy the transports: Cooke quickly drove them off.

As Holcomb's skirmishers deployed they were met by a brisk

fusillade from Vincent's men strongly posted in ambush behind a high fence in the thick wood that skirts the shore; but when Holcomb advanced his battalion Vincent's men fell back on their main body and left the wood to Holcomb, who immediately moved to the edge of the clearing and held it, observing the enemy on the farther border. This was Vincent with his regiment and the four guns of Corney; and from this moment all that was happening on the lake shore passed unseen by the Confederates.

Meanwhile the landing went on very slowly, for the transports could not come nearer to the beach than a hundred yards, and, although the foot-soldiers were able to jump overboard and scramble ashore, and the horses could also take to the water, it was necessary to make a bridge of flats for the guns and caissons of the artillery. Thus it was four o'clock in the afternoon before the whole division found itself assembled on the plantation of Duncan McWilliams on the shore of the lake, with the Teche at the upper reach of Irish Bend four miles to the southward, and Charenton in the hollow of Indian Bend lying but two miles toward the southwest. There were roads in either direction, but Irish Bend was the way to Franklin, and to Franklin Grover was under orders to go.

About nine o'clock in the morning Dwight had borrowed from Birge his two leading regiments, the 13th Connecticut and the 159th New York, to support the 1st Louisiana. Grover also gave Dwight Closson's battery and Barrett's troop of cavalry. Toward noon, moving a detachment by his left, Dwight seized the bridge that crosses the Teche in approaching Madame Porter's plantation from the northward, just in time to extinguish the flames that Vincent's men had lighted to destroy it. After seizing the bridge at Oak Lawn, Barrett galloped down the left bank of the Teche and seized the bridge a mile or two below, by which the same small plantation is reached from the eastward; probably by the shell road that Grover had been told to take, and at which he had tried to land. Barrett was in time to save the bridge from Vincent, and to hold the advantage thus gained Dwight soon sent Holcomb with the 1st Louisiana, 131st New York, 6th New York, 22nd Maine, and Closson's battery.

Meanwhile, the division being entirely without wagons, save a few that were loaded with the reserve ammunition, still another wait took place while the men's haversacks were being filled with hard bread and coffee. All these delays were now having their effect upon Grover's own calculations. He now knew nothing of Banks's movements or his situation. Of his own movements he was bound to suppose that Taylor had received early and full information. Moreover, the topography of the country where Grover found himself was obscure and to him unknown. Instead, therefore, of marching forward as fast as his troops could land, boldly and at all hazards to seize the roads by which Taylor must retreat, Grover now took counsel with prudence and concealing his force behind the natural screen of the wood, waited till his whole division should be fully ready.

Thus it was six o'clock and the sun stood low among the treetops when Grover, with Birge and Kimball, took up the line of march for the Teche. Crossing the upper of the two bridges, he went into bivouac on the right bank on the plantation of Madame Porter, and called in Dwight's detachment. Before setting out to rejoin the division Holcomb burned the lower bridge, under orders, and then marching up the left bank, crossed the upper bridge at a late hour of the night. In Grover's front stood Vincent alone, for Reily had not yet come; but in the darkness it was impossible for Grover to make out the enemy's force, or even to find his exact position.

When about nine o'clock that night, as related in the last chapter, Taylor heard the news from Reily, he supposed Grover to be already in strong possession of the only road by which the Confederates could make good their retreat up the Teche; yet desperate as the situation seemed, Taylor at once made up his mind to try to extricate himself from the toils. Sending his wagon train ahead, soon after midnight he silently moved out of the lines of Bisland and marched rapidly on Franklin, leaving Green to cover the rear and retard the pursuit. These dispositions made, Taylor himself rode at once to his reversed front, a mile east of Franklin. With him were Reily, whom he had picked up on the road below Franklin, Vincent who with the four guns of Cornay was still watching Grover, and Clack's Louisiana battalion, which had come in from New Iberia just in the nick of time. The plantation with the sugar-house, then belonging to McKerrall, is now known as Shaffer's. The grounds of Oak Lawn adjoin it toward the east and north, and along its western boundary stand Nerson's Woods, whence the coming battle takes the name given to it in the Confederate accounts. Here, beneath the trees, along their eastern skirt and behind a stout fence, Taylor formed his line of battle, facing toward the east, and waited for the coming of Grover. South of the bayou road stood Clack; on his left, two pieces of Cornay's battery, next Reily, then Vincent with a second section of Cornay's guns. The task before them was simple but desperate. They were to hold off Grover until all but they had safely passed behind the living barrier. Then they were to extricate themselves as best they could, and falling in the rear of the main column of the Confederate army try to make good their own escape. Before this could happen, Grover might overwhelm them or Banks might overtake them; yet there was no other way.

As early on the morning of Tuesday the 14th of April as it was light enough to see, Grover marched on Franklin by the winding bayou road. Preceded by Barrett and a strong line of skirmishers, Birge with Rodgers's battery led the column; Dwight with Closson's battery, followed; while Kimball with Nims's battery brought up the rear.

The head of Grover's column had gone about two miles, and in a few moments more would have turned the sharp corner of the bayou and faced toward Franklin, when, on the right, near the sugar-house, Birge's skirmishers ran into those of Clack's battalion, and the battle of Irish Bend began.

Between Birge and the concealed Confederate ranks, past which he was in fact marching, while his line of direction gave his right flank squarely to the hostile front, lay the broad and open fields of McKerrall's plantation, where the young sugar-cane stood a foot high above the deep and wide furrows. From recent ploughing and still more recent rains the fat soil was soft and heavy under foot, and here and there the cross-furrows, widening and deepening into a ditch, added to the toil and difficulty of movement, both for men and guns. On the left flowed the dark and sluggish Teche. On the right lay the swamp, thickly overgrown and nearly impassable, whence the waters of the Choupique begin to ooze toward the Gulf. Along the southern border of this morass ran a great transverse ditch that carried off the gathered seepage of the

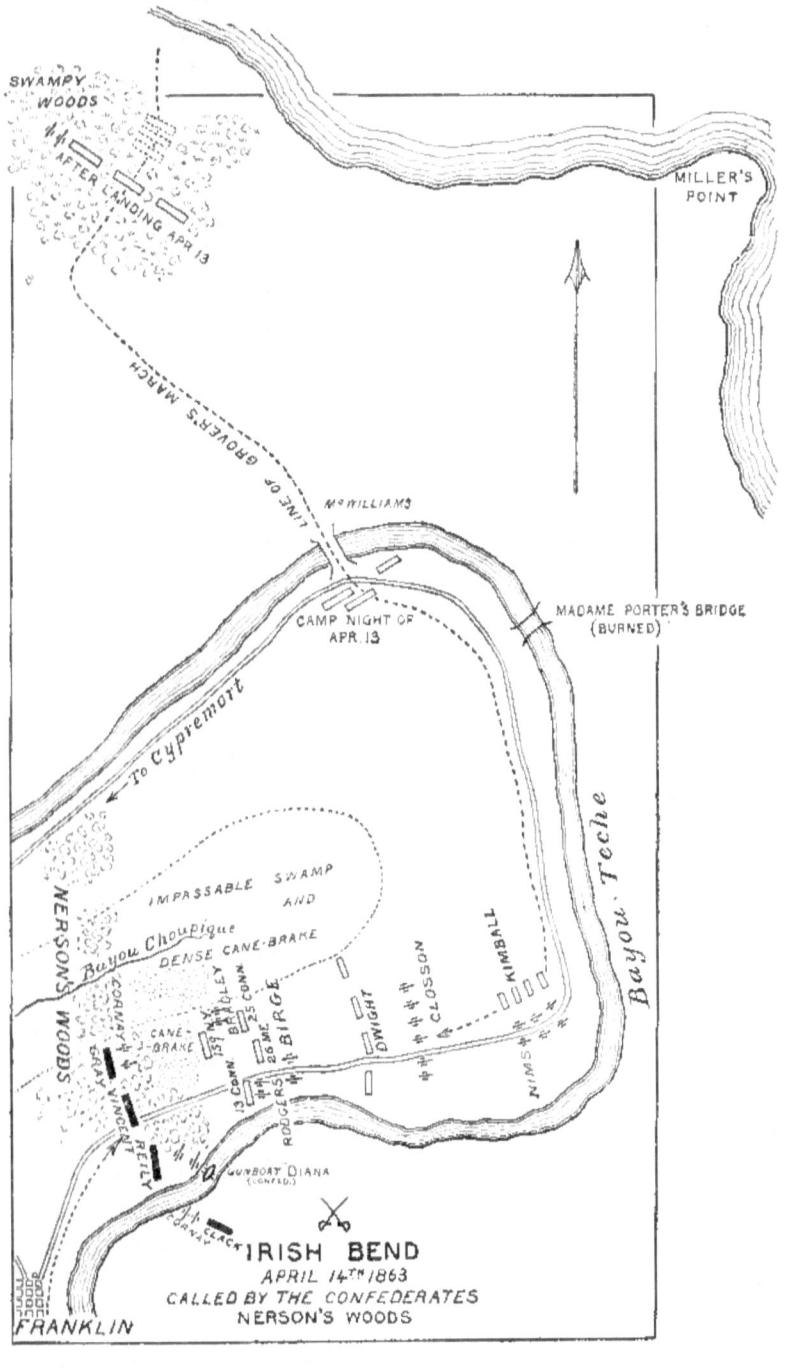

lesser drains. In front, on the western edge of the cane-field, stood Nerson's woods, where, as yet unseen, the Confederates lay in wait; while before them, like a screen, stretched a low fringe of brake and undergrowth.

Birge's order of march placed the 25th Connecticut in the advance, one wing deployed as skirmishers across the road, the other wing in reserve. Next came the 26th Maine with Bradley's section of Rodgers's battery, then the 159th New York, then the remainder of Rodgers's battery, while the 13th Connecticut brought up the rear. When he saw his skirmishers briskly engaged and by the sound and smoke discovered the position of the enemy, Birge made the reserved battalion of the 25th Connecticut change front forward and move across the field against the Confederate left. Bissell led his men quickly to within a hundred yards of the wood, where they lay down under the partial cover of a ditch and began firing. Hubbard, with the 26th Maine, came up on Bissell's left and took up the same tactics. At once the enfilade fire of the Confederate line became vigorous and annoying, until Bradley took his two guns at a gallop to the skirt of the undergrowth opposite the interval between the infantry battalions and, opening fire at five hundred yards' range, engaged for a time the whole attention of the Confederate cannoneers. Then Grover, who rode with Birge, sent in the 159th New York on the left of the 26th Maine, with orders to take the wood, while the 13th Connecticut, marching round the bend of the bayou, formed on the extreme left between the stream and the road.

Molineux promptly deployed his regiment, and gallantly led it forward at the double-quick over and beyond the left of the line already formed, until the men were within short point-blank range of the enemy's musketry; there, finding them exhausted by the rapid advance over the rough and heavy ground, as well as suffering severely from the bullets of the enemy, he made the men throw off their blankets and overcoats, lie down, and open a vigorous fire. Perhaps under the stress of this, but more probably in preparation for the counter-attack, the Confederates slackened their fire, and Molineux, perceiving his opportunity, as it seemed, was in the act of uttering the command "Forward!" when a bullet struck him in the mouth and he fell, painfully wounded, leaving the command of the regiment, for the time, to Captain Dayton. Lieutenant-Colonel Draper had already fallen, and Major Burt was with Grover, serving on the staff.

At the word the men sprang to their feet, but before the command could be carried out, suddenly came the crisis of the battle. About seven o'clock, Gray had brought up the 28th Louisiana to Taylor's aid, and with it the news that the rest of the forces from Bisland were close at hand and all was well with them. Under cover of the wood, Taylor moved Gray quietly to the left, and perceiving that his line now overlapped Grover's right, promptly determined to gain the brief time he still needed for the safe retreat of his main body by a bold and vigorous attack with the whole force he had under his hand. The order was obeyed with spirit. Out of the wood beyond the right, and from the main ditch, well in the rear of the 159th, the Confederates came charging strongly, and halting, they poured in a hot volley. Seeing that the situation was critical Dayton ordered the regiment to retire. Under a severe fire it fell back quickly, yet in good order, to the road. There it promptly re-formed on its colours, and Burt rejoining took command.

In their retreat the New Yorkers swept over the position of the 26th Maine and the 25th Connecticut and carried these already shaken regiments with them, in some natural disorder; but his lasted hardly longer than was needed for Dwight to hear and obey the command that now came back from Grover, to deploy the first brigade and take up the broken battle.

Bradley held his ground stoutly to the last moment, and when finally the choice was narrowed to retreat or capture, he retired in good order to a fresh position, and there serving his canister with coolness and deliberation, held off the enemy's advance. At this point, Rodgers, who with his centre section was in the road on the left, engaged at 800 and 400 yards with Cornay's right section, turned his attention to the Confederate infantry on the right, and crossing with spherical case-shot the canister fire of his Lieutenant, made good the check.

Almost at the moment when Taylor's left was thus roughly bearing down the right of Birge, on his left his own 13th Connecticut, under Lieutenant-Colonel Warner, enveloped in a grove, was moving steadily on the Confederate right, where Clack stood and the two guns of Cornay. Emerging from the grove into an open field that still lay between them and the enemy in the wood, Warner's men instantly replied to the volleys of cannon and small-arms that greeted their appearance and pushed on, firing as they went. More fortunate than their comrades in the direction and the moment of their attack, they pressed back Clack, drove off Cornay's guns, and took two of his caissons, a limber, and a colour presented to his battery by the ladies of Franklin. Nearly 60 prisoners at the same time fell into their hands. They were still advancing when Grover's orders recalled them to the restored line of battle of the brigade.

As Birge's right retired, Dwight deployed in two lines, the 6th New York and the 91st New York in front, the 22nd Maine, 1st Louisiana, and 131st New York in support, and advancing against Taylor's left flank and overlapping it in its turn pushed it back into and beyond the woods. In this movement Dwight took 70 prisoners. The resistance he encountered was feeble compared with the vigour with which Birge had been met and turned back, for in that effort the Confederate line of battle had practically gained its main object and had now only to extricate itself and make good its own withdrawal.

Birge, at the same time that he drew back the 13th Connecticut, once more moved forward his three other regiments and reformed the brigade in two lines on Dwight's left.

Kimball, whose brigade was in two lines in reserve, brought up the 12th Maine to the support of the 13th Connecticut.

This done, Grover advanced the whole division through the woods to the open fields on their farther or western verge, and seeing the Confederates in force on the knoll beyond, to which they had retired, halted and began to observe and reconnoitre.

To cover the right flank of the last Confederate position Semmes brought up the *Diana*, whose injuries of the day before he had during the night partly made good by repairs. Her 30-pounder Parrott now opened a slow fire without great effect other than to add to Grover's caution.

Shortly after eight o'clock Mouton rode up. To him Taylor turned over the command of the force confronting Grover, and then rode into Franklin to direct the retreat. By half-past nine Green with the rear-guard moved out on the direct road toward New Iberia. The last of Green's troopers had not quitted the little town at the upper end when the first of Weitzel's entered at the lower end.

Some time passed before Mouton knew of this. Then for a brief space his peril was great; but fortunately for him the unlooked-for situation of affairs raised a momentary doubt in the minds of Green's pursuers. Should they go to the right or to the left? And where was Grover? After questioning prisoners and townspeople, Banks directed Weitzel to follow by the cut-off road and Emory to move up the bayou. The interval, short as it was, enabled Mouton to fall back quickly, and taking a by-way across country to strike into the cut-off road beyond the northern outskirts of Franklin. Not an instant too soon, for in the confusion Sibley had fired the bridge over the Choupique and across the blazing timbers lay Mouton's last hope of escape. Hardly had his men reached the north bank in safety when Weitzel's advance guard came in sight down the road. They galloped to the bridge only to find it impassable.

Before retiring the Confederates blew up the *Diana* and applied the match to all their transport steamers on the Teche save the hospital boat, the *Cornie*, which loaded with the sick and wounded of Bisland fell into the hands of the Union forces. Captain Semmes, who had but the day before left his battery to command the *Diana*, was taken prisoner, with all his crew. He and Weitzel had been friends and classmates at West Point; he now refused the offered courtesies of his captor, and a few hours later, finding himself rather loosely guarded, cleverly managed to regain his liberty.

To return to Grover. The situation of the enemy's force in his front, the vigorous resistance encountered in his advance, and lastly, the information gathered from the prisoners he had taken, had convinced him that he had to deal with Taylor's whole force, save a small rear-guard, and that Taylor had already succeeded in passing him, so that it was no longer possible to cut the Confederate line of retreat. Indeed, Grover seems rather to have thought that Taylor meant to attack him. It was while careful reconnoissances were being conducted to develop the true facts that Taylor slipped away, as we have seen, having thus adroitly extricated himself from the net spread in his sight.

About two o'clock, however, as Taylor did not attack, Grover moved forward, and as he marched down the bayou road soon met Emory coming up, as related in the last chapter.

Banks, seeing that the bridge could not be made passable before morning, and that nothing was to be gained by marching his tired troops over the long roundabout of the bayou road, went into bivouac early in the afternoon, covering the northern approaches of Franklin. Grover occupied his battle-field of the morning, Emory held the bayou road between Grover and the town, and Weitzel the cut-off road. Taylor crossed the Cypremort and having marched fifteen miles since quitting Franklin, or twenty-five since midnight, rested near Jeannerette.

Grover reported his loss during the 13th, 14th, and 17th as 53 killed, 270 wounded, and 30 captured or missing; in all 353. In the battle of Irish Bend, according to the nominal lists as complied in the Official Records, his loss was 6 officers and 43 men killed, 17 officers and 257 men wounded, and 30 men missing; in all 353; agreeing with the first statement covering the three days, yet differing slightly in the details. Of this total Dwight's brigade lost 3 killed and 9 wounded on the 13th, 1 killed and 5 wounded on the 17th, and only 2 killed and 13 wounded in the battle. Both statements seem to leave out the 1st Louisiana, which had 2 men killed and the lieutenant-colonel and 2 men wounded on the 13th. In Birge's brigade the loss in the battle, according to Grover's report, was 46 killed, 236 wounded, 49 missing; in all 312. The official reports show 16 less in the columns of wounded and in the total: these are probably the 16 wounded officers accounted for in the nominal lists. Of the regiments engaged the heaviest loss fell upon the 159th New York, in which the nominal lists show 4 officers and 15 men killed, 5 officers and 73 men wounded, and 20 men captured or missing; in all 117.[1] But this fine regiment suffered even more severely than these figures indicate, for besides having to mourn the death of the gallant and promising Draper, Molineux received a grievous wound that for many weeks deprived the regiment of one of the best colonels in the service, while of the wounded officers two were mortally hurt and died soon

---

1. According to the regimental history (MS.), 4 officers and 22 men killed; 5 officers and 76 men wounded; 11 men missing; in all, 118: of the wounded, 2 officers and 10 men mortally.

afterward. Birge's loss was nearly one man in four or five, for his strength did not exceed 1,500, and it is probable that his fighting line numbered not more than 1,200.

The Confederate loss is not reported. They left on the field, to be cared for by their adversary, 21 of their dead and 35 of their wounded. Among these were Gray, Vincent, and Reily.

Taylor gives the number of his infantry engaged in the charge on Birge's right as less than 1,000. The disparity of the opposing forces in that affair was, therefore, not important, and Birge's somewhat greater numbers may fairly be considered as off-set by the advantages of Taylor's position and the familiarity with the country common to nearly all the Confederate soldiers there engaged, while to their antagonists it was an unknown land. Grover's whole force was about 5,000, of all arms, but of these, though all are to be taken into account, nearly a third were in reserve, neither firing nor under fire, while another third met a resistance so light that its loss was no more than one per cent. of its numbers—hardly more than it had suffered in the skirmishes of the day before. Grover had eighteen pieces of artillery, of which but four were in action; Taylor also had four guns of which he made good use, and these, toward the close of the battle, were reinforced by the five heavy guns of the *Diana*, of which, however, it is probable that but one, or at most two, could be brought to bear.

The field of battle was so contracted that Taylor's strength sufficed to occupy its front, while Grover was hindered or prevented from deploying a force large enough to outflank and crush his antagonist at a blow.

Viewed from a Confederate standpoint, the issue forms an instructive example of the great results that may be achieved by a right use of small forces. If, on the other hand, one turns to consider the lost opportunity of Grover, two things stand out in strong relief: the one, the positive disadvantage of employing forces, too large for the affair in hand or for the scene of operations; the other, that bold adventures must be carried boldly to the end.

Instead of making the campaign with four brigades and twenty-four guns, as Weitzel's original plan had contemplated, Banks, for greater security, set out with seven brigades and fifty-six guns. So far as concerned the main body ascending the Teche, this excess of strength could do no harm, but it was otherwise with the turning column by the lake; for to the needless augmentation of the artillery were directly due not only the day and night first lost, but also the still more precious hours of daylight consumed in landing guns that were not to fire a shot. Two brigades of infantry, with six guns at most, landing at Indian Bend, and marching directly toward the Cypremort, and quickly entrenching across both roads at or near their upper fork, would have been enough to hold the position against the best efforts of the whole of Taylor's army, with Emory close on their heels; and thus Taylor must have been lost and the war in Western Louisiana brought to an end. Consequences many and far-reaching would have followed. Moreover, when it was determined to use more than two divisions one of these was naturally Grover's, and thus it happened that to Grover, who knew nothing of the country, was assigned the delicate duty first cut out for Weitzel, while Weitzel, who had studied to the last point every detail of the topography and of the plan, stayed behind as the third in command of the column destined to butt its nose against the breastworks of Bisland and wait for the real work to be done a day's march on their farther side.

Grover has been often criticised and much misunderstood for alleged over-caution and for taking the wrong direction after quitting the borders of the lake. Both criticisms are unjust. Generals, like other men, act according to their temperaments. In the whole war no braver man than Grover ever rode at the head of a division, nor any more zealous, more alert, more untiring in his duty. No troops of his ever went into battle but he was with them. But he was by nature cautious, and the adventure was essentially one that called for boldness. Moreover, he was by nature conscientious. That his orders, based as they were on misinformation of a date much later than Weitzel's intelligence, required him to land at Irish Bend instead of at Indian Bend, as first arranged, and to march on Franklin instead of toward the Cypremort, was not his affair. Surely no soldier is to be blamed, least of all in combined and complex operations, for choosing to obey the clearly expressed orders of those set over him, rather than to follow the illusory inspirations of the will-o'-the-wisp commonly mistaken for genius.

As for the orders themselves, they were correct upon the information at hand when they were given and the state of affairs then existing. To land at Madame Porter's and to seize the roads at Franklin was better than to go farther afield to gain the same end; for the distance was less, and while on the march Grover was enabled to offer his front instead of his flank to the enemy. But the information proved inexact; when Madame Porter's road was tried it was found impassable, and with this and the unforeseen delays it happened that the orders became inapplicable.

CHAPTER 12

Opelousas

Cooke, after detaching the *Clifton* to go up the Teche after the *Diana*, as already related, remained at anchor in Grand Lake opposite Grover's landing-place and awaited developments. He had not long to wait. The first news of Banks's movement across Berwick Bay had overtaken and recalled Taylor on his way up the Atchafalaya to bring down the *Queen of the West* and her consorts, the *Grand Duke* and *Mary T*, to join in the intended operations against Weitzel. Although Taylor at once sent a staff officer to urge despatch, yet from some cause more than two full days had passed before, on the afternoon of the 13th, the distant smoke of the Confederate gun-boats coming down Lake Chicot was seen by the lookouts of the Union navy in Grand Lake. At daylight the *Queen of the West* and the *Mary T*, were seen approaching from Chicot Pass. Cooke at once got the *Estrella*, *Calhoun*, and *Arizona* under way, opened fire at long range, and forming his boats in a crescent began to close with the enemy. Soon, however, the *Queen of the West* was seen to be in flames, from the explosion of the Union shells, and, her consort having promptly taken to flight, Cooke ceased firing and lowered all his boats to save the crew of the burning vessel from drowning. Captain Fuller, who had formerly commanded the *Cotton*, was rescued with 90 of his men, but nearly 30 were lost. Then with a loud explosion the eventful career of the *Queen of the West* came to an end, leaving her five guns, however, once more in the hands of the Union navy. This fortunate stroke gave the mastery of the Atchafalaya into Cooke's hands with nothing save Butte-à-la-Rose and two feeble gunboats to hinder his taking possession.

Once safely across the Cypremort, Taylor's army began to melt away and his men, as they passed their homes, to fall out without hindrance. Many were of the simple class called Acadians, with scant sympathy for either side of the great war into which they found themselves drawn, and in all the regiments there were many conscripts.

On the 15th of April, Taylor marched ten miles to New Iberia. While there, he had the unfinished ironclad gunboat *Stevens*, previously known as the *Hart*, floated two miles down the Teche, destroyed by fire, and the wreck sunk in the channel.

On the 16th he marched twenty miles, crossed the Vermilion River, went into camp on high ground on the north bank, and burned the bridges behind him.

Early in the morning of the 15th of April, Banks took up the pursuit with his united force, now outnumbering Taylor's as three to one. Weitzel led the advance of the main column on the direct road. Emory followed him, and Grover marching at first on the bayou road fell in the rear after passing the fork. The army halted for the night at Jeannerette.

On the following afternoon Banks entered New Iberia. Here the ways parted, the right-hand road by Saint Martinville following for many miles the windings of the Teche, while the left-hand road leads almost directly to Opelousas, by way of Vermilionville, now called Lafayette.

Beyond Indian Bend the lowlands, in many places below and nowhere much above the level of the adjacent waters, may be said to end and the plains to begin; and soon after leaving New Iberia and Saint Martinville the troops found themselves on the broad prairies of Western Louisiana, where the rich grasses that flourish in the light soil sustain almost in a wild state vast herds of small yet fat beeves and of small yet strong horses; where in favoured spots the cotton plant is cultivated to advantage; where the ground, gently undulating, gradually rises as one travels northward; where the streams become small rivers that drain the land upon their borders, instead of merely bayous taking the back waters of the Mississippi and the Red. Near the right bank of the Teche runs even a narrow ribbon of bluffs that may be said to form the western margin of the great swamps of the Atchafalaya. Along the streams live-oaks, magnolias, pecans, and other trees grow luxuriantly; but, for the most part, the prairies are open to the horizon, and at this time, though the gin-houses were full of cotton, the fields were mainly given over to the raising of corn for the armies and the people of the Confederacy.

From New Iberia Banks ordered Grover to send a detachment to destroy the famous Avery salt-works, on Petit Anse Island, distant about twelve miles toward the southwest. On the 17th of April, Grover accordingly dispatched Kimball on this errand, with his 12th Maine, the 41st Massachusetts, one company of the 24th Connecticut, and Snow's section of Nims's battery. The extremely rich natural deposit of rock salt was, at that time, in the hands of the Confederate government, being, indeed, the main source of supply of this indispensable article for the whole Confederacy, especially for the region between the Mississippi and the Atlantic. The works required for its extraction are, however, very simple, for the deposit lies close to the surface, and has only to be quarried in blocks of convenient size. These, always as clear and beautiful as crystal, have only to be crushed or broken to be ready to use for common purposes, and when pulverized, however rudely, yield the finest table salt. Kimball burned all the buildings, destroyed the engines and implements, with six hundred barrels of salt, and marched back to New Iberia, and, on the 19th, rejoined Grover on the Vermilion. The Confederates having drawn off the detachment and the guns previously posted to guard the works, Kimball met with no opposition.

On the 17th of April, Grover, with the main body of his division, reinforced by Gooding's brigade, temporarily commanded by Colonel John W. Kimball, of the 53rd Massachusetts, continued the pursuit toward Vermilion, while Banks, with Weitzel and Emory, marched to Saint Martinville, on the Teche.

Early in the afternoon Grover caught sight of Green's rear-guard of Taylor's retreating forces, then about two miles distant, and in the act of crossing the Vermilion. Before Grover could overtake them, the bridges were in flames. Dwight's skirmishers deployed on the right and left of the road, and, with the help of the guns of Closson and Nims, drove off the enemy, posted to hinder or prevent the work of reconstruction. In this affair Dwight lost one killed and five wounded. The next day, the 18th of April, was spent by Grover in rebuilding the main bridge.

Then began to be felt the need of such a force of mounted troops as on these plains formed the main strength of Taylor's little army, and the source of its safety; for Banks's cavalry, taken as a whole, with some splendid exceptions, was at this time greatly inferior, not only in numbers but in fitness for the work at hand, to the rough riders led by the restless and indomitable Green. A few more horsemen, under leaders like Barrett, Williamson, and Perkins, would have saved the bridge and insured the dispersion or the destruction of Taylor's force.

Weitzel, who, as far as Saint Martinville, had led the advance of the main column, followed by Emory with Paine and Ingraham, there took the road to the left and halted on the evening of the 17th of April at Côte Geleé, four miles in the rear of Grover. The next morning Weitzel moved up to Grover's support, while Banks, with Emory, rested at Côte Geleé to await the rebuilding of the bridge.

From St. Martinville, Emory sent the 173rd New York, under Major Gallway, with Norris's section of Duryea's battery, to follow the Teche road to Breaux Bridge and endeavour to capture the bayou steamboats, five in number, that were still left to the Confederates. Five miles below the village of that name, Gallway met a small Confederate picket, and pushing it aside, soon afterward found the bridge over the bayou in flames. On the morning of the 18th he learned that four of the boats had been burned by the Confederates, and about the same time his farther advance was stopped by orders from Banks, despatched as soon as it was known that Grover had been brought to a stand. A courier from headquarters having lost his way in the night of the 18th, on the following morning Gallway found himself in the air without any apparent object. He accordingly marched along the banks of the Teche and the Bayou Fusilier, and taking the road to Opelousas, there rejoined Paine on the 1st.

On the 19th of April the army crossed the Vermilion and the Carencro, and marched unopposed sixteen miles over the prairie to Grand Coteau. Gooding's brigade rejoined Emory during the day.

On the 20th the march was continued about eight miles to Opelousas. Just outside the town the Corps went into bivouac, after throwing forward all the cavalry, the 13th Connecticut, and a section of Rodgers's battery, to Washington, on the Courtableau.

On the same day, after a brief engagement, Cooke, with the gunboats *Estrella*, *Arizona*, and *Calhoun*, and a detachment of four companies of the 16th New Hampshire from Brashear, captured Fort Burton at Butte-à-la-Rose, with its garrison of 60 men of the Crescent regiment and its armament of two 32-pounders; thus at last gaining the complete control of the Atchafalaya, and at the same time opening communication with Banks by way of Port Barré or Barré's Landing on the Courtableau, distant about nine miles north-easterly from Opelousas. Then Cooke steamed up the Atchafalaya to make his report to Farragut, lying in the Mississippi off the mouth of the Red River, and to seek fresh orders.

At the outset of the campaign the 16th New Hampshire had been detached from Ingraham's brigade of Emory and left at Brashear to guard the main depots and the surplus baggage. After the battle of Bisland, the 4th Massachusetts was turned back to Brashear to relieve the 16th New Hampshire. This regiment having assisted in the capture of Butte-à-la-Rose, now formed the garrison of that desolate and deadly hummock.

While at Opelousas the army could draw its supplies from Brashear by the Atchafalaya and the Courtableau, but so long as the direction of the future operations remained uncertain, it was necessary to keep a firm hold of the communications by the Teche. Accordingly, the 175th New York took post at Franklin and the 22nd Maine at New Iberia.

On the 22nd of April the 162nd New York, under Blanchard, with a section of the 1st Maine battery and one troop of the 2nd Rhode Island cavalry, marched to Barré's Landing, seized the position, and captured the little steamboat *Ellen*, the last of the Teche fleet.

On the 23rd of April the little *Cornie* arrived at Barré's Landing from the depot at Brashear, and the next day the first wagon-train came into camp laden with the supplies now sadly needed. At sight of the white-covered wagons winding over the plain, the men gave way to those demonstrations of delight so familiar to all who have ever seen soldiers rejoice. For fifteen days they had been subsisting upon an uncertain issue of hard bread, coffee, and salt, eked out by levies, more or less irregular, upon the countryside. They were sick of chickens and cornbread, and fairly loathed the very sight, to say nothing of the smell, of fresh-killed beef; tough at best, even in the heart of the tenderloin, the flesh had to be eaten with the odour and the warmth of the blood still in it, under penalty of finding it fly-blown before the next meal. Thus it was that, as Paine relates in his Diary, the men now "howled for salt pork and hard tack."

Although the army had now a double line of communication with its base, yet the long haul from New Iberia and the scarcity of light-draught steamboats adapted to the navigation of the narrow and tortuous bayous made the task of supplying even the urgent wants of the troops both tedious and difficult. The herds near Opelousas were fast disappearing under the ravages of the foragers, authorized and unauthorized, yet had it not been for the beef obtained from this source and for the abundant grass of the prairie men and horses must soon have suffered greatly.

On the 24th of April, Banks reviewed his army in the open plain, near Opelousas. The troops, not as yet inured to the long and hard marches, were indeed greatly diminished in numbers by the unaccustomed toil and exposure, as well as by the casualties of battle and the enervating effects of the climate, yet they presented a fine appearance, and were in the best of spirits.

On learning of Cooke's success at Butte-à-la-Rose, Banks detached Dwight, posted him at Washington in observation, and placed Grover with his remaining brigades at Barré's Landing, to secure the depots, while Emory and Weitzel covered Opelousas.

Having by burning the Vermilion bridge gained a day's rest for his tired soldiers, Taylor resumed the retreat at noon on the 17th of April, and passing through Opelousas and Washington on the 18th and 19th, on the following day found himself with all his trains behind the Cocodrie and the Boeuf. On the 20th he sent Mouton, with all the cavalry except Waller's battalion, westward over the prairie toward Niblett's Bluff, on the Sabine. Then, with Waller and the frayed remnant of the infantry, day by day wearing away at the edges, Taylor continued his retreat toward Alexandria, halting with what may be called his main body at Lecompte. To hinder the pursuit he burned the bridges over the Bayou Cocodrie and the Bayou Boeuf.

Opelousas, miles away from every thing, in the heart of a vast prairie, presented in itself no object for an invading army. Even the temptation of a good position was wanting.

Banks meant merely to halt there a day or two for rest, and then, if it should be found practicable to obtain the necessary supplies, to push on rapidly to Alexandria, and dispose for the season of Taylor's disordered fragments. Whether this could have been done will never be known, for although the army had now far out-marched its supplies, and even from its secondary base at Brashear was separated by nearly a hundred miles, and although the campaign had so far been made upon less than half the regular rations for men and animals, supplemented from farm, sugar-house, and prairie, the country on the line of march was no longer to be counted on for any thing save sugar in plenty and a little corn; nevertheless, it might have been possible, by great exertions, to replenish the trains and depots, as well as to fill up the haversacks. Moreover, a three days' march would find the army on the banks of Red River, with a new and ample source of supply open to them, and within easy reach of Grant, provided only the navy might be counted upon to control the waters of that stream and its larger tributaries. Of this Banks had no doubt whatever. To open communication with Grant and to dispose of Taylor had been the chief ends that Banks had proposed to himself in setting out on the campaign. These ends he now held almost in his hand. But on the 21st of April an event occurred that, slight as was its apparent importance, was destined, in the train of consequences, vitally to affect the operations of the Army of the Gulf.

This was the arrival at headquarters of Lieutenant Joseph T. Tenney, one of Dudley's *aides-de-camp*, who had been sent by Augur to find Banks, wherever he might be. With him Tenney brought important despatches from Grant and Farragut. What the contents were and what came of them will be related in the next chapter.

From Opelousas Bean, with the 4th Wisconsin, a section of Duryea's battery, and a squadron of the 2nd Rhode Island cavalry, went a day's march toward the southwest, to the crossing of the Plaquemine Brulé, and discovered that Mouton was retreating beyond the Mermentau. From Washington, Dwight moved out twenty miles along the Bayou Boeuf to Satcham's plantation without finding the enemy in force. After learning these things, on the 25th of April, Banks turned over the command of the forces to Emory and went to New Orleans to give his attention to affairs of urgency, chiefly affecting the civil administration of the department. He returned to headquarters in the field on the evening of the 1st of May.

Meanwhile Emory sent Paine, who, when crossing the Carencro, had seen the last of the Confederates disappearing in the distance, with his brigade and a section of Duryea's battery far out on the Plaquemine Brulé road, in order to find and disperse some cavalry, vaguely reported to be moving about somewhere in that quarter, a constant menace to the long trains from New Iberia. In fact Mouton, with the Texans, was now on the prairie, beyond the Calcasieu eighty miles away, in good position to retreat to Texas or to hang on the flank and rear of the Union army, as circumstances might suggest. On the 26th of April Paine marched sixteen miles to the Plaquemine Brulé, and on the following day sent four companies on horseback twenty miles farther toward the southwest across Bayou Queue de Tortue, and another detachment to Bayou Mallet to reconnoitre. Seeing nothing of the enemy, on the 28th Paine rejoined his division and resumed the command of it at Opelousas. Some time before this orders had been given to mount the 4th Wisconsin, and when the army finally marched from Opelousas this capital regiment made its appearance in the new role of mounted infantry. To say nothing of the equipments, a wide divergence in the size, colour, and quality of the horses, hastily gathered from the four quarters of the prairie, gave to these improvised dragoons rather a ludicrous appearance it must be confessed; yet marching afoot or standing to horse, the 4th Wisconsin was always ready and equal to the work cut out for it.

From his advanced camp, on Shields's plantation, twenty-three miles beyond Washington and twenty-nine from Opelousas, Dwight fell back on the 28th of April to his bivouac at Washington and waited for the movement of the army to begin.

In preparation for this, on the evening of the 1st of May, Bean, with the 4th Wisconsin, mounted, was sent forward to join the main body of the cavalry, under Major Robinson, in front of Washington. That night Dwight, with the cavalry, his own brigade, and a section of Nims's battery, marched out some distance to discover the position of the Confederate outposts. These, in the interval that elapsed, had been advanced to the junction of the Cocodrie and the Boeuf. After driving them in Dwight returned the next morning to Washington.

The advance of the column from Franklin to Opelousas had been disfigured by the twin evils of straggling and marauding. Before the campaign opened, Banks had taken the precaution to issue stringent orders against pillage, yet no means adequate to the enforcement of these orders were provided, and the marches were so long and rapid, the heat at times so intense, and the dust so intolerable, that comparatively few of the men were able to keep up with the head of the column. This contributed greatly to disorder of the more serious kind. One regiment, neither the best nor the worst, halting at the end of a particularly hard day's march, found itself with scarcely fifty men in the ranks. Then, too, the men were on short rations, in what they considered the enemy's country; the whole region was sparsely populated; and the residents had, for the most part, fled from their homes at the news of the approach of the Union army.

With these disorders there sprang up a third, less prevalent indeed, but to the last degree annoying and not without its share of danger, for when the straggler chanced to find himself in easy range of any thing, from a steer to a chicken, that he happened to fancy for his supper, he was not always careful in his aim or accurate in his judgment of distance; thus a number of officers and men were wounded and the lives of many put in peril.

As if to complete the lesson so often taught in all wars, that discipline, care, and efficiency go hand in hand, when the army moved out from Opelousas, though but a fortnight later, a different state of things was seen. This must be ascribed to the fact that immediately after entering Opelousas the most stringent and careful orders were given for the regulation of future marches, and the punishment of stragglers and marauders. By these orders was provided for the first time a system adequate to their enforcement, and sufficiently elastic to meet without annoyance and difficulty all those cases, of hourly and even momentary occurrence in the movement of an army, that require officers or men to quit the column. In the rear of each regiment was posted a surgeon, without whose permission no sick man was allowed to fall out. In the rear of each brigade and division marched a detachment of cavalry, under the orders of the provost marshal of the brigade or division, charged with the duty of picking up as stragglers all men found out of the ranks without a written permit from the surgeon or the company commander. The vital importance of a strict enforcement of these arrangements was personally impressed upon the division and brigade commanders; yet this was not now necessary, for there were but few persons in the column of any rank that did not realize, in part at least, the evil consequences resulting from the irregular practices that had hitherto prevailed. Thus the march to the Red River was made rapidly and in order, and now for the first time the soldiers of the Nineteenth Army Corps marched with that swift and regulated movement of the column as a unit that was to be ever afterwards a source of comfort to the men, of satisfaction to their officers, and of just pride to every one belonging to the corps.

Unhappily, on the 25th of April, before the result of these arrangements had had a chance to show themselves, Dwight, while on detached service in the advance, caught an unfortunate man of the 131st New York, Henry Hamill by name, absent from his regiment under circumstances that pointed him out as a plunderer. Then, without pausing to communicate with the general commanding, Dwight took upon himself the task of trial and judgment on the spot, and becoming satisfied of the man's guilt, caused him to be shot to death at sunset in front of the brigade. This action Banks, who was just setting out for New Orleans, sustained in special orders as soon as he returned. Indeed, between this course and the instant delivery of Dwight to punishment, Banks had practically no choice. Nevertheless, whatever may have been the excuse or how extreme the provocation, the act was altogether wrong. The rules and articles of war lay down the penal code of armies in all its severity, in terms too clear to be misunderstood and too ample to warrant an attempt on the part of any one in the service, however exalted his rank, to enlarge or evade them. The offender should have been tried by court-martial. No emergency or exigency existed to delay the assembling of the court. Had he been found guilty, his death might swiftly have followed. Then the terrible lesson would have been impressive. Then none would have thought it hasty, needless, violent, or unlawful.

As it was, the wretched man's punishment furnished chiefly matter for regret, and an example to be avoided.

CHAPTER 13

Banks and Grant

The first effect of the despatches from Grant and Farragut, referred to in the preceding chapter, was to cause Banks to reconsider his plan of campaign, and to put the direction of his next movement in suspense. While waiting for fresh advices in answer to his own communications and proposals Banks halted, and while he halted Taylor got time to breathe and Kirby Smith to gather new strength.

This correspondence has been so much discussed, yet so little understood, that, chronology being an essential part of history, the narrative of the events now at hand may be rendered clearer, if we turn aside for a moment to consider not only the substance of what was said upon both sides, but, what was even more important, the time at which it was heard.

Farragut's letter, written from the *Hartford* above Port Hudson on the 6th of April, was the first communication Banks had received from Farragut, save a brief verbal message brought to him by the Admiral's secretary, Mr. E. C. Gabaudan, on the 10th of April, just before the army set out from Brashear. Mr. Gabaudan had come straight from the Admiral, but without any thing in writing, having floated past Port Hudson by night in a skiff covered with twigs so as to look like a drift log. Farragut's letter gave assurance of the complete control of the Red River and the Atchafalaya by the navy of the Union.

Grant's despatch bore date the 23rd of March. It was the first writing received from him. It conveyed the answer to the letter addressed to him by Banks on the 13th of March, and placed in the hands of Farragut just before the *Hartford* ran the batteries of Port Hudson. Thus on either side began a correspondence clearly intended by both commanders to bring about an effective co-operation between the two armies, aided by the combined fleets of Farragut and Porter. Yet in the end, while the consequences remained unfelt in the Army by the Tennessee, upon the Army of the Gulf the practical effect, after the first period of delay and doubt, was to cause its commander to give up the thought of moving toward Grant and to conform all his movements to the expectation that Grant would send an army corps to Bayou Sara to join in reducing Port Hudson. Thus, quite apart from the confusion and the eventual disappointment, much valuable time was lost while the matter was in suspense; and so was demonstrated once more the impossibility, well established by the history of war, of co-ordinating the operations of two armies widely separated, having different objectives, while an enemy strongly holds the country between them.

When Banks wrote his despatch of the 13th of March, he was at Baton Rouge, about to demonstrate against Port Hudson. When Grant received this despatch he was on the low land opposite Vicksburg, with the rising river between him and his enemy, laboriously seeking a practical pathway to the rear of Vicksburg, and in the meantime greatly troubled to find dry ground for his seventy thousand men to stand on. Grant's first idea, derived from Halleck's despatches, was that Banks should join him before Vicksburg, with the whole available force of the Army of the Gulf. When he learned from Banks that this would be out of the question so long as Port Hudson should continue to be held by the Confederates, Grant took up the same line of thought that had already attracted Banks, and began to meditate a junction by the Atchafalaya, the Red, the Tensas, and the Black rivers. What Grant then needed was not more troops, but standing-room for those he had. Accordingly, he began by preparing to send twenty thousand men to Banks, when the Ohio River steamers he had asked for should come.[1] They never came, yet even after he had embarked upon the campaign, alike sound in conception and splendid in execution, that was to become the corner-stone of his great and solid fame, Grant kept to his purpose.

---

1. "I sent several weeks ago for this class of steamers, and expected them before this. Should they arrive and Admiral Porter get his boats out of the Yazoo, so as to accompany the expedition, I can send a force of say 20,000 effective men to co-operate with General Banks on Port Hudson."—Grant to Farragut, March 23rd; received by Banks, April 21st. The cipher message that followed seemed to Banks a confirmation of this.

On the 14th of April he penned this brief telegram to Banks:

> I am concentrating my forces at Grand Gulf; will send an army corps Bayou Sara by the 25th, to co-operate with you on Port Hudson. Can you aid me and send troops after the reduction of Port Hudson to assist me at Vicksburg?

This message, although Banks and Grant were then only about two hundred miles apart, had to travel three thousand miles to reach its destination. Banks received it just before marching from Opelousas on the 5th of May, twenty-one days after it left Grant's hands. As received, the message was in cipher and without a date. As the prevailing practice was, in conformity with the orders of the Secretary of War, the only persons in the Department of the Gulf who held the key to the cipher were the Superintendent of Military Telegraphs and such of his assistants as he chose to trust, and Mr. Bulkley was at New Iberia, where the wires ended. The code employed was the route cipher in common use in the service, and with the help of the words "Bayou" and "Sara" as guides the meaning was not hard to make out. Banks did not trust to this, however, and waited until, late at night, he received from the Superintendent an official translation, still without date, as indeed was the original document received at headquarters from New Orleans. The 25th Banks naturally took to mean the 25th of May. Grasping eagerly at the first real chance of effective co-operation, he at once replied: "By the 25th probably, by the 1st, certainly, I will be there." This despatch was not in cipher, because he had no code. Captain Crosby carried it to the *Hartford* at the mouth of Red River. Captain Palmer, who was found in command, the Admiral having crossed Fausse Point and joined his fleet below, at once forwarded the despatch. Near Natchez Crosby met Captain Uffers of Grant's staff and turned back with him bringing Grant's despatch of the 10th of May, written at Rocky Springs. This Banks received at Alexandria on the 12th of May. From it he learned that Grant was not coming. Having met the Confederates after landing at Grand Gulf and followed on their heels to the Big Black, he could not afford to retrace his steps; but he urged Banks to join him or to send all the force he could spare "to co-operate in the great struggle for opening the Mississippi River." The reasons thus assigned by Grant for his change of mind were certainly valid; yet it must be doubted whether in these hurried lines the whole of the matter is set forth, for three weeks earlier, on the 19th of April, five days after the promise to send an army corps to Bayou Sara by the 25th, Grant had reported to Halleck: "This will now be impossible." Moreover, until the moment when he crossed the river with his advance on the 30th of April he not only held firmly to his intention to send the twenty thousand men to join Banks at Bayou Sara as soon as the landing should have been secured, but the corps for this service had been designated; it was to be made up of the main body of McClernand's corps and McPherson's, and Grant himself meant to go with it. It was indeed the 2nd of May when Grant received at Port Gibson Banks's despatch sent from Brashear on the 10th of April indicating his purpose of returning to Baton Rouge by the 10th of May, and although Grant also attributes to this despatch the change of his plans, the 10th of May had already come before he made known the change to Banks.

All this time Banks bore with him Halleck's instructions of the 9th of November, and more than once studied with care and solicitude these significant words:

> As the ranking general in the Southwest you are authorized to assume the control of any military force from the upper Mississippi which may come within your command. The line of division between your department and that of Major-General Grant is, therefore, left undecided for the present, and you will exercise superior authority as far north as you may ascend the river.

By the articles of war, without these words, Banks would have been entitled to the command they gave him, but the words showed him plainly what was expected of him by his government. To the incentives of patriotism and duty were thus superadded one of the most powerful motives that can affect the mind of the commander of an army,—the hope and assurance of power and promotion. If, then, he held back from joining Grant in Mississippi, it was because he hesitated to take the extraordinary risks involved in the movement. In this he was more than justified.

Since the miscarriage of Sherman's attempt at the beginning of the year, Grant had been engaged in a series of tentative efforts, steadily prosecuted in various directions, yet all having a common object, the finding of a foothold of dry ground for a decisive movement against Vicksburg. Four of these experimental operations had failed completely, and Grant was now entering upon a fifth, destined indeed to lead to a great and glorious result, yet in itself conveying hardly more assurance of success than the most promising of its predecessors, while involving perils greater than any that had been so far encountered. Of these, the greatest danger was that the enemy, after allowing him to land on the east bank of the river and to penetrate, with a portion of his army, into the heart of Mississippi, might then concentrate all the available forces of the Confederacy in that region and fall upon him with vigour at the moment when his supplies should be exhausted and his communications interrupted. In such an event the fortune of war might have rendered it imperative for him to retire down the river; but what would have happened then if Banks, disregarding Port Hudson in his eagerness to join Grant before Vicksburg, should in his turn have abandoned his communications? Both armies would have been caught in a trap of their own making, whence not merit but some rare stroke of luck could alone have rescued either.

In the strong light of the great and decisive victory of Vicksburg, it is scarcely possible to reproduce, even in the mind of the most attentive reader, the exact state of affairs as they existed at the moment of Grant's landing below Grand Gulf. This phenomenal success was not foreshadowed by any thing that had gone before it, and it would have been the height of imprudence to stake upon it the fate of two armies, the issue of an entire campaign, and the mastery of the Mississippi River, if not the final result of the war. Nor should it be forgotten that Grant himself regarded this movement as experimental, like its forerunners, and that up to the moment he set foot upon the soil of Mississippi, he had formed no conception of the brilliant campaign on which he was about presently to embark. But instead of concentrating and acting with instant determination upon a single plan with a single idea, at the critical moment the Confederates became divided in council, distracted in purpose, and involved in a maze of divergent plans, cross purposes, and conflicting orders. While events caused the Confederate leaders to shift from one plan to the other, with the chances of the day, Grant was prompt to see and quick to profit by his advantage, and thus the campaign was given into his hands.

But on the 4th of May these great events were as yet hidden in the unknown future, and when, after waiting thirteen days at Opelousas, Banks began his march on Alexandria, it was with the earnest hope of a speedy meeting of the two Union armies on the Mississippi; then came the cipher telegram to exalt this hope into a firm and just expectation of finding three weeks later an entire corps from Grant's army at Bayou Sara, and as Banks mounted his horse to ride toward the head of his column, it was with the fixed purpose of being with his whole force at the appointed place at the appointed time.

Chapter 14

Alexandria

Every one was in high spirits at the prospect of meeting the Army of the Tennessee, and, to add to the general good-humour, just before quitting Opelousas two pieces of good news became known.

Grierson rode into Baton Rouge on the 2nd of May at the head of his own 6th Illinois and Prince's 7th Illinois cavalry, together 950 horse. Leaving La Grange on the 17th of April, he had within sixteen days ridden nearly 600 miles around the rear of Vicksburg and Port Hudson and along the whole line of the Jackson and Great Northern railroad. Beside breaking up the railway and the telegraph, and destroying for the time being their value to the Confederate army, Grierson's ride had an indirect effect, perhaps even more important than the direct objects Grant had in view when he gave his orders. That the railway should be rendered useless for the movement of troops and supplies, and the telegraph for the transmission of orders and intelligence, was of course the essential purpose of the operation, yet no one could have foreseen the extent of the confusion that followed, aided by Grierson's rapid movements, amid the fluttering and distracted councils at Vicksburg. Thus it happened that, when he heard of Grant's landing below Grand Gulf, Pemberton actually thought himself menaced by the advance of Banks, and this misapprehension was the parent of the first of those mistakes of his adversary of which Grant made such good use.

Lieutenant Sargent,[1] the *aide-de-camp* sent to communicate with

---

1. Professor Charles Sprague Sargent, of Harvard University, Director of the Arnold Arboretum, the distinguished author of the great book on Forest Trees of North America. At this time he was serving zealously as a volunteer aide-de-camp without pay.

Admiral Farragut, as stated in the last chapter, found at the mouth of the Red River Admiral Porter, with the gunboats *Benton*, *Lafayette*, *Pittsburg*, and *Price*, the ram *Switzerland*, and the tugboat *Ivy*, with which he had run the batteries of Vicksburg in preparation for Grant's movement. Porter brought, indeed, no despatches, but he brought the great news that Grant had secured his landing at Grand Gulf and had begun his victorious march on Vicksburg. When Sargent returned to headquarters at Opelousas, he brought with him a despatch from Porter, promising to meet the army at Alexandria.

Banks had already broken up the depots at Barré's Landing and New Iberia. On the afternoon of the 4th of May, he set Dwight in motion from his advance post at Washington. Weitzel marched from Opelousas at five o'clock the same afternoon, and Emory's division under Paine followed on the morning of the 5th. Emory, who had been suffering for some weeks, had at last consented to obey his surgeon's orders and go to New Orleans for a brief rest. Grover followed from Barré's Landing early in the afternoon of the same day. Banks himself remained at Opelousas until early in the morning of the 6th, having waited to receive and answer the translation of the cipher telegram from Grant; then he rode forward rapidly and joined his troops near Washington. From this time the communications of the army were to be by the Atchafalaya and the Red River.

On the 4th of May, while riding to the front to join the advance commanded by his brother, Captain Howard Dwight, Assistant Adjutant-General, was surprised and cut off at a sharp turn in the Bayou Boeuf by a party of armed men on the opposite bank. Having no reason to apprehend any special danger so far in the rear of the advance, the little party was proceeding along the road without precaution. At the moment of the encounter Captain Dwight was quite alone, concealed by the turn in the road from the ambulance and the few orderlies that were following at leisure. Armed only with his sword, and seeing that escape was hopeless, he instantly declared his readiness to surrender. "Surrender be damned!" cried the guerrillas, and, firing a volley without further parley, shot him dead. When the orderlies who were with the ambulance heard the firing they galloped forward, only to find poor Dwight's lifeless body lying in the dusty road. The murderers had fled.

By this painful event the service lost a brave and promising young officer and the staff a pleasant and always cheerful comrade. The distinguished family to which this gallant gentleman belonged had given four brothers to the service of their country. Of these Howard himself most nearly resembled in character, looks, and bearing his elder brother Wilder, who fell at Antietam, honoured and lamented by all that knew him.

Upon hearing the news, Banks instantly sent order to Brigadier-General Dwight to arrest all the white men he might find near the line of his march to the number of one hundred, and to send them to New Orleans to be held as hostages for the delivery of the murderers. "The people of the neighbourhood who harbour and feed these lawless men," Banks wrote, "are even more directly responsible for the crimes which they commit, and it is by punishing them that this detestable practice will be stopped." There were not a hundred white men in the region through which Dwight was marching, but many were punished by imprisonment after this order—a harsh measure, it must be admitted, yet not without the justification that the countryside was infested by men wearing no uniform, who acted in turn the part of soldiers in front of the Union army, of citizens on its line of march, and of guerrillas in its rear. When, under a flag of truce, Dwight presently demanded from Taylor the surrender of his brother's murderers, the Confederate officers not only disavowed but severely condemned the crime, declaring themselves, however, unable to pick out the criminals.

Two miles beyond Washington the Bayous Boeuf and Cocodrie unite to form the Bayou Courtableau, out of which again, below the town, flows the Bayou Maricoquant, forming a double connection with the Teche at its head. For a long distance the Boeuf and the Cocodrie keep close company, each following a crooked channel cut deeply into the light soil. Crossing the Courtableau above Washington, the line of march now lay along the east bank of the Boeuf, by Holmesville and Cheneyville, through a country of increasing richness and beauty, gradually rising with quickened undulations almost until the bluffs that border the Red River draw in sight.

Banks had promised that he would be in Alexandria on the morning of the 9th of May; but no opposition was encountered;

the roads were good, dry, and easy under foot; the weather fine, and the men were filled with a desire to push the march, and with an eager rivalry to be first in Alexandria. Early on the afternoon of the 7th of May the brigades of Dwight and Weitzel, both under Weitzel's command, arrived at the beautiful plantation of Governor Moore, and went into bivouac. Here the cavalry, who had ridden well forward, returned, bringing the news that Porter, with his gunboats, was already in the river off Alexandria, where the fleet had cast anchor early that morning, a full day before its time. This made Banks desire to push on, and he at first ordered Paine to continue the march, preceded by all the cavalry. When Weitzel heard this, his spirit rose for the honour of his brigade, and in emphatic yet respectful terms he protested against being deprived at the last moment of the post he had held almost since leaving Brashear. Banks yielded to Weitzel's wishes, and his men, not less eager than their commander, notwithstanding the long march of twenty miles they had already made, at once broke camp and with a swinging stride set out the accomplish the twelve miles that still separated them from the river. One of the ever-present regimental wits sought to animate the spirits and quicken the flagging footsteps of his comrades by offering a turkey ready trussed upon his bayonet to the man that should get to Alexandria before him. For a long part of the way the men of the 8th Vermont and the 75th New York amused themselves by taking advantage of the wide and good roadway to run a regimental race. As the eager rivals came swinging down the hill, they found their progress checked by a momentary halt of the horsemen in their front, while watering their jaded animals. Then, "Get out of the way with that cavalry," was the cry, "or we'll run over you!"

It was ten o'clock at night when Weitzel's men led the way into Alexandria. A full ration of spirits was served out to the men, who then threw themselves on the ground without further ceremony and used to the full the permission to enjoy for once a long sleep mercifully unbroken by a reveille. Paine followed and encamped near Alexandria on the following morning; Grover rested near Lecompte, about twenty miles in the rear.

Beside his own vessels, Porter brought with him to Alexandria the *Estrella* and *Arizona* from the flotilla that had been operating on the Atchafalaya under Cooke. Porter was thus fully prepared to deal with any opposition he might encounter from the Confederate batteries at Fort De Russy; but, although only the day before the *Albatross*, *Estrella*, and *Arizona* had been driven off after a sharp fight of forty minutes, when, on the 5th of May, Porter arrived at Fort De Russy, he found the place deserted and the guns gone.[2]

On the 8th of May, finding that the river was falling, Porter, after conferring freely with Banks, withdrew all his vessels except the *Lafayette*, and descending the Red River, sent four of the gunboats seventy miles up the Black and its principal affluent, the Washita, to Harrisonburg. This latter expedition had no immediate result, but it served to show the ease with which the original plan of campaign might have been followed to its end.

While Banks was still at Opelousas, Kirby Smith, taking Dwight's approach to signify a general advance of the Union army, had arranged to retire up the Red River and to concentrate at Shreveport. Thither, on the 24th of April, he removed his headquarters from Alexandria and called in not only Taylor but a division of infantry under Walker, and three regiments of Texans already on the Red River. All the troops that Magruder could spare from the 8,000 serving in Eastern Texas he was at once to put in march to the Sabine. These orders, though too late for the emergency, brought about the concentration that was presently to threaten the ruin of Banks's main campaign on the Mississippi.

Weitzel, with Dwight, followed the Confederate rear-guard to Lawson's Ferry, forty-one miles by the river beyond Alexandria, taking a few prisoners. Taylor himself appears to have had a narrow escape from being among them.

During the week spent at Alexandria, Banks was for the first time in direct and comparatively rapid communication with Grant, now in the very heart of his Vicksburg campaign, and here, as we

---

2. Under orders from Kirby Smith to Taylor, dated April 22nd: "The General is of the opinion that if a portion of the force pursuing you should move against Fort De Russy by the road from Hauffpaur, it would be impossible to hold it." See also Smith to Cooper, April 23rd: "The people at Fort De Russy cannot stand a land attack. The advance of the enemy's column to the Hauffpaur . . . will ensure its speedy fall, with loss of guns and garrison. Under these circumstances, General Taylor has ordered the removal of the 32-pounder rifle and 11-inch columbiads to a position higher up the Red River."

have seen, the correspondence was brought to a point. When he first learned that Grant had given up all intention of sending to him any portion of the Army of the Tennessee, Banks was greatly cast down, and his plans rapidly underwent many changes and perturbations. At first he was disposed to think that nothing remained but to retrace his steps over the whole toilsome way by Opelousas, the Teche, Brashear, New Orleans, and the Mississippi River to Baton Rouge, and thence to conduct a separate attack upon Port Hudson. This movement would probably have consumed two months, and long before the expiration of that time it was fair to suppose the object of such an operation would have ceased to exist. What led Banks to this despondent view was the fact that he had been counting upon Grant's steamboat transportation for the crossing of the Mississippi to Bayou Sara, and at first, he did not see how this deficiency could now be met.

Indeed, on the 12th of May, he went so far as to issue his preparatory orders for the retrograde movement; but the next day careful reconnoissances by his engineers, Major Houston and Lieutenant Harwood, led him to change his mind and to conclude that it would, after all, be possible to march to Simmesport, and there, using the light-draught boats of the Department of the Gulf, supplemented by such steamers as Grant might be able to spare for this purpose, to transfer the whole column to Grand Gulf and thence march to join Grant in the rear of Vicksburg. Accordingly, on the 13th of May, Banks gave orders for the immediate movement of his whole force in accordance with this plan, and set aside all the preparations that had previously been made.

When the news reached Washington that Grant had gone to Jackson and Banks to Alexandria, great was the dissatisfaction of the Government and emphatic its expression. On the 19th of May Halleck wrote to Banks:

> These operations are too eccentric to be pursued. I must again urge that you co-operate as soon as possible with General Grant east of the Mississippi. Your forces must be united at the earliest possible moment. Otherwise the enemy will concentrate on Grant and crush him. Do all you can to prevent this. . . .

> We shall watch with the greatest anxiety the movements of yourself and General Grant. I have urged him to keep his forces concentrated as much as possible and not to move east until he gets control of the Mississippi River.

And again, on the 23rd of May, still more pointedly:

> If these eccentric movements, with the main forces of the enemy on the Mississippi River, do not lead to some serious disaster, it will be because the enemy does not take full advantage of his opportunity. I assure you the Government is exceedingly disappointed that you and General Grant are not acting in conjunction. It thought to secure that object by authorizing you to assume the entire command as soon as you and General Grant could unite.

When the despatches were penned, Grant and Banks were already committed to their own plans for the final campaign on the Mississippi. When they were received, Grant was before Vicksburg, Banks before Hudson; each had delivered his first assault and entered upon the siege. The censure was withdrawn as soon as, in the light of full explanations, the circumstances came to be understood.

CHAPTER 15

Back to Port Hudson

On the 7th of May Porter relieved Farragut in the guardianship of the Mississippi and its tributaries above the mouth of the Red River. This left Farragut free to withdraw his fleet so long blockading and blockaded above Port Hudson. Accordingly he gave discretionary orders to Palmer to choose his time for once more running the gauntlet, and Palmer was only watching his opportunity when he yielded to the earnest entreaty of Banks, and agreed to remain and co-operate if the General meant to go against Port Hudson.

Grover began the movement on the 14th of May; Paine followed early on the morning of the 15th, while Weitzel, still retaining Dwight, was ordered to hold Alexandria until the 17th, and then to retire to Murdock's plantation, where the east and west road along the Bayou Hauffpaur crosses the road from Alexandria to Opelousas, and there await further orders.

Besides the ordinary duty of a rear-guard, the object of this disposition of Weitzel's force was to cover the withdrawal toward Brashear of the long train of surplus wagons for which there was now no immediate need, and which would only have encumbered the proposed movement of the Corps by water. All the troops took the road by Cheneyville instead of that by Marksville, in order to conceal from the Confederates as long as possible the true direction of the movement.

Having given these orders, Banks embarked on one of the river steamboats on the evening of the 15th and transferred his headquarters to Simmes's plantation on the east bank of the Atchafalaya opposite Simmesport. Thence he proceeded down the Atchafalaya to Brashear, and so by rail to New Orleans.

Grover broke camp at Stafford's plantation on the 14th of May, and marched seventeen miles to Cheneyville; on the 15th, fourteen miles to Enterprise; on the 16th, sixteen miles to the Bayou de Glaise; and, on the morning of the 17th, twelve miles to Simmesport, and immediately began to cross on large flatboats rowed by negro boatmen. To these were presently added a little, old, slow, and very frail stern-wheel steamboat, named the *Bee*, which, a short time afterwards, quietly turned upside down, without any observable cause, while lying alongside the levee; then the *Laurel Hill*, one of the best boats in the service of the quartermaster; afterward gradually but very slowly the other steamers began to come in. Grover finished crossing on the morning of the 18th, and went into camp near the Corps headquarters.

Paine, with the 6th New York added to his command for the few remaining days of its service, followed in the footsteps of Grover. Leaving Alexandria on the morning of the 15th, Paine marched twenty miles and halted at Lecompte. On the 16th, he marched twenty-five miles to the Bayou Rouge; on the 17th, twenty miles to the Bayou de Glaise, where the Marksville road crosses it; on the 18th, seven miles to Simmesport, and on the following morning began to cross.

Before leaving Alexandria, Weitzel, on the 14th May, sent two companies of cavalry to reconnoitre a small force of the enemy said to be near Boyce's Bridge on Bayou Cotile. The Confederates were found in some force. A slight skirmish followed, with trifling loss on either side, and when, the next day, Weitzel sent the main body of the cavalry with one piece of Nims's battery, accompanied by the ram *Switzerland* with a detachment of 200 men of the 75th New York, the Confederates once more retired beyond Cane River.

Weitzel moved out of Alexandria at four o'clock on the morning of the 17th of May, and, lengthening his march to thirty-eight miles during the night, encamped on Murdock's plantation on the following morning. The gunboats *Estrella* and *Arizona* and the ram *Switzerland* stayed in the river off Alexandria until noon of the 17th to cover Weitzel's withdrawal, and then dropped down to the mouth of Red River and the head of the Atchafalaya. The Confederates slowly followed Weitzel at some distance, observing his movements, and, on the morning of the 20th, attacked his pickets. Then Bean, who commanded Weitzel's advanced guard, consisting of his own 4th Wisconsin, mounted, the 12th Connecticut, and all the cavalry, threw off the attack and pursued the Confederates nearly to Cheneyville, where Barrett, advancing too boldly after the main body had halted, was cut off, with a detachment of seventeen of his troop, and, finding himself surrounded, was forced to surrender. Barrett himself and several of his men afterwards succeeded in making their escape. The attacking party of the Confederates consisted of Lane's regiment, fresh from Texas, Waller's battalion, and a part of Sibley's brigade, with a battery of artillery.

On the morning of the 22nd, Weitzel, having completed the object of his halt at Murdock's plantation, marched at a stretch the thirty-four miles to Simmesport without further molestation, and arriving there on the morning of the 23rd, at once began the crossing.

Chickering marched from Barré's Landing on the morning of the 21st of May. His force consisted of his own regiment, the 41st Massachusetts, commanded by Lieutenant-Colonel Sargent and mounted on prairie horses, the 52nd Massachusetts, the 22nd Maine, the 26th Maine, the 90th New York, the 114th New York, under Lieutenant-Colonel Per Lee, Company E of the 13th Connecticut, and Snow's section of Nims's battery.

The 90th New York, Colonel Joseph S. Morgan, was among the older regiments in the Department of the Gulf, having been mustered into the service in December, 1861. In January, 1862, it went to Florida with Brannan, on his appointment to command the Department of Key West; and in June, 1862, it formed the garrison of Fort Jefferson on the Dry Tortugas and of Key West; in November it was relieved by the 47th Pennsylvania, and joined Seymour's brigade on Port Royal Island, South Carolina. In March, 1863, it was back at Key West. There both regiments remained together until May. Meanwhile the district, then commanded by Woodbury, had been transferred from the Department of the South to the Department of the Gulf by orders from the War Office dated the 16th of March. These Banks received on the 10th of April, just before leaving Brashear, and as soon as he learned the condition and strength of the post, he called in the 90th New York. The regiment arrived at Barré's Landing just in time to go back to Brashear with Chickering. Morgan, though Chickering's senior in rank, waived his claim to the command and accepted a temporary brigade made up of all the infantry and the artillery.

The 114th New York, after quitting the column on the 19th of April, before passing the Vermilion, and performing the unpleasant duty of driving before it to Brashear all the beeves within its reach, was so unfortunate as to arrive at Cheneyville, on the return march, on the 12th of May, at the moment when Banks had made up his mind to retire to Brashear, and so just in time to face about and once more retrace its weary steps. Passing through Opelousas and Grand Couteau, the 114th turned to the left by the Bayou Fusilier and fell in with Chickering on the Teche.

The way was by the Teche, on either bank. By this time Mouton, reinforced by a brigade of three regiments under Pyron, with a light battery, probably Nichols's, had recrossed the Calcasieu under orders sent him by Kirby Smith on the 14th of May, before he knew of Banks's latest movement, and was approaching the Vermilion just in time to harry the flank and rear of Chickering's column, scattered as it was in the effort to guard the long train that stretched for eight miles over the prairies, with a motley band of 5,000 negroes, 2,000 horses, and 1,500 beeves for a cumbrous accompaniment. With the possible exception of the herd that set out to follow Sherman's march through Georgia, this was perhaps the most curious column ever put in motion since that which defiled after Noah into the ark.

On the 21st of May, Chickering halted near Breaux Bridge; on the 22nd, above Saint Martinville; on the 23rd, above New Iberia; on the 24th, at Jeannerette. On the following afternoon the column had halted five miles beyond Franklin, when a small force of the enemy, supposed to be part of Green's command or of Fournet's battalion, fell upon the rear-guard and a few shots were exchanged, with slight casualties on either side, save that Lieutenant Almon A. Wood, of the 110th New York, fell with a mortal wound. However, although the troops had already traversed twenty-five miles, this decided Morgan, who seems by this time to have taken the command, to push on, and the march being kept up throughout the night, the wearied troops, after a short rest for breakfast arrived at

Berwick Bay at eleven o'clock on the following morning. In the last thirty-one hours the command had marched forty-eight miles. In the forty-one days that had passed since the campaign opened the 114th New York had covered a distance of almost 500 miles, nearly every mile of it afoot and with but three days' rest. The same afternoon the crossing began, and by the 28th every living thing was in safety at Brashear.

Banks had sent his despatches of the 13th of May to Grant by the hands of Dwight, with instructions to lay the whole case before Grant and to urge the view held by Banks with regard to the co-operation of the two armies. Dwight proceeded to Grand Gulf by steamboat, and thence riding forward, overtook Grant just in time to witness the battle of Champion's Hill on the 16th of May. That night he sent a despatch by way of Grand Gulf, promising to secure the desired co-operation, but urging Banks not to wait for it. The message arrived at headquarters at Simmes's plantation on the evening of the 17th, and was at once sent on to Brashear to be telegraphed to the commanding general at New Orleans. This assurance sent by Dwight really conveyed no more than his own opinion, but Banks read it as a promise from Grant, and once more convinced that it would be futile to attempt a movement toward Grand Gulf with the limited means of transport he had at hand, he again changed his plan and determined to go directly to Bayou Sara, hoping and trusting to meet there on the 25th of May a corps of 20,000 men from Grant's army.

The effective strength of the force now assembled near the head of the Atchafalaya was 8,400 infantry, 700 cavalry, 900 artillery; in all, 10,000. This great reduction was not wholly due to the effects of the climate, hardships, and long marches, but is partly to be ascribed to heavy detachments. These included the six regiments with Chickering, one at Butte-à-la-Rose, and one at Brashear.

At Simmesport the Corps sustained its first loss by expiration of service. The 6th New York, having completed the two years' term for which it had enlisted, went by the Atchafalaya and the railway to New Orleans, and there presently took transport for New York to be mustered out.

The movements of the army, though pressed as much as possible, were greatly retarded by the scanty means of water transportation and the pressing need of coal. From this cause the navy was also suffering, and urgent means had to be taken to supply the deficiency.

Reconnoissances, conducted by Lieutenant Harwood, in the course of which the enemy's cavalry was seen but not engaged, showed the roads from the Atchafalaya to Waterloo to be practicable for all arms. A detachment of cavalry sent out on the 18th to ascertain whether the Confederates had any force on the west bank of the Mississippi, encountered near Waterloo about 120 men of the 1st Alabama regiment, under Lieutenant-Colonel Locke, who had been sent over the day before from Port Hudson in skiffs to prevent any communication between the upper and the lower fleets. A skirmish followed, with slight loss on either side.

First placing Emory in command of the defences of New Orleans, and ordering Sherman to take Dow and Nickerson and join Augur before Port Hudson, Banks left the city on the 20th of May, rejoined his headquarters on the 21st, and at once set his troops in motion toward Bayou Sara. At half-past eight o'clock on the morning of the 21st of May, Paine broke up his bivouac on the Atchafalaya and marched to Morganza, after detaching the 131st New York and the 173rd New York with a section of artillery to guard the ammunition train. Grover followed by water as fast as the steamboats could be provided. At two o'clock on the morning of the 22nd of May, Banks and Grover, with the advance of Grover's division, landed at Bayou Sara without meeting any opposition from the enemy, who, up to this time, seems not to have suspected the movement. The other troops followed as rapidly as the means of transport permitted. Grover's division was sent ashore, followed by two brigades of Paine's division from Morganza. The wagon train went on down the road to the landing directly opposite Bayou Sara, under the escort of the 110th New York, and the 162nd New York, with one section of Carruth's battery, all under the command of Benedict.

Soon after the landing at Bayou Sara, a party of cavalry rode in, bringing the news of Augur's battle of the 21st. Hearing that Augur was at that moment engaged with the enemy, Banks pressed forward his troops. In a violent storm of wind and rain Grover pushed on until he met Augur's outlying detachments. Then, finding all quiet, he went into bivouac near Thompson's Creek, north-west of Port Hudson. Paine followed, and rested on the Perkins plantation, a mile in the rear of Grover. Banks made his headquarters with Grover. Augur covered the front of the position taken up by the enemy after the battle of Plains Store. On the same day, the 22nd, Sherman came up the river, landed at Springfield, and went into position on the Bayou Sara road on Augur's left. Thus at night on the 22nd the garrison of Port Hudson was practically hemmed in.

On the 18th, Banks had ordered Augur to march with his whole disposable force to the rear of Port Hudson to prevent the escape of the garrison. As early as the 13th of May, while yet the plan of campaign was in suspense, Augur had sent Grierson with the cavalry and Dudley with his brigade to Merritt's plantation, near the junction of the Springfield Landing and Bayou Sara roads, to threaten the enemy and discover his movements. Dudley then took post near White's Bayou, a branch of the Comite, and remained in observation, covering the road to Clinton and the fork that leads to Jackson. On the 20th of May Augur moved the remainder of his force up to Dudley, in order to be ready to cover T. W. Sherman's landing at Springfield, as well as to meet the advance of the main column under Banks from Bayou Sara, now likely to occur at any moment. With Augur now were Dudley, Chapin, Grierson, Godfrey's squadron composed of troops C and E of the Louisiana cavalry, two sections of Rawles's battery, Holcomb's battery, and one section of Mack's commanded by Sergeant A. W. McCollin. At six o'clock on the morning of the 21st of May Augur marched toward the crossing of the Plains Store and Bayou Sara roads to seize the enemy's line of retreat and to open the way for Banks. When Grierson came to the edge of the wood that forms the southern boundary of the plain, his advance fell in with a detachment of the garrison under Colonel S. P. Powers of the 14th Arkansas regiment, and a brisk skirmish followed. The same afternoon Gardner sent out Miles, with his battalion, about 400 strong, and Boone's battery, to feel Augur's advance and perhaps to drive it away. This brought on the action known as the battle of Plains Store. Unfortunately, no complete reports of the affair were made and the regimental narratives are meagre.

In the heavy forest that then masked the crossroads and formed the western border of the plain, Miles met Augur moving into position; Dudley, on the right of the road that leads from Plains Store to Port Hudson, supporting Holcomb's guns, and Chapin on the left supporting Rawles's guns. For about an hour the artillery fire was brisk. The 48th Massachusetts, being badly posted in column on either side of the Port Hudson road, gave way in some confusion under the sharp attack of Miles's men coming on through the thicket, and thus exposed the guns of Beck's section of Rails. As the 48th fell back through the advancing ranks of the 49th Massachusetts, the progress of that regiment was momentarily hindered, but a brisk charge of the 116th New York restored the battle. On the right, a section of Boone's battery got an enfilade fire on Rails and Chapin, and enabled Miles to draw off and retire behind the breastworks. Thus the affair was really ended before Augur, whose duty it was to act with prudence, had time to complete the proper development of his division as for a battle with the full force of the enemy, which he was bound to suppose was about to engage him. Then he completed the task of making good his position, and proceeded to open communication with Banks and with Sherman.

The main loss fell upon Chapin, Dudley's casualties numbering but 18, Grierson's but 2. The total casualties were 15 men killed, 3 officers and 69 men wounded, and 25 men missing—in all, 102. Miles reports his loss as 8 killed, 23 wounded, and 58 missing,—in all, 89.

When Augur quitted Baton Rouge he placed Drew with the 4th Louisiana Native Guards in Fort Williams to hold the place, supported by the fleet, and ordered Nelson with the 1st and 3rd Louisiana Native Guards to be ready to follow the division to Port Hudson.

Chapter 16

The Twenty-Seventh of May

Port Hudson was now held by Gardner with a force of about seven thousand of all arms. During the interval that had elapsed since its first occupation a formidable series of earthworks had been thrown up, commanding not only the river but all the inland approaches that were deemed practicable. The first plan for land defence was mainly against the attack expected to come from the direction of Baton Rouge. Accordingly, about four miles below Port Hudson a system of works was begun that, if completed, according to the original trace, would have involved a defensive line eight miles in length, requiring thirty-five thousand men and seventy guns to hold it. As actually constructed, the lines were four and a half miles long, and ran in a semicircular sweep from the river near Ross Landing, below Port Hudson, to the impassable swamp above. Following this line for thirteen hundred yards after leaving the river on the south, the bluff is broken into irregular ridges and deep ravines, with narrow plateaus; thence for two thousand yards the lines crossed the broad cotton fields of Gibbons's and of Slaughter's plantations; beyond these for four hundred yards they were carried over difficult gullies; beyond these again for fourteen hundred yards their course lay through fields and over hilly ground to the ravine at the bottom of which runs Sandy Creek. Here, on the day of the investment, the line of Confederate earthworks stopped, the country lying toward the northeast being considered so difficult that no attack was looked for in that quarter. Sandy Creek finds its way into the marshy bottom of Foster's Creek, and from Sandy Creek, where the earthworks ended, to the river at the mouth of Foster's Creek, is about twenty-five hundred yards. Save where the axe had been busy, nearly the whole country was covered with a heavy growth of magnolia trees of great size and beauty. This was a line that, for its complete defence against a regular siege, conducted according to the strict principles of military science, as laid down in the books, should have had a force of fifteen thousand men. At the end of March the garrison consisted of 1,366 officers, 14,921 men of all arms present for duty, making a total of 16,287. The main body was organized in 5 brigades, commanded by Beall, Buford, Gregg, Maxey, and Rust. The fortifications on the river front mounted 22 heavy guns, from 10-inch columbiads down to 24-pounder siege guns, manned by 3 battalions of heavy artillerists, while 13 light batteries, probably numbering 78 pieces, were available for the defence of all the lines: of these batteries only 5 were now left, with 30 guns.

When, early in May, Pemberton began to feel the weight of Grant's pressure, he called on Gardner for reinforcements; thus Rust and Buford marched to the relief of Vicksburg on the 4th of May, Gregg followed on the 5th, and Maxey on the 8th. Miles was to have followed Maxey; in fact the preparations and orders had been given for the evacuation of Port Hudson; but now the same uncertainty and vacillation on the part of the Confederate chiefs that were to seal the doom of Vicksburg began to be felt at Port Hudson. Gardner, who had moved out with Maxey, had hardly arrived at Clinton when he was met by an order from Pemberton to return to Port Hudson with a few thousand men and to hold the place to the last. But ten days later, on the 19th of May, Johnston, who was then engaged in carrying out his own ideas, which differed radically from those of Davis and Pemberton, ordered Gardner to evacuate Port Hudson and to march on Jackson, Mississippi. This order, sent by courier as well as by telegraph, Gardner received just as Augur was marching from Baton Rouge to cut him off. Then it was too late, and when on the 23rd Johnston peremptorily renewed his order for the evacuation, even the communication was closed.

The investment was made perfect by the presence in the river, above and below Port Hudson, of the ships and gunboats of the navy. Just above the place and at anchor around the bend lay the *Hartford*, now Commodore Palmer's flagship, with the *Albatross*,

Sachem, *Estrella*, and *Arizona*. Below, at anchor off Prophet's Island, were the *Monongahela*, bearing Farragut's flag, the *Richmond*, *Genesee*, *Essex*, and the mortar flotilla. Both the upper and the lower fleets watched the river at night by means of picket-boats in order to discover any movement and to intercept any communication with the garrison.

At the Hermitage plantation, on the west bank of the river, Benedict was stationed with his own regiment, the 162nd New York, the 110th New York, and a section of artillery to prevent the escape of the Confederates by water. As soon as Weitzel joined, on the 25th of May, Banks began to close in his lines along the entire front. Weitzel moved up to the sugar-house on the telegraph road near the bridge over Foster's Creek; Paine advanced into the woods on Weitzel's left; Grover moved forward on the north of the Clinton Railway, crossed the ravine of Sandy Creek, and occupied the wooded rest of the steep hill in front. Augur prolonged the line across the Plains Store road under cover of the woods, yet in plain view of the Confederate entrenchments. Sherman held the Baton Rouge road, occupying the skirt of woods that formed the eastern edge of Slaughter's and Gibbons's fields.

The 1st and 3rd Louisiana Native Guards, under Nelson, having come up from Baton Rouge, were posted at the sugar-house near Foster's Creek, forming the extreme right of the line of investment.

Banks now placed Weitzel in command of the right wing of the army, comprising his own brigade under Thomas, Dwight's brigade of Grover's division under Van Zandt, together forming a temporary division under Dwight, the six regiments that remained of Paine's division after the heavy detachments, and the two coloured regiments under Nelson. During the day of the 25th Weitzel gained the wooded slope covering the Confederate left front. The Confederate advanced guard on this part of their line, composed in part of the 9th battalion of Louisiana partisan rangers, under Lieutenant-Colonel Wingfield, resisted Weitzel's advance stoutly, but was steadily and without difficulty pushed back into the entrenchments.

When night fell on the 26th of May the division commanders met at headquarters at Riley's on the Bayou Sara road to consider the question of an assault. No minutes of this council were kept, and to this day its conclusions are a matter of dispute. They may safely be regarded as sufficiently indicated by the orders for the following day. By at least one of those present any immediate movement in the nature of an assault was objected to because of the great distance that still separated the lines of investment from the Confederate earthworks; it was urged that the troops would have to move to the attack over ground the precise character of which was as yet unknown to them or to their commanders, although it was known to be broken and naturally difficult and to be obstructed by felled timber. The general opinion was, however, that prompt and decisive action was demanded in view of the unusual and precarious nature of the campaigns on which the two armies of Grant and Banks were now embarked, the uncertainty as to what Johnston might do, and the certainty that a disaster at Vicksburg would bring ruin in Louisiana. Moreover, officers and men alike were in high spirits and full of confidence in themselves, and they outnumbered the Confederates rather more than two to one. This was the view held by Banks himself. Upon his mind, moreover, the disapproval and the repeated urgings of the government acted as a goad. Accordingly, as soon as the council broke up he gave orders for an assault on the following morning.

All the artillery was to open upon the Confederate works at daybreak. For this purpose the reserve artillery was placed under the immediate orders of Arnold. He was to open fire at six.

Weitzel was to take advantage of the attacks on the left and centre to force his way into the works on his front, since it was natural to expect that, whether they should prove successful or not, these attacks would distract the attention of the enemy and serve to relieve the pressure in Weitzel's front.

Grover was thus left with five regiments to support the left centre, to reinforce either the right or left, and to support the right flank of the reserve artillery, or to force his way into the works, as occasion might require.

Augur, holding the centre, with Dudley's brigade forming his right and Chapin his left, and Sherman, at the extreme left, separated from Augur by a thick wood, were to begin the attack during the cannonade by advancing their skirmishers to kill the enemy's cannoneers and to cover the assault. They were to place their troops in position to take instant advantage of any favourable opportunity, and, if possible, to force the enemy's works at the earliest moment.

Each division commander was to provide his own means for passing the ditch. These, for the most part, consisted of cotton bags, fascines, and planks borne by detachments of men, furnished by detail or by volunteering.

It will be observed that no time was fixed for the assault of either column nor any provision made to render the several attacks simultaneous. Moreover, although the order wound up with the emphatic declaration that "Port Hudson must be taken to-morrow," an impression prevailed in the minds of at least two of the division commanders that there were still to be reconnoissances by the engineers, and that upon the results of these would depend the selection of the points of attack.

There were no roads along the front or rear of the investing army, and the only means by which communication was maintained between the left, the centre, and the right was either by wide detours or through dense and unknown woods and thickets. It was impossible to see the troops in front or rear or on either flank. On no part of the line was either division in sight of the other.

The forest approached within 250 yards at the nearest point on Weitzel's front, within 450 yards on Grover's, within 500 yards on Augur's, and within 1,200 yards on Sherman's front. The field to be passed over was partly the cleared land of the plantations, crossed by fences and hedges, but in many places, especially on Augur's approach, the timber had been recently felled, and, lying thick upon the ground, made a truly formidable obstacle.

The morning of the 27th of May broke bright and beautiful. As the early twilight began to open out along the entire front the artillery began a furious cannonade. At first the Confederate guns replied with spirit, but it soon became apparent that they were over-weighted, and, moreover, the necessity of husbanding their scanty store of ammunition no doubt impressed itself upon the minds of the Confederate commanders.

About six o'clock, when Weitzel judged that the movement on the left must be well advanced, he put his columns in motion through the dense forest in his front, forming his command, as far as the nature of the ground admitted, in column of brigades, Dwight's brigade under Van Zandt leading, followed by Weitzel's brigade under Thomas. Paine formed his division in two lines in support, his own brigade under Fearing in front, and Gooding's in reserve. The Confederate skirmishers and outposts continued to occupy the forest and the ravines on this part of their front, and the first hour was spent in pressing them back behind their entrenchments. Then Thomas moved forward through Van Zandt's intervals, and deploying from right to left the 160th New York, Lieutenant-Colonel Van Petter; 8th Vermont, Lieutenant-Colonel Dillingham; 12th Connecticut, Lieutenant-Colonel Peck; and 75th New York, Lieutenant-Colonel Babcock, advanced to the attack. Van Zandt, owing to the inequalities of the ground and the difficulty of finding the way, drifted somewhat toward the right. Thereupon Paine, finding his front uncovered, moved forward into the interval. Then began what has been aptly termed a "huge bushwack."

Until within three days a part of the Confederate lines in front of Weitzel had not been fortified at all, the defence resting on the great natural difficulties of the approaches no less than of the ground to be held; but in the interval Gardner had taken notice of the indications that pointed to an advance in this quarter, and had caused light breastworks to be constructed in all haste. This the great trees that covered the hill rendered an easy task. On the morning of the 27th of May, therefore, the works that Weitzel was called upon to attack consisted mainly of big logs on the crest and following the contour of the hill, rendered almost unapproachable by the felled timber that choked the ravines. Thus, while Weitzel's men could not even see their enemy, they were themselves unable to move beyond the cover of the hollows and the timber without offering an easy mark for a destructive fire of small-arms, as well as of grape, shell, shrapnel, and canister. When finally, after climbing over hills, logs, and fallen trees, and forcing the ravines filled with tangled brush and branches, Weitzel had driven the Confederates into their works, he held the ridge about two hundred yards distant from the position to be attacked.

Paine's position at this time was to the right and rear of battery No. 6, as shown on the map; Weitzel and Dwight were on the same crest near batteries 3, 4, and 5. The pioneers worked like beavers to open the roads as fast as the infantry advanced, and with such skill and zeal that hardly had the infantry formed upon the crest than the guns of Duryea, Bainbridge, Nims, Haley, and Carruth unlimbered and opened fire by their side.

At length Thomas succeeded in making his way across the rivulet known as Little Sandy Creek, and, working gradually forward, began to fortify with logs the hill on the right, afterward known as Fort Babcock, in honour of the Lieutenant-Colonel of the 75th New York.

To support Weitzel's movement, Grover sent the 159th New York, Lieutenant-Colonel Burt, and the 25th Connecticut by a wide detour to the right to make their way in on Paine's left. Taking advantage of the protection afforded by the ravine, at the bottom of which ran or rather trickled Sandy Creek, these regiments, after the most difficult and exhausting scramble through the brush and over the fallen timber, came to the base of a steep bluff, near the position afterward occupied by siege battery No. 6. This, although the works directly opposite were as yet light, was naturally one of the ugliest approaches on the whole front. In spite of every exertion, it took the 159th an hour to move half a mile. Just before reaching the foot of the hill over which they were to charge, they captured a Confederate captain and six skirmishers, who lay concealed in the ravine, cut off by the advance and unable to retire. So crooked and obscure was the path and so difficult was it to see any thing, even a few feet ahead, that the officers had to stand at every little turning to tell the men which way to go. At last the regiment formed, and, with a rush, began the assault of the bluff, but they could get no farther than the crest, where they were met by a destructive flank fire from the Confederate riflemen. There, within thirty yards of the works, the men sought shelter.

To try the effect of a diversion, Grover put in the 12th Maine, supported by the remaining fragment of his division, reduced to the 13th and 25th Connecticut, against the partly exposed west face of the bastion that formed the left of the finished portion of the Confederate earthworks. The point of attack is shown at X. and XI., and the position whence Grover moved at 1 and 7.

After the first attack on the right had well-nigh spent itself, and when its renewal, in conjunction with an advance on the centre and left, was momentarily expected, Dwight thought to create a diversion and at the same time to develop the strength and position of the Confederates toward their extreme left, where their lines bent back to rest on the river, and to this end he ordered Nelson to put in his two coloured regiments. This portion of the Confederate line occupied the nearly level crest of a steep bluff that completely dominates the low ground by the sugar-house, where the telegraph road crosses Foster's Creek. Over this ground the coloured troops had to advance unsupported to receive their first fire. The bridge had been burned when the Confederates retired to their works. Directly in front of the crest, and somewhat below it, a rugged bluff stands a little apart, projecting boldly from the main height with a sharp return to the right, so as to form a natural outwork of great strength, practically inaccessible save by the road that winds along the bottom of the little rivulet at the foot of the almost perpendicular flank. This detached ridge is about four hundred yards in length. It was held by six companies of the 39th Mississippi regiment, under Colonel W. B. Shelby, while behind, in the positions of land batteries III. and IV., were planted six field pieces, and still farther back on the water front the columbiads of Whitfield and Seawell, mounted on traversing carriages, stood ready to rake the road with their 8-inch and 10-inch shell and shrapnel.

Shortly after seven o'clock, Nelson sent in the 1st Louisiana Native Guards, under Lieutenant-Colonel Bassett, in column, to force the crossing of the creek. The 3rd Louisiana Native Guards followed in close support. Just before the head of the column came near the creek, the movement was perceived by the Confederates, who immediately opened on the negroes a sharp fire of musketry from the rifle-pits on the detached bluff; at the same moment the field guns opened with shell and shrapnel from the ridge behind, and as the men struggled on through the creek and up the farther bank they became exposed to the enfilade fire of the columbiads. When, in mounting the narrow gorge that led up the hill, the head of the column, necessarily shattered as it was by this concentrated fire, had gained a point within about two hundred yards of the crest, suddenly every gun opened on them with canister. This was more than any man could stand. Bassett's men gave back in disorder on their supports, then in the act of crossing the creek, and the whole column retired in confusion to its position near the sugar-house on the north bank. Here both regiments were soon re-formed and again moved forward in good order, anticipating instructions to renew the attack; yet none came, and, in fact, the attack was not renewed, although the contemporary accounts, some of them even official, distinctly speak of repeated charges. In this abortive attempt, Captain Andrew Cailloux and Second Lieutenant John H. Crowder, of the 1st regiment, were instantly killed. Cailloux, who is said to have been a free man of colour, although all the officers of his race were at that time supposed to have resigned, fell at the head of the leading company of his regiment, while gallantly cheering on his men. The 1st regiment lost, in this brief engagement, 2 officers, and 24 men killed and 79 wounded—in all, 105. The 3rd, being far less exposed, as well as for a shorter time, lost 1 officer and 5 men killed, and 1 officer wounded—in all, 7.

The morning was drawing out when these movements were well spent, and the advanced positions simply held without further effort to go forward. The hour may have been about ten o'clock. Grover, Paine, and Weitzel listened in vain for any sounds of musketry on their left to indicate that either Augur or Sherman was at work, yet no sound came from that quarter save the steady pounding of the Union artillery. Now Weitzel believed that, by pursuing his advance in what might be called skirmishing order and working his way gradually forward from the vantage-ground of Fort Babcock, he might gain, without great addition to his losses, already heavy, a foothold on the high ground held by the Confederate left; yet of the character of the defences of this part of the line Weitzel knew but little, and of the nature of the ground behind these defences and the direction of the roads, neither he nor any one in the Union army knew any thing. The topography of the ground in sight afforded the only indication of what might be expected farther on, and this was confusing and difficult to the last degree. Weitzel had, therefore, strong reason for believing that his difficulties, instead of ending with the capture of the Confederate works, might be only beginning. There was, of course, the chance that the garrison along the whole front might throw down their arms or abandon their defences the moment they should find themselves taken in reverse at any point, for it was known that they had no reserves to be reckoned with after breaking through the line. Grover had been ordered to support either the right or the left, or to attempt to make his way into the works, as circumstances might suggest. This last he had tried, and failed to accomplish. On his left there was no attack to support. When riding toward the right he met Weitzel, who, although commanding the right wing, was his junior in rank as well as in experience, Grover gave Weitzel the counsel of prudence, and Weitzel fell in with these views. The two commanders decided to ask fresh orders or to wait for an assault on the centre or left before renewing the attack on the right.

All this time Augur stood ready, his division formed and all in perfect order, waiting for the word from Banks, who made his headquarters close at hand, and who, in his turn, waited for the sound of Sherman's musketry as the signal to put in Augur. With Sherman, Augur was in connection along the front, although not in easy communication. The precise nature of the causes that held Sherman back it is, even now, impossible to state, nor would it be easy, in the absence of the facts, to form a conjecture that should seem to be altogether probable and at the same time reasonable. The most plausible surmise seems to be that Sherman supposed he was to wait for the engineers to indicate the point of attack, and that he himself did not choose to go beyond what he conceived to be his orders to precipitate a movement whose propriety he doubted. Sherman was an officer of the old army, of wide experience, favourably known and highly esteemed throughout the service for his intelligence, his character, and his courage. He was known as one of the most distinguished of the chosen commanders of the few light batteries that the government of the United States had thought itself able to afford in the days before the war. Before coming to Louisiana he had commanded a department, and in that capacity had carried to a successful conclusion the brilliant operations that gave Hilton Head and Port Royal to the forces of the Union. Neither in his previous history was there any thing to his personal discredit as a man or as a soldier. The fact remains, however, account for it how we may, that when about noon, greatly disturbed by the check on the right, and still more by the silence on the left, Banks himself rode almost unattended to Sherman's headquarters, he found Sherman at luncheon in his tent, surrounded by his staff, while in front the division lay idly under arms, without orders. Hot words passed, the precise nature of which has not been recorded, and Banks returned to his headquarters determined to replace Sherman by the chief-of-staff of the department. The roads had not yet been opened, and it was half-past one before these orders could be given. Andrews rode directly to the left, accompanied by but a single *aide-de-camp*, Lieutenant Fiske. When he came on the ground he found Sherman's division deployed, and Sherman himself on horseback at the head of his men, ready to lead them forward. Then Andrews, with great propriety, deferred the delivery of the orders placing him in command, and, after a few words, at a quarter past two Sherman moved to the assault. Andrews remained to witness the operation.

Nickerson moved forward on the right in column of regiments. The 14th Maine, deployed as skirmishers, covered his front, followed by the 24th Maine, 177th New York, and 165th New York in line. After emerging from the woods, Nickerson's right flank rested on the road that runs past Slaughter's house, near the position of battery 16.

Dow formed the left of the division and of the army. He advanced at the same time as Nickerson, and in like order, his right resting near the position of battery 17 and his left near Gibbons's house, marked as the position of battery 18. The 6th Michigan led the brigade, followed by the 15th New Hampshire, 26th Connecticut, and 128th New York.

In the interval between the two brigades rode Sherman, surrounded by his whole staff and followed by his escort.

No sooner had the line emerged from among the trees than the Confederates opened upon every part of it, as it came in sight, a galling fire of musketry and artillery. At first the troops moved forward steadily and at a good pace, but as they drew nearer to the enemy and the musketry fire grew hotter, their progress was delayed and their formation somewhat broken by four successive and parallel lines of fence that had to be thrown down and crossed. Once clear of the young corn, they found themselves entangled with the abatis that covered and protected the immediate front of the Confederate works on this part of the line. This had been set on fire by the exploding shells, and the smoke and flame now added to the difficulty of the movement. Here the men suffered greatly, many being shot down in the act of climbing the great trunks of the fallen trees, and many more having their clothing reduced to tatters and almost torn from their bodies in the attempt to force their way through the entangled branches. The impetus was soon lost, the men lay down or sought cover; numbers of Dow's men made their way to the grove in their rear and into the gully on their left; of Nickerson's, many drifted singly and in groups into the ravine on their right.

Long before this, indeed within a few minutes after the line first marched out from the wood, Sherman had fallen from his horse, severely wounded in the leg; under the vigorous fire concentrated upon this large group of horsemen in plain sight of the Confederates and in easy range, two of his staff officers had shared the same fate. This would have brought Dow to the command of the division; but nearly at the same instant Dow himself was wounded and went to the rear, and so the command fell to Nickerson, who was with his brigade, and, in the confusion of the moment, was not notified. Thus, for some interval, there was no one to give orders for fresh dispositions among the regiments. Many officers had fallen; the 128th New York had lost its colonel, Cowles; the 165th New York, at last holding the front of Nickerson's line, had lost two successive commanders, Abel Smith and Carr, both wounded, the former mortally, while standing by the colours. To retire was now only less difficult than to advance. Nickerson's men, lying down, held their ground until after dark; but Dow's, being nearer the cover of the woods, fell back to their first position.

Andrews now took command of the division, in virtue of the written orders of the commanding general, and prepared to obey whatever fresh instructions he might receive. None came; there was, indeed, nothing to be done but to withdraw and to restore order.

As soon as Banks heard the rattle of the musketry on the left, and saw from the smoke of the Confederate guns that Sherman was engaged, he ordered Augur forward. Augur, as has been said, had been ready and waiting all day. His arrangements were to make the attack with Chapin's brigade, deployed across the Plains Store road, and to support it with Dudley's, held in reserve under cover of one of the high and thick hedges of the Osage orange that crossed and divided the fields on the right of the road. Chapin's front was covered by the skirmishers of the 21st Maine; immediately in their rear were to march the storming column of two hundred volunteers, under Lieutenant-Colonel O'Brien, of the 48th Massachusetts. The stormers rested and waited for the word in the point of the wood on the left of the Plains Store road, nearly opposite the position of battery 13. Half their number carried cotton bags and fascines to fill the ditch. On the right of the road the 116th New York was deployed; on its left the 49th Massachusetts, closely supported by the 48th Massachusetts, the 2nd Louisiana, of Dudley's brigade, and the reserve of the 21st Maine.

O'Brien shook hands with the officer who brought him the last order, and, turning to his men, who were lying or sitting near by, some on their cotton bags, others on the ground, said in the coolest and most business-like manner: "Pick up your bundles, and come on!" The movement of the stormers was the signal for the whole line. A truly magnificent sight was the advance of these battalions, with their colours flying and borne sturdily toward the front; yet not for long. Hardly had the movement begun when the whole force—officers, men, colours, stormers, and all,—found themselves inextricably entangled in the dense abatis under a fierce and continuous discharge of musketry and a withering cross-fire of artillery. Besides the field-pieces bearing directly down the road, two 24-pounders poured upon their flank a storm of missiles of all sorts, with fragments of railway bars and broken chains for grape, and rusty nails and the rakings of the scrap-heap for canister. No part of the column ever passed beyond the abatis, nor was it even possible to extricate the troops in any order without greatly adding to the list of casualties, already of a fearful length. Banks was all for putting Dudley over the open ground directly in his front, but, before any thing could be done, came the bad news from the left, and at last it was clear to the most persistent that the day was miserably lost. When, after nightfall, the division commanders reported at headquarters, among the wounded under the great trees, it was known that the result was even worse than the first accounts.

The attempt had failed without inflicting serious loss upon the enemy, save in ammunition expended, yet at a fearful cost to the Union army. When the list came to be made up, it was found that 15 officers and 278 men had been killed, 90 officers and 1,455 men wounded, 2 officers and 155 men missing, making the total killed 293, total wounded 1,545, total missing 157, and an aggregate of 1,995. Of the missing, many were unquestionably dead. Worse than all, if possible, the confidence that but a few hours before had run so high, was rudely shaken. It was long indeed before the men felt the same faith in themselves, and it is but the plain truth to say that their reliance on the department commander never quite returned.

The heavy loss in killed and wounded taxed to the utmost the skill and untiring exertions of the surgeons, who soon found their preparations and supplies exceeded by the unlooked-for demand upon them. All night long on that 27th of May the stretcher-bearers were engaged in removing the wounded to the field-hospitals in the rear. These were soon filled to overflowing, and many rested under the shelter of the trees. Hither, too, came large numbers of men not too badly hurt to be able to walk, and to all the tired troops the whole night was rendered dismal to the last degree by the groans of their suffering comrades mingled everywhere, the wounded with the well, the dying with the dead.

Among the killed were: Colonel Edward P. Chapin, of the 116th New York; Colonel Davis S. Cowles, of the 128th New York; Lieutenant-Colonel William L. Rodman, of the 38th Massachusetts; Lieutenant-Colonel James O'Brien, of the 48th Massachusetts; Captain John B. Hubbard, Assistant Adjutant-General, of Weitzel's brigade; Lieutenant Ladislas A. Wrotnowkski, Topographical Engineer on Weitzel's staff. Lieutenant-Colonels Oliver W. Lull, of the 8th New Hampshire, and Abel Smith, Jr., of the 165th New York, were mortally wounded. The long list of the wounded included Brigadier-General Thomas W. Sherman, Brigadier-General Neal Dow, Colonel Richard E. Holcomb, of the 1st Louisiana; Colonel Thomas S. Clark, of the 6th Michigan; Colonel William F. Bartlett, of the 49th Massachusetts; Major Gouverneur Carr, of the 165th New York.

Farragut's ships and mortar-boats, which had been harassing the garrison at intervals, day and night, for more than ten days, joined hotly in the bombardment, but ceased firing, by arrangement, as soon as the land batteries slackened. The fire of the fleet, especially that of the mortars, was very annoying to the garrison, especially at first, yet the actual casualties were not great.

The Confederate losses during the assault are not known. In Beall's brigade all the losses up to the 1st of June numbered 68 killed, 194 wounded, and 96 missing; together, 358; most of these must have been incurred on the 27th of May. The Confederate artillery was soon so completely overpowered, that it became nearly useless, save when the Union guns were masked by the advance of assaulting columns. Three 24-pounders were dismounted, and of these one was completely disabled.

With the result of this day the last hope of a junction between the armies of Banks and Grant vanished. It may therefore be convenient to retrace our steps a little in order to note the closing incidents of this strange chapter of well-laid plans by fortune brought to naught.

Dwight returned from his visit to Grant on the 22nd of May, and reported to Banks in person at his headquarters with Grover on Thompson's Creek. In his account of what had taken place, Dwight confirmed the idea Banks had already derived from the despatch that Dwight had sent from Grand Gulf on the 16th, before he had seen Grant. Grant would send 5,000 men, Dwight reported, but Banks was not to wait for them. Practically this had no effect whatever upon the campaign, and how little impression it made upon the mind of Grant himself may be seen from his description, written in 1884, of his interview with Dwight. It was the morning of the 17th of May and Grant's troops were standing on the eastern bank of the Big Black ready to force the passage of the river:

> While the troops were standing as here described, an officer from Banks's staff came up and presented me with a letter from General Halleck, dated the 11th of May. It had been sent by way of New Orleans to Banks to forward to me. He ordered me to return to Grand Gulf and to co-operate from there with Banks against Port Hudson, and then to return with our combined forces to besiege Vicksburg. I told the officer that the order came too late and that Halleck would not give it then if he knew our position. The bearer of the despatch insisted that I ought to obey the order, and was

giving arguments to support his position when I heard great cheering to the right of our line, and looking in that direction, saw Lawler, in his shirt-sleeves, leading a charge upon the enemy. I immediately mounted my horse and rode in the direction of the charge, and saw no more of the officer who delivered the despatch, I think not even to this day.[1]

Here two mistakes are perhaps worth noting as curious rather than important: Dwight was not a member of Banks's staff, and the letter from Halleck, dated the 11th of May, which General Grant strangely supposed to have come by way of New Orleans, was, in fact, Halleck's telegram of that date, sent by way of Memphis, which Dwight had picked up as he passed through Grand Gulf, after Grant had cut his communications. Dwight's account may have taken colour from his hopes, yet the course of events gives some reason to think he may have had warrant for his belief.

On the 19th of May Grant's first assault of Vicksburg was repulsed with a loss of 942. Three days later he delivered his second assault, which likewise failed, at a cost of 3,199 killed, wounded, and missing. This drove him to the siege and put him in need of more troops; yet when, on the 25th of May, he sat down to write to Banks, it was with the purpose of offering to send down a force of 8,000 or 10,000 men if Banks could now provide the means of transport. But even while Grant wrote, word came that Johnston was gathering in his rear; and so the whole thing was one more given up, and instead, once again he called on Banks for help; and this time he sent down two large steamers, the *Forest Queen* and *Moderator*, to fetch the men. But Banks had now no men to spare; he too was cast for a siege; he could only echo the entreaty and send back the steamboats empty as they came. So the affair ended.

---

1. *Personal Memoirs of U. S. Grant*, vol. I., p. 524.

CHAPTER 17

The Fourteenth of June

Banks at once ordered up the ammunition and the stores from the depot at Riley's, near the headquarters of the day before, and early on the morning of the 28th of May established his headquarters in tents at Young's, in rear of the centre, and began his arrangements to reduce Port Hudson by gradual approaches. At six o'clock in the morning he sent a flag of truce to Gardner, from Augur's front on the Plains Store road, bearing a request for a suspension of hostilities until two o'clock in the afternoon, to permit the removal of the dead and wounded. To this Gardner at once refused to agree unless Banks would agree to withdraw at all points to a distance of eight hundred yards. He also demanded that the fleet should drop down out of range. Banks was unable to consent. A long correspondence followed, twelve letters in all, crossing and re-crossing, to the utter confusion of time. At length, shortly after half-past three o'clock, Banks received Gardner's assent to an armistice extending till seven o'clock. The conditions were that the besiegers were to send to the lines of the defence, by unarmed parties, such of the Confederate killed as remained unburied, and such of their wounded as had not already been picked up and sent to the rear. The killed and wounded of the Union army, lying between their lines and the Confederate works, were to be cared for in the same way.

Arnold was ordered to bring up the siege train, manned by the 1st Indiana heavy artillery, and Houston to provide entrenching tools and siege materials. When all the siege artillery was in position there were forty pieces, of which six were 8-inch sea-coast howitzers on siege carriages, eight 24-pounders, seven 30-pounder Parrotts, four 6-inch rifles, four 9-inch Dahlgren guns, four 8-inch mortars, three

10-inch mortars, and four 13-inch mortars. To these were added twelve light batteries of sixty pieces, namely, six 6-pounder Sawyer rifles, two 10-pounder Parrotts, twenty-six 12-pounder Napoleons, two 12-pounder howitzers, twelve 3-inch rifles, and twelve 20-pounder Parrotts. The Dahlgren guns were served by a detachment of fifty-one men from the *Richmond* and seventeen from the *Essex*, under Lieutenant-Commander Edward Terry, with Ensign Robert P. Swann, Ensign E. M. Shepard, and Master's Mates William R. Cox and Edmund L. Bourne for chiefs of the gun divisions.

In the course of the next few days the eight regiments that had been left on the Teche and the Atchafalaya rejoined the army before Port Hudson, coming by way of Brashear, Algiers, and the river. This gave to the cavalry under Grierson one more regiment, the 41st Massachusetts, now mounted, and henceforth known as the 3rd Massachusetts cavalry, the three troops of the old 2nd battalion being merged in it; Weitzel got back the 114th New York; Paine recovered the 4th Massachusetts and the 16th New Hampshire of Ingraham's brigade, now practically broken up; and Grover the 22nd Maine and 90th New York of Dwight's brigade, the 52nd Massachusetts of Kimball's, and the 26th Maine of Birge's, while losing the 41st Massachusetts by its conversion into a mounted regiment. The 16th New Hampshire, however, had suffered so severely during its six week's confinement in the heart of the pestilential swamp that it was reduced to a mere skeleton, without strength either numerical or physical. It was easy to see that officers and men alike were suffering from some aggravated form of hepatic disorder, due to malarial poison. Many were added to the sick-report every day. Few that went to the regimental or general hospital returned to duty, while of the men called well all were yellow, emaciated, and restless, or so drowsy that the sentries were found asleep on their posts at noonday. This unfortunate regiment was therefore taken from the front and set to guard the general ammunition depot, near headquarters. Without being once engaged in battle, so that it had not a single gunshot wound to report, the 16th New Hampshire suffered a loss by disease during its seven months' service in Louisiana of 5 officers and 216 men—in all, 221; and nearly the whole of this occurred in the last two months. This regiment was replaced in Paine's division by the 28th Connecticut, from Pensacola.

Dwight was now given the command of Sherman's division, relieving Nickerson, who had assumed command the morning after the assault of the 27th. Dow being disabled by his wounds, his brigade fell to Clark. The 2nd Louisiana was transferred from Dudley's brigade to Chapin's, bringing Charles J. Paine in command. Halbert E. Paine's division was withdrawn from the earlier formation of the right wing under Weitzel, and was established in position on Grover's left, covering the Jackson road and the second position of Duryea's battery at No. 12. Grover was placed in command, from the afternoon of the 27th, of the whole right wing, but Dwight's brigade, under Morgan, remained with Weitzel as part of a temporary division under his command, Thomas retaining the command of Weitzel's brigade. Finally, the 162nd New York and the 175th New York were temporarily taken from Paine and lent to Dwight, who, directly after the 14th of June, united them with the 28th Maine of Sherman's division to form a temporary 2nd brigade. At the same time he transferred the 6th Michigan to Nickerson's brigade, evidently meaning to take the command of the 1st brigade from Clark; but these arrangements were promptly set aside by orders from headquarters. The left wing, comprising Augur's division and Sherman's, now Dwight's, was placed under the command of Augur.

Along the whole front the troops now held substantially the advanced positions they had gained on the 27th of May. This shortened the line, and, as it was on the whole better arranged and the connections and communications better, Augur took ground a little to the left and held, with Charles J. Paine's brigade, a part of the field that had been in Sherman's front on the 27th; while Dwight, in closing up and drawing in his left flank, moved nearer to the river and covered the road leading in a southerly direction from the Confederate works around the eastern slope of Mount Pleasant and past Troth's house.

The cavalry, being of no further use to the divisions, but rather an encumbrance upon them, was massed, under Grierson, behind the centre, and assigned to the duty of guarding the rear, the depots, and the communications against the incursions of the Confederate cavalry, under Logan, known to be hovering between Port Hudson and Clinton, and supposed to be from 1,500 to 2,000 strong. Logan's actual force at this time was about 1,200 effective. Grierson had about 1,700, including his own regiment, the 6th Illinois, the 7th Illinois, Colonel Edward Prince, a detachment of the 1st Louisiana, the 3rd Massachusetts cavalry, and the 14th New York.

As fast as the engineers were able to survey the ground and the working parties to open the roads, Arnold and Houston chose with great care the positions for the siege batteries, and heavy details were soon at work upon them, as well as upon the long line of rifle-pits, connecting the batteries and practically forming the first parallel of the siege works. The positions of some of these batteries, especially on the left, were afterward changed; but as finally constructed and mounted, they began at the north, near the position of the coloured regiments on the right bank of Foster's Creek, and extended, at a distance from the Confederate works varying from six hundred to twelve hundred yards, to the Mount Pleasant road, across which was planted siege battery No. 21. The first position of siege battery No. 20 is marked "old 20," and the three formidable batteries on the extreme left, Nos. 22, 23, and 24, were not established till later, the attack of the Confederate works in their front being at first left to the guns of the fleet. Two epaulements for field artillery were thrown up on either side of the road at Foster's Creek to command the passage of the stream, but no siege guns were mounted there. The extreme right of the siege batteries was at No. 2.

While all eyes were turned upon the siege works and every nerve strained for their completion, Logan's presence in the rear, though at no time so hurtful as might fairly have been expected, was a continual source of anxiety and annoyance. To find out just what force he had and what he was about, Grierson moved toward Clinton on the morning of the 3rd of June with the 6th and 7th Illinois, the old 2nd Massachusetts battalion, now merged in the 3rd, a squadron of the 1st Louisiana, two companies of the 4th Wisconsin, mounted, and one section of Nims's battery. Grierson took the road by Jackson, and, when within three miles of that place, sent Godfrey, with 200 men of the Massachusetts and Louisiana cavalry, to ride through the town, while the main column went direct to Clinton. Godfrey pushing on briskly through Jackson, captured and paroled, after the useless fashion of the time, a number of prisoners, and rejoined the column two miles beyond.

When eight miles west of Clinton, Grierson heard a report that Logan had gone that morning toward Port Hudson, but pushing on toward Clinton, after crossing the Comite Grierson found Logan's advance and drove it back on the main body, strongly posted on Pretty Creek. A three hours' engagement followed, resulting in Grierson's retirement to Port Hudson, with a loss of 8 killed, 28 wounded, and 15 missing; 3 of the dead and 7 of the wounded falling into the hands of the enemy. Logan reports his loss as 20 killed and wounded, and claims 40 prisoners. Among the killed, unfortunately, was the young cavalry officer, Lieutenant Solon A. Perkins, of the 3rd Massachusetts, whose skill and daring had commended itself to the notice of Weitzel during the early operations in La Fourche, and whose long service without proper rank had drawn out the remark: "This Perkins is a splendid officer, and he deserves promotion as much as any officer I ever saw."

Banks determined to chastise Logan for this; accordingly, at daylight on the morning of the 5th of June, Paine took his old brigade under Fearing, with the 52nd Massachusetts, the 91st New York, and two sections of Duryea's battery, and preceded by Grierson's cavalry, marched on Clinton by way of Olive Branch and the plank road. That night Paine encamped at Redwood creek; on the 6th he made a short march to the Comite, distant nine miles from his objective, and there halted till midnight. Then, after a night march, the whole force entered Clinton at daylight on the morning of the 7th, only to find that Logan, forewarned, had gone toward Jackson. Then Paine countermarched to the Comite, and, remaining till sunset, marched that evening to Redwood, and, there going into bivouac, at two o'clock on the following morning, the 8th of June, returned to the lines before Port Hudson. On this fruitless expedition the men and horses suffered severely from the heat, and there were many cases of sunstroke.

By the 1st of June the artillery and the sharp-shooters of the besieged had obtained so complete a mastery over the guns of the defenders, that on the whole line these were practically silent, if not silenced. In part, no doubt, this is to be ascribed to a desire on the part of the Confederate artillerists to reserve their ammunition for the emergency, yet something was also due to the effect of the Union fire, by which, in the first week, twelve heavy guns were disabled. The 10-inch columbiad in water battery 4 was dismounted at long range. This gun was known to the Union soldiers, and perhaps to the Confederates first, as the "Lady Davis," and great was the dread awakened by the deep bass roar and the wail of the big shells as they came rolling down the narrow pathway, or searched the ravines where the men lay massed. The fire of the navy also did great damage among the heavy batteries along the river front. When the siege batteries were nearly ready, on the evening of the 10th of June, Banks ordered a feigned attack at midnight by skirmishers along the whole front, for the purpose, as stated in the orders—

> . . . . of harassing the enemy, of inducing him to bring forward and expose his artillery, acquiring a knowledge of the ground before the enemy's front, and of favouring the operations of pioneers who may be sent forward to remove obstructions if necessary.

None of these objects can be said to have been accomplished, nor was any advantage gained beyond a slight advance of the lines, at a single point on Weitzel's front, by the 131st New York. The full loss in this night's reconnaissance is not known; in Weitzel's own brigade, there were 2 killed, 41 wounded, 6 missing—in all, 49; in Morgan's, a partial report accounts for 12 wounded and 59 missing, including two companies of the 22nd Maine that became entangled and for the moment lost in the ravines.

On the evening of the 12th of June, all arrangements being nearly complete, Banks ordered a vigorous bombardment to be begun the next morning. Punctually at a quarter past eleven on the morning of the 13th, every gun and mortar of the army and navy that could be brought to bear upon the defences of Port Hudson opened fire, and for a full hour kept up a furious cannonade, limited only by the endurance of the Union guns and gunners, for the Confederates hardly ventured to reply, save at first feebly. When the bombardment was at its fiercest, more than one shell in a second could be seen to fall and explode within the narrow circuit of the defences visible from the headquarters on the field. The defenders had three heavy guns dismounted during the day, yet suffered little loss in men, for long before this nearly the whole garrison had accustomed themselves to take refuge in their caves and "gopher-holes" at the first sound of Union cannon, and to await its cessation as a signal to return to their posts at the parapet. They were not always so fortunate, however, for more than once it happened that three or four men were killed by the bursting of a single shell.

When the hour was up the cannonade ended as suddenly as it began, and profound silence followed close on the intolerable din. Then Banks sent a flag of truce summoning the garrison to surrender in these words:

> Respect for the usages of war and a desire to avoid unnecessary sacrifice of life, impose on me the necessity of formally demanding the surrender of the garrison at Port Hudson. I am not unconscious, in making this demand, that the garrison is capable of continuing a vigorous and gallant defence. The events that have transpired during the pending investment exhibit in the commander and garrison a spirit of constancy and courage that, in a different cause, would be universally regarded as heroism. But I know the extremities to which they are reduced.... I desire to avoid unnecessary slaughter, and I therefore demand the immediate surrender of the garrison, subject to such conditions only as are imposed by the usages of civilized warfare.

To this Gardner replied:

> My duty requires me to defend this position, and therefore I decline to surrender.

In the evening the generals of division met in council at headquarters. In anticipation of what was to come, Dudley had already been ordered to send the 50th Massachusetts, and Charles J. Paine the 48th Massachusetts, to Dwight; and Dudley himself, with the 161st and 174th New York, was to report to Grover. This left under Augur's immediate command only five regiments of his division, namely, one, the 30th Massachusetts, of Dudley's brigade, and four of C. J. Paine's. Shortly before midnight a general assault was ordered for the following morning. At a quarter before three Augur was to open a heavy fire of artillery on his front, following it up half and hour later by a feigned attack of skirmishers. Dwight was to take two regiments, and, with a pair of suborned deserters for guides, was to try and find an entrance on the extreme left of the works near the river. But the main attack was to be made by Grover on the priest-cap. Its position is shown on the map at XV. and XVI., and the approach was to be from the cover of the winding ravine, near the second position of Duryea's battery, at No. 12. The artillery cross-fire at this point was to begin at three o'clock, and was to cease at a signal from Grover. At half-past three the skirmishers were to attack. The general formation of each of the two columns of attack had been settled in orders issued from headquarters on the morning of the 11th. Each column, assumed to consist of about 2,000 men, was to be preceded and covered by 300 skirmishers; immediately behind the skirmishers were to be seventy pioneers, carrying thirty-five axes, eighteen shovels, ten pickaxes, two handsaws, and two hatchets; next was to come the forlorn hope, or storming party, of 300 men, each carrying a bag stuffed with cotton; following the stormers, thirty-four men were to carry the balks and chesses to form a bridge over the ditch, in order to facilitate the passage of the artillery, as well as of the men. The main assaulting column was to follow, marching in lines-of-battle, as far as the nature of the ground would permit, which, as it happened, was not far. The field-artillery was to go with the assaulting column, each battery having its own pioneers. To the cavalry, meanwhile, was assigned the work of picketing and protecting the rear, as well as of holding the telegraph road leading out of Port Hudson toward Bayou Sara, by which it was thought the garrison might attempt to escape, on finding their lines broken through, or even to avoid the blow.

As was the uniform custom during the siege, all watches at division and brigade headquarters were set at nine o'clock, by a telegraphic signal, to agree with the adjutant-general's watch.

These final orders for the assault bear the hour of 11.30 p.m. This was in fact the moment at which the earliest copies were sent out by the *aides-de-camp*, held in readiness to carry them. There were seven hundred and fifty words to be written, and eleven o'clock had already passed when the council listened to the reading of the drafts and broke up. From the lateness of the hour, as well as from the distance and the darkness of the night, it resulted that one o'clock came before the last orders were in the hands of the troops that were to execute them. Many arrangements had still to be carried out and many of the detachments had still to be moved over long distances and by obscure ways to the positions assigned to them. In some instances all that was left of the night was thus occupied, and it was broad daylight before every thing was ready.

A dense fog prevailed in the early morning of Sunday, the 14th of June, strangely veiling, while it lasted, even the sound of the big guns, so that in places it was unheard a hundred yards in the rear. Punctually at the hour fixed the cannonade opened. It was an hour later, that is to say, about four o'clock, when the first attack was launched.

For the chief assault Grover had selected Paine's division and had placed the main body of his own division with Weitzel's brigade, in close support. Paine determined to lead the attack himself. Across his front as skirmishers he deployed the 4th Wisconsin, now again dismounted, and the 8th New Hampshire. The 4th Massachusetts was told off to follow the skirmishers with improvised hand-grenades made of 6-pounder shells. Next the 38th Massachusetts and the 53rd Massachusetts were formed into line of battle. At the head of the infantry column the 31st Massachusetts, likewise deployed, carried cotton bags, to fill the ditch. The rest of Gooding's brigade followed, next came Fearing's, then Ingraham's under Ferris. In rear of the column was posted the artillery under Nims. At a point on the crest of the ridge, ninety yards distant from the left face of the priest-cap, Paine's advance was checked. Then Paine, who had previously gone along the front of every regiment, addressing to each a few words of encouragement and of preparation for the work, passed afoot from the head of the column to the front of the skirmish line, and exerting to the full his sonorous voice, gave the order to the column to go in. At the word the men sprang forward, but almost as they did so, the Confederates behind the parapet in their front, with fairly level aim and at point-blank range, poured upon the head of the column a deadly volley. Many fell at this first discharge; among them, unfortunately, the gallant Paine himself, his thigh crushed by a rifle-ball. Some of the men of the 4th Wisconsin, of the 8th New Hampshire, and of the 38th Massachusetts gained the ditch, and a few even climbed the parapet, but of these nearly all were made prisoners. The rear of the column fell back to the cover of the hill, while all those who had gained the crest were forced to lie there, exposed to a pitiless fire of sharp-shooters and the scarcely more endurable rays of the burning sun of Louisiana, until night came and brought relief. In this unfortunate situation the sufferings of the wounded became so unbearable, and appealed so powerfully to the sympathy of their comrades, that many lives were risked and some lost in the attempt to alleviate the thirst, at least, of these unfortunates. Two men, quite of their own accord, took a stretcher and tried to reach the point where Paine lay, but the attempt was unsuccessful, and cost both of them their lives. These heroes were E. P. Woods, of Company E of the 8th New Hampshire, and John Williams, of Company D, 31st Massachusetts. Not less nobly, Patrick H. Cohen, a private soldier of the 133rd New York, himself lying wounded on the crest, cut a canteen from the body of a dead comrade and by lengthening the strap succeeded in tossing it within reach of his commander; this probably preserved Paine's life, for unquestionably many of the more seriously hurt perished from the heat and from thirst on that fatal day.

It was about seven o'clock, and the fog had lifted, when Weitzel advanced to the attack on the right face of the priest-cap. The 12th Connecticut and the 75th New York of his own brigade were deployed to the left and right as skirmishers to cover the head of the column. Two regiments of Morgan's brigade, loosely deployed, followed the skirmishers; in front the 91st New York, with hand-grenades, and next the 24th Connecticut, every man carrying two cotton bags weighing thirty pounds each. In immediate support came the remainder of Weitzel's brigade in column of regiments, in the order of the 8th Vermont, 114th New York, and 160th New York, followed by the main body of Morgan's brigade. Birge was in close support and Kimball in reserve. Finally, in the rear, as in Paine's formation, was massed the artillery of the division.

Toward the north face of the priest-cap the only approach was by the irregular, but for some distance nearly parallel, gorges cut out from the soft clay of the bluffs by Sandy Creek and one of its many arms. The course of these streams being toward the Confederate works, the hollows grew deeper and the banks steeper at every step. At most the creeks were but two hundred yards apart, and the ridge that separated them gave barely standing room. Within a few feet of the breastworks the smaller stream and its ravine turned sharply toward the north and served as a formidable ditch until they united with the main stream and ravine below the bastion. This larger ravine near its outlet and the natural ditch throughout its length were mercilessly swept by the fire of the bastion on the right, the breastworks in front, and the priest-cap on the left. The smaller ravine led toward the south to the crest from which Paine's men had recoiled, where their wounded and their dead lay thick, and behind which the survivors were striving to restore the broken formations.

Weitzel therefore chose the main ravine. Bearing to the right from the Jackson road, the men moved by the flank and cautiously, availing themselves of every advantage afforded by the timber or the irregularities of the ground, until they gained the crest of the ridge at points varying from twenty to fifty yards from the works near the north face of the priest-cap. In advancing to this position the column came under fire immediately on filing out of the ravine and the wood in front of the position of battery No. 9. Then, in such order as they happened to be, they went forward with a rush and a cheer, but beyond the crest indicated few men ever got. From this position it was impossible either to advance or retire until night came.

At the appointed hour Dwight sent the 6th Michigan, under Lieutenant-Colonel Bacon, and the 14th Maine, to the extreme left to make an attempt in that quarter, the arrangements for which have been already described; but either Dwight gave his orders too late, or the column mistook the path, or else the difficulties were really greater than they had been thought beforehand or than they afterward seemed, for nothing came of it. Then recalling this detachment to the Mount Pleasant road, Dwight tried to advance in that direction. The 14th Maine was sent back to its brigade and Clark deployed his own regiment, the 6th Michigan, as skirmishers, supported by the 128th New York, now commanded by Lieutenant-Colonel James Smith. The 15th New Hampshire followed and the 26th Connecticut, under Lieutenant-Colonel Joseph Selden, brought up the rear. These two regiments went forward in column of companies on the main road, but as the Confederates immediately opened a heavy artillery fire upon the head of the column, they had to be deployed. However, the ground, becoming rapidly narrower, did not long permit of an advance in this order, so that it soon became necessary to ploy once more into column. About 350 yards from the outer works the Mount Pleasant road enters and crosses a deep ravine by a bridge, then destroyed. The hollow was completely choked with felled timber, through which, under the heavy fire of musketry and artillery, it was impossible to pass; so here the brigade stayed till night enabled it to retire. Nickerson's brigade supported the movement of Clark's, but without becoming seriously engaged. Thus ended Dwight's movement. It can hardly be described as an assault, as an attack, or even as a serious attempt to accomplish any valuable result; yet indirectly it was the means of gaining, and at a small cost, the greatest, if not the only real, advantage achieved that day, for it gave Dwight possession of the rough hill, the true value of which was then for the first time perceived, and on the commanding position of its northern slope was presently mounted the powerful array of siege artillery that overlooked and controlled the land and water batteries on the lower flank of the Confederate defences.

Of Augur's operations in the centre, it is enough to say that the feigned attack assigned to this portion of the line was made briskly and in good order at the appointed time, without great loss.

The result of the day may be summed up as a bloody repulse; beholding the death and maiming of so many of the bravest and best of the officers and men, the repulse may be even termed a disaster. In the whole service of the Nineteenth Army Corps darkness never shut in upon a gloomier field. Men went about their work in a silence stronger than words.

On this day 21 officers and 182 men were killed, 72 officers and 1,245 men were wounded, 6 officers and 180 men missing; besides these, 13 were reported as killed, 84 as wounded, and 2 as missing without distinguishing between officers and men, thus making a total of 216 killed, 1,401 wounded, 188 missing—in all, 1,805. Among the wounded many had received mortal hurts, while of the missing, as in the first assault, many must now be set down as killed.

Paine, as we have seen, fell seriously hurt while in the very act of leading his division to the assault. Nine days earlier he had received his well-earned commission as brigadier-general. He was taken to New Orleans, and there nine days later, at the Hotel de Dieu Hospital, after vain efforts to save the limb, the surgeons performed amputation of the thigh. A few days after the surrender, in order to avoid the increasing dangers of the climate, Paine was sent to his home in Wisconsin on the captured steamer *Starlight*, the first boat that ascended the river. Thus the Nineteenth Corps lost one of its bravest and most promising commanders, one who had earned the affection of his men, not less through respect for his character than by his unfailing sympathy and care in all situations, and who was commended to the confidence and esteem of his associates and superiors by talent and devotion of the first order joined to every quality that stamps a man among men.

The fiery Holcomb, wounded in the assault of the 27th, yet refusing to leave his duty to another, fell early on this fatal morning at the head of his regiment and brigade, in the first moment of the final charge of Weitzel's men. This was another serious loss, for Holcomb had that disposition that may, for want of a better term, be described as the fighting character. All soldiers know it and respect it, and every wise general, seeing it anywhere among his officers, shuts his eyes to many a blemish and pardons many a fault that would be severely visited in another; yet in Holcomb there was nothing to overlook or forgive. As he was the most prominent and the most earnest of the few officers of the line that to the last remained eager for the fatal assault, so he was among the earliest and noblest of its victims.

Mortally wounded at the head of Weitzel's brigade fell Colonel Elisha B. Smith, of the 114th New York. Barely recovered from a serious illness, his spirit could not longer brook the restraint of the hospital at New Orleans with the knowledge that his men were engaged with the enemy. Thomas was ill and had received a slight wound of the scalp; this brought Smith to the head of the brigade; his fall devolved the command upon Lieutenant-Colonel Van Petten, for though Thomas, unable to bear the torture inflicted upon him by the sounds of battle, rose from his sick-bed and resumed the command, his weakness again overcame him when the day's work was done.

No regiment at Port Hudson approached the 8th New Hampshire in the number and severity of its losses, no brigade suffered so much as Paine's, to which this regiment belonged, and no division so much as Emory's, under the command of Paine. On this day, Fearing commanded the brigade, and later the division, and Lull having fallen in the previous assault, the regiment went into action 217 strong, led by Captain William M. Barrett; of this number, 122, or 56 per cent., were killed or wounded. On the 27th of May, out of 298 engaged, the regiment lost 124, or 41 per cent.

Next to the 8th New Hampshire on the fatal roll stands the 4th Wisconsin. This noble regiment, at all times an honour to the service and to its State, whence came so many splendid battalions, was a shining monument to the virtue of steady, conscientious work and strict discipline applied to good material. Bean had been instantly killed by a sharp-shooter on the 29th of May; the regiment went into action on the 14th of June 220 strong, commanded by Captain Webster P. Moore; of these, 140 fell, or 63 per cent. In the first assault, however, it had fared better, its losses numbering but 60.

The eccentric Currie, who came to the service from the British army, with the lustre of the Crimea still about him, rather brightened than dimmed by time and distance, fell severely wounded on the same fatal crest. He was struck down at the head of his regiment, boldly leading his men and urging them forward with the quaint cry of "Get on, lads!" so well known to English soldiers, yet so unfamiliar to all Americans as to draw many a smile, even in that grim moment, from those who heard it.

To the cannonade that preceded the assault and announced it to the enemy must be attributed not only the failure but a great part of the loss. The wearied Confederates were asleep behind the breastworks when the roar of the Union artillery broke the stillness of the morning, and gave them time to make ready. Such was their extremity that in Grover's front they burned their last caps in repelling the final assault, and, for the time, were able to replenish only from the pouches of the fallen.

Under cover of night all the wounded that were able to walk or crawl made their way to places of safety in the rear; while, disregarding the incessant fire of the sharp-shooters, heavy details and volunteer parties of stretcher-bearers, plying their melancholy trade, carried the wounded with gentle care to the hospitals and the dead swiftly to the long trenches. The proportion of killed and mortally wounded, already unusually heavy, was increased by the exposure and privations of the long day, while many, whom it was impossible to find or reach during the night, succumbed sooner or later during the next forty-eight hours. For although when, on the morning of the 15th, Banks sent a flag of truce asking leave to send in medical and hospital supplies for the comfort of the wounded of both armies, Gardner promptly assented, and in his reply called attention to the condition of the dead and wounded before the breastworks, yet it was not until the evening of the 16th that Banks could bring himself to ask for a suspension of hostilities for the relief of the suffering and the burial of the slain. But three days and two nights had already passed; most of the hurt, and these the most grievously, were already beyond the need of succour. The same thing had already occurred at Vicksburg.

The operations at Vicksburg and Port Hudson were so far alike in their character and objects that no just estimate of the events at either place can well be formed without considering what happened at the other. In this view it is instructive to observe that Grant assaulted the Confederate position at Vicksburg within a few hours after the arrival of his troops in front of the place, on the afternoon of the 19th of May, when two determined attacks were easily thrown off by the defenders, with a loss to their assailants of 942 men. On the 22nd of May Grant delivered the second assault, in which about three fourths of his whole effective force of 43,000 of all arms were engaged. The full corps of Sherman and McPherson, comprising six divisions, were repulsed by four brigades of the garrison, numbering probably 13,000 effectives. In this second assault Grant's loss was 3,199. These are the reasons he gives for his decision to attack:

> Johnston was in my rear, only fifty miles away, with an army not much in inferior in numbers to the one I had with me, and I knew he was being reinforced. There was danger of his coming to the assistance of Pemberton, and, after all, he might defeat my anticipations of capturing the garrison, if, indeed, he did not prevent the capture of the city. The immediate capture of Vicksburg would save sending me the

reinforcements which were so much wanted elsewhere, and would set free the army under me to drive Johnston from the State. But the first consideration of all was—the troops believed they could carry the works in their front, and they would not have worked so patiently in their trenches if they had not been allowed to try.

Having tried, he now "determined upon a regular siege—to 'outcamp the enemy,' as it were, and to incur no more losses. The experience of the 22nd convinced officers and men that this was best, and they went to work on the defences and approaches with a will."[1]

It has also to be remembered, in any fair and candid consideration of the subject, that at this comparatively early period of the war even such bloody lessons as Fredericksburg had not sufficed to teach either the commanders or their followers on either side, Federal or Confederate, the full value, computed in time, of even a simple line of breastworks of low relief, or the cost in blood of any attempt to eliminate this value of time by carrying the works at a rush. Indeed, it may be doubted whether, from the beginning of the war to the end, this reasoning, in spite of all castigations that resulted from disregarding it, was ever fully impressed upon the generals of either army, although at last there came, it is true, a time when, as at Cold Harbor, the men had an opinion of their own, and chose to act upon it. It is also very questionable whether earthworks manned by so much as a line of skirmishers, prepared and determined to defend them, have ever been successfully assaulted save as the result of a surprise. Sedgwick's captures of the Rappahannock redoubts and of Marye's Heights have indeed been cited as instances to the contrary, yet on closer consideration it is apparent that although in the former case the Confederates had been looking for an attack, they had given up all expectation of being called on to meet it that day, when, just at sunset, Russell fell suddenly upon them and finished the affair handsomely before they had time to recover. Marye's Heights, again, may be described as a moral surprise, for no Confederate officer or man that had witnessed the bloody repulse of Burnside's great army on the very same ground, but a few weeks before, could have expected to be

---

1. *Personal Memoirs of U. S. Grant*, pp. 530, 532.

called on so soon to meet the swift and triumphant onset of a single corps of that army. Moreover, Sedgwick's tactical arrangements were perfect.

The truth is, the insignificant appearance of a line of simple breastworks has almost always caused those general and staff-officers especially that viewed them through their field-glasses, with the diminishing power of a long perspective, to forget that an assault upon an enemy behind entrenchments is not so much a battle as a battue, where one side stands to shoot and the other goes out to be shot, or if he stops to shoot it is in plain sight of an almost invisible foe. European examples, as usual misapplied or misunderstood, have contributed largely to the persistency of this fatal illusion, and Ciudad Rodrigo and Badajos have served but as incantations to confuse many a mind to which these sounding syllables were no more than names; ignorant, therefore, of the stern necessities that drove Wellington to these victories, forgetful of their fearful cost, and above all ignoring or forgetting the axiom, on which rests the whole art and science of military engineering—that the highest and stoutest of stone walls must yield at last to the smallest trench through which a man may creep unseen. Vast, indeed, is the difference between an assault upon a walled town, delivered as a last resort after crowning the glacis and opening wide the breach, and any conceivable movement, though bearing the same name, made as the first resort, against earthworks of the very kind whereby walled towns are taken, approached over ground unknown and perhaps obstructed.

Even so, in the storm of Rodrigo the defenders struck down more than a third of their own numbers; Badajos was taken by a happy chance after the main assault had miserably failed; at both places the losses of the assailants were in proportion less, and in number but little greater, than at Port Hudson; yet, in the contemplation of the awful slaughter of Badajos, even the iron firmness of Wellington broke down in a passion of tears.

CHAPTER 18

Unvexed to the Sea

With that quick appreciation of facts that forms so large a part of the character of the American soldier, even to the extent of exercising upon the fate of battles and campaigns an influence not always reserved for considerations derived from a study of the principles of the art of war, the men of the Army of the Gulf had now made up their minds that the end sought was to be attained by hard work on their part and by starvation on the part of the garrison. Criticism and denunciation, by no means confined to those officers whose knowledge of the art of war is drawn from books, have been freely passed upon this peculiarity, yet both alike have been wasted, since no proposition can be clearer than that a nation, justly proud of the superior intelligence of its soldiers, cannot expect to reap the full advantage of that intelligence and at the same time escape every disadvantage attending its exercise. Among these drawbacks, largely overbalanced by the obvious gains, not the least is the peculiar quality that has been aptly described in the homely saying, "They know too much." When, therefore, the American volunteer has become a veteran, and has reached his highest point of discipline, endurance, and the simple sagacity of the soldier, it is often his way to stay his hand from exertions that he deems needless and from sacrifices that he considers useless or worse than useless, although the same exertions and the same sacrifices would, but a few months earlier in the days of his inexperience, have been met by him with the same alacrity that the ignorant peasant of Europe displays in obeying the orders of his hereditary chief in the service of the king.

After the 14th of June the siege progressed steadily without farther attempt at an assault. This was now deferred to the last resort.

At four points a system of comparatively regular approaches was begun, and upon these labour was carried on incessantly, night and day; indeed, as is usual with works of this character, the greatest progress was made in the short hours of the June nights. The main approach led from Duryea's battery No. 12 toward the priest-cap, following the winding of the ravines and the contour of the hill. When at last the sap had, with great toil and danger, been carried to the crest facing the priest-cap, and only a few yards distant, the trench was rapidly and with comparative ease extended toward the left, in a line parallel with the general direction of the defences. The least distance from this third parallel, as it was called by an easy stretch of the language, to the enemy's parapet was about twenty yards, the greatest about forty-five.

About two hundred yards farther to the right of the elbow of the main sap, a zigzag ran out of the ravine on the left flank of Bainbridge's battery, No. 8, toward the bastion. Upon this approach, because of its directness, the use of the sap-roller, or some equivalent for it, could never be given up until the ditch was gained.

From the extreme left, after the northern slope of Mount Pleasant had been gained, a main approach was extended from the flank of Roy's battery of 20-pounder Parrotts, No. 20, almost directly toward the river, until the trench cut the edge of the bluff, forming meanwhile a covered way that connected all the batteries looking north from the left flank. Of these No. 24 was the seventeen-gun battery, including two 9-inch Dahlgrens removed from the naval battery of the right wing, and commanded by Ensign Swann. On the 2nd of July, Lieutenant-Commander Terry took command of the *Richmond* and turned over the command of the right naval battery to Ensign Shepard. These "blue-jacket" batteries, with their trim and alert gun crews, were always bright spots in the sombre line. From the river bank the sap ran with five stretches of fifty or sixty yards, forming four sharp elbows, to the foot and well up the slope of the steep hill on the opposite side of the ravine, where the Confederates had constructed the strong work known to both combatants as the Citadel. From the head of the sap to the nearest point of the Confederate works the distance was about ninety-five yards.

From the ravine in front of the mortar battery of the left wing,

No. 18, a secondary approach was carried to a parallel facing the advanced lunette, No. XXVII., and distant from it 375 yards. The object of this approach was partly to amuse the enemy, partly to prevent his breaking through the line, now drawn out very thin, and partly also to serve as a foothold for a column of attack in case of need.

From the ravine near Slaughter's house a zigzag, constructed by the men of the 21st Maine, under the immediate direction of Colonel Johnson, led to the position of battery No. 16, where were posted the ten guns of Rails and Baines. The distance from this battery to the defences was four hundred yards.

On the 15th of June, on the heels of the bloody repulse of the previous day, Banks issued a general order congratulating his troops upon the steady advance made upon the enemy's works, and expressed his confidence in an immediate and triumphant issue of the contest: "We are at all points on the threshold of his fortifications," the order continues:

> Only one more advance, and they are ours!
>
> For the last duty that victory imposes, the Commanding General summons the bold men of the corps to the organization of a storming column of a thousand men, to vindicate the flag of the Union, and the memory of its defenders who have fallen! Let them come forward!
>
> Officers who lead the column of victory in this last assault may be assured of the just recognition of their services by promotion; and every officer and soldier who shares its perils and its glory shall receive a medal to commemorate the first great success of the campaign of 1863 for the freedom of the Mississippi. His name will be placed in General Orders upon the Roll of Honour.

Colonel Henry W. Birge, of the 13th Connecticut, at once volunteered to lead the stormers, and although the whole project was disapproved by many of the best officers and men in the corps, partly as unnecessary and partly because they conceived that it implied some reflection upon the conduct of the brave men that had fought and suffered and failed on the 27th and the 14th, yet so general was the feeling of confidence in Birge that within a few days the ranks of the stormers were more than filled. As nearly as can now be ascertained, the whole number of officers who volunteered was at least 80; of enlisted men at least 956. Of these, 17 officers and 226 men belonged to the 13th Connecticut. As the different parties offered and were accepted, they were sent into camp in a retired and pleasant spot, in a grove behind the naval battery on the right. On the 15th of June Birge was ordered to divide his column into two battalions, and to drill it for its work. On the 28th this organization was complete. The battalions were then composed of eight companies, but two companies were afterwards added to the first battalion. To Lieutenant-Colonel Van Petter, of the 160th New York, Birge gave the command of the first battalion, and to Lieutenant-Colonel Bickmore, of the 14th Maine, that of the second battalion. On that day, 67 of the officers and 826 men—in all, 893, were present for duty in the camp of the stormers. Among those that volunteered for the forlorn hope but were not accepted were 54 non-commissioned officers and privates of the 1st Louisiana Native Guards, and 37 of the 3rd. From among the officers of the general staff and staff departments that were eager to go, two were selected to accompany the column and keep up the communication with headquarters and with the other troops; these were Captain Duncan S. Walker, assistant adjutant-general, and Lieutenant Edmund H. Russell, of the 9th Pennsylvania Reserves, acting signal officer.

Then the officers and men quietly prepared themselves for the serious work expected of them. Those that had any thing to leave made their wills in the manner sanctioned by the custom of armies, and all confided to the hands of comrades the last words for their families or their friends.

Meanwhile an event took place, trifling in itself, yet accenting sharply some of the more serious reasons that had, in the first instance, led Banks to resist the repeated urging to join Grant with his whole force, and afterward had formed powerful factors in determining him to deliver and to renew the assault. Early on the morning of the 18th of June a detachment of Confederate cavalry rode into the village of Plaquemine, surprised the provost guard, captured Lieutenant C. H. Witham and twenty-two men of the 28th Maine, and burned the three steamers lying the bayou, the *Sykes*, *Anglo-American*, and *Belfast*. Captain Albert Stearns, of the 131st New York, who was stationed at Plaquemine as provost marshal of the parish, made his escape with thirteen men of his guard. The Confederates were fired upon by the guard and lost one man killed and two wounded. In their turn they fired upon the steamboats, and wounded two of the crew. Three hours later the gunboat *Winona*, Captain Weaver, came down from Baton Rouge, and, shelling the enemy, hastened their departure. In the tension of greater events, little notice was taken at the moment of this incident; yet it was not long before it was discovered that the raiders were the advance guard of the little army with which Taylor was about to invade La Fourche, intent upon the bold design of raising the siege of Port Hudson by blockading the river and threatening New Orleans.

Thus Banks was brought face to face with the condition described in his letter of the 4th of June to Halleck:

> The course to be pursued here gives me great anxiety. If I abandon Port Hudson, I leave its garrison, some 6,000 or 7,000 men, the force under Mouton and Sibley, now threatening Brashear City and the Army of Mobile, large or small, to threaten or attack New Orleans. If I detach from my command in the field a sufficient force to defend that city, which ought not to be less than 8,000 or 10,000, my assistance to General Grant is unimportant, and I leave an equal or larger number of the enemy to reinforce Johnston. If I defend New Orleans and its adjacent territory, the enemy will go against Grant. If I go with a force sufficient to aid him, my rear will be seriously threatened. My force is not large enough to do both. Under these circumstances, my only course seems to be to carry this post as soon as possible, and then to join General Grant. If I abandon it I cannot materially aid him.

Taylor's incursion caused Banks some anxiety and appreciable inconvenience, without, however, exercising a material influence on the fortunes of the siege; accordingly, it will be better to reserve for another chapter the story of this adventure.

About the same time, Logan again became troublesome. At

first he seems to have thought of retiring on Jackson, Mississippi; but this Johnston forbade, telling him to stay where he was, to observe and annoy the besiegers, and if pressed by too strong a force, to fall back only so far as necessary, hindering and retarding the advance of his assailants. By daylight, on the morning of the 15th of June, Logan dashed down the Clinton road, surprised the camp of the 14th New York cavalry, who made little resistance, and the guard of the hospital at the Carter House, who made none. In this raid Logan took nearly one hundred disabled prisoners, including six officers, and carried off a number of wagons. However, finding Grierson instantly on his heels, Logan promptly "fell back as far as necessary." On the evening of the 30th of June, while hovering in the rear of Dwight, Logan captured and carried off Brigadier-General Dow, who, while waiting for his wound to heal, had taken up his headquarters in a house some distance behind the lines. At daylight, on the morning of the 2nd of July, Logan surprised the depot at Springfield Landing, guarded by the 162nd New York, Lieutenant-Colonel Blanchard, and a small detachment of the 16th New Hampshire, under Captain Henry. Careless picket duty was the cause, and a great stampede the consequence, but Logan hardly stayed long enough to find out exactly what he had accomplished, since he reports that, besides burning the commissary and quartermasters' stores, he killed and wounded 140 of his enemy, captured 35 prisoners, fought an entire brigade, and destroyed 100 wagons, with a loss on his part of 4 killed and 10 wounded; whereas, in fact, the entire loss of the Union army was 1 killed, 11 wounded, 21 captured or missing, while the stores burned consisted of a full supply of clothing and camp and garrison equipment for about 1,000 men. The wagons mentioned by Logan were part of a train met in the road, cut out, and carried off as he rapidly rode away, and the number may be correct.

    The end of June was now drawing near, and already the losses of the besiegers in the month of constant fighting exceeded 4,000. At least as many more were sick in the hospitals, while the reinforcements from every quarter barely numbered 3,000. There were no longer any reserves to draw from; the last man was up. The effective strength of all arms had at no time exceeded

17,000.[1] Of these less than 12,000 can be regarded as available for any duty directly connected with the siege, and now every day saw the command growing smaller in numbers, as the men fell under the fire of the sharp-shooter, or succumbed to the deadly climate, or gave out exhausted by incessant labour and privation. The heat became almost insupportable, even to those who from time to time found themselves so fortunate as to be able to snatch a few hours' rest in the dense shade of the splendid forest, until their tour of duty should come again in the trenches, where, under the June sun beating upon and baking all three surfaces, the parched clay became like a reverberating furnace. The still air was stifling, but the steam from the almost tropical showers was far worse. Merely in attempting to traverse a few yards of this burning zone many of the strongest men were sun struck daily. The labour of the siege, extending over so wide a front, pressed so severely upon the numbers of the besieging army, always far too weak for such an undertaking in any climate at any season, above all in Louisiana in June, that the men were almost incessantly on duty, either in digging, as guards of the trenches, as sharp-shooters, or on outpost service; and as the number available for duty grew smaller, and the physical strength of all that remained in the ranks daily wasted, the work fell the more heavily. When the end came at last the effective force, outside of the cavalry, hardly exceeded 8,000, while even of this small number nearly every officer and man might well have gone on the sick-report had not pride and duty held him to his post.

This will seem the less remarkable when it is remembered that the garrison during the same period suffered in the same proportion, while from like causes less than a year before Breckinridge had, in a much shorter time, lost the use of half his division. Butler's experience had been nearly as severe.

To the suffering and labours that are inseparable from any operation in the nature of a siege were added insupportable torments, the least of which were vermin. As the summer days drew out and

---

1. The figures here given do not agree with those of the monthly and tri-monthly returns for May and June. These returns are, however, simply the returns for March carried forward, owing to the impossibility of collecting and collating the reports of regiments, brigades, and divisions during active operations.

the heat grew more intense, the brooks dried up; the creek lost itself in the pestilential swamp; the wells and springs gave out; the river fell, exposing to the almost tropical sun a wide margin of festering ooze. The mortality and the sickness were enormous.

The animals suffered in their turn, the battery horses from want of exercise, the train horses and mules from over-work, and all from the excessive heat and insufficiency of proper forage. There was never enough hay; the deficiency was partly eked out by making fodder of the standing corn, but this resource was quickly exhausted, and after the 3rd of July, when Taylor sealed the river by planting his guns below Donaldsonville, all the animals went upon half or quarter rations of grain, with little hay or none. At length, for two or three days, the forage depots fairly gave out; the poor beasts were literally starving when the place fell, nor was it for nearly a week after that event that, by the raising of Taylor's blockade below and the arrival of supplies from Grant above, the stress was wholly relieved.

The two coloured regiments, the 1st and 3rd Louisiana Native Guards, besides strongly picketing their front, were mainly occupied, after the 27th of May, in fatigue duty in the trenches on the right. While the army was in the Teche country, Brigadier-General Daniel Ullmann had arrived at New Orleans from New York, bringing with him authority to raise a brigade of coloured troops. With him came a full complement of officers. A few days later, on the 1st of May, Banks issued, at Opelousas, an order, which he had for some time held in contemplation, for organizing a corps of eighteen regiments of coloured infantry, to consist, at first, of five hundred men each. These troops were to form a distinct command, to which he gave the name of the Corps d'Afrique, and in it he incorporated Ullmann's brigade. By the end of May Ullmann had enrolled about 1,400 men for five regiments, the 6th, 7th, 8th, 9th, and 10th. These recruits, as yet unarmed and undrilled, were now brought to Port Hudson, organized, and set to work in the trenches and upon the various siege operations.

About the same time the formation of a regiment of engineer troops was undertaken, composed of picked men of colour, formed in three battalions of four companies each, under white officers carefully chosen from among the veterans. The ranks of this regiment, known as the 1st Louisiana engineers, were soon recruited to above a thousand; the strength for duty was about eight hundred. Under the skilful handling of Colonel Justin Hodge it rendered valuable service throughout the siege.

Company K of the 42nd Massachusetts, commanded by Lieutenant Henry A. Harding, had for some months been serving as pontoniers, in charge of the bridge train. During the siege it did good and hard work in all branches of field engineering under the immediate direction of the Chief Engineer.

While at Opelousas, Banks had applied to Halleck to order Brigadier-General Charles P. Stone to duty in the Department of the Gulf. Stone had been without assignment since his release, in the preceding August, from his long and lonely imprisonment in the casemates of the harbour forts of New York, and, up to this moment, every suggestion looking to his employment had met the stern disapproval of the Secretary of War. Even when in the first flush of finding himself at last at the top notch of his career, Hooker, in firm possession, as he believed, of the post he had long coveted, as commander of the Army of the Potomac, had asked for Stone as his Chief of Staff, the request had been met by a flat refusal. A different fate awaited Banks's application. On the 7th of May Halleck issued the orders asked for, and in the last days of the month Stone reported for duty before Port Hudson. At first Banks was rather embarrassed by the gift he had solicited, for he saw that he himself was falling into disfavour at Washington; the moment was critical; and it was easy to perceive how disaster, or even the slightest check, might be magnified in the shadows of Ball's Bluff and Fort Lafayette. Moreover, Stone was equally unknown to and unknown by the troops of the Nineteenth Army Corps. Instead, therefore, of giving him the command of Sherman's division, for which his rank indicated him, Banks kept Stone at headquarters without special assignment, and made every use of his activity, as well as of his special knowledge and ready skill in all matters relating to ordnance and gunnery.

On the evening of the 26th of June a strange thing happened. While it was yet broad daylight Colonel Provence of the 16th Arkansas, posted in rear of the position of battery XXIV, discovering and annoyed by the progress made on battery 16 in his front, sent out, one at a time, two bold men, named Mieres and Parker, to see what was going on. After nightfall, on their report, he despatched thirty volunteers, under Lieutenant McKennon, to drive off the guard and the working party and destroy the works. The position was held by the advance guard of the 21st Maine, under Lieutenant Bartlett, who, for some reason hard to understand, ordered his men not to fire. The Arkansas party, therefore, accomplished its purpose, without further casualty than having one man knocked down, as he was leaping the parapet of the trench, by a soldier who happened to consider his orders as inapplicable to this method of defence. Then Major Merry, with the reserves of the 21st, coming promptly to the rescue, easily drove out the enterprising assailants, with whom went as prisoners Lieutenant Bartlett and five of his men, with fourteen muskets that had not been fired.[2]

As the saps in front of Bainbridge's and Duryea's batteries drew every day nearer to the bastion and the priest-cap, the working parties were harassed and began to be greatly delayed by the unceasing fire of the Confederate sharp-shooters. Moreover, in spite of the vigilance of the sharp-shooters in the trenches, their adversaries had so much the advantage of ground that they were able to render the passage of certain exposed points of the approaches slow and hazardous. At first, cotton bales were used to protect the head of the sap, but these the adventurous enemy set alight with blazing arrows or by sallies of small parties under cover of darkness. In the short night it was impossible to raise a pile of sand-bags high enough to overlook the breastworks. Toward the end of June this was changed in a single night by the skill and ingenuity of Colonel Edward Prince, of the 7th Illinois cavalry.

Happening to be at headquarters when the trouble was being talked about, he heard an officer suggest making use of the empty hogsheads at the sugar-house; how to get them to the trenches was the next question. This he promptly offered to solve if simply ordered to do it and left to himself. Cavalry had never been of any use in a siege, he said; it was time for a change. The order was instantly given. Prince swung himself into the saddle and rode away. Before daylight his men had carried through the woods and over the hills to the mouth of the sap, opposite the southern angle of the

---

2. Colonel Provence, in his report, claims 7 prisoners, and says: "The enemy fired but once, and then at a great distance." (*Official Records*, vol. xxvi., part I., p. 150.)

priest-cap, enough sugar hogsheads to make two tiers. The heads had been knocked in, a long pole thrust through each hogshead, and thus slung, it was easy for two mounted troopers to carry it between them. Quietly rolled into position by the working parties and rapidly filled with earth, a rude platform erected behind for the sharp-shooter to mount upon, with a few sand-bags thrown on top to protect his head,—this was the beginning of the great trench cavalier, whose frowning crest the astonished Confederates awoke the next morning to find towering high above their heads. Afterwards enlarged and strengthened, it finally dominated the whole line of defence not only in its immediate front, but for a long distance on either side.

Not less ingenious was the device almost instinctively resorted to by the artillerists for the safety of the gunners when, after the siege batteries opened, the Confederate sharp-shooters began picking off every head that came in sight. The first day saw a number of gunners stricken in the act of taking aim, an incident not conducive to deliberation or accuracy on the part of their successors at the guns. The next sunrise saw every exposed battery, from right to left, protected by a hinged shutter made of flat iron chiefly taken from the sugar troughs, covered with strips of rawhide from the commissary's, the space stuffed tight with loose cotton, and a hole made through all, big enough for the gunner's eye, but too small for the sharp-shooter's bullet. Such was substantially the plan simultaneously adopted at three or four different points and afterwards followed everywhere. The remedy was perfect.

On the 3rd of July arrangements were made for the daily detail of a brigade commander to act as General of the Trenches during a tour of twenty-four hours, from noon to noon. His duties were to superintend the siege operations, to post the guards of the trenches, to repulse sorties, and to protect the works. The works to be constructed were indicated and laid out by the Chief Engineer, whose duties, after the 17th of June, when Major Houston fell seriously ill, were performed by Captain John C. Palfrey, aided and overlooked by General Andrews, the Chief of Staff. Daily, at nine o'clock in the morning, the General of the Trenches and the Chief Engineer made separate reports to headquarters of everything that had happened during the previous day. Each of these officers made five reports, yet of the ten but two are to be found printed among the Official Records. These are the engineer's reports of work done on the 5th and 6th of July. They contain almost the only details of the siege to be gathered from the record, notwithstanding the fact that every paper, however small, or irregular in size or form, or apparently unimportant in substance, that related in any way to the military operations of the Army of the Gulf was carefully preserved on the files of its Adjutant-General's office, where, for safety as well as convenience, documents of this character were kept separate from the ordinary files covering matters of routine and requiring to be handled every day or hour. The proof is strong that these important records were in due time delivered into the custody of the War Office, where, for a considerable period after the close of the war, little or no care seems to have been taken of the documents thus turned in by the several Corps and Departments, as these were discontinued; and although the care and management of the War Records division of the Adjutant-General's Office at Washington has, from its earliest organization, been such as to deserve the highest admiration, yet many of these papers are not to be found there. The probability is that they were either mislaid or else swept away and destroyed before this office was organized.

Palfrey's report for the 5th of July shows the left cavalier finished and occupied, and the right cavalier nearly finished, but constantly injured by a 24-pounder gun that had so far escaped destruction by the artillery of the besiegers. The sap in front of Bainbridge's battery, No. 8, was advanced about twenty yards during this day, and the parallel in front of the priest-cap extended to the left eleven yards; work was greatly retarded by a heavy rain in the night. The mine was so far advanced that a shaft was begun to run obliquely under the salient, this course being chosen instead of the usual plan of a vertical shaft with enveloping galleries, as shorter in time and distance, although more dangerous.

On the 6th the sap was pushed forward forty-two feet, and the parallel carried to the left sixty-nine feet. The mine shaft, begun the day before, was carried about twenty-seven feet underground, directly toward the salient. The cavaliers were finished.

During the 7th, although there is no report for that day, the shaft for the mine under the priest-cap was finished, the chamber itself excavated and charged with about twelve hundred pounds of powder, and the mine tamped with sand-bags. The mine on the left had been ready for some days; it was now charged with fifteen hundred pounds of powder and tamped.

Heavy thunder-storms, accompanied by warm rain, had been frequent of late, and the night dews had been at times heavy. Accordingly it was thought best not to trust so delicate an operation as the explosion of the mines to the chance of a damp fuse. Daybreak on the 9th of July having been set as the hour for the simultaneous explosion of the mines, to be instantly followed by one last rush through the gaps, Captain Walker was sent on the evening of the 7th, to the *Richmond* to ask for dry fuses from the magazines of the Navy.

Meanwhile events were moving rapidly to an end. In the early morning of Tuesday, the 7th, the gunboat *General Price* came down the river bringing the great news that Vicksburg had surrendered to Grant on the 4th of July. Commodore Palmer, on board the *Hartford*, was the first to receive the news, but for some reason it happened that signal communication was obstructed or suspended between the *Hartford* and headquarters, so that it was not until a quarter before eleven that Colonel Kilby Smith, of Grant's staff, delivered to Banks the welcome message of which he was the bearer.

In less time than it takes to tell, an *aide-de-camp* was on his way to the General of the Trenches bearing the brief announcement, "Vicksburg surrendered on the 4th of July." This note, written upon the thin manifold paper of the field order-books, the General of the Trenches was directed to wrap securely around a clod of clay—the closest approach to a stone to be found in all the lowlands of Louisiana—and toss it over into the enemy's works. At the same time the good news was sped by wire and by staff officers to the commanders of divisions. At noon a national salute was to be fired and all the bands were to play the national airs; but the men could not wait for these slow formalities. No sooner was the first loud shout of rejoicing heard from the trenches, where for so many weary nights and days there had been little to rejoice at, than by a sort of instinct the men of both armies seem to have divined what had happened. From man to man, from company to company, from regiment to regiment, the word passed, and as it passed, once more the cheers of the soldiers of the Union rang out, and again the forest echoed with the strains of *The Star-Spangled Banner* from the long-silent bands. Many a rough cheek, unused to tears, was wet that morning, and the sound of laughter was heard from many lips that had long been set in silence; but when the first thrill was spent, it gave way to a deep-drawn sigh of relief. The work was done; all the toil and suffering was over. Nor was this feeling restricted to the outside of the parapet; the defenders felt it even more strongly. At first they received the news with real or affected incredulity. An officer of an Arkansas regiment, to whom was first handed the little scrap of tissue paper on which the whole chapter of history was told in seven words, acknowledged the complement by calling back, "This is another damned Yankee lie!" Yet before many minutes were over the firing had died away, save here and there a scattering exception, although peremptory orders were even given to secure its renewal. In spite of everything the men began to mingle and to exchange story for story, gibe for gibe, coffee for corn-beer, and when night fell there can have been few men in either army but believed the fighting was over.

That evening Gardner summoned his commanders to meet him in council. Among them all there was but one thought—the end had come.

Shortly after half-past twelve the notes of a bugle were heard on the Plains Store road sounding the signal, "Cease firing." A few seconds later an officer with a small escort approached, bearing a lantern swung upon a long pole, with a white handkerchief tied beneath it, to serve as a flag of truce. At the outpost of Charles J. Paine's brigade the flag was halted and its purpose ascertained. This was announced to be the delivery of an important despatch from Gardner to Banks. Thus it was that a few minutes after one o'clock the hoofs of two horses were heard at the same instant at headquarters, yet each with a sound of its own that seemed in keeping with its story. One, a slow and measured trot, told of duty done and stables near; the other, quick and nervous, spoke of pressing news. Two officers dismounted; the clang of their sabres was heard together; together they made their way to the tent where the writer of these lines lay awake and listening. One was Captain Walker, with the fuse, the other was Lieutenant Orton S.

Clark, of the 116th New York, then attached to the staff of Charles J. Paine. The long envelope he handed in felt rough to the touch; the light of a match showed its colour a dull gray; every inch of it said, "Surrender."

When opened it was found to contain a request for an official assurance as to the truth of the report that Vicksburg had surrendered. If true, Gardner asked for a cessation of hostilities with a view to consider terms. At a quarter-past one Banks replied, conveying an exact copy of so much of Grant's despatch as related the capitulation of Vicksburg. He told when and how the despatch had come, and wound up by regretting that he could not consent to a truce for the purpose indicated. In order to avoid all chance of needless excitement or disturbance, as well as of the premature publication of the news, the Adjutant-General carried this despatch himself, and, accompanied by Lieutenant Clark, as well as, at his own request, by General Stone, rode first to Augur's headquarters to acquaint him with the news and to borrow a bugler, and then to the outposts to meet the Confederate flag of truce. A blast upon the bugle brought back the little party of horsemen, with the lantern swaying from the pole; but it was nearly daylight before they again returned with Gardner's reply. Meanwhile, right and left word had been quietly passed to the pickets to cease firing.

In his second letter Gardner said:

> Having defended this position so long as I deem my duty requires, I am willing to surrender to you, and will appoint a commission of three officers to meet a similar commission, appointed by yourself, at nine o'clock this morning, for the purpose of agreeing upon and drawing up the terms of surrender, and for that purpose I ask a cessation of hostilities. Will you please designate a point outside of my breastworks where a meeting shall be held for this purpose?

To this Banks answered at 4:30 a.m.:

> I have designated Brigadier-General Charles P. Stone, Colonel Henry W. Birge, and Lieutenant-Colonel Richard B. Irwin as the officers to meet the commission appointed by

you. They will meet your officers at the hour designated at a point near where the flag of truce was received this morning. I will direct that all active hostilities shall entirely cease on my part until further notice for the purpose stated.

The division commanders, as well as the commanders of the upper and lower fleets, were at once notified, and at six o'clock Captain Walker was sent to find Admiral Farragut, wherever he might be, and to deliver to him despatches conveying the news of the surrender, outlining Banks's plans for moving against Taylor in La Fourche, and urging the Admiral to send all the light-draught gunboats at once to Berwick Bay.

Banks meant to march Weitzel directly to the nearest landing, which was within the lines of Port Hudson, as soon as the formal capitulation should be accomplished, and to send Grover after him as fast as steamboats could be found. This called for many arrangements; the occupying force had also to be seen to; and finally, it was necessary that the starving garrison should be fed. Colonel Irwin was therefore relieved, at his own request, from duty as one of the commissioners, and Brigadier-General Dwight was named in his stead. This drew an objection from Weitzel, who naturally felt that there were claims of service as well as of rank that might have been considered before those of the temporary commander of the second division; however, it was too late to make any further change, and when Banks offered to name Weitzel, whose protest had been not for himself but for his brigades, as the officer to receive Gardner's sword, the offer was declined. Among the officers of the navy, too, especially those of higher grades, great cause of offense was felt that, after all their services in the siege, they were left unrepresented in the honours of the surrender. This feeling was natural enough; yet before determining how far the complaints based on it were just, it is necessary to consider how important was every hour, almost every moment, with reference to the operations against Taylor, while three and a half hours were required to make the journey between headquarters and the upper fleet, and four and a half hours to reach the lower fleet. Moreover, the Admiral had gone to New Orleans the evening before.

At nine the commissioners met under the shade of the beautiful trees, nearly on the spot where O'Brien had rested among his men while waiting for the word on the 27th of May. On the Confederate side the commissioners were Colonel William R. Miles, commanding the right wing of the garrison, Colonel I. G. W. Steedman, of the 1st Alabama, commanding the left wing, and Lieutenant-Colonel Marshall J. Smith, Chief of Heavy Artillery.

Among those thus brought together there was more than one gentleman of marked conversational talent; the day was pleasant, the shade grateful, and, to one side at least, the refreshment not less so; and thus the time passed pleasantly until two o'clock, when the commissioners signed, with but a single change, the articles that had been drawn up for them and in readiness since six in the morning. The alteration was occasioned by the great and unexpected length to which the conference had been protracted. Five o'clock in the afternoon had been named as the time when the besiegers were to occupy the works; this had to be changed to seven o'clock on the morning of the 9th. The terms, which will be found in full in the Appendix, were those of an unconditional surrender. Gardner, who was in waiting conveniently near, at once approved the articles, and at half-past two they were completed by the signature of Banks. A few minutes later the long wagon-train, loaded with provisions, that had been standing for hours in the Plains Store road, was signalled to go forward. The cheers that welcomed the train, as it wound its way up the long-untravelled road and through the disused sally-port, were perhaps not so loud as those with which the besiegers had greeted the news from Vicksburg, yet they were not less enthusiastic. From this moment the men of the two armies, and to some extent the officers, mingled freely.

Andrews was designated to receive the surrender, and from each division two of the best regiments, with one from Weitzel's brigade, were told off to occupy the place.

Punctually at seven o'clock on the morning of the 9th of July the column of occupation entered the sally-port on the Jackson road. At its head rode Andrews with his staff. Next, in the post of honour, came the stormers with Birge at their head, then the 75th New York of Weitzel's brigade, followed by the 116th New York and the 2nd Louisiana of Augur's division, the 12th Maine, and the 13th Connecticut of Grover's division, the 6th Michigan and the 14th Maine of Dwight's division, and 4th Wisconsin and the 8th New Hampshire of Paine's.[3] With the column was Duryea's battery. The 38th Massachusetts was at first designated for this coveted honour, but lost it through some necessary changes due to the intended movement down the river. Weitzel, with his own brigade under Thomas, on the way to the place of embarkation, closely followed the column and witnessed the ceremonies.

These were simple and short. The Confederate troops were drawn up in line, Gardner at their head, every officer in his place. The right of the line rested on the edge of the open plain south of the railway station; the left extended toward the village. At the word "Ground arms" from their tried commander, followed by the command of execution from the bugles, every Confederate soldier bowed his head and laid his musket on the ground in token of submission, while Gardner himself tendered his sword to Andrews, who, in a few complimentary words, waived its acceptance. At the same instant the Stars and Bars, the colours of the Confederacy, were hauled down from the flagstaff, where they had so long waived defiance; a detachment of sailors from the naval batteries sprang to the halyards and rapidly ran up the flag of the United States; the guns of Duryea's battery saluted the colours; the garrison filed off as prisoners of war, and all was over.

The last echo of the salute to the colours had hardly died away when Weitzel, at the head of the First Division, now for the first time united, marched off to the left, and began embarking on board the transports to go against Taylor.

With the place were taken 6,340 prisoners of war, of whom 405 were officers and 5,935 enlisted men. The men were paroled with the exact observance of all the forms prescribed by the cartel then in form; yet the paroles were immediately declared void by the Confederate government, and the men were required to return to duty in the ranks. The officers, in accordance with the retaliatory orders of the period, had to be kept in captivity; they were, however, given the choice of their place of confinement.

---

3. No record exists of these details, but the list here given is believed to be nearly correct.

About 211 elected to go to Memphis, and were accordingly sent up the river a few days after the surrender, the remainder were sent to New Orleans with instructions to Emory to keep them safely under guard in some commodious house or houses, to be selected by him, and to make them as comfortable as practicable.[4] There were also captured 20 pieces of light artillery and 31 pieces of field artillery; of these 12 heavy guns and 30 light guns were in comparatively good order.

The total losses of the Corps during the siege were 45 officers and 663 men killed, 191 officers and 3,145 men wounded, 12 officers and 307 men captured or missing; in all, 4,363. Very few prisoners were taken by the Confederates, and little doubt remains that a large proportion of those set down as captured or missing in reality perished.

Of the Confederate losses no complete return was ever made. A partial return, without date, signed by the chief surgeon, shows 176 killed, 447 wounded, total 632. In this report the number of those that had died in the hospital is included among the wounded. Nor does this total include the losses at Plains Store, which, according to the surgeon's return, were 12 killed and 36 wounded, or, according to Colonel Miles's report, 8 killed, 23 wounded, 58 missing; in all, 89. Major C. M. Jackson, who acted as assistant inspector-general under Gardner, and, according to his own account, came out through the lines of investment about an hour after the surrender, reported to Johnston that the total casualties during the siege were 200 killed, between 300 and 400 wounded, and 200 died from sickness.

---

4. As evidence of the considerate manner in which these gentlemen were treated, see the interesting article, "Plain Living on Johnson's Island," by Lieutenant Horace Carpenter, 4th Louisiana, printed in the *Century* for March, 1891, page 706.

CHAPTER 19

Harrowing La Fourche

It will be remembered that when Banks marched to Opelousas, Taylor's little army, greatly depleted by wholesale desertion and hourly wearing away by the roadside, broke into two fragments, the main body of the cavalry retiring, under Mouton, toward the Sabine, while the remainder of the troops were conducted by Taylor himself toward Alexandria and at last to Natchitoches. As soon as Kirby Smith became aware that his adversary was advancing to the Red River, he prepared to meet the menace by concentrating on Shreveport the whole available force of the Confederacy in the Trans-Mississippi from Texas to Missouri, numbering, according to his own estimate, 18,000 effectives. He accordingly called on Magruder for two brigades and drew in from the line of the Arkansas the division of John G. Walker. However, this concentration became unnecessary and was given up the instant Smith learned that Banks had crossed the Atchafalaya and the Mississippi and had sat down before Port Hudson.

While this movement was in progress, Walker was on the march toward Natchitoches or Alexandria, by varying routes, according as the plans changed to suit the news of the day. Taylor observed Banks and followed his march to Simmesport, while Mouton hung upon the rear and flank of Chickering's column, guarding the big wagon-train and the spoils of the Teche campaign.

Then Kirby Smith, not caring as yet to venture across the Atchafalaya, ordered Taylor to take Walker's division back into Northern Louisiana and try to break up Grant's campaign by interrupting his communications opposite Vicksburg; but this attempt turned out badly, for Grant had already given up his communications on the west bank of the Mississippi and restored them on the east, and Taylor's forces, after passing from Lake Catahoula by Little River into the Tensas, ascending that stream to the neighbourhood of Richmond and occupying that town on the 3rd of May, were roughly handled on the 7th in an ill-judged attempt to take Young's Point and Milliken's Bend. Then, leaving Walker with orders to do what damage he could along the river bank—which was not much—and, if possible, as it was not, to throw supplies of beef and corn into Vicksburg, Taylor went back to Alexandria and prepared for his campaign in La Fourche, from which Kirby Smith's superior orders had diverted him. Meanwhile nearly a month had passed and Walker, after coming down to the Red River, a week too late, was once more out of reach.

Taylor's plan was for Major, with his brigade of cavalry, to cross the Atchafalaya at Morgan's Ferry, while Taylor himself, with the main body under Mouton, should attempt the surprise and capture of Brashear: then, if successful, the whole army could be thrown into La Fourche, while in case of failure Major could easily return by the way he came.

Major left Washington on the 10th of June, marched twenty-eight miles to Morgan's Ferry, by a road then high and dry although in April Banks had found it under water, and crossing the Atchafalaya on the 14th rode along the Bayou Fordoche with the intention of striking the river at the Hermitage; but a broken bridge turned him northward round the sweep of False River toward Waterloo. Sage was at False Point with six companies of his 110th New York, a squadron of the 2nd Rhode Island cavalry, and a section of Carruth's battery. As soon as he found the enemy approaching in some force he moved down the levee to the cover of the lower fleet and thus lost the chance of gaining and giving timely notice of Major's operation. Major on his part rode off by the Grosstête through Plaquemine, as already related, and so down the Mississippi to Donaldsonville, having passed on the way three garrisons without being seen by any one on board. Making a feint on Fort Butler, Major, under cover of the night, took the cut-off road and struck the Bayou La Fourche six miles below Donaldsonville; thence he rode on to Thibodeaux, entering the town at daylight on the 21st of June. At Thibodeaux Major picked up all the Union soldiers in the place to the number of about 100, mostly convalescents.

Soon after taking command in New Orleans, Emory had begun to look forward to what might happen in La Fourche, as well as to the possible consequences to New Orleans itself. The forces in the district were the 23rd Connecticut, Colonel Charles E. L. Holmes, and the 176th New York, Colonel Charles C. Nott, both regiments scattered along the railroad for its protection, Company F and some odd men and recruits of the 1st Indiana, under Captain F. W. Noblett, occupying the field works at Brashear, and two companies of the 28th Maine at Fort Butler. About this time Holmes, who as the senior colonel had commanded the district since Weitzel quitted it to enter on the Teche campaign, resigned on account of ill-health. Nott and Wordin, the lieutenant-colonel of the 23rd, were on the sick-list. Finding the country thus feebly occupied and the service yet more feebly performed, as early as the 7th of June, Emory had chosen a very intelligent and spirited young officer of the 47th Massachusetts, Lieutenant-Colonel Albert Stickney, placed him in command of the district, without regard to rank, and sent him over the line to Brashear to put things straight. In this work Stickney was engaged, when, at daylight on the morning of the 20th of June, he received a telegram from Emory conveying the news that the Confederates were advancing on La Fourche Crossing; so he left Major Anthony, of the 2nd Rhode Island cavalry, in command at Brashear and went to the point where the danger threatened. When, on the afternoon of the 21st of June, the Confederate force drew near, Stickney found himself in command of a medley of 838 men belonging to eight different organizations—namely, 195 of the 23rd Connecticut, 154 of the 176th New York, 46 of the 42nd Massachusetts, 37 of the 26th Maine, 306 of the 26th Massachusetts, 50 troopers of the 1st Louisiana cavalry, 20 artillerymen, chiefly of the 1st Indiana, and one section, with 30 men, of Grow's 25th New York battery.

The levee at this point was about twelve feet high, forming a natural fortification, which Stickney took advantage of and strengthened by throwing up slight rifle-pits on his flanks. These had only been carried a few yards, and were nowhere more than two feet high, when, about seven o'clock in the evening, under cover of the darkness, Major attacked. The attack was led by Pyron's regiment, reported by Major as 206 strong, and was received and thrown off by about three quarters of Stickney's force. For this result the credit is largely due to the gallantry and good judgment of Major Morgan Morgan, Jr., of the 176th New York, and the steadiness of his men, inspired by his example. Grow's guns being separated and one of them without support, this piece was abandoned by its gunners and fell for the moment into the hands of the Confederates; the other piece, placed by Grow himself to protect the flank, poured an effective enfilade fire upon Pyron's column.

Stickney's loss was 8 killed and 41 wounded, including Lieutenant Starr, of the 23rd Connecticut, whose hurt proved mortal. The Confederate loss is not reported, but Stickney says he counted 53 of their dead on the field, and afterward found nearly 60 wounded in the hospitals at Thibodeaux. The next morning, June 22nd, their dead and wounded were removed under a flag of truce.[1]

While the flag was out, Cahill came up from New Orleans with the 9th Connecticut, a further detachment of the 26th Massachusetts, and the remainder of Grow's battery. This gave Stickney about 1,100 men, with four guns in position and six field-pieces. Cahill's arrival was seen by Major, who, after waiting all day in a drenching rain, began to think his condition rather critical; accordingly, at nine o'clock in the evening he set out to force his way to Brashear, where he was expecting to find Green. Riding hard, he arrived at the east bank of Bayou Boeuf late the next afternoon, and, crossing by night, at daylight on the 24th he had completely surrounded the post of Bayou Boeuf, and was just about to attack, when he saw the white flag that announced the surrender of the garrison to Mouton. Before this, Captain Julius Sanford, of the 23rd Connecticut, set fire to the sugar-house filled with the baggage and clothing of the troops engaged at Port Hudson.

Meanwhile, for the surprise of Brashear, Mouton had collected thirty-seven skiffs and boats of all sorts near the mouth of the Teche, and manned them with 325 volunteers, under the lead of Major Sherod Hunter. At nightfall on the 22nd of June Hunter set out, and by daylight the next morning his whole party had safely

---

1. The history of the 23rd Connecticut says: "We delivered to them 108 dead. We captured 40 prisoners."—*Connecticut in the War*, p. 757.

landed in the rear of the defences of Brashear, while Green, with three battalions and two batteries of his command, stood on the western bank of Berwick Bay, ostentatiously attracting the attention of the unsuspicious garrison, and three more regiments were in waiting on Gibbon's Island, ready to make use of Hunter's boats in support of his movement.

Banks meant to have broken up the great depot of military stores at Brashear, and to have removed to Algiers or New Orleans all regimental baggage and other property that had gone into store at Brashear and the Boeuf before and after the Teche campaign; such were his orders, but for some reason not easy to explain they had not been carried out. Besides the Indianans, who numbered about 30 all told, there were at Brashear four companies—D, G, I, K—of the 23rd Connecticut, two companies of the 176th New York, about 150 strong, and one company, or the equivalent of a company, of the 42nd Massachusetts, making in all rather less than 400 effectives; there were also about 300 convalescents, left behind by nearly thirty regiments. Notwithstanding the vast quantity of stores committed to their care, including the effects of their comrades, and in spite of all warnings, so slack and indifferent was the performance of duty on the part of the garrison of Brashear that, on the morning of the 23rd of June, the reveille was sounded for them by the guns of the Valverde battery. Thus sharply aroused, without a thought of what might happen in the rear, the garrison gave its whole attention to returning, with the heavy guns, the fire of Green's field-pieces across Berwick Bay. Soon the gunboat *Hollyhock* backed down the bay and out of the action, and thus it was that about half-past six Hunter's men, running out of the woods toward the railway station, and making known their presence with their rifles, took the garrison completely by surprise, and, after a short and desultory fight, more than 700 officers and men gave up their swords and laid down their arms to a little less than one half of their own number. Of the men, nearly all were well enough to march to Algiers four days later, after being paroled. Worse still, they abandoned a fortified position with 11 heavy guns—24-, 30-, and 32-pounders. The Confederate loss was 3 killed and 18 wounded. Hunter says the Union troops lost 46 killed and 40 wounded, but about this there seems to be some mistake, for the proportion is unusual, and the whole loss of the 23rd Connecticut in killed and wounded was but 7, of the 176th New York but 12.

Green crossed Berwick Bay as fast as he could, and pushing on found the post at Bayou Ramos abandoned. The Union troops stationed there had retired to Bayou Boeuf, and so at daylight on the 24th, without feeling or firing a single shot, the united guards of the two stations, numbering 433 officers and men, with four guns, commanded by Lieutenant-Colonel Duganne, of the 176th New York, promptly surrendered to the first bold summons of a handful of Green's adventurous scouts riding five miles ahead of their column. Taylor now turned over the immediate command of the force to Mouton and hastened back to Alexandria to bring down Walker, in order to secure and extend his conquests. Mouton marched at once on Donaldsonville.

When the Union forces at La Fourche Crossing found the Confederates returning in such strength, they made haste to fall back on New Orleans, and were followed as far as Boutte Station by Waller's and Pyron's battalions.

On the 27th of June, Green, with his own brigade, Major's brigade, and Semmes's battery appeared before Donaldsonville, and demanded the surrender of the garrison of Fort Butler. This was a square redoubt, placed in the northern angle between the bayou and the Mississippi, designed to command and protect the river gateway to La Fourche, mounting four guns, and originally intended for a garrison of perhaps 600 men. The parapet was high and thick, like the levee, and was surrounded by a deep ditch, the flanks on the bayou and the river being further protected by stout stockades extending from the levees to the water, at ordinary stages. The work was now held by a mixed force of 180 men, comprising two small companies of the 28th Maine—F, Captain Edward B. Neal, and G, Captain Augustine Thompson,—besides a number of convalescents of various regiments. Major Joseph D. Bullen, of the 28th, was in command, and with him at the time was Major Henry M. Porter, of the 7th Vermont, provost-marshal of the parish of Iberville, whose quarters in the town on the other side of the bayou were no longer tenable.

Farragut, who had gone down to New Orleans and hoisted his

flag on the *Pensacola*, leaving Palmer and Alden in command of the upper and lower fleets before Port Hudson, had disposed his gunboats so as to patrol the river in sections. The *Princess Royal*, Lieutenant-Commander M. B. Woolsey, was near Donaldsonville; the *Winona*, Lieutenant-Commander A. W. Weaver, near Plaquemine; and the *Kineo*, Lieutenant-Commander John Watters, between Bonnet Carré and the Red Church. As soon as the Confederates appeared before Donaldsonville, Woolsey was notified, and couriers were sent up and down the river to summon the *Winona* and the *Kineo*.

Green brought to the attack six regiments and one battery, between 1,300 and 1,500 strong,[2] including three regiments of his own brigade, the 4th, 5th, and 7th Texas, and three regiments of Major's brigade—Lane's, Stone's, and Phillips's. The river, and therefore the bayou, were now low, exposing wide margins of *batture*, and Green's plan was, while surrounding and threatening the fort on its land faces, to gain an entrance on the water front by crossing the *batture* and passing around the ends of the stockades.

At ten minutes past midnight the red light of a Coston signal from the fort announced to the Navy that the enemy were coming. At twenty minutes past one the fight was opened by the Confederates with musketry. Instantly the fort replied with the fire of its guns, and of every musket that could be brought to the parapet. Five minutes later the *Princess Royal*, which, since nightfall, had been under way and cleared for action, began shelling the woods on the right of the fort, firing a few 9-inch and 30-pounder shells over the works and down the bayou, followed presently by 30-pounder and 20-pounder shrapnel and 9-inch grape, fired at point-blank range in the direction of the Confederate yells. The assault was made in the most determined manner. Shannon, with the 5th Texas, passed some of his men around the end of the river stockade, others climbed and helped one another over, some tried to cut it down with axes, many fired through the loopholes; Phillips made a circuit of the fort and tried the bayou stockade, while Herbert's 7th Texas attempted to cross the ditch on the land side. The fight

---

2. When Green says 800, he of course refers to the four regiments actually engaged in the assault; for, after losing, as he says, 261 of these 800, he makes the four regiments of Major's brigade, with two sections of Faries's battery, number 800; while his own force, with one section of Gonzales's battery, he puts at 750. 800 + 750 + 261 = 1,811.

at the stockade was desperate in the extreme; those who succeeded in surmounting or turning this barrier found an impassable obstacle in the ditch, whose existence, strange to say, they had not even suspected. Here the combatants fought hand to hand; even the sick, who had barely strength to walk from the hospital to the rampart, took part in the defence. The Texans assailed the defenders with brickbats; these the Maine men threw back upon the heads of the Texans; on both sides numbers were thus injured. Lane, who was to have supported Phillips, somehow went adrift, and Hardeman, who was to have attacked the stockade on the bayou side, was delayed by his guide, but toward daylight he came up to join in the last attack. By way of a diversion, Stone had crossed the bayou to the east bank on a bridge of sugar coolers, and his part in the fight was confined to yells.

At a quarter before four the yelling, which had gone on continuously for more than two hours, suddenly died away, the fire slackened, and three rousing cheers went up from the fort. A few minutes later the *Winona* came down and opened fire, and at half-past four the *Kineo* hove in sight. The fight was ended. "The smoke clearing away," says Woolsey, "discovered the American flag flying over the fort. Gave three cheers and came to anchor." Yet the same sun rose upon a ghastly sight—upon green slopes gray with the dead, the dying, and the maimed, and the black ditch red with their blood.

Green puts his loss at 40 killed, 114 wounded, 107 missing, in all 261. However, during the 28th, the *Princess Royal* and the *Kineo* received on board from the provost-marshal 124 prisoners, by actual count, including 1 lieutenant-colonel, 2 major, 3 captains, and 5 lieutenants; and Lieutenant-Commander Woolsey says the garrison buried 69 Confederates and were "still at it." Among the Confederates killed was Shannon, and among the missing Phillips. Of the garrison, 1 officer, Lieutenant Isaac Murch, of the 28th Maine, and 7 men were killed, 2 officers and 11 men wounded—in all 21. The *Princess Royal* had 1 man killed, 2 wounded. The vessel was struck in twenty places by grape-shot.

Green has been sharply criticised for the apparent recklessness with which he delivered his assault, even after having announced to Mouton his intention of waiting; yet it is clear that he was sent there to attack; if he was to attack at all, he had nothing to gain by waiting; an assault by daylight would have been wholesale suicide; while, on the other hand, the garrison would unquestionably be reinforced by troops and gunboats before another night. Having paid this tribute to his judgment, and to his daring and the intrepidity of his men the homage that every soldier feels to be his due, one may be allowed to quote without comment this passage from Green's report of the affair, in naked frankness hardly surpassed even among the writings of Signor Benvenuto Cellini:

> At daylight I sent in a flag of truce, asking permission to pick up our wounded and bury our dead, which was refused, as I expected. My object in sending the flag so early was to get away a great number of our men, who had found a little shelter near the enemy's works, and who would have been inevitably taken prisoners. I must have saved one hundred men by instructing my flag-of-truce officer, as he approached the fort, to order our troops to steal away.

Bullen's message to Emory has the true ring: "The enemy have attacked us, and we have repulsed them. I want more men; I must have more men." Emory responded with the remaining two companies of the 28th Maine, that had been left near New Orleans when the regiment moved to Port Hudson, and Banks relieved the 1st Louisiana on the lines and sent it at once to Donaldsonville, with two sections of Closson's battery under Taylor, and Stone to command. This put the place out of peril.

Even this bright spot on the dull, dark background was not to be permitted to go untarnished, for, on the 5th of July, Bullen, the hero of this heroic defence, whose name deserves to live in the memory of all that love a sturdy man, a stout heart, a steady mind, or a brave deed, was murdered by a tipsy mutineer of the relieving force. On Friday, the 14th of August, 1863, this wretched man, Francis Scott, private of Company F, 1st Louisiana, suffered the military penalty of his crime.

Taylor now gave up the attempt to capture the position at Donaldsonville, and devoted his attention to a blockade of the river by establishing his batteries at various points behind the natural fortification formed by the levee. Seven guns, under Faries, were placed on Gaudet's plantation, opposite Whitehall Point, while the guns of Semmes, Nichols, and Cornay were planted opposite College Point and at Fifty-five Mile Point, commanding Grand View reach. On the 3rd of July Semmes opened fire on the Union transports, as they were approaching College Point on their way up the river. The steamer *Iberville* was disabled, and from this time until after the surrender no transport passed up, except under convoy, and it was only with great difficulty that even the fastest boats made their way down with the help of the current.

When this state of things was reported to Farragut, who had gone back to Port Hudson, he sent to New Orleans for his Chief of Staff, Captain Jenkins, to come up, in order that he himself might once more go down and give his personal attention to the affair. On the 7th of July the *Tennessee* started from New Orleans with Jenkins aboard; she had successfully run the gauntlet of the batteries, when, between eight and nine o'clock in the evening, as Faries was firing his last rounds, a solid shot struck and instantly killed Commander Abner Read. Captain Jenkins was, at the same time, wounded by a flying fragment of a broken cutlass. Of the crew two were killed and four wounded.

On the 8th the *Saint Mary's*, a fine seagoing steamer and one of the fastest boats in the department, was carrying Lieutenant Emerson, Acting-Assistant Adjutant-General, with important despatches from headquarters to Emory and to the Chief Quartermaster, when, about three o'clock in the morning, she drew the fire of all the Confederate guns. The *Princess Royal* and the *Kineo* convoyed her past the upper battery, but from this point she had to trust to her speed and her low freeboard. In rounding Fifty-five Mile Point she was struck five times, one conical shell and one shrapnel penetrating her side above the water-line and bursting inboard.

At half-past six on the morning of the 9th of July, Farragut, who had left Port Hudson on the *Monongahela* on the evening of the 7th, started from Donaldsonville with the *Essex*, *Kineo*, and *Tennessee* in company, ran the gauntlet of the batteries, swept and silenced them with his broadsides, and endured for nearly two hours a brisk musketry fire from the enemy without serious loss suffered or inflicted. At half-past one o'clock on the morning of the 10th of July, the gunboat *New London*, bearing Captain Walker, Assistant Adjutant-General, with a despatch announcing the surrender of Port Hudson, came under the fire of Faries's battery, opposite Whitehall. She was very soon disabled by a shot through her boilers, and was run ashore near the left bank, where the *Tennessee* and the *Essex* came to her assistance from below. Landing on the east bank, Captain Walker made his way afoot down the river along the levee until he came in sight of the *Monongahela*, when, at six o'clock in the morning, his signals being perceived, he was taken aboard in one of the ship's boats and communicated to the admiral the good news that the campaign was at an end. To dispose of Taylor could be but a matter of a few days; then once more, in the words of Lincoln, would the great river flow "unvexed to the sea."

Taylor's plans were well laid, and had been brilliantly executed. In no other way, with the force at his disposal, could he have performed a greater service for his cause. Save the severe yet not material check at Donaldsonville, he had had everything his own way: he had overrun La Fourche; his guns commanded the river; his outposts were within twenty miles of the city; he even talked of capturing New Orleans, but this, in the teeth of an alert and powerful fleet, was at best but a midsummer fancy.

In New Orleans, indeed, great was the excitement when it became known that the Confederate forces were so near. In Taylor's army were the friends, the brothers, the lovers, the husbands, even the fathers of the inhabitants. In the town were many thousands of registered enemies, and of paroled Confederate prisoners of all ranks. At one time there were no Union troops in the city, save a detachment of the 42nd Massachusetts, barely two hundred and fifty strong. But the illness that had deprived Emory's division of its leader in the field had given to New Orleans a commander of a courage and firmness that now, as always, rose with the approach of danger, with whom difficulties diminished as they drew near, and whose character had earned the respect of the townspeople. These, though their hearts beat high and their pulses were tremulous with emotion, conducted themselves with a propriety and an outward calmness that reflected the highest credit upon their virtue and their good sense. Yet, when all that was possible had been done, things were at such a pass that, on the 4th of July, Emory thought it imperative to speak out. "I respectfully suggest," he wrote to Banks, "that unless Port Hudson be already taken, you can only save this city by sending me reinforcements immediately and at any cost. It is a choice between Port Hudson and New Orleans."

Banks made the choice with serenity and without a moment's hesitation determined to run the remote risk of losing New Orleans for the moment, with the destruction of Taylor's army in reserve as a consolation, rather than to insure himself against this peril at the price of instant disaster at Port Hudson, even on the very eve of victory.

"Operations here," was the reply sent from headquarters on the 5th to Emory's urgent appeal, "can last but two or three days longer at the outside, and then the whole command will be available to drive back the enemy who is now annoying our communications and threatening New Orleans." So the event proved and such was now the task to be performed.

Augur, who had been ill for some time, yet unwilling to relinquish his command, now found himself unfitted for the summer campaign that seemed in prospect. He accordingly turned over his division to Weitzel, took leave of absence on surgeon's certificate, and went North to recruit his health. Shortly afterward he was assigned to the command of the Department of Washington and did not rejoin the Nineteenth Corps.

Weitzel, as has been said, took transport on the 9th of July immediately after the formal capitulation. Getting under way toward evening, he landed at Donaldsonville early the next morning. His presence there so threatened the flank and front of Taylor's forces, as to induce an immediate withdrawal of the guns from the river and the calling in of all detachments. Morgan, with Grover's First brigade and Nims's battery, followed Weitzel about midnight on the 10th, and Grover himself, with his other two brigades, on the 11th. During the night of that day, Grover therefore found himself before Donaldsonville, holding both banks of Bayou La Fourche with two divisions. He was confronted by Green with his own brigade and Major's, together with the batteries that had lately been annoying the transports and drawing the attention of the gunboats on the river. When, on the 10th, Green saw the transports coming down the Mississippi laden with troops, it did not at once occur to him that Port Hudson was lost; he simply thought these troops were coming to attack him. Concentrating his whole force, he posted Major with four regiments and four guns on the left or east bank of the bayou, and on the right or west bank three regiments and two guns of his own brigade. Green's pickets were within two miles of Donaldsonville. As Grover developed and took more ground in his front, Green drew back toward Paincourtville.

On the morning of the 13th of July, without any intention of bringing on a battle or of hastening the enemy's movements, but merely to gain a little more elbow-room and to find new fields for forage for his animals, Grover moved out an advance guard on either side of the bayou. "The enemy is evidently making preparation," he said in his despatch of the 12th before ordering this movement, "to escape if pursued by a strong force or to resist a small one. Our gunboats can hardly be expected at Brashear City for some days, and it is evidently injudicious to press them until their retreat is cut off." Dudley, with two sections of Carruth's battery under Phelps and with Barrett's troop, marched on the right bank of the bayou, supported by Charles J. Paine's brigade with Haley's battery. Morgan, under the orders of Birge, temporarily commanding Grover's division, moved in line with Dudley on the opposite bank. They went forward slowly until, about six miles out, they found themselves upon the estate of the planter whose name is variously spelled Cox, Koch, and Kock. Here, as Dudley and Morgan showed no disposition to attack, Green took the initiative, and, favoured by a narrow field, a rank growth of corn, dense thickets of willows, the deep ditches common to all sugar plantations in these lowlands, and his own superior knowledge of the country, he fell suddenly with his whole force upon the heads of Dudley's and Morgan's columns, and drove them in almost before they were aware of the presence in their front of anything more than the pickets, whom they had been seeing for two days and who had been falling back before them. Morgan handled his brigade badly, and soon got it, or suffered it to fall, into a tangle whence it could only extricate itself by retiring. This fairly exposed the flank of Dudley, who was making a good fight, but had already enough to do to take care of his front against the fierce onset of Green's Texans. The result of this bad mismanagement was that the whole command was in effect clubbed and on both banks driven back about a mile, until Paine came to its support; then Grover rode out, and, seeing what had happened, drew in his whole force.

Grover's losses in this affair, called the battle of Cox's Plantation, were 2 officers and 54 men killed, 7 officers and 210 men wounded, 3 officers and 183 men captured or missing; in all 465. To add to the reproach of this rough treatment at the hands of an inferior force, two guns were lost, one of the 1st Maine battery and one of the 6th Massachusetts, but without the least fault on the part of the artillerists.

After the close of the campaign Colonel Morgan was arraigned before a general court-martial upon charges of misbehaviour before the enemy and drunkenness on duty, and, being found guilty upon both charges, was sentenced to be cashiered and utterly disqualified from holding any office of employment under the government of the United States; but Banks disapproved the proceedings, findings, and sentence on the ground that the evidence appeared to him too conflicting and unsatisfactory. "The execution of this sentence," his order continue, "is suspended until the pleasure of the President can be known." When the record with this decision reached the Judge Advocate-General of the Army at Washington, he sent it back to Banks with instructions that, as no sentence remained for the action of the President, the proceedings were at an end and Colonel Morgan must be released from arrest. This was accordingly done on the 26th of October, 1863.

Green puts his loss at 3 killed and 30 wounded, including 6 mortally wounded. The Union loss, he says, was "little less than 1,000; there were over 500 of the enemy killed and wounded, of whom 200 were left out on the field, and about 250 prisoners."

When, on the evening of the 14th of July, at Port Hudson, Banks received this news, he went at once to Donaldsonville to confer with Grover and Weitzel on the situation and the plan of campaign. It was agreed on all hands that it was inexpedient to press Taylor hard or to hasten his movements in any way until time should have been allowed for the light-draught gunboats to re-enter Berwick Bay and thus gain control of Taylor's line of retreat. In thus refraining from any attempt to avenge promptly what must be regarded as a military affront, the depleted ranks and the wearied condition of the troops were perhaps taken into account, and, moreover, it must have been considered to the last degree inadvisable to entangle the command in the dense swamps that would have to be crossed, after pushing Taylor prematurely back from the fertile and comparatively high lands that border the Bayou La Fourche. Then Banks continued on to New Orleans, where he arrived on the 18th, and renewed his pressure on the admiral for the gunboats; but, unfortunately, the gunboats were not to be had. Of those that had accompanied the army in the campaign of the Teche, only one, the feeble *Hollyhock*, had remained in Berwick Bay after the army descended the Red River, crossed the Atchafalaya, and moved on Port Hudson. The others, with the transports, had followed the movements of the troops and had been caught above the head of the Atchafalaya when the waters fell. Thus they had long been without repairs and not one of them was now in condition for immediate service. The water on the bar at the mouth of the Atchafalaya was now nearly at its lowest point, so that even of the light-draught gunboats only the lightest could cross. Accordingly it was not until the 22nd of July that the *Estrella* and *Clifton* made their appearance in Berwick Bay and put an end to Taylor's operations.

On the afternoon of the 21st of July, knowing that the gunboats were coming, Taylor set the finishing touch to his incursion by burning the rolling-stock of the railway and running the engines into the bay. He had already destroyed the bridges as far back as Tigerville, thus rendering the road quite useless to the Union forces for the next five weeks.

On the morning of the 25th the advance of Weitzel's brigade, under Lieutenant-Colonel Peck, consisting of his own 12th Connecticut and the 13th Connecticut, commanded by Captain Comstock, arrived at Brashear by steamer from Donaldsonville, and, landing, once more took possession of the place; but in the meantime Taylor had safely withdrawn to the west bank, and gone into camp on the Teche with all of his army intact and all his materials and supplies and most of his captures safe.

CHAPTER 20

In Summer Quarters

Before Banks parted with Grover at Donaldsonville, he left orders for the troops to rest and go into "summer quarters" as soon as the pending operation should be decided. Accordingly, in the last days of July, Weitzel broke away from the discomforts of muddy, dusty, shadeless Donaldsonville, and marching down the bayou, once more took up his quarters near Napoleonville and Thibodeaux, and encamped his men at ease among the groves and orchards of the garden of La Fourche.

On the 16th of July the steamboat *Imperial*, from St. Louis on the 8th, rounded to at the levee at New Orleans in token that the great river was once more free. The next day she set out on her return trip. On the 5th of August a despatch from Halleck, dated the 23rd of July, was received and published in orders:

> I congratulate you and your army on the crowning success of the campaign. It was reserved for your army to strike the last blow to open the Mississippi River. The country, and especially the great West, will ever remember with gratitude their services.

Afterwards, on the 28th of January, 1864, Congress passed a joint resolution of thanks—

> .... to Major-General Nathaniel P. Banks and the officers and soldiers under his command for the skill, courage, and endurance which compelled the surrender of Port Hudson, and thus removed the last obstruction to the free navigation of the Mississippi River.

Admiral Porter now came down the river to New Orleans in his flagship *Black Hawk*, and arranged to relieve Admiral Farragut from the trying duty of patrolling and protecting the river, so long borne by the vessels of his fleet. Farragut then took leave of absence and went North, leaving the West Gulf Squadron to Commodore Bell.

When Port Hudson surrendered, two of the nine-months' regiments had already served beyond their time. The 4th Massachusetts claimed its discharge on the 26th of June, the 50th four days later, insisting that their time ran from the muster-in of the last company; but, being without information from Washington on this point, Banks counted the time from the muster-in of the field and staff, and therefore wished to hold these regiments respectively eighty-one and forty-two days longer, or at all events until the receipt of instructions or the end of the siege. To this view officers and men alike objected, many of them so strongly that whole companies refused duty. They were within their lawful rights, yet, better counsels quickly prevailing, all consented to stay, and did good service to the last. Of seven other regiments the term of enlistment was on the point of expiring. They were the 21st, 22nd, 24th, and 26th Maine, the 52nd Massachusetts, the 26th Connecticut, and the 16th New Hampshire. These nine regiments were now detached from the divisions to which they belonged and placed under the orders of Andrews to form part of the garrison of Port Hudson until the transports should be ready to take them home by sea or river.

As soon as the river was opened, Grant responded freely to all the urgent demands made upon him for steamboats, forage, beef, telegraph operators, and so on. He sent Ransom to occupy Natchez, and about the 25th of July Herron arrived at Port Hudson with his division of two brigades, 3,605 effectives, with 18 guns. Herron's command, the victor of Pea Ridge and Prairie Grove, formerly known as the Army of the Frontier, had been called to the aid of Grant at Vicksburg. It came to the Gulf as Herron's division, but was presently, by Grant's orders, merged in the 13th Corps as its Second Division.

At the close of July, in response to Banks's urgent appeals for more troops to replace the nine-months' men, Halleck ordered Grant to send down a corps of 10,000 or 12,000 men. Accordingly, between the 10th and 26th of August, Grant sent the reorganized Thirteenth Corps to Carrollton. Ord, the proper commander of the Thirteenth Corps, took sick leave, and the corps came to Louisiana under the command of Washburn, with Benton, Herron, Lee and Lawler commanding the divisions, and Colonel Mudd the brigade of cavalry. All told, the effective strength of the corps was 778 officers and 13,934 men; total, 14,712.

Chiefly in July and August the twenty-one nine-months' regiments and in November the nine-months' men of the 176th New York went home to be mustered out. This left of the Nineteenth Corps thirty-seven regiments, having an effective strength, daily diminishing, of less than 350 men each; in all, less than 15,000. From these it was indispensable to take one full and strong regiment for Key West and the Tortugas, another for Pensacola, and a third for Forts Jackson and Saint Philip. This disposed of 2,000; 2,500 more was the least force that could be expected to do the police and guard duty of a hostile town so great and populous as New Orleans, containing the main depots of the army; thus the movable force of infantry was cut down to 8,500, or, as Banks states it, 10,000, and for any operations that should uncover New Orleans, would be but half that number.

In the reorganization of the Nineteenth Corps, thus rendered necessary, the Second division was broken up and ceased to exist, its First and Third brigades being transferred to the Third division, the temporary command of which was given to Dwight, but only for a short time. The First and Third brigades of the First division were thrown into one; Weitzel's brigade at first resumed its original name of the Reserve brigade, and a new Second brigade was provided by taking Gooding's from the Third division, so that when a fortnight later Weitzel's brigade was restored to the First division, it became the Third brigade. The Fourth division, like the Third, was reduced to two brigades. Major-General William B. Franklin, who had just come from the North under orders from Washington, was assigned to command of the First division, while Emory was to retain the Third and Grover the Fourth; but when the Thirteenth Corps began to arrive, Banks found himself in the anomalous position of commanding a military department within whose limits two army corps were to serve, one, numerically the smaller, under his own immediate orders, the other under its proper commander. The approaching completion of the organization of the Corps d'Afrique would add a third element. It was therefore found convenient on every account to name an immediate commander of the Nineteenth Corps, and for this post Franklin's rank, service, and experience plainly indicated him. The assignment was made on the 15th of August, and Franklin took command at Baton Rouge on the 20th. Then Weitzel was designated to command the First division. However, there were during the next few months, among the commanders of all grades, so many changes, due to illness or absence, that only confusion could follow the attempt to tell them all.

The artillery of the corps was redistributed to correspond with the new organization, and the cavalry was concentrated at Baton Rouge, Plaquemine, Thibodeaux, and New Orleans, with orders that all details for orderly duty and the like were to be furnished from a single battalion, the 14th New York, attached to the defences of New Orleans.

Weitzel's division, except his old brigade under Merritt, took post at Baton Rouge, where also Emory's division was encamped, successively commanded by Nickerson and McMillan, while Grover's division, assigned to the defence of New Orleans, was separated, Birge occupying La Fourche, with headquarters at Thibodeaux, and Cahill forming the garrison of New Orleans.

At Port Hudson, after the departure of the nine-months' troops, Andrews had the 6th Michigan newly converted into the 1st Michigan heavy artillery, ten troops of the 3rd Massachusetts cavalry, Rawles's, Holcomb's, and Barnes's batteries; and besides these the infantry of the Corps d'Afrique, then in process of organization, including, at the end of August, the old 1st and 3rd regiments and the five regiments of Ullmann's brigade—the 6th to the 10th. The return of the post for the 31st of August accounts for an effective force of 5,427; of these 1,815 belonged to the white troops and 3,612 to the coloured regiments. The whole number of infantry regiments of the Corps d'Afrique, then authorized, was nineteen, of which only the first four were completed. Besides these there were two regiments of engineers, the 1st full, the 2nd about half full, and three companies of heavy artillery, making the whole muster of coloured troops in the department about 10,000. Towards the end of September the regiments of infantry numbered twenty, with ranks fairly filled. The Corps d'Afrique was then organized in two divisions of two brigades each, Ullmann commanding the First division and the senior colonel the Second. Rawles's battery was assigned to the First division and Holcomb's to the Second. This division, however, never became much more than a skeleton, its First brigade being from the first detached by regiments for garrison duty in the various fortifications.

Andrews at once took up the work of organization and instruction in earnest, rightly conceiving it not merely possible, but even essential, to give to the officers and men of the coloured regiments, thus formed into an army corps under his command, a degree of instruction, as well in tactics as in the details of a soldier's duty, higher then was to be found in any save a few picked regiments of the volunteer and regular service. The prejudice at first entertained against the bare idea of service with coloured troops had not entirely disappeared, yet it had so far lost its edge that it was now possible to select from a number of applicants for promotion, especially to the higher grades, officers who had already shown their fitness and their capacity, while holding inferior commissions or serving in the ranks of the white regiments. Thus the original source of weakness in the composition of the first three regiments was avoided, and, small politics and local influence being of course absent, and Banks's instructions being urgent to choose only the best men, the coloured regiments soon had a fine corps of officers. To the work now before him Andrews brought an equipment and a training such as few officers possessed. Experience had shown him the merit, the capacity, and the defects of the American volunteer officer. At the very bottom of these defects was the looseness of his early instruction in the elements of his duty; once wrongly taught by an instructor, himself careless or ignorant, he was likely to go on conscientiously making the same mistake to the end of his term. Realizing his opportunity, Andrews set about establishing uniformity in all details of drill and duty by establishing a school of officers. These he himself taught with the greatest pains and industry, correcting the slovenly, yet encouraging the willing, until the whole corps was brought up to a uniform standard, and on the whole a high one.

Stone succeeded Andrews as Chief of Staff at department headquarters on the 25th of July.

Franklin's staff, as commander of the Nineteenth Army Corps in the field, included Major Wickham Hoffman, Assistant Adjutant-General; Colonel Edward L. Molineux, Acting Assistant Inspector-General; Lieutenant-Colonel John G. Chandler, Chief Quartermaster; Lieutenant-Colonel Henry D. Woodruff, Chief Commissary of Subsistence; Surgeon John H. Rauch, Medical Director; Captain Henry W. Closson, Chief of Artillery; Lieutenant-Colonel Joseph Bailey, Acting Chief Engineer; Captain William A. Pigman, Chief Signal Officer.

CHAPTER 21

A Foothold in Texas

Banks now wished and proposed to move on Mobile, which he rightly supposed to be defended by about 5,000 men.[1] This had indeed been among the objects specially contemplated by his first instructions from the government, and in the progress of events had now become the next in natural order. Grant and Farragut were of the same mind; but other ideas had arisen, and now the government, anxious to avert the impending risk of European complications, deemed it of the first importance that the flag of the nation should, without delay, be restored at some point in Texas. The place and the plan were left discretionary with Banks, but peremptory orders were given him to carry out the object.[2]

Texas had no military value at that moment. To have overrun the whole State would hardly have shortened the war by a single day. The possession of Mobile, on the other hand, would, besides its direct consequences, have exercised an important if not a vital influence upon the critical operations in the central theatre of war; would have taken from the Confederates their only remaining line of railway communication between the Atlantic seaboard and the States bordering on the Mississippi; would have weakened the well-nigh fatal concentration against Rosecrans at Chickamauga and Chattanooga; would have eased the hard task of Sherman in his progress to Atlanta; and would have given him a safe line of retreat in the event of misfortune. What was it, then, that persuaded the government to put aside its designs on Mobile, to give up the

---

1. Banks to Halleck, July 30 and August 1, 1863: *Official Records*, vol. xxvi., part I, pp. 661, 666.
2. Halleck to Banks, July 24, 1863, July 31st, August 6th, August 10th, August 12th: *Official Records*, vol. xxvi., part I, pp. 652, 664, 672, 673, 675.

offensive, to refrain from gathering the fruits of its successes on the Mississippi, in order to embark in the pursuit of objects avowedly "other than military"?

A series of acts and events, more or less menacing in character, seemed to indicate a concerted purpose on the part of some, at least, of the leading nations of Europe to interfere in the domestic affairs of the United States against the government of the United States. The powerful rams, intended for the recapture of New Orleans, that were being almost openly built to the order of the Confederacy in the port of Liverpool, in the very shipyards whence the *Alabama* had gone to sea, were approaching completion. Other ironclads, not less powerful, were under construction in France, with the personal connivance of the Emperor, under the flimsy pretence that they were intended for the imperial government of China. Finally, on the 10th of June, casting all promises and pretexts to the winds, the French troops had marched into the capital of Mexico, made themselves masters of the country, vamped up a sham throne, and upon it set an Austrian puppet. That Napoleon III. nursed among his favourite dreams the vision of a Latin empire in America, built upon the ruins of Mexican liberty and taking in at least the fairest portion of the Louisiana that his illustrious uncle had parted with so cheaply, was well known. Against the inconvenient spread of his ambition the occupation of some part, of any part, of Texas, was intended as a diplomatic caution. That the warning cast its shadow even upon the dark mind of Louis Napoleon Bonaparte there can be no doubt; yet in the meantime there had occurred in quick succession three events that must have sounded in his ears with tones that even his dull imagination could not easily misunderstand. These were Gettysburg, Vicksburg, and Port Hudson. He had not the least notion of helping the unsuccessful.

The whole Confederate force under Kirby Smith in the trans-Mississippi region numbered at this time about 33,000 effective. Of these, about 4,000 were in the Indian country, 8,000 in Arkansas, less than 14,000 in Western Louisiana, and rather less than 7,000 in Texas. Of the forces in Louisiana under Taylor, about 3,000 were in the extreme northern district. Magruder, whose headquarters were at Houston, and who commanded not only the whole of Texas but nominally New Mexico and Arizona besides, was keeping rather more than two thirds of his forces for the defence of Galveston and the line of the Sabine, while the remainder were distributed on the Rio Grande, at Corpus Christi, San Antonio, and Indianola; he had not 2,000 men together anywhere, nor could even Kirby Smith have concentrated 20,000 at any single point without giving up all the rest of the vast territory confided to his care.

At the end of August Banks had nearly 37,000 officers and men for duty. Of these, about 13,000 belonged to the Thirteenth Corps and about 6,500 to that portion of the Nineteenth Corps, being the First and Third divisions, that was concentrated and ready for active service in the field. The defences of New Orleans, including La Fourche, absorbed 7,000; Port Hudson, 5,500; the rest were holding Baton Rouge, Key West, and Pensacola.

Yielding his own views as to Mobile, Banks entered heartily into the project of the government for gaining a foothold in Texas. Learning from the Navy that the mouth of the Sabine was but feebly defended, while the entrance was practicable for gunboats of light draught, he conceived the plan of descending suddenly upon the coast at that point with a force sufficient to march to Houston and take Galveston in reverse. He selected the troops, and collected the transports and the stores. When he was ready he gave the command of the expedition to Franklin, and caused Beckwith to replace Emory in command of the defences of New Orleans, to enable him to rejoin his division for service in the field.

Franklin had the brigades under Love and Merritt of Weitzel's First division, with Bainbridge's, Closson's, and Bradbury's batteries, and the two brigades, Nickerson's and McMillan's, of Emory's Third division, with Duryea's, Trull's, and Hebard's batteries. For cavalry there were the two squadrons of the 1st Texas. Commodore Bell, who then commanded the West Gulf Squadron, gave the command of the gunboats, destined to keep down the fire of the shore batteries and cover the landing of the troops, to Lieutenant Frederick Crocker, from whose personal observation while serving on the blockade the information that led to the choice of the point of attack had been largely drawn. Crocker, besides his own vessel, the *Clifton*, had the *Sachem*, Lieutenant Amos Johnson; the *Arizona*, Acting-Master Howard Tibbetts; the *Granite City*, Acting-Master

C. W. Lamson. Crocker's belief was that the defences ashore and afloat consisted of two 32-pounder guns in battery, and two small steamboats converted into rams.

Franklin's orders were to proceed to Sabine Pass; there, if the Navy should be able to secure the landing, he was to debark his whole force rapidly, take up a strong position, seize Beaumont, or some other point on the railroad to Houston, and then reconnoitre the enemy to learn their position and strength. He was not to go farther into the country until reinforced. After landing, he was to turn back the transports to Brashear, where Benton's division of the Thirteenth Corps would be found waiting to join him.

After many delays, due to the state and inadequacy of the transports, which, besides ten ocean steamers, fit and unfit, included six river steamers wholly of the latter class, Weitzel sailed from New Orleans on the evening of the 4th of September. Leaving the Southwest Pass on the morning of the 5th, under convoy of the *Arizona*, and steering westward, he was joined, early on the following morning, off Berwick Bay, by the *Clifton* and the *Sachem*. A detachment of about 100 sharp-shooters, mainly from Companies B and G of the 75th New York, under Lieutenants Root and Cox, was then sent aboard the *Clifton*, and to the *Sachem* an officer and 25 men from the 161st New York.

About daylight on the 7th, Crocker became convinced that he had overrun his distance and gone beyond Sabine Pass; but when all the vessels had put about and for three or four hours had been steering to the eastward, he found himself off the entrance to the Calcasieu, thirty miles east of the Sabine. Then he and Weitzel agreed that, under the circumstances, the best thing to be done was to intercept the remainder of the expedition, supposed to be following, under the immediate command of Franklin, and assembling the whole force where they were to wait until the next morning, the 8th of September, for the attempt at Sabine Pass. But the arrangement had been that the attack by the gunboats to cover Weitzel's landing was to be made early on the morning of the 7th. Accordingly Franklin, with his part of the fleet, carrying the supporting force, had already passed Berwick Bay; in fact, at eleven o'clock he was off Sabine Pass; and the *Suffolk*, bearing the headquarters flag of the Nineteenth Corps, had crossed the bar and was about to run in, the others following, when Franklin perceived that his advance had not yet come up, and therefore stopped the movement. In the afternoon Weitzel, seeing nothing of Franklin's fleet, made up his mind that he must have gone by, and once more setting his face toward the west, joined Franklin off the Sabine about nine o'clock that evening.

After the full and open notice thus given the enemy, all thought of anything like a surprise was at an end; yet it was agreed to go on and make the attempt the next morning. Accordingly, at daylight on the 8th, Crocker, with the *Clifton* and the other gunboats, followed by Weitzel with the 75th New York on the transport steamer *Charles Thomas*, entered the harbour, and after reconnoitring the landing-place and the defences, signalled the rest of the fleet to run in. Weitzel put a picked force of five hundred men on the transport *General Banks*, and following in the wake of the four gun-boats, made ready to land about a thousand yards below the fort.

Shortly before four o'clock the gunboats moved to the attack. Above the swamp through which the Sabine finds an outlet to the Gulf, the shore lies low and barren. The fort or sand battery was placed at the turn about one half mile below the hamlet called Sabine City, opposite the upper end of the oyster reef that for nearly a mile divides the channel into two parts, each narrow and neither straight. The *Sachem*, followed by the *Arizona*, took the eastern or Louisiana channel, and was hardly under fire before a shot struck her steam pipe and completely disabled her. The *Clifton* moved at full speed up the western or Texas channel until, when almost directly under the guns of the fort, she also received a shot through her boilers, grounding at the same time; and thus, nearly at the same instant, before the action had fairly begun, the two leading gunboats were completely disabled and at the mercy of the enemy. The Louisiana channel was too narrow for the *Arizona* to pass the *Sachem* or to turn about; so at the moment when the *Clifton* received her fatal injury, the *Arizona* was backing down the eastern channel to ascend the western to her assistance; but in doing this she also took the ground. The *Sachem* hauled down her colours and hoisted the white flag at the fore, and after bravely continuing the fight for twenty minutes longer the *Clifton* followed suit.

The place where the *Clifton* grounded was fairly in range of the beach where Weitzel was expected to land his troops. There may have been a minute, or even ten, during which it might have been possible for Weitzel, breaking away from the concerted plan, to have thrown his picked men ashore while the attention of the Confederates was fixed upon the *Clifton*; yet, although this criticism has been suggested by high authority, the point would have been a fine one at best; and under the actual circumstances, with the *Granite City* in the channel ahead, the *Arizona* aground, and the guns of the *Sachem* and the *Clifton* about to be added to those with which the enemy had opened the action, the problem becomes one of pure speculation. What is clear is that the landing depended upon the gunboats; that these were cruelly beaten before they had a chance to prove themselves; and that nothing really remained to do but what was actually done: that is, to give up the expedition and go home.

It is true that the orders under which Franklin was acting indicated that if he found a landing impracticable at Sabine Pass he was to attempt to land at some other place near by; and it is also true that the infantry might have been set ashore almost anywhere in the soft salt marsh that serves for the neighbouring coasts of Louisiana and Texas; but this must have been without their guns and wagons and with no fresh water save what they carried with them until they should have moved successfully into the interior; while on the transports the stock of water was already running so low that the men and animals were on short allowance. Therefore, with the loss of 3 officers and 94 men captured, of the 75th New York, 6 killed, 2 drowned, and 4 wounded, and 200 mules and 200,000 rations thrown into the sea, the expedition returned to New Orleans, whence, by reason of unseaworthiness of transports, part of it had not yet started. The transports came back in a sorry plight, the *Cahawba* on one wheel, the river steamboat *Laurel Hill* without her smokestacks, and all the others of her class with their frail sides stove. The *Clifton* and the *Sachem*, whose losses are but partially reported, lost 10 killed, 9 wounded, and 39 missing. Nearly all the rest of their crews were taken prisoners.

The Confederate work, known as Fort Griffin, mounted six guns, of which two were 32-pounder smooth bores, two 24-pounder smooth bores, and two 32-pounder howitzers, manned by a single company of Cook's regiment of Texas artillery, whose strength is stated variously, though with great precision, as 40, 41, 42, and 44 men. This company was commanded by Lieutenant Richard W. Dowling, and the post by Captain Frederick H. Odlum. There was a supporting body of about 200 men, as well as the gunboat *Uncle Ben*, but Dowling's company was the only force actually engaged. They received, and certainly deserved, the thanks of the Confederate Congress.

Still intent on executing the instructions of the government, and having in mind Halleck's strong preference for an overland operation, Banks at once gave orders to concentrate at Brashear for a movement up the Teche as far as Lafayette, or Vermilion, and thence across the plains by Niblett's Bluff into Texas. The route by the Atchafalaya and the Red River, Halleck's favourite, was now impracticable, for both rivers were at their lowest stage, and the great length of this line put out of the question the movement of any large force dependent upon land transport.

During the last fortnight of September, Banks concentrated Weitzel's and Emory's divisions of the Nineteenth Corps, under Franklin, on the lower Teche, near Camp Bisland, supporting them with Washburn's and McGinnis's divisions of the Thirteenth Corps, under Ord. The cavalry division under A. L. Lee covered the front towards New Iberia.

Emory being forced to go North on sick-leave, his division was commanded by McMillan from the 17th of September until the 6th of October, when Grover relieved him after turning over the Fourth division to Beckwith. Birge, with his reorganized brigade, occupied La Fourche, with headquarters at Thibodeaux. Sharpe's brigade of Weitzel's division remained at Baton Rouge, with Gooding as the post commander. Burbridge's division of the Thirteenth Corps remained at Carrollton, while Herron's, at the time of the Sabine Pass expedition, had been posted at Morganza to observe and prevent any fresh movement by the Confederates across the upper Atchafalaya. This division was about 2,500 strong, and Herron, being ill, had just turned over the command to Dana, when on the 29th of September Green swept down with Speight's and Mouton's brigades and the battalions of Waller and Rountree upon the outposts on Bayou Fordoche, at Sterling's plantation, killed 16, wounded 45, and took 454 prisoners, including nearly the full strength of the 19th Iowa and 26th Indiana. Green's loss was 26 killed, 85 wounded, and 10 missing; in all, 212.

On the 3rd of October Franklin broke camp at Bisland and moved by easy marches to a position near the south bank of the Bayou Carencro, meeting with no resistance beyond slight skirmishing at the crossing of the Vermilion. On the 11th the Nineteenth Corps encamped within two miles of the Carencro, its daily marches having been, on the 3rd to Franklin, twelve miles; on the 4th to Sorrell's plantation, eleven miles; on the 5th to Olivier's, near New Iberia, thirteen miles; on the 8th to the Vermilion, fifteen miles; on the 9th, crossing the Vermilion, eight miles; on the 11th ten miles; in all, sixty-nine miles.

Ord with the Thirteenth Corps, meanwhile augmented by Burbridge's division from Carrollton, set out from Berwick at the same time that Franklin left Bisland, and, following at an interval of a day's march, encamped on the 10th of October on the Vermilion. On the 14th Ord closed up on Franklin at the Carencro. A week later, Ord being ill, Washburn took command of the detachment of the Thirteenth Corps, his division falling to Lawler.

Banks with his staff left New Orleans on the 7th of October. On the following afternoon he joined the forces near New Iberia, remaining near headquarters in the field until the evening of the 11th, when he returned to New Orleans. Stone stayed two days longer and then followed his chief. This left Franklin in command of all the forces in Western Louisiana, numbering about 19,500 for duty, namely, 11,000 of the Thirteenth Corps, 6,000 of the Nineteenth Corps, and 2,500 of the cavalry division. Banks's object in returning to New Orleans was to organize a second expedition for the coast of Texas. The advance to the Carencro had not only brought his army face to face with Taylor's forces, but also with the well-known conditions that would have to be met and overcome in the movement beyond the Sabine. All idea of this march of more than two hundred miles across a barren country, with no water in the summer and fall, while in the winter and spring there is plenty of water but no road, was now given up once for all. Besides the natural obstacles, there was Magruder to be reckoned with at the end of the march and Taylor in the rear.

Taylor had now about 11,000 effectives in the divisions of Mouton, Walker, and Green, with eleven batteries. To occupy him and to push him farther away, Franklin marched to Opelousas on the 21st of October, skirmishing by the way, and until the end of the month continued to occupy a position covering that town and Barré's Landing.

On the 26th of October, with a force of about 4,000 effectives of the Second division of the Thirteenth Corps under Dana, augmented by the 13th and 15th Maine, the 1st Engineers and 16th infantry of the Corps d'Afrique, and the 1st Texas cavalry, Banks embarked at New Orleans for the mouth of the Rio Grande. After long delays and great peril from bad weather, the expedition landed at Brazos Santiago between the 3rd and 5th of November, and on the 6th occupied Point Isabel and Brownsville, distant thirty miles on the main land.

Having thus at last secured the foothold in Texas so urgently desired by the government, Banks, who had now entered heartily into the expansive scheme, set about occupying successively all the passes or inlets that connect the Gulf of Mexico with the landlocked lagoons or sounds of the Texas coast from the Rio Grande to the Sabine.

Accordingly, he sent for the rest of the Thirteenth Corps, and by the end of December had taken possession of the fringe of the coast as far east and north as Matagorda Bay. So far he had met with little opposition, the Confederate force in this part of Texas being small. The Brazos and Galveston were still to be gained, and here, if anywhere in Texas, a vigorous resistance was to be counted on. Banks was bending everything to the attempt when, as the new year opened, the government stopped him, and turned his head in a new direction.

During these operations on the Texas coast the 13th Maine, commanded by Lieutenant-Colonel Hesseltine, and the 15th Maine formed part of the Second division of the Thirteenth Corps. Both regiments did good service, especially under Ransom, in the expedition that, led by Washburn, landed on Mustang Island on the 16th of November, took the Confederate battery commanding Aransas Pass, and then, crossing to Matagorda Island, rapidly reduced Fort Esperanza, and thus gained the control of Matagorda Bay before the month was out.

CHAPTER 22

Winter Quarters

In preparation for Washburn's departure on the 27th of October, Franklin began to draw back from Opelousas to New Iberia. Lawler led off, and was followed on the 1st of November by McGinnis, Grover, Weitzel, and the cavalry under Fonda, in the order named. Burbridge, followed by Mudd's cavalry brigade, took the Teche road, by Grand Coteau.

On the 3rd, while the Nineteenth Corps rested at the Vermilion and McGinnis at the Carencro, Burbridge, who was in camp on Bayou Bourbeau, was surprised by the sudden descent of Green with two brigades. Burbridge had with him only his First brigade, about 1,200 strong, with 500 men of the 118th Illinois mounted infantry and the 14th New York cavalry, under Fonda, Rice's 17th Ohio battery, and Marland's section of Nims's battery; in all, 1,625 men. The 23rd Wisconsin, 96th Ohio, 60th Indiana, and the gunners of Rice and Nims fought hard to prevent a rout and to save the wagon-trains and the cavalry; and, McGinnis coming up in good time, Green drew off, taking with him nothing save one of the Ohio 10-pounder Parrotts. At one moment both of Marland's guns, abandoned by their supports, were completely cut off by the Confederate cavalry, but Marland, rising to the occasion, bade his cannoneers draw their revolvers, and charged at a full gallop directly through the lines of Green's cavalry, to the complete astonishment of both armies, and came into battery on the right of the 46th Indiana. "The bringing off of the section of Nims's battery, commanded by Lieutenant Marland," says Washburn, "after the regiment sent to its support had surrendered, extorted the admiration of every beholder."

Marland's loss in this brilliant little affair was but two men missing. Burbridge had 25 killed, 129 wounded, and 562 captured or missing; in all, 716. Green reports his loss as 22 killed, 103 wounded, and 53 missing. Green's report shows that he had in the fight three regiments of infantry, seven of cavalry, and two sections of artillery.

With frequent skirmishing, but without serious molestation, the march was continued, and on the 17th of November, the Nineteenth Corps went into camp at New Iberia.

By the end of December the Thirteenth Corps, except Sheldon's brigade which was at Plaquemine, had been gradually transferred to the Texas coast. Thus Franklin was left to hold the line of the Teche with little more than 5,000 men of the Nineteenth Corps and about 3,500 of Lee's cavalry. This, with the winter nights and the winter roads, was too small a force to hold a position so advanced and so exposed as New Iberia, even if there had been any longer an object in doing so.

Accordingly, on the evening of the 5th of January, marching orders were issued for the following morning; but in the night a drizzling rain came on and, freezing as it fell, coated the deep, dense mud with a glaze of ice. The march was therefore put off a day, and on the morning of the 7th, through a frozen bog, a biting norther blowing, and the weather unusually cold for this region, the Nineteenth Corps floundered back to Franklin. The best of the roads were bad enough, but those across the bends, used in ordinary seasons as cut-offs, were now impassable sloughs, so the troops had to march nearly the full length of the bayou. Here a novel form of straggling was introduced through the ever industrious ingenuity of the lazy, many of whom contrived to leave the ranks, and, crossing the levee, seized canoes or made rafts, and tranquilly floated down the bayou ahead of their plodding comrades.

On the morning of the 9th of January the corps went into winter quarters at Franklin. Tents were not issued until a month later, but meanwhile the men built shelters and huts for themselves of such materials as they could find on the plantations or in the wooded swamps; and with branches of live oak and boughs of laurel and the long gray Spanish moss, they constructed for their camps a lavish ornamentation of arbours and arches, mimic forts and sham monitors.

The terms of service of the older regiments enlisted in the early days of 1861 being about to expire, the government now offered a bounty and a furlough for thirty days to all veterans who should again enlist for three years or during the war; and in carrying out this plan Banks arranged to send home in each month, beginning with February, at least two regiments of re-enlisted veterans from each corps. Of the nineteen regiments and six batteries of the Nineteenth Corps raised in 1861, every one promptly embraced these terms. In some regiments nearly every man present re-enlisted. The 7th Vermont enrolled every survivor, save 59, of the original muster; in the 13th Connecticut out of 406 present 400 signed; the 26th Massachusetts returned 546. To make up, in part, for the temporary loss to be accounted for from this cause, the government sent down four fine regiments, well commanded, the 29th Maine, the 30th Maine, the 153rd New York, and the 14th New Hampshire, and, these being assigned to the Nineteenth Corps, the first three joined the First division, but the 14th New Hampshire came too late for the campaign, and was assigned to temporary duty near New Orleans. About the same time Nields's 1st Delaware battery and Storer's 7th Massachusetts battery joined the corps.

The idea of a foothold in Texas had been gradually swelling until at length it had attained the dimensions of an overland army of occupation. For this the nature of the region to be traversed, as well as the character of the enemy to be met, demanded a large mounted force. Therefore the government sent from Washington and from other Northern stations the 2nd New York veteran cavalry, the 11th New York, the 18th New York, the 2nd Maine, the 3rd Rhode Island, the 12th Illinois, and the 3rd Maryland, and from the West many horses. Banks also mounted seven more regiments of infantry, and having thus raised Lee's cavalry division, when all had joined, to nineteen regiments, they were finally organized in five brigades, with three batteries of horse artillery, namely, Duryea's, Rawles's, and Nims's. These three batteries were lost to the Nineteenth Corps, and with them four of the mounted infantry regiments, the 2nd Louisiana, the 75th New York, the 8th New Hampshire, and the 31st Massachusetts; the last three only for a time.

Returning from sick-leave, Emory relieved Weitzel in command of the First division on the 13th of December. Weitzel presently went North on special service and did not resume his command but was transferred in the spring to the Army of the James.

In February, 1864, while the Nineteenth Corps lay in camp at Franklin, it was once more re-organized by breaking up the First, Third, and Fourth divisions, and forming two new divisions, the First, commanded by Emory, comprising the brigades of Dwight, McMillan and Benedict; the Second division, commanded by Grover, composed of the brigades of Nickerson, Birge, and Sharpe. Emory's division was already concentrated on the Teche, but Grover's brigades were separated, Nickerson's being in the defences of New Orleans, Birge's in La Fourche, and Sharpe's at Baton Rouge. The first intention was to concentrate the division at Madisonville, and move it by rail to join Franklin; but events interposed.

The Corps staff serving at this time at headquarters in the field included Colonel Charles C. Dwight, acting assistant inspector-general; Surgeon Eugene F. Sanger, medical director; Captain J. G. Oltman, topographical engineer; Captain Thomas H. Annable, commissary of musters; Captain A. W. Chapman, judge-advocate; Lieutenant John J. Williamson, ordnance officer; Captain Henry C. Inwood, provost-marshal; Captain John P. Baker, Captain George M. Franklin, and Lieutenant David Lyon, *aides-de-camp*.

CHAPTER 23

The Red River

Seven months had thus been spent in desultory adventures and in multitudinous preparations without a serious military object, and still the capture of Mobile was to be put off, and still the dream of a foothold in Texas was to be pursued. As for Texas, if the government had, especially at this time, any settled plan, it is by no means easy to make out what it was. In the previous July the occupation of some point in Texas had been put forward by Halleck as an object of paramount importance. At first the particular place and manner were of no consequence; yet, when the mouth of the Rio Grande had been seized, with the effect of cutting off the contraband trade of Matamoras, Seward, who may be supposed to have known the diplomatic purposes of the government, was frankly delighted, while Halleck, who must be regarded as expressing its military views, was as frankly disgusted. Finally, when not one foothold but many footholds had been gained along the coast of Texas, Halleck wound up the long correspondence[1] by renewing his instructions of the previous summer, looking to a combined naval and military operation on the Red River upon a scale even greater than that originally contemplated; for now, besides the great fleet of ironclads under Porter, the project was to absorb the available strength of three armies. Banks was to move northward by the Atchafalaya; Steele was to advance from the line of the Arkansas; and from Vicksburg Grant was to send Sherman, with such troops as he could spare. Grant, Banks, Sherman, and Steele, as well as Admiral Porter, received corresponding instructions at the same time, and, understanding them in the same sense, the Red River expedition was fairly launched.

---

1. January 4, 1864—*Official Records*, vol. xxxiv, part ii., p. 15.

Once committed to the scheme, Banks devoted himself loyally to the arrangements necessary for prosecuting it on a scale at least commensurate with the magnitude of the undertaking and with the expectations of the government, as he understood them. Texas was to be his objective, and he was the lead his army up the Red River, as the shortest and best way to Texas. From the outset he was committed to the use of a large body of cavalry able to operate on the plains that lie beyond the Sabine, as well as to overcome the opposition of the mounted forces of the Confederacy in that region. Not only was forage scarce in the Red River country, but Shreveport once taken and passed, the march would lie for three hundred miles across a desert; an immense forage train was therefore indispensable. It was also reasonable to suppose that, before passing Shreveport, the combined armies of the Confederacy in the trans-Mississippi would have to be met and beaten, and for this end a large force of infantry and artillery must also form part of the expedition, at least as far as Shreveport. The co-operation of the Navy was necessary, in its turn, if only to keep open the long line of supply by the Red River. Finally the usual time of the highest water in the upper Red River fixed the date of the movement.

Sherman came from Vicksburg to New Orleans on the 1st of March, and within a few hours reached a distinct agreement with Banks as to the aid expected from the Army of the Tennessee. Admiral Porter had already arranged to be at the mouth of the Red River with a large fleet of gunboats in time for the rising of the waters; and now Sherman promised to send with the fleet ten thousand picked men of his army, to be at Alexandria on the 17th of March. Banks, on his part, agreed that his troops, marching north by the Teche, should meet Sherman's at Alexandria. Steele, who was at Little Rock, undertook to move at the same time to meet the combined forces and the fleet on the Red River. Confronting Steele was Price; across Banks's line of advance stood Taylor; with the whole or any part of his force, Sherman and Porter might have to reckon, and in any case Fort De Russy must be neutralized or reduced before they could get to Alexandria.

Thus upon a given day two armies and a fleet, hundreds of miles apart, were to concentrate at a remote point far within the enemy's lines, situated on a river always difficult and uncertain of navigation, and now obstructed and fortified. Not often in the history of war is the same fundamental principle twice violated in the same campaign; yet here it was so, and even in the same orders, for after once concentrating within the enemy's lines at Alexandria, the united forces of Banks, Sherman, and Porter were actually to meet those of Steele within the enemy's lines at Shreveport, where Kirby Smith, strongly fortified moreover, was within three hundred miles, roughly speaking, of either Banks or Steele, while Steele was separated from Banks by nearly five hundred miles of hostile territory, practically unknown to any one in the Union armies, and neither commander could communicate with the other save by rivers in their rear, over a long circuit, destined to lengthen with each day's march, as they should approach their common enemy in his central stronghold.

Perhaps the most remarkable thing about all this was Sherman's ready and express assent to the disregard of the first rule of the great art of which he had always been an earnest student and long past a master; yet it is to be observed that Sherman knew the Red River country better than any one in the Union armies; he knew well the scanty numbers and the scattered state of the hostile forces; with him, as well as with Admiral Porter, this movement had long been a favourite; he had indeed hoped and expected to undertake it himself; but he evidently had in mind a quick and bold movement, having for its object the destruction of the Confederate depots and workshops at Shreveport, without giving the enemy notice, breathing space, or time to concentrate. But this was not to be. On learning, at New Orleans, that Banks meant to command in person, Sherman naturally gave up all thought of accompanying the expedition, and went back to Vicksburg to get his troops ready. The contingent he had promised to send from the Army of the Tennessee he now made up of two divisions of the Sixteenth Corps, united under Mower, with Kilby Smith's division of the Seventeenth Corps, and the command of the whole he gave to A. J. Smith.

As early as the 2nd of March Porter assembled at the mouth of the Red River a great fleet of nineteen ironclads, including fifteen of the heavier class and four of the lighter. The fleet carried 162 guns, of which 62 were of the higher calibres, from 80-pounder

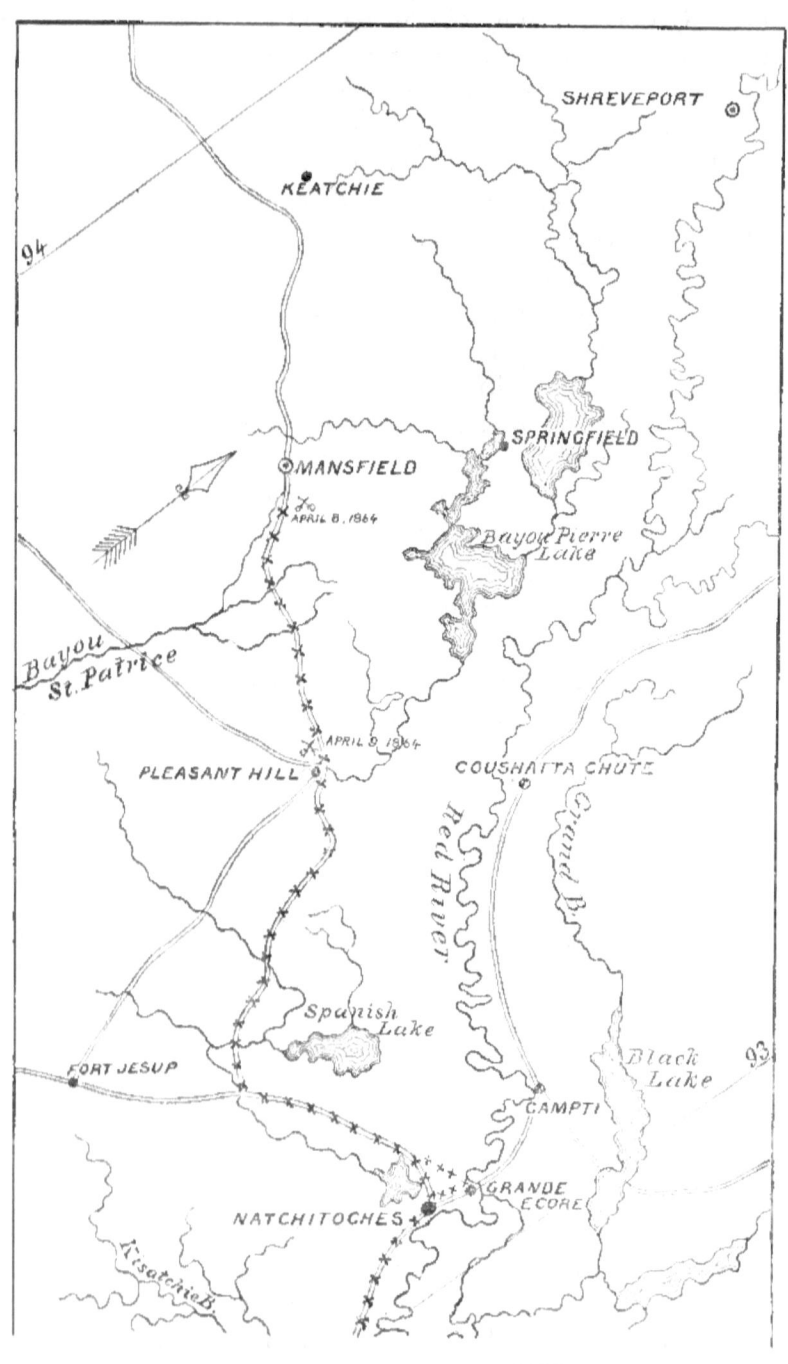

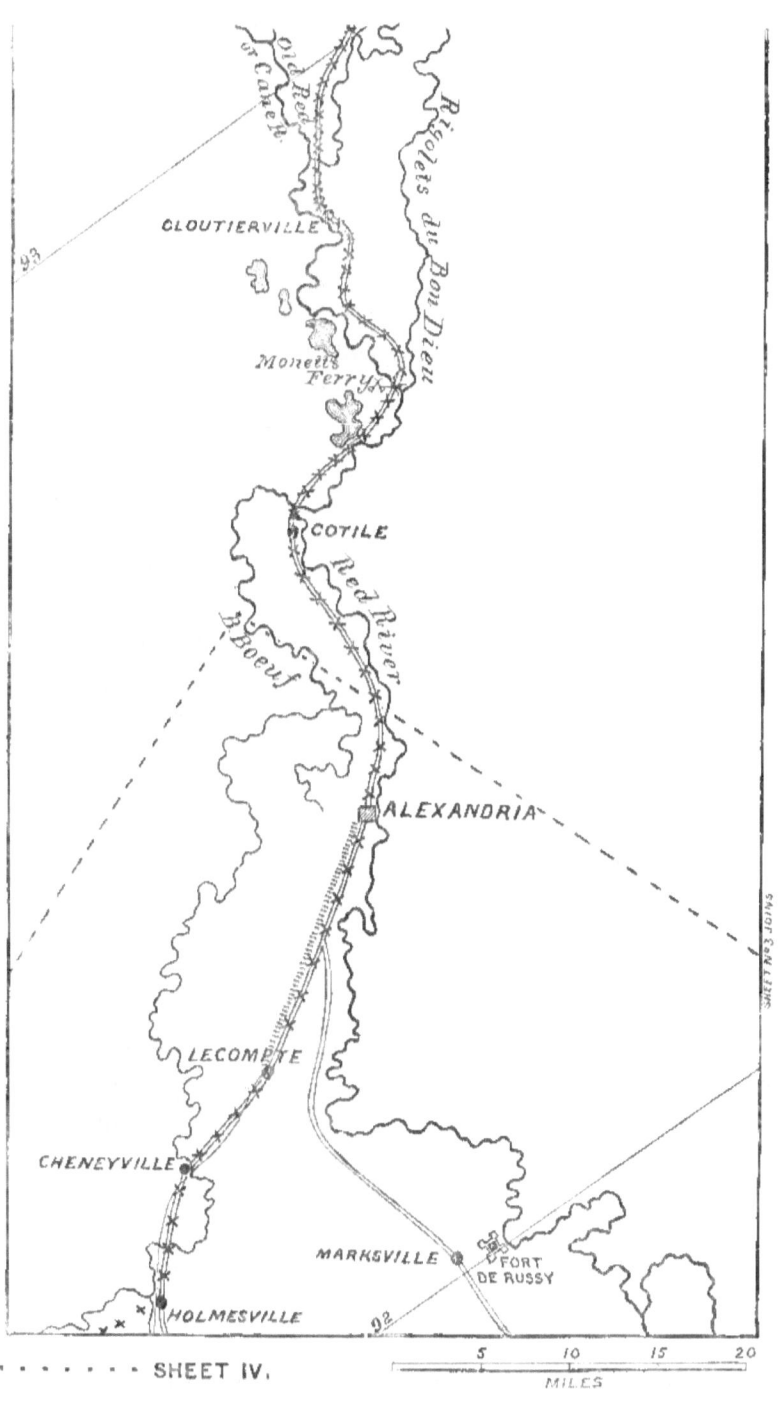

rifles up to 11-inch Dahlgrens, and the combined weight of projectiles was but little less than five tons.

On the 10th of March, A. J. Smith embarked his force at Vicksburg on an admirably organized fleet of nineteen river transports, controlled by a simple system of signals from the flagship *Clara Bell*. When, the next day, Smith joined Porter at the mouth of the Red River, six days were still left until the time when Banks had agreed to be at Alexandria with his army. Sherman's orders to Smith required him to make use of the interval by co-operating with the navy in an expedition up the Black and the Washita, for the destruction of Harrisonburg, but Porter had already done the work single-handed. Naturally supposing that Banks's troops were in march up the Teche toward the point of meeting, although they knew that Banks himself was still detained at New Orleans, Smith and Porter determined at once to take or turn Fort De Russy, and then to push on to Alexandria. On the morning of the 12th of March, the combined fleet entered the Red River. At the head of the Atchafalaya, Porter, with nine of the gunboats, turned off to the left and descended that stream as far as Simmesport, followed by the army transports, while Phelps, with the *Eastport* and the remainder of the fleet, continued the ascent of the Red River, with a view of threatening Fort De Russy, and occupying the attention of its defenders until Smith could land and march across country to attack them.

On the morning of the 13th of March Smith landed, and toward nightfall took up the line of march for Fort De Russy, distant by land twenty-eight miles, although by the windings of the river nearly seventy. In his front, Smith found Scurry's brigade of Walker's division partly entrenched on Yellow Bayou; but Mower quickly brushed Scurry aside, and Walker, after observing the strength of his enemy, concentrated on the Bayou De Glaze, to avoid being shut up in the elbow at Marksville, as well as to get Mouton in support; and thus the way was open to Smith. On the afternoon of the 14th, Mower arrived before Fort De Russy, and just before nightfall the brigades of Lynch and Shaw swept over the parapet and forced a surrender, with a loss of 3 killed and 35 wounded. The captures included 25 officers and 292 men, and ten guns, of which two were 9-inch Dahlgrens from the spoils of the *Indianola* and the *Harriet Lane*, once more restored to their first owners.

Phelps, who had with great energy burst through the formidable raft nine miles below Fort De Russy, came up in *Eastport* in time to fire one shot from his 100-pounder Parrott, and to see the white flag displayed.

When this news reached him, Porter at once ordered his fastest boats to hasten to Alexandria. The advance of the fleet arrived off the town on the 15th of March, just as the last of the Confederate boats were making good their escape above the falls. Kilby Smith and his division followed on the transports with the remainder of the fleet, and, landing at Alexandria during the afternoon of the 16th, relieved the naval detachment sent ashore some hours earlier to occupy the town. On the 18th of March, A. J. Smith marched in with Mower's two divisions. Thus the advance of Porter's fleet was in Alexandria two days, and the head of A. J. Smith's column one day, ahead of the appointed time.

Walker retreated on Natchitoches, accompanied by Gray's brigade of Mouton's division from the Huffpower. Taylor, quitting his headquarters at Alexandria, called in Polignac's brigade from the line of the Tensas and concentrated his force at Carroll Jones's plantation, on the road between Opelousas and Fort Jesup, distant forty-six miles in a south-south-easterly direction from Natchitoches, twelve miles south from Cotile, and twenty miles south-westerly from Alexandria. Here he was in a good position for receiving supplies and reinforcements, for covering Natchitoches, and for observing any approach of the Union forces either from Opelousas or from Alexandria.

Meanwhile Banks had called in from Texas the divisions of Cameron and Ransom of the Thirteenth Corps and sent them to join Franklin on the lower Teche. The command of this detachment being given to Ransom, his division fell to Landram. Lee's cavalry was given the same direction, excepting Fonda's brigade, which stayed at Port Hudson. His last brigade, that of Dudley, marched from Donaldsonville on the 6th of March, crossed Berwick Bay on the 9th, and arrived at the cavalry camp near Franklin on the 10th. Cameron's wagons reached him at Berwick on the 12th, and he marched to join the army in the field on the morning of the 13th. On the evening of the same day Lee led the advance of the army from the town of Franklin, but, his column being quite nine miles long, it was not until the following morning that his rear-guard filed into the road. On the morning of the 15th of March he was followed by Emory and Ransom. Lee arrived at Alexandria on the 19th, Emory on the 25th, and Ransom on the 26th. The troops were, with some exceptions among the newly mounted regiments, in admirable condition, all were in fine spirits, and the long march of one hundred and sixty miles was well ordered and well executed, without confusion, haste, or delay, so that when, with closed ranks and bands playing, and with measured tread and all intervals observed, the column entered Alexandria, the appearance of the men drew exclamations of admiration even from critics the least friendly.

When the news of A. J. Smith's and Porter's arrival in the Red River and of the capture of Fort De Russy reached New Orleans on the 16th of March, it found Banks himself preparing to set out on the following morning to join Franklin near New Iberia. He at once despatched Stone to Alexandria by the river, and following him on the 23rd on the transport steamer *Black Hawk*, arrived at Alexandria on the 24th, and took command of the combined forces of Franklin and A. J. Smith.

Grover, as has been said, was to have moved with Franklin, or close upon his heels, but the 7th of March had come before the first preparatory orders were given for the movement of Sharpe's brigade from Baton Rouge, and not until the 10th was Grover told to concentrate his division at Thibodeaux. His route was now changed to the river. Accordingly Sharpe's brigade debarked at Alexandria on the 26th, and the Second brigade under Molineux on the 28th, but Nickerson stayed for a fortnight longer at Carrollton.

Vincent, who with the 2nd Louisiana cavalry had been watching and reporting Lee's movement and regularly falling back before his advance, joined Taylor at Carroll Jones's on the 19th. Then Taylor sent Vincent with his regiment and Edgar's battery to watch the crossing of Bayou Jean de Jean and to hold the road by which Banks was expected to advance on Shreveport. Vincent encamped on the high ground known as Henderson's Hill, commanding the junction of the Bayou Rapides and Cotile twenty-three miles above Alexandria. Here he was in the air, and A. J. Smith, realizing the importance of seizing the passage without loss of time, at once proceeded to dislodge him. Accordingly, on the 21st of

March he sent out Mower with his two divisions of the Sixteenth Corps and Lucas's brigade of cavalry. Mower made his dispositions with great skill and promptness, and that night, during a heavy storm of rain and hail, completely surprised Vincent's camp and captured the whole regiment bodily, together with four guns of Edgar's battery. A few of Vincent's men managed to escape in the darkness and confusion, but about 250 were brought in and with them 200 horses. This was a heavy blow to Taylor, since it deprived him of the only cavalry he had with him and thus of the means of scouting until Green should come from Texas. Mower returned to Alexandria on the 22nd, and Taylor, probably unwilling to risk a surprise in his exposed position, withdrew about thirty miles to Kisatchie, still covering the Fort Jesup road; but a week later he sent his cavalry northward twenty-six miles to Natchitoches and with his infantry retired to Pleasant Hill.

Banks has been blamed for his delay in meeting A. J. Smith and Porter at Alexandria, yet, whatever may be the theoretical merits of such a criticism, in fact no loss of time that occurred up to the moment of quitting Alexandria had the least influence on the course of the campaign, for even after the concentration was completed the river, though very slowly rising by inches, was still so low that the gunboats were unable to pass the rapids. The *Eastport* hung nearly three days on the rocks in imminent peril, and at last had to be hauled off by main force, a whole brigade swaying on her hawsers to the rhythm of the field music. This was on the 26th of March, and the *Eastport* was the first of the gunboats to pass the rapids, the Admiral being naturally unwilling to expose the boats of lighter draught as well as of lighter armament to the risk of capture if sent up alone. The hospital steamer *Woodford*, which was the first boat to follow the *Eastport*, was wrecked in the attempt. The next five boats took three days to pass, nor was it until the 3rd of April that the last of the twelve gunboats and thirty transports, selected to accompany the expedition to Shreveport, floated in safety above the obstructions. Several of the transports drew too much water to permit them to pass the rapids; these, therefore, stayed below, and with them the remaining seven gunboats.

And now occurred the first important departure from the original plan of operations. The season of high water had been looked forward to as insuring constant communication along the whole length of the Red River as far as the fleet should be able to ascend. But the Red is a treacherous river at best, and this year it was at its worst. There was to be no March rise worth speaking about. Thus the rapids presented an obstacle, impassable, or only to be passed with difficulty; the bare rocks divided the fleet in twain, the only communication was overland by the road around the falls. The supplies had to be landed at Alexandria, loaded into wagons, hauled around, and re-shipped, and this made it necessary to establish depots in the town as well as above the falls, and to leave behind Grover's division, 4,000 strong, to protect the stores and the carry. At the same time McPherson recalled Ellet's marine brigade to Vicksburg, and thus the expedition lost a second detachment of 3,000 men; but this loss was partly made up by Dickey's brigade of coloured troops, 1,500 strong, which joined the column from the garrison of Port Hudson. Withal the force was ample, for at the end of March there were 31,000 officers and men for duty, including about 4,800 under Ransom, 6,600 under Emory, 9,000 under A. J. Smith, and Lee's cavalry, 4,600. Here was a superb fighting column of 25,000 officers and men of all arms, with ninety guns. This more than met the calculations of Banks and Sherman on which the campaign was undertaken. In the three columns there were to be 40,000 men; of these, Sherman was to furnish 10,000, Banks 15,000, and Steele 15,000.

Steele had already sent word that he could not be counted upon for more than 7,000, all told. He had expected to march from Little Rock by the 14th of March on Arkadelphia, there to be joined by Thayer moving at the same time from Fort Smith. Thayer marched on the 21st with 4,000 effectives and 14 guns, Steele on the 23rd with 7,500 effectives and 16 guns; besides these, he left Clayton with 1,600 men and 11 guns to hold Pine Bluff.

We have seen how, in one movement, three divergent ideas were being carried out without either having been distinctly decided on: a foothold in Texas, an overland occupation in force, and a swift raid by the river. To these there was now to be added a fourth idea, in itself sound, yet fatally inconsistent with the others.

On the 27th of March, before setting out from Alexandria, Banks received, by special messenger, the orders of Lieutenant-

General Grant, dated the 15th of March, on taking command of the armies of the United States. For the first time during the war, all the armies were to move as one, with a single purpose, ruled by a single will; along the whole line, from the Mississippi to the Atlantic, a combined movement was to take place early in May, and in this the entire effective force of the Department of the Gulf was to take part. A. J. Smith was to join the Army of the Tennessee for the Atlanta campaign, and Banks was to go against Mobile. Sherman had lent A. J. Smith to Banks for thirty days. This limit Grant was willing to extend by ten or fifteen days, but if Shreveport were not to be taken by that time—that is, by the 25th of April at the very latest,—then Banks was to send A. J. Smith's detachment back to Vicksburg in season to arrive there at the date originally named—that is, by the 10th of April,—even if this should lead to the abandonment of the expedition. The orders for the expedition given by Halleck, while occupying nominally the supreme command that had now in truth fallen into the strong hand of Grant, were not revoked; the expedition was to go on; only, to make sure that it should not be gone too long, it was to be put in irons.

Grant may easily be excused if, while as yet hardly warm in the saddle, he hesitated to revoke orders that he must have known to be those of the President himself; yet, since a door must be either open or shut it would have been far better to revoke the orders than to trammel their execution with conditions so hard that Banks might well have thrown up the campaign then and there. However, Banks on his part had good reason to know the wishes of the government and not less the consequences of disregarding them; moreover, as the case must have presented itself to him, there was an off chance that Kirby Smith might not be able to concentrate in time to save Shreveport; another, still more remote, that he might give up the place without a fight; and a third, more unlikely than either, that Steele might join Banks in time to make short work of it, or at all events to make Banks strong enough to spare A. J. Smith by the appointed time. Two weeks remained until the earliest date set for A. J. Smith to be at Vicksburg; twenty-nine days to the latest day allowed for the taking of Shreveport. In his dilemma Banks decided to run these chances.

After seeing the first of the gunboats safely over the falls, on the 26th of March Banks set his column in motion. A. J. Smith marched on Cotile Landing to wait for his boats. On the 28th Lee, with the main body of the cavalry, preceded Smith to Henderson's Hill, in order to hold the road and the crossing of Bayou Jean de Jean. Franklin with Emory and Ransom and the main supply trains followed on the same day.

Twenty miles above Cotile Landing the Red River divides, and, for sixty miles, until Grand Ecore is reached, the waters flow in two unequal channels; the most southerly of these, along which the road runs, is known as Cane River, or Old Red River. This was formerly the main stream, but the more northerly branch, at once deeper and less tortuous, now forms the only navigable channel, and is called the Rigolets du Bon Dieu, or more familiarly the Bon Dieu.

Lee crossed Cane River at Monett's Ferry, and, re-crossing above Cloutierville, entered Natchitoches on the 31st of March. At Monett's Ferry on the 29th, Cloutierville on the 30th, and again at Natchitoches he encountered slight opposition from the enemy's skirmishers. Franklin, marching by the same road, encamped at Natchitoches on the 2nd of April.

Embarking on his transports as they came, A. J. Smith set out from Cotile Landing on the 2nd of April in company with Porter's fleet, and landed at Grand Ecore on the 3rd.

The river was still rising slowly, and it was not until the 7th of April that Porter considered the draught of water sufficient to justify him in going farther. Then, leaving at Grand Ecore the six heavy boats that had come with him thus far, he began the ascent of the upper reach of the river with the *Carondelet*, *Fort Hindman*, *Lexington*, *Osage*, *Neosho*, and *Chillicothe*, convoying and closely followed by a fleet of twenty transports, bearing Kilby Smith's division and a large quantity of military stores of all kinds. Porter expected to be at Springfield Landing, 110 miles above Grand Ecore, on the 9th. On arriving there, Kilby Smith was to reconnoitre towards Springfield, and if practicable, to send a regiment to seize the bridge across the Bayou Pierre in the direction of Mansfield.

On the 6th of April, as soon as the movement of the fleet was decided on, Banks resumed the march on Shreveport. Shortly after leaving Natchitoches the main road, with which the road from Grand Ecore unites, strikes off from the river toward the west to avoid Spanish Lake, and, traversing a barren wilderness, affords neither position nor resting-place until Shreveport is reached. Banks meant to be at Mansfield, holding the roads that there converge, simultaneously with the arrival at the fleet at Springfield Landing. Lee, who was encamped at Natchitoches with the brigades of Lucas, Robinson, and Dudley, led the advance, and marching twenty-three miles encamped that night at Crump's Corner. Ransom broke camp at Natchitoches at six o'clock in the morning, and marched sixteen miles. Emory followed closely upon Ransom. A. J. Smith remained at Grand Ecore till the next day, to await the departure of the fleet, and then marching eight miles on the Shreveport road fell into the rear of the column. Dickey's coloured brigade formed the guard of the main wagon train, and Gooding's brigade of cavalry covered the rear and left flank. From this time Lee's movements were to be directed by Franklin.

Meanwhile, between the 3rd and 5th of April, Taylor, after consuming the forage for twenty miles around Pleasant Hill, had withdrawn his infantry to Mansfield. Green's cavalry, long expected, was now beginning to come in, largely augmented, from Texas, whither it had been hastily sent, early in the winter, to meet the threatened invasion from the coast.

On the morning of the 7th of April, Lee advanced on Pleasant Hill, Robinson leading, supported by Lucas. Robinson easily drove before him the advance guard of the Confederate cavalry until about two o'clock in the afternoon, at Wilson's farm, three miles beyond Pleasant Hill, he came upon the main body of Green's force, comprising Major's brigade, under Lane, posted in the skirt of the wood, on rising ground, behind a clearing. Robinson dismounted his men and engaged the enemy, who resisted so firmly that Lucas was sent to Robinson's support just in time to save him from being driven off the field by a determined charge. Lucas likewise dismounted his men, and the two brigades, charging together afoot, drove the Confederates from their position, and pursued them to Carroll's saw-mill, on the southerly branch of Bayou St. Patrice, about seven miles beyond Pleasant Hill, where, toward nightfall, they made a strong stand. In this action, Lee took 23 prisoners, and suffered a loss of 11 killed, 42 wounded, and 9 missing.

Ransom marched at half-past five in the morning, and at two

o'clock in the afternoon the head of his column was at Pleasant Hill, nineteen miles distant, where he went into camp, having overtaken the cavalry train during the march, and Dudley's brigade at the close. Emory, closely following Ransom, arrived at Pleasant Hill about five o'clock in the afternoon, and went into camp. The last of the infantry and all the wagons were much retarded by a heavy storm that broke over the rear of the column and cut up the road badly. The night was far spent when Ransom's train joined him, and Emory's, in spite of every exertion, could not be brought up until late on the following morning. A. J. Smith was now a good day's march behind Ransom and Emory.

When Lee found himself so obstinately opposed, and so hindered by these dilatory tactics, he sent a message to Franklin, through Banks's senior *aide-de-camp*, who had been riding with the advance, asking that a brigade of infantry might be sent forward to his assistance. Lee's view was that the infantry, advancing in skirmish order, could make better progress than the cavalry, which, in a country so thickly wooded, found itself reduced to the same tactics, with the added drawback that as often as they dislodged the enemy they had to run back after their horses before they could follow. Franklin declined to accede to this request without orders, justly reflecting that infantry thus advanced at night, after a hard day's march, must be worn out in the attempt to keep touch with the cavalry, while, in the history of these mixed forces, the instances are rare indeed in which the mounted men have not, after bringing on the action, left it, as the proper thing, for the infantry to finish. However, late in the evening Banks joined Franklin, and an hour or two before midnight ordered him to send a brigade to Lee, to report to him at dawn. Upon this Franklin directed Ransom to send either a brigade or a division, at his discretion, and Ransom, in his turn, ordered Landram to take Emerson's brigade of his division and join the cavalry for the service indicated.

CHAPTER 24

Sabine Cross-Roads

Landram accordingly marched at three o'clock on the morning of the 8th of April, and reported to Lee about five.

Soon after sunrise Lee moved forward against the enemy, Lucas leading, with one regiment of his brigade dismounted and deployed as skirmishers, supported by two regiments of Landram's infantry, in line of battle. Green's men still adhering to the obstructive policy of the day before, after a time the two remaining regiments of Emerson's brigade were deployed and required to drive the enemy more rapidly, while the cavalry covered the flanks. About one o'clock in the afternoon, when half the distance that separated Mansfield from his camp of the night before had been accomplished, Lee found himself at the edge of a large clearing on the slope of a hill, with the Confederates in force in his front and on his right flank.

Ransom marched from Pleasant Hill at half-past five, and at half-past ten was ten miles distant on the northerly branch of the Bayou St. Patrice, designated as his camp for the day. He was just going into bivouac when, on a request from Lee for a fresh force of infantry to relieve the exhausted men of Emerson's brigade, Franklin directed Ransom to go forward himself with Vance's brigade, and thus to make sure of Emerson's return.

Franklin's arrangements for the day's march of his command, as well as Banks's for the whole force, contemplated a short march for the head of the column and a longer one for the rear, so that a comparatively early hour in the day the army would be closed up, ready to encounter the enemy in good order. Accordingly, shortly before three o'clock in the afternoon, Emory went into camp on the banks of the south branch of the St. Patrice, within easy supporting distance of Ransom, while A. J. Smith continued his march, until at night, having accomplished twenty-one miles, he went into bivouac about two miles before reaching Pleasant Hill.

At last nearly the whole of Green's cavalry corps had joined Taylor, and at the same time two divisions of Price's army had come in from Arkansas and taken post in supporting distance of Taylor at Keachie, which is about half-way between Mansfield and Shreveport, or about twenty miles from either. With his own force, under Walker and Mouton, Green's Texans, Churchill's Arkansas division, and Parsons's Missouri division, Taylor now had at least sixteen thousand good men, with whom, if permitted, he might give battle in a chosen position, while Banks's force was stretched out the length of a long day's march on a single narrow road in a dense pine forest, with no elbow-room save such as was to be found in the narrow and infrequent clearings. In such a region excess of numbers was a hindrance rather than a help, and cavalry was worse then useless for offence. Banks was, moreover, encumbered by twelve miles of wagons bearing all his ammunition and stores, and was weakened by the necessity of guarding this long train through the barren wilderness deep in the heart of the enemy's country. Of these conditions Kirby Smith was planning to take advantage, and it was to guard against such an enterprise that Banks's column was closing up in readiness to meet the enemy with its full strength, when suddenly on both sides events took the bit in their teeth and precipitated a battle that was in the plans of neither.

It was about eleven o'clock when Ransom set out to go to the front with Vance's brigade. The distance to be passed over was about five and a half miles. Riding ahead, Ransom himself arrived on the field about half-past one in the afternoon. At this time, by Lee's orders, Landram had pushed forward the 19th Kentucky, deployed as skirmishers, and supporting it strongly with the rest of Emerson's brigade, had driven Green's troopers across the open ground, over the hill, and well into the woods beyond, and had taken position on the crest. Here he was joined by Nims, who brought his guns into battery across the road. On the left of Nims were placed two of Rottaken's howitzers, detached from the 6th Missouri cavalry. On the right and left of the horse artillery Emerson formed, and

Vance, as soon as he came up, took position on Emerson's right, but as Banks undertook to hasten the movement through the direct action of his own staff-officers, it resulted that the regiments of the two brigades were sandwiched. Lucas, dismounted, extended the line of battle to the right. With him were a section of Rawles's battery and another of Rottaken's.

To cover the flanks in the forest Dudley deployed as skirmishers the 8th New Hampshire on the right, and on the left the 3rd and the 31st Massachusetts, supported by the 2nd Illinois. Robinson was with the cavalry train, which was rather closely following the march of its division, in order to clear the head of the infantry without starving the cavalry.

Neither side could move forward without bringing on a battle. But Lee, instead of being able and ready to disengage his cavalry advance-guard and to fall back to a chosen field, was now anchored to the ground where he found himself, not alone by the concentration of the main body of the cavalry at the very front, but also and even more firmly by the presence of the infantry with its artillery and their employment, naturally enough, to form the centre of his main line.

The clearing, the largest yet seen by the Union Army since entering the interminable wilderness of pines, was barely half a mile in width; across the road it stretched for about three quarters of a mile, and down the middle it was divided by a ravine.

Directly in front of Banks stood Taylor in order of battle, covering the crossing of the ways that lead to Pleasant Hill, to Shreveport, to Bayou Pierre, and to the Sabine. On his right was the cavalry of Bee, then Walker's infantry astride of the main road, and on Walker's left Mouton, supported on his left by the cavalry brigades of Major and Bagby, dismounted. To this position, well selected, Taylor had advanced from Mansfield early in the morning, with the clear intention of offering battle, and, regardless of Kirby Smith's purpose of concentrating nearer Shreveport, had sent back orders for Churchill and Parsons to come forward. They marched early, and were by this time well on the way, but a distance of twenty-five miles separated their camp of the night before from the field of the approaching combat.

As on the previous day's march, Stone had been with Lee's advance since the early morning, without, however, being charged with the views of his chief and without attempting to issue orders in his name; but now Banks himself rode to the extreme front, as his habit was. Arriving on the ground not long after Ransom, and seeing the enemy before him in force, Banks at once ordered Lee to hold his ground and sent back orders to Franklin to bring forward the column. The skirmishing that had been going on all the morning, as an incident of the advance and retreat of the opposing forces, had become the sharp prelude of battle, and through the openings of the forest the enemy could be seen in continuous movement toward his left. This was Major and Mouton feeling their way to the Union right, beyond which and diagonally across the front ran the road that leads from Mansfield to Bayou Pierre.

Whether Taylor, as he says, now became impatient at the delay and ordered Mouton to open the attack, or whether, as others have asserted, Mouton attacked without the knowledge or orders of Taylor, is not quite clear, nor is it here material. About four o'clock, when the two lines had looked at each other for two hours or more, Taylor suddenly delivered his attack by a vigorous charge of Mouton's division on the east of the road. Ransom's infantry on the field numbered about 2,400 officers and men; including Lucas, Banks's fighting line fell below 3,500, and the whole force he had at hand was not above 5,000 strong. Against this, Taylor was now advancing with nearly 10,000. It was therefore inevitable that on both flanks his line must widely overlap that of Banks as soon as the two should meet.

When Ransom perceived Mouton's movement, he threw forward his right to meet it with such spirit that Mouton's first line was driven back in confusion on his second; then rallying and returning to the charge, Mouton's men halted, lay down, and began firing at about two hundred yards' range. The two batteries of Landram's division, Cone's Chicago Mercantile, and Klauss's 1st Indiana, now came on the field, and were posted by Ransom on the ridge near the centre, to oppose the enemy's advance on the left, before which Dudley's men were already falling back. Bee and Walker had in fact turned the whole left flank, and were rapidly moving on, breaking in the line as they advanced. This soon left Nims's guns without support, and at the same time Klauss and

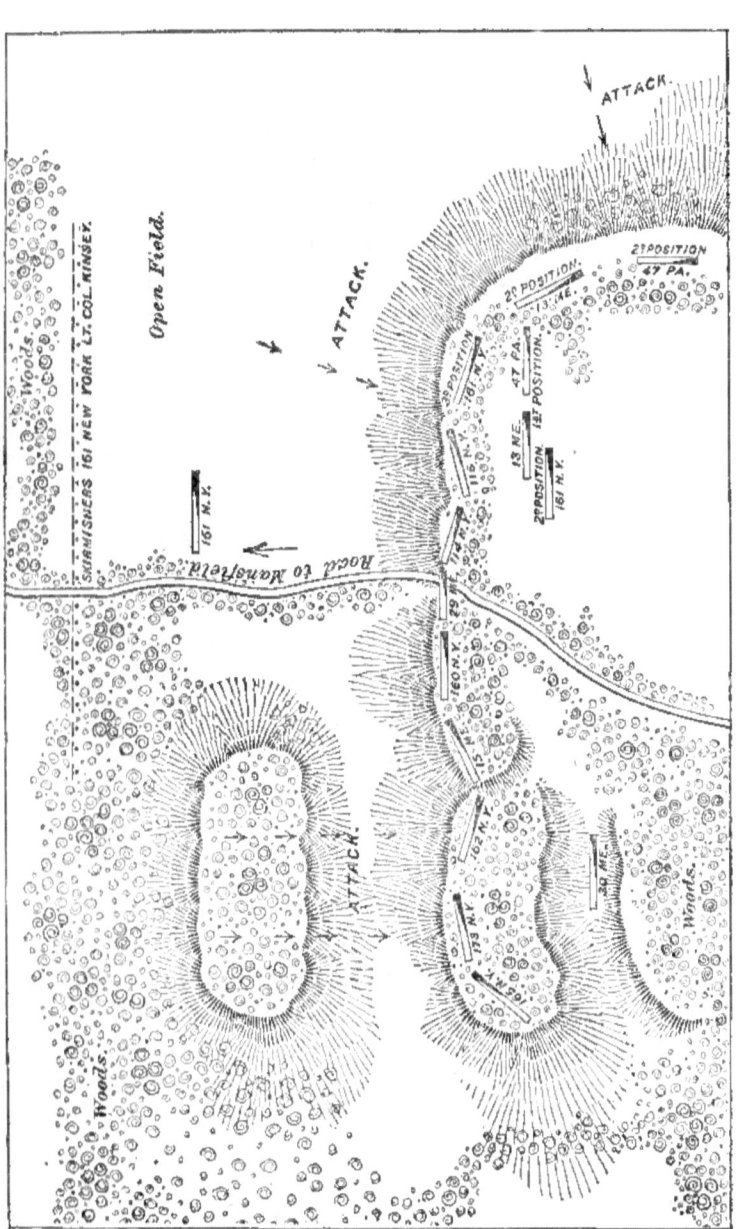

SABINE CROSS-ROADS.
APRIL 8, 1864. ATTACK ON EMORY'S DIVISION. FROM GENERAL EMORY'S MAP.

Cone came under a fire so severe from Walker's men, that Ransom determined to withdraw to the cover of the wood in his rear at the edge of the clearing. Unfortunately, Captain Dickey, his assistant adjutant-general, fell mortally wounded in the act of communicating these orders, and thus some of the regiments farther toward the right, being without orders, and fighting stubbornly against great odds, stood their ground until they were completely surrounded and taken prisoners. While aiding Landram to rally and reform the remnants of his division in the skirt of timber, Ransom was severely wounded in the knee, and had to be carried off the field. Vance and Emerson were wounded and taken prisoners, each at the head of his brigade.

Meanwhile, shortly after three o'clock, at his quarters, near Ransom's camp of the forenoon, Franklin received his first suggestion of an impending battle, in Banks's order to bring all the infantry to the front. First sending back word to Emory, Franklin set out at once and rode forward rapidly, followed by Cameron's division. When, some time after four o'clock, he entered the clearing and galloped to the hill where the guns of Nims still stood grimly defiant and Ransom's men were still desperately struggling to hold their first ground, the situation was already hopeless. Hardly had he arrived on the ground, than, by a single volley from Walker's advancing lines, Franklin's horse was killed, and he himself and Captains Chapman and Pigman of his staff were wounded.

Cameron came up just as Landram was striving hard to rally his men and to hold a second position in the lower skirt of the wood, to prevent the enemy from coming on across the clearing; but for this, time and numbers and elbow-room were alike wanting. Moreover, every movement of the Confederate troopers must be gaining on the flanks. Nor was Cameron's handful, barely 1,300, enough to enable the remnant of the Thirteenth Corps to hold for many minutes so weak a position against such odds. Cameron deployed his four battalions and tried hard, but the whole line soon crumbled and fell apart to the rear.

Until this moment, Banks and Franklin, as well as every officer of the staff of either, beginning with Stone, had exerted themselves to the utmost to second the efforts of Ransom and of Landram to save the day. The retreat once fairly began, all attempt to stay its course was for a time given up as idle, for every man knew just how far back he must go to find room to form a line of battle longer than the road was narrow. Green's cavalry having been for the most part dismounted and on the flanks, as well as in the forest, the pursuit was not very vigorous and was now and then retarded by the successive covering lines of Lucas and of Dudley, so that the prospect seemed fair of bringing off the remnants of the fighting force without much more loss, when about a mile behind the battle-field, at the foot of a slight descent, the retreating column came upon a knot of wagons inextricably tangled and stuck fast in a slough. This was the great cavalry train trying to escape. Instantly what had been a severe check became a serious disaster. Already, by holding so stiffly to his first position, in the front line, in the road, Nims had lost more than half his horses, and thus in quitting the field he found himself compelled to abandon three of his guns; yet not until he had inflicted vast injuries on his enemy, and to the last furnished a noble example of coolness in the performance of duty and the highest courage in the hour of trial. Now the remnant of this fine battery was swallowed up in the wreck of the wagons, and soon fourteen more guns went to swell the ruin. Thus Rails and Rottaken lost each a section, Cone and Klauss their whole batteries. In all twenty guns were lost; three on the field and seventeen at the jam. With them went 175 wagons, 11 ambulances, and 1,001 draught animals. To pass the obstruction the infantry had to turn widely out of the road and for a long distance push their way through the woods. No semblance of order survived. After this there was only one mass of men, wagons, and horses crowding to the rear.

How little expectation there had been of fighting a battle that day, especially on the line where the extreme outposts chanced to be, and how suddenly all was changed, is aptly shown by what was happening in Emory's camp when, at a quarter before four o'clock, he received Franklin's order to go to the front. The wagons of the Thirteenth Corps were in the road in the act of passing the lines of the Nineteenth Corps on the way to join their proper command. Emory's wagons had been with him for some little time and several of the quartermasters were even engaged in issuing clothing when the summons came. There had been no heavy firing as yet, such as indicates a battle, and the exact degree of urgency may be best represented by saying that the marching orders were delivered to Emory in writing by a mounted orderly and were in these words:

> Move your infantry immediately to the front, leaving one regiment as guard to your batteries and train. If your train has got up, you will take two days' rations and the cooking utensils.

The language of this order, which may fairly be taken as an authentic reflection of the oral message from Banks, on which it was directly based, would have justified Emory in taking an hour or more for the issue of the rations; but Emory, whose nature it was to forecast danger, had from the first hour of the campaign been apprehensive of some sudden attack that should find the army unprepared; and thus it was that, merely stopping to take a double ration of hard bread, twelve minutes later the head of his column filed into the road and marched to the front. At this hour the battle was just beginning, and the first sounds, rolling to the rear, served to quicken the march of Emory's men. About a quarter before five he was met by an aide-de-camp with orders to hasten, coupled with the first direct information that an engagement was in progress. A mile farther on an ambulance was met bearing Ransom to the rear. Emory exchanged a few words with the wounded officer, and then ordered his division to take the double-quick. A mile beyond, the usual rabble of camp followers and stragglers was encountered, and soon the road was filled with the swollen stream of fugitives, crying that the day was lost.

And now from Emory down to the smallest drummer-boy every man saw that the hour had come to show what the First division was made of. The leading regiments and flankers instantly fixed bayonets; the staff-officers drew their swords; hardly a man fell out, but at a steady and even quickened pace, Emory's men forced their way through the confused mass in the eager endeavour to reach a position where the enemy might be held in check. This, in that country, was not an easy task, and it was not until the last rush of the flying crowd and the dropping of stray bullets here and there told that the pursuing enemy was close at hand, that Emory found room to deploy on ground affording the least advantage for the task before him. He was now less than three miles from the field where Lee had been beaten back and Ransom had been overwhelmed. The scene was a small clearing with a fenced farm, traversed by a narrow by-road and by a little creek flowing toward the St. Patrice. Here the Confederates could be plainly seen coming on at such a pace that for some moments it was even doubtful whether Emory might not have delayed just too long the formation of his line of battle. Such was his own though as in the dire need of the crisis he determined to sacrifice his leading regiment in order to gain time and room for the division to form. Happily the Confederates helped him by stopping to loot the train and the rejoice loudly over each discovery of some special luxury to them long unfamiliar.

Then rapidly sending orders to Dwight to hold the road at any cost, to McMillan to form on the right, to Benedict to deploy on Dwight's left, Emory himself rode up to Kinsey, and together they led forward the 161st New York and deployed the regiment widely as skirmishers across the whole front of the division, in the very teeth of the Confederate line of battle, rapidly advancing with wild yells and firing heavily as they came. Not a man of the division, not one of the 161st, but felt as well as Emory the imposing duty laid on that splendid regiment and the hard sacrifice expected of it; yet they stood their ground so well and so long that not only had the whole division time to deploy, but, when at last the Confederate line of battle refused any longer to be held back by a fringe of skirmishers, it became a serious question whether friend and foe might not enter the Union lines together. Then, when Emory saw that his line was formed, he gave to word to Kinsey to retire. For some seconds his skirmishers masked fire of their own lines, but, as the Confederates followed with great impetuosity, Dwight's whole line, kneeling, waiting, and ready, opened a fierce fire at point-blank range and soon threw off the attack with heavy loss to their assailants. The brunt of the attack was borne by the 28th Maine, holding the centre and the road. An attempt followed to turn Emory's right flank; in this Dwight's right was pressed so heavily that Emory was obliged to deploy McMillan nearly at right angles to the main front, and thus the onset was easily checked. About the same time the Confederates, whose line was longer than Emory's, made a like attempt to turn the left, but Benedict held on firmly, and although his position was a bad one, soon drove off his assailants. The whole fight was over in twenty minutes, but while it lasted it was sharp. It rolled back the pursuit and changed the fortunes of the evil day.

In no other battle of the war was so little use made of artillery. In Ransom's fight only a few guns could be brought into action on either side, though these indeed were served with vigour. As for Emory, he left his batteries and his baggage to the safekeeping of the 153rd New York and swept to the front with all the rest of his infantry, while the same jam of wagons that entrapped the guns of Lee and Ransom likewise held back the guns of Taylor. Thus Emory's fight was fought by infantry alone against infantry and dismounted cavalry, and no roar of cannon was heard to break the rattle and the wail of the musketry.

So great a change had these few hours wrought that the same sun rose upon an army marching full of confidence that within two days Shreveport would be in its grasp, and set up the same army defeated, brought to bay, its campaign ruined, saved only by a triumph of valour and discipline on the part of a single division and of skill on the part of its intrepid commander from complete destruction at the hands of an enemy inferior in everything and outnumbered almost as two to one. The passage of a wood is the passage of a defile; there, then, was a blind defile, where of six divisions four were suffered to be taken in detail and attacked in fractions on ground of the enemy's choosing. Hardly any tactical error was wanting to complete the discomfiture. Ransom was overwhelmed and double outflanked by two or three times his numbers; even Emory had but five thousand against a force reduced by casualties and straggling, yet still half as large again as his and flushed with victory; moreover, his position was, whether for offence or defence, worthless beyond the passing hour. Banks's losses in the battle of Sabine Cross-Roads were as follows:

	Killed	Wounded	Missing	Total
Cavalry Division	39	250	144	433
Cameron's Division	24	99	195	318
Landram's Division	28	148	909	1,085
Emory's Division	24	148	175	347
Staff of 19th Corps	0	3	0	3
In all	115	648	1,423	2,186

By Taylor the action is called the battle of Mansfield. He puts his losses at 1,000, all told. Foremost among the slain, while leading the fierce onset against Ransom's right, Mouton fell, a regimental colour in his hand, and with him perished many of his brave Louisianans.

Clearly the next thing, whatever might be the next after, was to concentrate and reform on the first fair ground in the rear. Such were Banks's orders. Accordingly at midnight Emory marched in orderly retreat, with all his material intact, and at eight o'clock the next morning, the 9th of April, went into bivouac at Pleasant Hill, where A. J. Smith was found near his resting-place of the night before, and with him Gooding. Thither Lee and the shattered remnants of Ransom's Corps, now under Cameron, had already retired, and there they now reformed in comparative order.

CHAPTER 25

Pleasant Hill

The scenes and events of the 8th produced a deep effect on Banks. At first he was disposed to look on the campaign as lost. Whatever hope he might have had that morning of taking or even reaching Shreveport within the time fixed for the breaking up of the expedition, was at an end before night fell. Not only must A. J. Smith be sent back to Vicksburg within two days, but Banks himself must be on the Mississippi with his whole force ready to move against Mobile by the 1st of May. Such were his orders from Grant, peremptory and repeated. Therefore Banks at once made up his mind to retreat to Grand Ecore, and sent messenger after messenger across the country to tell Kilby Smith and Porter what had happened and what he was about to do. In thus deciding he chose the second best course, and the one that Taylor wished for; it would have been far better to cover Blair's Landing and thus make sure of the safety as well as the support of the gunboats and Kilby Smith.

Pleasant Hill was a village of a dozen houses dispersed about a knoll in a clearing. Beside the main highway between Natchitoches and Shreveport, by which Banks had come and was now going back, fairly good roads radiate to Fort Jesup and Many on the south to the crossings of the Sabine on the west, and on the north and east towards the Red River. The nearest point on the river was Blair's Landing, distant sixteen miles from Pleasant Hill by the road and forty-five miles by water above Grand Ecore.

Though a good place to fight a battle, Pleasant Hill was not a position that could be held for any length of time, even if there had been an object in holding it. It was too far even from the immediate base of supplies, and there was no water to be had save from the cisterns in the village. These were merely sufficient, in ordinary times, for the storage of rain water for the daily use of the inhabitants. Now two armies had been drawing from them, and there was not enough left in them to supply the wants of Banks's men, to say nothing of the animals, for a single day; and for this reason, if for no other, it was impossible for the army to stay there an hour longer than was really necessary to cover a safe and orderly withdrawal of the train.

Accordingly, early on the 9th of April, Banks gave orders for the wagon train to be set in motion toward Grand Ecore, escorted by Lee with the cavalry and Dickey's coloured brigade, and put his army into position at Pleasant Hill to cover the movement.

Churchill with Tappan and Parsons had accomplished the march of twenty miles from Keachie to Mansfield too late in the evening of the 8th to take any part in the battle of Sabine Cross-Roads. At two o'clock the next morning he marched toward the front in order to arrive on the ground in time to renew the fight. By the earliest light of morning Taylor saw that his adversary had already left the field. Then he promptly advanced his whole force, feeling his way as he went. Green led with the cavalry; next came Churchill with his own division, under Tappan; then Parsons, Walker, and Polignac. The morning was well-nigh spent, when Taylor with the head of his column drew near Pleasant Hill and discovered his adversary in position. The last of his infantry did not come up until after noon. Churchill's men were so fagged by their early start and their long march of forty-five miles since the morning of the 8th that Taylor thought it best to give them two hours' rest before attempting anything more.

Two miles to the southward, across the main road, stood Emory, firmly holding the right of the Union lines. Dwight's brigade formed the extreme right flank, thrown back and resting on a wooded ravine that runs almost parallel with the road. Squarely across the road and somewhat more advanced, in the skirt of the wood before the village, commanding an open approach, was posted Shaw's brigade, detached from Mower's Third division, to strengthen the exposed front of Emory. Benedict occupied a ditch traversing a slight hollow, the course of which was nearly perpendicular to the Logansport road, on which his right rested in echelon behind the left of Shaw. Benedict's front was generally hidden by a light growth of reed and willow, but his left was in the open and was completely exposed. Grow's battery, under Southworth, held the hill between Dwight and Shaw, and Closson's battery, under Franck Taylor, was planted so as to fire over the heads of Benedict's men. McMillan's brigade was in reserve behind Dwight and Shaw. The position thus occupied by Emory was a short distance north of the village in front of the fork of the roads that lead to Mansfield and to Logansport.

About four hundred yards behind Benedict, and slightly overlapping his left, the line was prolonged by A. J. Smith, with the two divisions of Mower, strongly posted in the wood, to cover the crossing of the roads to Fort Jesup, to Natchitoches, and to Blair's Landing. Near Mower's right, Closson placed Hebard's battery.

The extreme left flank on the Fort Jesup road was for a time held by Cameron; but, through some uncertainly or misunderstanding of orders, he appears to have considered himself charged with the duty of protecting the right flank and rear of the retreating trains, rather than the left flank of the army. Accordingly five o'clock found him with the wagons, two hours' march from the field of battle.

Lucas, with about 500 picked men of his own brigade, taken from the 16th Indiana, the 6th Missouri, and the 14th New York, and a like number from Gooding's brigade, was detached from the cavalry division for service under the immediate orders of Franklin. With these detachments Lucas skilfully watched all the approaches.

Thus matters rested until the afternoon was well advanced, the long train steadily rolling on its way, and the prospects of being molested seeming to grow by degrees fainter as hour after hour passed and gave no sign of movement on the part of the Confederates.

Taylor formed his line of battle and set his troops in motion between three and four o'clock in the afternoon. Bee with two brigades of cavalry was on the left or east of the Mansfield road, supported by Polignac, on whose division had fallen the heaviest losses of the day before. On the right or west of the road was Walker, while Churchill, with three regiments of cavalry on his right flank, moved under cover and out of sight on the right or south of the upper road to the Sabine.

As early as the previous evening Taylor had considered the chances of Banks's retreat on Blair's Landing, and had sent a detachment of cavalry to gather intelligence of such a movement and to seize the crossing of Bayou Pierre. Now, hearing nothing from this detachment, he sent Major, with his own brigade and Bagby's, to the right of the Union army in time to seize and hold the road to the landing.

Taylor's intention was that Churchill should gain the Fort Jesup road and fall upon the flank and rear of the Union army, while at the same instant Walker was to deliver a direct attack in echelon of brigades from the right. As soon as Churchill should have thrown the Union left into disorder, Bee was to charge down the Mansfield road, while Major and Bagby were to turn the flank of Emory.

It was after three o'clock when Churchill took up his line of march through the woods, Parsons leading. Whether for want of a good map of the country or from whatever cause, it seems probable that, when the head of Churchill's column had gained the lower Sabine road, which enters Pleasant Hill from the southwest, he mistook it for the Fort Jesup road, which approaches the village from the south. Thus, changing front to the left, the double lines of Parsons and Tappan charged swiftly down on the left flank and diagonally upon the front of Benedict, instead of falling, as Taylor meant, upon the flank and rear of Mower. Emory says the attack began at a quarter after five; other reports name an earlier hour. However that may be, night was approaching, and the Union army had practically given up the idea of being attacked that day, when suddenly the battle began.

Benedict's position was, unavoidably, a bad one, and this oblique order of attack was singularly adapted for searching out its weakness. When once Benedict's skirmishers had been driven back through the skirt of the woods that masked his right and centre, Churchill's men had but to descend the slope, firing as they came on, but without checking their pace, and it was a mere question of minutes when the defenders of a line so exposed and overlapped must be crushed by the weight of thrice their numbers. For one brief moment, indeed, the fight was hand to hand; then Benedict's men were driven out of the ditch, and forced in more or less disorder up the reverse slope. So they drifted to the cover of the

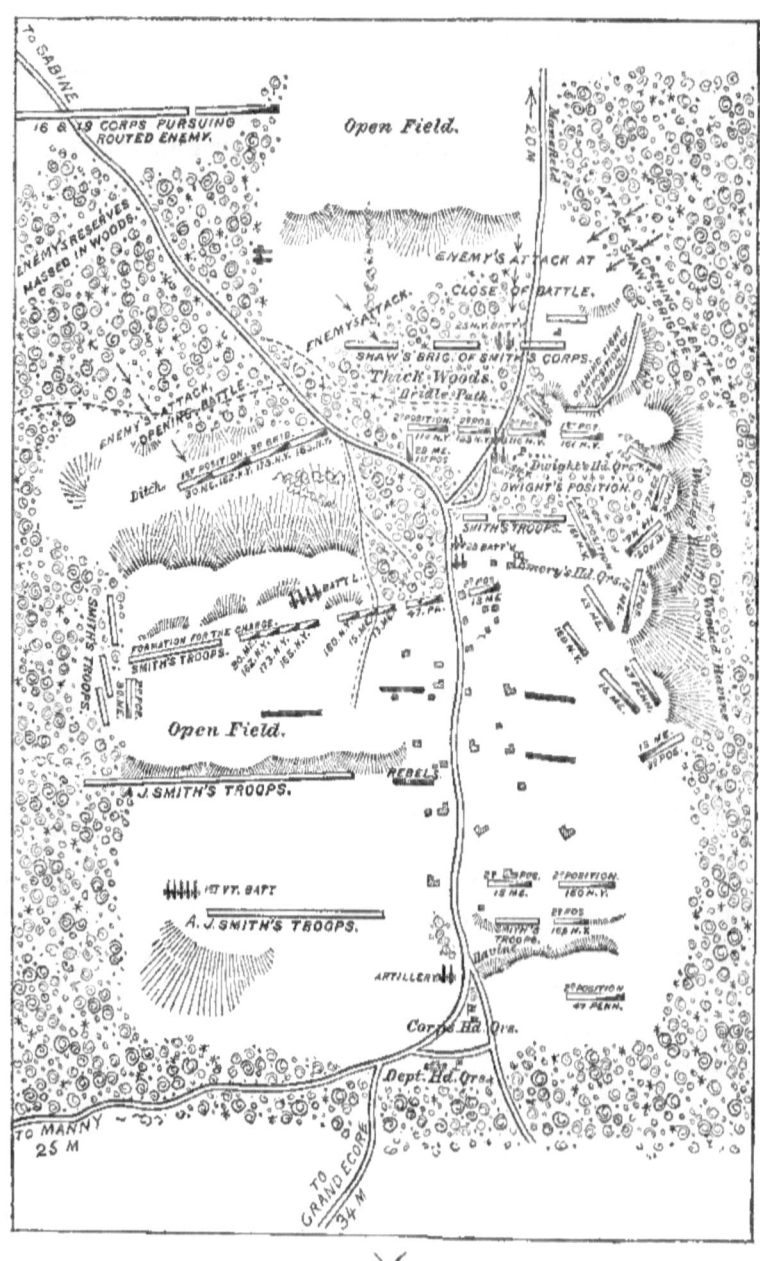

PLEASANT HILL.
APRIL 9, 1864. FROM GENERAL EMORY'S MAP.

wood, where Mower lay in wait, and there by regiments they reformed and sought fresh places in the front of battle; for Benedict had fallen, and the night followed so quickly that darkness had closed in before the discreet and zealous Fessenden had gathered the brigade and held it well in hand. The whole brigade bore the searching test like good soldiers, yet conspicuous in steadiness under the shock and in prompt recovery were the 30th Maine and the 173rd New York, inspired by the example and the leadership of Fessenden and of Conrady.

When Green heard the sound of Churchill's musketry he launched Bee with Debray's and Buchel's regiments in an impetuous charge against the left of Shaw's line; but this wild swoop was quickly stopped by the muskets of the 14th Iowa and the 24th Missouri at close range. Many saddles were emptied; Bee, Buchel, and Debray were among the victims, and in great disorder the beaten remnants fled.

Eighteen guns, among them, sad to say, trophies of Sabine Cross-Roads, concentrated their fire upon the six pieces of Southworth and presently overcame him by sheer weight. The giving way of Benedict had already exposed Shaw's left when Walker closed with him. Vigorously attacked in front, and menaced in flank, Shaw made a stout fight, but he was in great danger of being cut off. Not a moment too soon A. J. Smith recalled him.

When Shaw gave back, Dwight suddenly found himself attacked in front by Walker and in flank and rear by Major. At this trying moment the 114th New York and the 153rd New York were covering the fork of the roads to Mansfield and to Logansport, while beyond the Mansfield road, on the right, stood the 116th New York. To protect the left and right flanks of this little line, Dwight quickly moved the 29th Maine and the 161st New York. Fortunately his men stood firm under the trial of a fire that seemed to come from all quarters at once. For a moment, indeed, the exultant and still advancing Confederates seemed masters of the plain. Along the whole Union front nothing was to be seen in place save Dwight's men far off on the right, standing as it were on a rocky islet, with the gray floods surging on every side.

But far away, out of sight from the plain, an event had already occurred that was to cost the Confederates the battle. Parsons, following up the overthrow of Benedict, offered his own right flank to Lynch, who stood alert and observant in the skirt of the woods, beyond the left of Mower. Lynch struck hard and began doubling up the Missourians. Seeing this, and noting the condition of affairs on the other flank, A. J. Smith instantly ordered forward his whole line. Shaw had already re-formed his brigade on the right of Mower. Across Dwight's rear Emory was leading McMillan from his position in reserve, to restore the line on Dwight's left. Then, just at the instant when to one standing on the plain the day must have seemed hopelessly lost, the long lines of A. J. Smith, with Mower riding at the head, were seen coming out of the woods and sweeping, with unbroken front and steady tread, down upon the front and flank of the enemy. To the right of this splendid line McMillan joined his brigade, and among its intervals here and there the rallied fragments of Benedict's brigade found places. Under this impetuous onset, Parsons and Tappan and Walker melted away, and before anything could be done with Polignac, the whole Confederate army was in hopeless confusion. Their disordered ranks were pushed back about a mile, with a loss of five guns, and after nightfall Taylor's infantry and part of his cavalry fell back six miles to the stream on which Emory had encamped on the morning of the previous day, while the cavalry retired to Mansfield, but Taylor himself slept near the field of battle with the remnant of Debray's troopers. In the superb right wheel, three of the guns lost at Sabine Cross-Roads were retaken.

As soon as the news of the battle of Sabine Cross-Roads reached Kirby Smith at Shreveport, he rode to the front and joined Taylor after nightfall on the 9th of April. The earliest Confederate despatches and orders of Kirby Smith and Taylor claimed a signal and glorious victory, and to this view Taylor seems to have adhered; but in a report dated August 28, 1864, Smith says, in giving his reasons for not adopting Taylor's ambitious plan of pursuing Banks to New Orleans, that Taylor's troops

> . . . . were finally repulsed and thrown into confusion . . . The Missouri and Arkansas troops, with the brigade of Walker's division, were broken and scattered. The enemy recovered cannon which we had captured, and two of our

pieces were left in his hands. To my great relief I found in the morning that the enemy had fallen back during the night. . . . Our troops were completely paralyzed by the repulse at Pleasant Hill.

In an article written in 1888[1] he adds:

> Our repulse at Pleasant Hill was so complete and our command was so disorganized that had Banks followed up his success vigorously he would have met with but feeble opposition to his advance on Shreveport. . . . Polignac's (previously Mouton's) division of Louisiana infantry was all that was intact of Taylor's force. . . . Our troops were completely paralyzed and disorganized by the repulse at Pleasant Hill.

Again, in an intercepted letter, very clear and outspoken, Lieutenant Edward Cunningham, one of Kirby Smith's aides-de-camp, is even more emphatic:

> That it was impossible for us to pursue Banks immediately—under four or five days—cannot be gainsaid. It was impossible . . . because we had been beaten, demoralized, paralyzed, in the fight of the 9th.

The losses of the Union army in the battle of Pleasant Hill were 152 killed, 859 wounded, 495 missing; in all, 1,506. Of these, nearly one half fell upon Emory's division, which reported 8 officers and 47 men killed, 19 officers and 275 men wounded, 4 officers and 374 men missing; in all, 725. The Confederate losses were estimated by Taylor at 1,500.

Each side claims to have fought a superior force, yet the numbers engaged seem to have been nearly equal. Including the thousand horsemen, who were not seriously engaged at any time during the day, and in the battle not at all, the Union army can hardly have numbered more than 13,000 nor less than 11,000. Taylor's force must have been about the same, for, although Kirby Smith's figures account for 16,000, on the one hand the attrition of battle and march is to be reckoned, and on the other hand Taylor himself owns to 12,000.

---

1. *Century War Book*, vol. iv., p. 372.

CHAPTER 26

Grand Ecore

In the first moments of elation that succeeded the victory, Banks was all for resuming the advance, but later in the evening, after consulting his corps and division commanders, he determined to continue the retreat to Grand Ecore. Unfortunately by some mistake the ambulances had gone off with the wagon train, so that there were no adequate means of relieving the wounded on the field. Indeed, all the wounded had not been gathered, and most of the dead lay still unburied, when, about midnight, Banks gave the orders to march. Then from each corps a detail of surgeons was ordered to stay behind, with such hospital stores as they had at hand, and two hours later, in silence and in darkness, unobserved and unmolested, the army marched to the rear, leaving the dead and wounded of both sides on the ground. In the order of march Emory had the head of the column, Mower the rear. Early in the afternoon of the 10th, after a march of twenty miles, the column halted at the Bayou Mayon. At sunrise on the 11th the march was resumed; and the same afternoon found the whole army in camp at Grand Ecore.

Great was the astonishment of Taylor when daylight revealed to him the retreat of the victors of Pleasant Hill. He sent Bee with some cavalry to follow, and this Bee did, yet not rashly, for in twenty miles he came not once near enough to Mower's rear-guard to exchange a shot. Green, with all the rest of the cavalry, was then brought back to Pleasant Hill to carry on operations against the fleet in the direction of Blair's Landing, while the main body of the infantry was drawn in to Mansfield to reorganize.

The fleet was now in great peril. Pushing slowly up the river, constantly retarded by the low stage of water, the gunboats and the transports arrived at Loggy or Boggy Bayou at two o'clock on the afternoon of the 10th of April. Kilby Smith at once landed a detachment of his men, and was proceeding to carry out his orders with regard to opening communication with Banks by way of Springfield, when about four o'clock, Captain Andrews, of the 14th New York cavalry, rode in with his squadron, bringing word of the battles of Sabine Cross-Roads and Pleasant Hill, and bearing a message from Banks to Kilby Smith that directed his return to Grand Ecore. He was at the moment consulting with Porter how best they might get rid of the obstructions caused by the sinking by the Confederates of a large steamboat, called the *New Falls City*, quite across the channel from bank to bank, and they had just decided to set fire to her and blow her up; the bad news made it clear that nothing remained to be done but to go back down the river with all speed.

The natural obstacle presented by the deep waters and by the steep banks of the Bayou Pierre would have formed a complete defence against any assault on the fleet from the west bank of the Red River, had it not been for the fact that there are three good ferries across the bayou, approached by good roads. The upper of these ways led to the river a long distance above the point attained by the fleet; the second struck the bank at Grand Bayou, fifteen miles below where the fleet stopped; the third was the road from Pleasant Hill to Blair's Landing, which is fifty miles below Grand Bayou. Liddell was already watching the east bank of the river, and Taylor now sent Bagby across from Mansfield to Grand Bayou with his brigade and Barnes's battery, to cut off the fleet. However, Bagby did not start from Mansfield until after daybreak on the 11th, so that his arrival at the mouth of Grand Bayou was many hours too late to catch the fleet, which at eight that evening tied up for the night at Coushatta Chute. Here Kilby Smith received a second order of recall from Banks, this time in writing, and dated "On the road, April 10th."

By noon on the 12th, Bagby, riding fast and making use of the short cuts, overtook the rear of the fleet; and somewhat later Green, who had marched from Pleasant Hill early on the morning of the 11th, with Woods's and Gould's regiments and Parsons's brigade of Texans, and the batteries of Nettles, West, McMahan, and Moseley, struck the river at Blair's Landing almost simultaneously with the arrival of the fleet. Here, about four o'clock in the afternoon, in the bend between the high banks, Green caught the rear of the transport fleet at a disadvantage. Making the most of his opportunity, he attacked with vigour. Instantly Kilby Smith and Porter responded and a sharp fight followed, but by sunset they succeeded, without great loss, in driving off their assailants. Indeed the total casualties in Kilby Smith's division above Grand Ecore were but 19, and Porter mentions only one. Chief among the Confederate killed was the brave, impetuous, and indomitable Green.

About noon on the 13th, several of the boats being aground in mid-stream, they were attacked by Liddell, strongly posted on the high bluff known as Bouledau Point. However, all passed by without loss or serious injury, and on the morning of the 14th, the fleet reached the bar at Campti, where A. J. Smith was met marching up the left bank of the river to its relief. But, although Campti is barely twenty miles above, so crooked and shallow was the river that it was midnight on the 15th before the last of the fleet lay in safety at Grand Ecore.

Below Grand Ecore there was a bad bar. As the river continued to fall, the larger gunboats were sent down as fast as possible to Alexandria, whither Porter followed them on the 16th, leaving the *Osage* and *Lexington* at Grand Ecore, and the big *Eastport* eight miles below, where, on the 15th, she had been sunk to her gun-deck either by a torpedo or by a snag. The admiral brought up his pump boats and after removing the guns got the *Eastport* afloat on the 21st.

As Banks realized that his campaign was ruined, he grew earnest in trying to meet Grant's expectations and orders, requiring him to be on the Mississippi by the first of May. For ten days he had been waiting at Grand Ecore, only to see the last of the fleet pass down in safety. Meanwhile he had entrenched his position, thrown a pontoon bridge across the river, placed a strong detachment from Smith's command on the north bank, and sent urgent orders to Alexandria, to New Orleans, and to Texas for reinforcements. Birge, with his own brigade and the 38th Massachusetts and 128th New York of Sharpe's brigade, embarked at Alexandria on the 12th of April, and joined Emory on the 13th. Nickerson's brigade came from New Orleans to join Grover at Alexandria. On the 20th of

April, learning that the *Eastport* was expected to float within a few hours, Banks sent A. J. Smith to take position covering Natchitoches, and when the next day he heard from the admiral that the *Eastport* was actually afloat, he lost not a moment in beginning the march on Alexandria.

An hour later the *Eastport* again struck the bottom; eight times more she ran hard aground; at last on the 25th she lay immovable on a raft of logs, and the next day her crew gave her to the flames.

For some time the relations between the commanding general and his chief-of-staff had been strained, and in spite of Stone's zeal and gallantry in the late battles, Banks had determined on a change, indeed had already announced it in orders, when on the 16th of April he received an order of the War Office bearing date the 28th of March, whereby Stone was relieved from duty in the Department of the Gulf, deprived of his rank of brigadier-general, and ordered to go to Cairo, Illinois, and thence to report by letter to the adjutant-general of the army. For this action neither cause nor occasion has ever been made known. Then Banks recalled his own order and published this instead, and on the following day he made Dwight his chief-of-staff, the command of Dwight's brigade falling to Beal.

Chapter 27

The Crossing of Cane River

Banks broke camp at Grand Ecore at five o'clock in the afternoon of the 21st of April and turned over the direction and control of the march to Franklin.

The cavalry corps, now commanded by Arnold, was separated by brigades. Gooding took the advance; Crebs, who had succeeded to Robinson's command, rode with Birge; E. J. Davis, with Dudley's brigade, covered the right flank; and Lucas, reporting to A. J. Smith, formed the rear-guard.

Birge led the main column with a temporary division formed of the 13th Connecticut and the 1st Louisiana of his own brigade under Fiske, the 38th Massachusetts and the 128th New York of Sharpe's brigade under James Smith, and Fessenden's brigade of Emory's division. Next were the trains, in the same order as the troops. Emory followed with the brigades of Beal and McMillan and the artillery reserve under Closson. Then came Cameron, and last A. J. Smith, in the order of Kilby Smith and Mower.

Crossing Cane River about two miles below Grand Ecore, the line of march traversed the length of the long island formed by the two branches of the Red River, and recrossed the right arm at Monett's Ferry. For the whole distance the army was once more separated from the fleet.

It was half-past one on the morning of the 22nd before the last of the wagons had effected the first crossing of Cane River. By three o'clock Emory was on the south bank, and A. J. Smith at five.

As early as the 14th of April, at Mansfield, Kirby Smith had withdrawn Churchill and Walker from Taylor and sent them to aid in driving Steele back into Arkansas. This left Taylor only the infantry of Polignac, reduced to 2,000 muskets, and the reorganized cavalry corps under Wharton, comprising the divisions of Bee, Major, and William Steele. With this handful, Taylor undertook to hurry Banks by blocking his communications and beating up his out-posts; but just at that moment Banks moved and thus, by the merest chance, brought Bee and Major, with four brigades and four batteries, directly across his path, on the high ground at Monett's bluff, commanding the ford and the ferry. At three o'clock in the afternoon of the 22nd, Wharton with Steele's division, supported by Polignac, engaged Lucas sharply, compelling A. J. Smith to deploy and the rest of the column to halt for an hour; and thus began a series of almost continuous skirmishes that lasted nearly to Alexandria, yet without material result.

At seven o'clock in the evening of the 22nd of April, Birge halted for the night two miles beyond Cloutierville. Under orders inspired by the urgency, he had been pushing on at all speed to seize the crossing; in spite of the heat and the dust, he had led the column at the furious pace of thirty-eight miles, perhaps forty, in twenty-six hours; but Gooding had already found the Confederates in strong possession, and now it seemed clear that the passage must be forced. At nine o'clock Emory and Cameron closed on Birge and halted, and at three in the morning A. J. Smith came up.

At daylight on the 23rd of April, Franklin moved down to the ferry and began to reconnoitre. His wound had now become so painful as to disable him; accordingly, after maturing his plans, he turned over his command to Emory, with orders to dislodge the enemy and to open the way. With equal skill, care, and vigour, Emory instantly set about this critical task, upon which the fate of the army may almost to have said depended, and with this the safety of the fleet.

The grounds on which the Union army found itself was, like the whole island, low and flat and largely covered with a thick growth of cane and willow. Near the river the soil was moreover swampy and the brakes were for the most part impenetrable. On the high bluff opposite, masked by the trees, stood Bee with the brigades of Debray and Terrell, Major with his two brigades under Baylor and Bagby, and the twenty-four guns of McMahon, Moseley, West, and Nettles. The position was too strong and too difficult of ap-

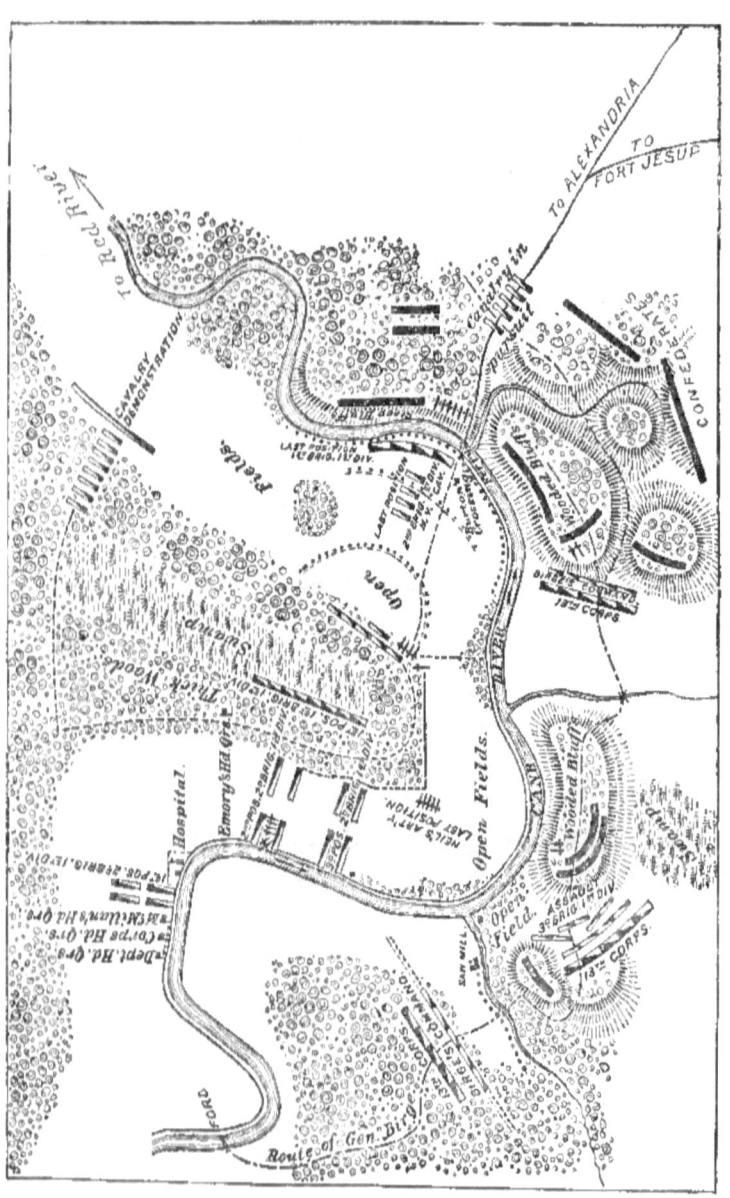

CANE RIVER CROSSING.

OR MONETT'S BLUFF, APRIL 23, 1864. FROM GENERAL EMORY'S MAP.

proach to be taken by a direct attack save at a great cost. Through the labyrinthine morass that lay between the ferry and the river's mouth Bailey and E. J. Davis searched in vain for a practicable ford. Nothing remained but to try the other flank.

Birge with his temporary division augmented by Cameron's, without artillery and with no horsemen save a few mounted men of the 13th Connecticut, was to march back, to ford Cane River two miles above the bluff, and by a wide detour to sweep down upon the Confederate left.

To amuse the enemy and to draw his attention away from Birge, Emory, who had yielded his division to McMillan, caused him to deploy the First and Second brigades under Beal and Rust, and to threaten the crossing directly in front, while Closson advanced his guns and kept up a steady and well judged fire against the Confederate position on the hill.

Birge took up the line of march at nine o'clock. His progress was greatly delayed not only by the passage of Cane River, where the water was waist-deep, but also by the swampy and broken ground, and by the dense undergrowth through which he had to force his way. Thus the afternoon was well advanced before he found the position of the Confederates on a hill, with their right flank resting on a deep ravine, and their left upon a marsh and a small lake, drained by a muddy bayou that wound about the foot of the hill. Up to this point Fiske had led the advance. Now, in deploying, after emerging from the thicket, he found himself before the enemy's centre, while Fessenden confronted their left. Fiske formed his men in two lines, the 13th Connecticut and the 1st Louisiana in front, supported by James Smith with the 38th Massachusetts and the 128th New York. To Fessenden Birge gave the duty of carrying the hill.

Behind a hedge and a high fence Fessenden deployed his brigade from right to left in the order of the 165th New York, the 173rd New York, the 30th Maine, and the 162nd New York. Directly before them, on the other side of the fence, was an open field inclining toward the front in a gentle slope, and traversed at the foot by a second and stouter fence, beyond which a sandy knoll arose, covered with trees, bushes, and fallen timber. On the crest the enemy stood, Bee having changed front to the left and rear as soon as he made out the movement of Birge.

Stopping but to throw down the fence, at the word Fessenden's whole line ran across the field to the foot of the hill. There the brigade quickly re-formed for the ascent, and then, with Fessenden at the head, charged stiffly up the difficult slope straight in the teeth of the hot fire of Bee's dismounted troopers. Many fell, among them Fessenden with a bad hurt, the 165th New York found itself hindered by the marsh, but gallantly led on by Hubbard, by Conrady, and by Blanchard the 30th Maine, the 173rd New York, and the 162nd New York won the crest and opened fire on the retreating foe. Once more halting to re-form his lines, Birge swept on, gained the farther hill without much trouble, and moving to the left uncovered the crossing. Birge's loss in this engagement was about 200, of whom 153 were in Fessenden's brigade, and of these 86 in the 30th Maine. In leading the charge across the open ground Fessenden was severely wounded in the leg, and the command of his brigade fell to Lieutenant-Colonel Blanchard.

As soon as Emory, on the north bank of Cane River, heard the noise of the battle on the opposite heights, he posted five guns under Closson (two of Hinkle's twenty-pounder Parrotts, one gun of Nields' 1st Delaware, one of Hebard's 1st Vermont, and one of the 25th New York battery), to silence the Confederate artillery on their right, in front of the crossing, well supported by the 116th New York, and deployed his skirmishers as if for an assault. Tempted by the exposed position of these guns, Bee sent a detachment across the river to capture them, but Love easily threw off the attack; and, seeing this, Chrysler, whose regiment, the 2nd New York Veteran Cavalry, was dismounted in skirmishing order on the left, at once led his men in pursuit and seized the crossing.

Bee retreated rapidly to Beasley's, thirty miles away to the southward on the Fort Jesup road, without making any further effort to stay or trouble the retreat of Banks.

Word coming from Davis that he had been unable to find a crossing below, Emory, when he saw the enemy in retreat, sent Chrysler and Crebs in pursuit, supported by Cameron. However, this came to nothing, for Chrysler naturally enough followed the small Confederate rear-guard that held to the main road toward Alexandria.

The pontoon bridge was at once laid, and being completed

soon after dark, the march was continued by night, McMillan, with Beal and Rust, moving six miles to the reversed front to cover the trains.

About ten o'clock on the same morning Wharton charged down on Kilby Smith, who was moving up to the rear of A. J. Smith's command and of the army, but was driven off after a fight lasting an hour.

By two o'clock on the afternoon of April 24th, Beal's men being on the south bank of Cane River, the bridge was taken up and the march continued without further molestation by Cotile and Henderson's Hill, the head of the column resting at night near the Bayou Rapides.

Marching thence at six o'clock on the morning of the 25th of April, the head of the column arrived at Alexandria at two o'clock that afternoon, and on the following day A. J. Smith brought up the rear. Here the fleet, with the exception of the ill-fated *Eastport*, was found lying in safety, yet unfortunately above the falls.

Here, too, early on the 27th came Hunter, with fresh and very positive orders from Grant to Banks, bearing date the 17th, requiring him to bring the expedition to an immediate end, to turn over his command at once to the next in rank, and to go himself to New Orleans. In truth, this was but the culmination of an earnest and persistent wish on Grant's part, shown even as far back as the beginning of the campaign, to replace Banks in command by Hunter or another. When, afterward, Grant came to learn of the perilous situation of the fleet, and moreover perceived that none of the troops engaged in the expedition could be in time to take part in the spring campaigns east of the Mississippi, he suspended these orders, and, without recalling that portion of them that required Banks to go to New Orleans, directed the operations for the rescue of the navy to go on under the senior commander present. In any case, however, it was now clearly impossible to abandon the fleet in its dangerous and helpless position above the rapids, with the river falling, and an active enemy on both banks.

And Steele,—where was Steele all this time? Having rejected Banks's advice to join him near Alexandria, marching by way of Monroe and so down the Ouachita, Steele set out from Little Rock on the 24th of March, moved by his right on Arkadelphia, and arrived there on the 28th. His object in preferring this direction was, not only to avoid the heavy roads in the low lands of the Ouachita, but to take up Thayer, who was already on the march from Fort Smith, thus making a fourth concentration in the enemy's country. The exigencies of the wretched farce called a State election in Arkansas had reduced Steele's effective force by fully 3,000, so that he now moved with barely 7,000 of all arms, and six batteries. Opposed to Steele was Price, with the cavalry divisions of Fagan and Marmaduke, the former at Spring Hill to meet the advance from Arkadelphia, and the latter at Camden, to guard the line of the Ouachita. To strengthen himself, Price drew in Cabell and Maxey, who with three brigades were at first engaged in watching Thayer.

On the 1st of April, hearing nothing from Thayer, Steele advanced from Arkadelphia, crossed the Little Missouri at Elkin's Ferry on the 3rd, was joined by Thayer on the 6th, and on the 10th had a sharp engagement with an outlying brigade, under Shelby, of Price's army. Price was then at Prairie d'Ane, covering the crossing of the roads that led to Camden and to Shreveport, but on the evening of the 11th he drew back beyond the prairie to a strong position eight miles north of Washington. To have followed Price would have been to put Steele's long and lengthening line of communication at the mercy of Marmaduke. This was what Price wanted; but when, on the 12th, Steele saw the road to Camden left open, he promptly took it, and, harried by Price in his rear, and not seriously impeded by Marmaduke in his front, he marched into Camden on the 15th, and occupied the strong line of the Confederate defences. This was four days after the return of Banks to Grand Ecore, which of course put an end to any farther advance of Steele in the direction of Shreveport, and while he was waiting for authentic news, Price was busy on his line of communication with Pine Bluff, and Kirby Smith, with Churchill and Walker, was moving rapidly to join Price. On the 20th of April Kirby Smith appeared before the lines of Camden; but Steele had already begun his inevitable retreat a few hours earlier, and having destroyed the bridge across the Ouachita, gained so long a start that he was enabled make good the difficult crossing of the Saline at Jenkins's Ferry, but only after a hard fight on the

30th of April with the combined forces of Smith and Price. Finally, the 2nd of May saw Steele back at Little Rock with his army half starved, greatly reduced in men and material in these six ineffectual weeks, thinking no longer of Halleck's wide schemes of conquest, or even of Grant's wish to hold the line of the Red River, but rather hoping for some stroke of good fortune to enable him to defend the line of the Arkansas and to keep Price out of Missouri.

CHAPTER 28

The Dam

Directly after the capture of Port Hudson, Bailey offered to float the two Confederate transport steamers, *Starlight* and *Red Chief*, that were found lying on their sides high and almost dry in the middle of Thompson's Creek. With smiles and a shrug or two permission was given him to try; he tried; he succeeded; and this experience it undoubtedly was that caused his words to be listened to so readily when he now proposed to rescue the fleet in the same way. But to build at leisure and unmolested a pair of little wing-dams in the ooze of Thompson's creek and to close the opening by a central boom against that sluggish current was one thing; it was quite another to repeat the same operation against time, while surrounded and even cut off by a strong and active enemy, this too on the scale required to hold back the rushing waters of the Red River, at a depth sufficient for the passage of the heaviest of the gunboats and for a time long enough to let the whole fleet go by. Yet, bold as the bare conception seems, and stupendous as the work looks when regarded in detail, no sooner had it been suggested by Bailey then every engineer in the army at once entered heartily into the scheme. Palfrey, who had previously made a complete survey of the rapids, examined the plan carefully, and approved it. Franklin, to whose staff Bailey was attached, himself an engineer of distinguished attainments and wide experience, approved it, and Banks at once gave orders to carry it out.

In the month that had elapsed since the fleet ascended the rapids, the river had fallen more than six feet; for more than a mile the rocks now lay bare. In the worst places but forty inches of water were found, while with seven feet the heavy gunboats could barely float, and in some places the channel, shallow as it was, narrowed to a thread. The current ran nine miles an hour. The whole fall was thirteen feet, and at the point just above the lower chute, where Bailey proposed to construct his dam, the river was 758 feet wide, with a fall of six feet below the dam. The problem was how to raise the water above the dam seven feet, backing it up so as to float the gunboats over the upper rapids.

Heavy details were made from the troops, the working parties were carefully selected, and on the 30th of April the work was begun. From the north bank a wing-dam was constructed of large trees, the butts tied by cross logs, the tops laid towards the current, covered with brush, and weighted, to keep them in place, with stone and brick obtained by tearing down the buildings in the neighbourhood. On the south bank, where large trees were scarce, a crib was made of logs and timbers filled in with stone and with bricks and heavy pieces of machinery taken from the neighbouring sugar-houses and cotton-gins. When this was done there remained an open space of about one hundred and fifty feet between the wings, through which the rising waters poured with great velocity. This gap was nearly closed by sinking across it four of the large Mississippi coal-barges belonging to the navy.

When on the 8th of May all was thus complete, the water was found to have risen five feet four and a half inches at the upper fall, giving a measured depth there of eight feet eight and one half inches. Three of the light-draught gunboats, *Osage*, *Neosho*, and *Fort Hindman*, which had steam up, took prompt advantage of the rise to pass the upper fall, and soon lay in safety in the pool formed by the dam; yet for some reason the other boats of the fleet were not ready, and thus in the very hour when safety was apparently within their reach, suddenly they were once more exposed to a danger even greater than before. Early on the morning of the 9th the tremendous pressure of pent-up waters surging against the dam drove out two of the barges, making a gap sixty-six feet wide, and swung them furiously against the rocks below. Through the gap the river rushed in a roaring torrent. At sight and sound of this, the Admiral at once mounted a horse, galloped to the upper fall, and called out to the *Lexington* to run the rapids. Instantly the *Lexington* was under way, and as, with a full head of steam she made the plunge, every

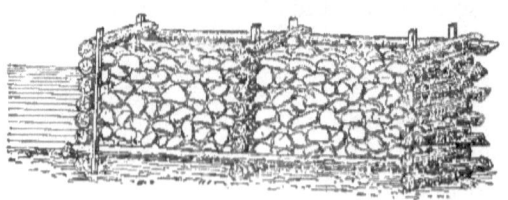

STONE CRIB.

TREE DAM.

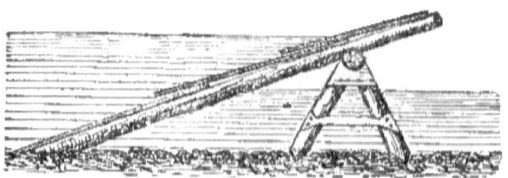

BRACKET DAM.

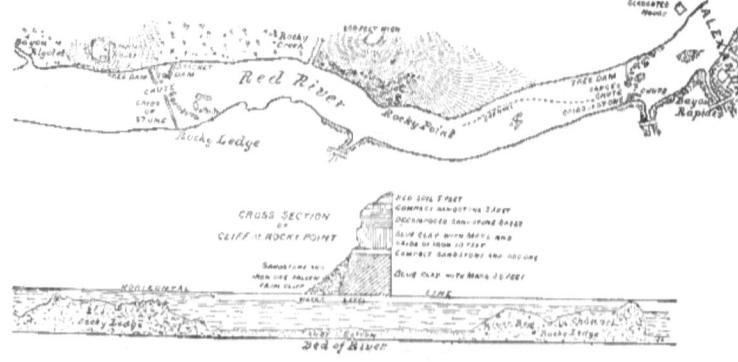

THE RED RIVER DAM.

man in the army and the fleet held his breath in the terrible silence of suspense. For a moment she seemed lost as she reeled and almost disappeared in the foam and surge, but only to be greeted with a mighty cheer, such as brave men give to courage and good fortune, when she was seen to ride in safety below. The *Osage*, the *Neosho*, and the *Fort Hindman* promptly followed her down the chute, but the other six gunboats and the two tugs were still imprisoned above by the sudden sinking of the swift rushing waters; the jaws of danger, for an instant relaxed, had once more shut tightly on the prey. Doubt and gloom took the place of exultation. As for the army, hard as had been the work demanded of it, still greater exertions were before it, nor was their result by any means certain, for the volume of the river was daily diminishing, and there would be no more rise that year.

So far Bailey had substantially followed, though on a larger scale, the same plan that had worked so successfully the year before at Port Hudson. But against a weight, a volume, and a velocity of water such as had to be encountered here, it was now plainly seen that something else would have to be tried. No emergency, however great or sudden, ever finds a man of his stamp unready. As soon therefore as the collapse showed him the defect in his first plan, he instantly set about remedying it by dividing the weight of water to be contended with. At the upper fall three wing-dams were constructed. Just above the rocks a stone crib was laid on the south side, and directly opposite to this on the north side a tree-dam, like those already described when speaking of the original dam. Just below the rocks, projecting diagonally from the north bank, a bracket-dam was built, made of logs having one end sunk to meet the current, the other end raised on trestles, and the whole then sheathed with plank. By this means the whole current was turned into one very narrow channel, and a new rise of fourteen inches was gained, giving in all six feet six and one half inches of water. Every man bending himself to this task to his utmost, by the most incredible exertions this new work was completed in three days and three nights, and thus during the 12th and 13th the remainder of the fleet passed free of the danger.

The cribs were washed away during the spring rise in 1865; but it is said that the main tree-dam survives to this day, having driven the channel towards the south shore, and washed away a large slice of the bank at the upper end of the town of Alexandria.

For his part in the conception and execution of this great undertaking, Bailey received the thanks of Congress on the 11th of June, 1864, and was afterward made a brigadier-general by the President.

The troops engaged in constructing the dam were the 97th coloured, Colonel George D. Robinson; the 99th coloured, Lieutenant-Colonel Uri B. Pearsall; the 29th Maine, Lieutenant-Colonel Charles S. Emerson; the 133rd New York, a detail of 300 men, under Captain Anthony J. Allaire; the 161st New York, Lieutenant-Colonel Wm. B. Kinsey; the pioneers of the Thirteenth Army Corps, 125 in number, commanded by Captain John B. Hutchens of the 24th Indiana, and composed of men detailed from the 11th, 24th, 34th, 46th, 47th, and 67th Indiana, the 48th, 56th, 83rd, and 96th Ohio, the 24th and 28th Iowa, the 23rd and 29th Wisconsin, 130th Illinois, and 19th Kentucky; 460 men of the 27th Indiana, 29th Wisconsin, 19th Kentucky, 130th Illinois, 83rd Ohio, 24th Iowa, 23rd Wisconsin, 77th Illinois, and 16th Ohio, commanded by Captain George W. Stein of the latter regiment.

Bailey was also greatly assisted by a detail from the navy, under Lieutenant Amos R. Langthorne, commanding the *Mound City*. Besides these officers, all of whom rendered service the most laborious and the most valuable, Bailey acknowledges his indebtedness to Brigadier-General Dwight, Colonel James Grant Wilson, and Lieutenant Charles S. Sargent of Banks's staff; to Major W. H. Sentell, 160th New York, provost-marshal; Lieutenant John J. Williamson, ordnance officer of the Nineteenth Corps; and Lieutenant Sydney Smith Fairchild, 161st New York.

All this time the army lying about Alexandria, to secure the safety of the navy, was itself virtually invested by the small but active forces under Taylor, who now found himself, not only foot loose, but once more able to use for his supplies the channel of the upper Red River, whence he had caused the obstructions to be removed as soon as the withdrawal of Banks relieved all fears of invasion, and turned the thoughts of the Confederate chiefs to dreams of conquest.

On the 31st of March Grant had peremptorily ordered the evacuation of the coast of Texas save only the position held at the mouth of the Rio Grande, and Banks, as soon as he received this order, had ordered McClernand to join him with the bulk of his troops, consisting of the First and Second divisions of the Thirteenth Corps. McClernand, with Lawler's brigade of the former, arrived at Alexandria on the 29th of April; Warren, with the rest of his division, was on his way up the Red River, when he found himself cut off near Marksville. Then he seized Fort De Russy and held it until the campaign ended.

Brisk skirmishing went on from day to day between the outposts and advanced guards, yet Banks, though he had five men to one of Taylor's,[1] held fast by his earthworks without making any real effort to crush or to drive off his adversary, while on their part the Confederates refrained from any serious attempt to interrupt the navigation of the lower Red River until the evening of the 3rd of May, when near David's Ferry Major attacked and, after a sharp fight, took the transport *City Belle*, which he caught coming up the river with 425 officers and men of the 120th Ohio. Many were killed or wounded, and many others taken prisoner, a few escaping through the forest. Major then sunk the steamboat across the channel and thus closed it. Early on the morning of the 5th of May Major, with Hardeman's and Lane's cavalry brigades and West's battery, met just above Fort De Russy the gunboats *Signal* and *Covington*, and the transport steamer *Warner*, and after a short and hard fight disabled all three of the boats. The *Covington* was set on fire by her commander and destroyed, but the *Signal* and *Warner* fell into the hands of the Confederates with many of the officers and men of the three boats, and of a detachment of about 250 men of the 56th Ohio, on the *Warner*. These captured steamers, also, were sunk across the channel.

On the 2nd of May, Franklin's wound compelling him to go to New Orleans and presently to the North, Banks assigned Emory to the command of the Nineteenth Army Corps. This brought McMillan to the head of the First division and gave his brigade to Beal. Captain Frederic Speed was announced as Assistant Adjutant-General of the Corps. A few days later, in consequence of McClernand's illness, Lawler was given the command of the Thirteenth Corps.

---

1. Banks's return for April 30th shows 33,502 officers and men for duty. May 10th, Taylor says: "To keep this up with my little force of scarce 6,000 men, I am compelled to 'eke out the lion's skin with the fox's hide.'" (*Official Records*, vol. xxxiv., part I., p. 590.) He does not count his cavalry.

CHAPTER 29

Last Days in Louisiana

On the 13th of May Banks marched from Alexandria on Simmesport, Lawler leading the infantry column, Emory next, and A. J. Smith's divisions of the Sixteenth and Seventeenth Corps bringing up the rear. As far as Fort De Russy the march followed the bank of the river, with the object of covering the withdrawal of the fleet of gunboats and transports against any possible molestation. Steele's cavalry division hung upon and harassed the rear, Polignac, Major, and Bagby hovered in front and on the flanks, while Harrison followed on the north bank of the Red River, but no serious attempt was made to obstruct the movement. On the afternoon of the 15th the Confederates were seen in force in front of the town of Marksville, but were soon driven off and retired rapidly through the town.

On the morning of the 16th of May an event took place, described by all who saw it as the finest military spectacle they ever witnessed. On the wide and rolling prairie of Avoyelles, otherwise known as the Plains of Mansura, the Confederates stood for the last time across the line of march of the retreating army. As battery after battery went into action and the cavalry skirmishers became briskly engaged, it seemed as if a pitched battle were imminent. The infantry rapidly formed line of battle, Mower on the right, Kilby Smith next, Emory in the centre, Lawler on the left, the main body of Arnold's cavalry in column on the flank. Save where here and there the light smoke from the artillery hindered the view, the whole lines of both armies were in plain sight of every man in either, but the disparity in numbers was too great to justify Taylor in making more than a handsome show of resistance on a field like this, where defeat was certain, and destruction must have followed close upon defeat; and so when our lines were advanced he prudently withdrew. Banks's losses were small, but Lieutenant Haskin's horse-battery F, 1st U. S., being unavoidably exposed in spite of its skilful handling, to a hot enfilade fire of the Confederate artillery, to cover their flank movement in retreat, suffered rather severely.

In the afternoon the troops halted for a while on the banks of a little stream to enjoy the first fresh, clear water they had so much as seen for many weeks. At the sight the men broke into cheers, and almost with one accord rushed eagerly to the banks of the rivulet. That night the army bivouacked eight miles from the Atchafalaya, and early the next morning, the 17th of May, marched down to the river at Simmesport, where the transports and the gunboats, having arrived two days earlier, lay waiting. Near Moreauville on the 17th the rear-guard of cavalry was sharply attacked by Wharton; at the same time Debray, lying in ambush with two regiments and a battery, opened fire on the flank of the moving column. While this was going on the two other regiments of Debray made a dash on the wagon-train near the crossing of Yellow Bayou, and threw it into some momentary confusion. Neither of these attacks were serious, and all were easily thrown off.

The next day, the 18th, A. J. Smith's command was in position near Yellow Bayou to cover the crossing of the Atchafalaya, and he was himself at the landing at Simmesport, in the act of completing his arrangements for crossing, when Taylor suddenly attacked with his whole force. Mower, who commanded in Smith's absence, advanced his lines as soon as he found his skirmishers coming in, and thus brought on one of the sharpest engagements of the campaign. With equal judgment, skill, and daring, Mower finally drove the Confederates off the field in confusion and with heavy loss, and so brought to a brilliant close the part borne by the gallant soldiers of the Army of the Tennessee in their trying service in Louisiana. Mower's loss was 38 killed, 226 wounded, and 3 missing, in all 267. Taylor reports his loss as about 500, including 30 killed, 50 severely wounded, and about 100 prisoners from Polignac's division. The Confederate returns account for 452 killed and wounded.

At Simmesport the skill and readiness of Bailey were once more put to good use in improvising a bridge of steamboats across the

Atchafalaya. In his report, Banks speaks of this as the first attempt of the kind, probably forgetting, since it did not fall under his personal observation, that when the army moved on Port Hudson the year before, the last of the troops and trains crossed the river at the same place in substantially the same way. However, the Atchafalaya was then low: it was now swollen to a width of six hundred or seven hundred yards by the back water from the Mississippi, and thus the floating bridge, which the year before was made by lashing together not more than nine boats, with their gangways in line, connected by means of the gangplanks and rough boards, now required twenty-two boats to close the gap. Over this bridge, on the 19th of May, the troops took up their march in retreat, and so brought the disastrous campaign of the Red River to an end just a year after they had begun, in the same way and on the same spot, the triumphant campaign of Port Hudson.

On the 20th A. J. Smith crossed, the bridge was broken up, and in the evening the whole army marched for the Mississippi. On the 21st, at Red River landing, the Nineteenth Corps bade farewell to its brave comrades of the Sixteenth and Seventeenth.

A. J. Smith landed at Vicksburg on the 23rd of May too late for the part assigned him in the spring campaign of Sherman's army, and the operations on the Mississippi being now reduced to the defensive, he remained on the banks of the river until called on to repulse Price's invasion of Missouri. Then, having handsomely performed his share of this service, he joined Thomas just in time to take part in the decisive battle of Nashville.

At Simmesport Banks was met by Canby, who on the 11th of May, at Cairo or on the way thence to Memphis, had assumed command of the new-made Military Division of West Mississippi, in virtue of orders from Washington, dated the 7th. The President still refused to yield to Grant's repeated requests that Banks might be altogether relieved from his command, nor did Grant longer persist in this; accordingly Banks remained the titular commander of the Department of the Gulf, with a junior officer present as his immediate superior and his next subordinate in actual command of his troops.

The Thirteenth and Nineteenth Corps, the cavalry, and the trains continued the march, under Emory, and on the 22nd of May went into camp at Morganza.

From the Arkansas to the Gulf, from the Atchafalaya to the Rio Grande there was no longer a Union soldier, save the insignificant garrison kept at Brownsville to preserve the semblance of that foothold in Texas for the sake of which so much blood and treasure had been spilled into this sink of shame.

When Steele's retreat to Little Rock had put an end to all hopes of a successful pursuit, Kirby Smith faced about and set Walker in rapid motion toward Alexandria with Churchill closely following. A day or two after Banks had left the place Walker arrived at Alexandria, too late to do anything more in Louisiana.

Taylor quarrelled bitterly with Kirby Smith, who ended by ordering him to turn over his command to Walker. Leaving a small force to hold the country and to observe and annoy the Union army of occupation in Louisiana, Kirby Smith then gathered his forces, and passing by Steele's right flank, invaded Missouri.

After arriving at Morganza, Emory, by Canby's orders, put his command in good condition for defence or for a movement in any direction by sending to other stations all the troops except the Nineteenth Corps and the First division, Lawler's, of the Thirteenth Corps, as well as all the extra animals, wagons, and baggage of the army. For the sedentary defensive, the position at Morganza had many advantages, but except that good water for all purposes was to be had in plenty for the trouble of crossing the levee, the situation was perhaps the most unfortunate in which the corps was ever encamped. The heat was oppressive and daily growing more unbearable. The rude shelters of bushes and leaves, cut fresh from the neighbouring thicket and often renewed, gave little protection; the levee and the dense undergrowth kept off the breeze; and such was the state of the soil that when it was not a cloud of light and suffocating dust, it was a sea of fat black mud. The sickly season was close at hand, the field and general hospitals were filled, and the deaths were many. The mosquitoes were at their worst; but worse than all were the six weeks of absolute idleness, broken only by an occasional alarm or two, such as led to the brief expedition of Grover's division to Tunica and Natchez.

At first Canby intended to use the Nineteenth Corps as a sort of marine patrol or coast-guard, with its trains and artillery and cavalry reduced to the lowest point, and the main body of the infantry kept always ready to embark on a fleet of transports specially assigned for the service and to go quickly to any point up or down the Mississippi or the adjacent waters that might be menaced or attacked by the enemy. The orders for the organization and equipment of the corps in this manner form a model of forethought and of minute attention to detail, yet as events turned out, they were never put in practice.

Toward the end of June the corps underwent at the hands of Canby the last of its many reorganizations.[1] The First and Second divisions were left substantially as they had been during the campaign just ended, but the Thirteenth Corps being broken up,[2] seventeen of its best regiments were taken to form for the Nineteenth Corps a new Third division, under Lawler. Emory, who was suffering from the effects of the climate and the hardships of the campaign, had just applied for leave of absence, supposing that all idea of a movement during the summer was at an end, and Canby, having granted this, assigned Reynolds to command the corps, to which, in truth, his rank and record entitled him, and gave the First division, Emory's own, to Roberts, a total stranger. Upon this, and learning of the movement about to be made, Emory at once threw up his leave of absence, and Reynolds, noting with the eye of a soldier the deep and widespread disappointment among the officers and men of the corps, magnanimously persuaded Canby to leave the command of the Nineteenth Army Corps, for the time being, to Emory, while Reynolds himself commanded the forces at Morganza. The brigades of the First division were commanded by Beal, McMillan, and Currie. Grover kept the Second division with Birge, Molineux, and Sharpe as brigade commanders, and afterward a fourth brigade was added, made up of four regiments from the disbanded Thirteenth Corps, under Colonel David Shunk of the 8th Indiana, and comprising, in addition to his own regiment, the 24th and 28th Iowa, and the 18th Indiana. At this later period also the 1st Louisiana was taken from Molineux's brigade to remain in the Gulf, and its place was filled by the 11th Indiana and the 22nd Iowa. Lawler's new Third division had Lee, Cameron, and Colonel F. W. Moore of the 83rd

---

1. Begun about June 16th. The final orders are dated June 27th.
2. By orders from Washington, issued at Canby's request, June 11th.

Ohio for brigade commanders. This was a splendid division, on both sides congenial; unfortunately it was not destined to see service with the corps.

Three great reviews broke the torrid monotony of Morganza. On the 11th of June Emory reviewed the corps in a tropical torrent, which suddenly descending drenched every man to the skin and reduced the field music to discord, without interrupting the ceremony. On the 14th the troops again passed in review before Sickles, who had been sent to Louisiana on a tour of inspection, and finally on the 25th Reynolds reviewed the forces at Morganza on taking the command.

Grant's orders to Canby were the same as those he had given to Banks, to go against Mobile.

This was indeed an integral and important, though strictly subordinate, part of the comprehensive plan adopted by the lieutenant-general for the spring campaign. Besides distracting the attention of the Confederates, and either drawing off a large part of their forces from Sherman's front or else causing them to give up Mobile without a struggle, the control of the Alabama River would give Sherman a secure base of supplies and a safe line of retreat in any contingency, while the occupation of a line from Atlanta to Mobile would, as Grant remarked, "once more split the Confederacy in twain."

But while in Louisiana the troops stood still, awaiting the full completion of Canby's exhaustive preparations, elsewhere events were marching with great rapidity. On the 3rd of June Grant's campaign from the Rappahannock to the James came to an end in the bloody repulse of Cold Harbor, with the loss of 12,737 officers and men. On the 14th he crossed the James and sat down before Petersburg. In the six weeks that had passed since the Army of the Potomac made its way into the Wilderness, Grant had lost from the ranks of the two armies of the Potomac and the James nearly as many men as Lee had in the Army of Northern Virginia.[3]

While he was himself directing the movement of Meade and

---

[3]. From the 5th of May to the 15th of June Meade's losses were 51,908, and Butler's 9,234, together 61,142. The best estimates give 61,000 to 64,000 as Lee's strength at the Wilderness, or 78,400 from the Rappahannock to the James,—*Century War Book*, vol. iv., pp. 182-187.

Butler against Richmond and Petersburg, Grant ordered Hunter, who commanded in the Shenandoah Valley, to march by Charlottesville on Lynchburg, and sent Sheridan, with the cavalry on a great raid to Charlottesville to meet Hunter; but Lee sent Early to intercept the movement, and Early, moving with the speed and promptness to which Jackson's old corps was well used, got to Lynchburg in time to head Hunter off. Then Hunter, rightly deeming his position precarious, instead of retreating down the valley, made his escape across the mountains into West Virginia. This left the gates of the great valley thoroughfare wide open for Early, who, instantly marching north, once more invaded Maryland, harried Pennsylvania, and menaced Washington.

It was at this crisis, when nothing was being accomplished in Louisiana and everything was happening in Virginia, that Grant ordered Canby to put off his designs on Mobile and to send the Nineteenth Corps with all speed to Hampton Roads.[4] Canby understood this to mean the First and Second divisions, and placed Emory in command of this detachment. On the 30th of June the two divisions began moving down the river to Algiers, and on the 3rd of July the advance steamed out of the river into the Gulf of Mexico with sealed orders. When the steamer *Crescent*, which led the way, carrying the 153rd New York and four companies of the 114th, had dropped her pilot outside of the passes, Davis broke the seal and for the first time learned his destination. Within a few days the remainder of the First division followed, without Roberts, Emory accompanied by the headquarters of the expedition going on the *Mississippi* on the 5th of July, with the 30th Massachusetts, the 90th New York, and the 116th New York, but transferring himself at the Southwest Pass to the *Creole*, in his impatience at finding the *Mississippi* aground and his anxiety to come up with the advance of his troops. The *Crescent* was the first to arrive before Fortress Monroe. The last regiment of the Third brigade sailed on the 11th. Grover's division began its embarkation about the 10th and finished about the 20th.

---

4. The first suggestion seems to have come from Butler to Stanton, May 29th, Weitzel concurring. Grant disapproved this in a telegram dated 3 p.m., June 3rd: the second assault had been made that morning. The movement across the James for the surprise and seizure of Petersburg came to a stand-still on the 18th. On the 23rd Grant made the request and the orders were issued the next day.

In this movement some of the best regiments of the corps were left behind, as well as all the cavalry and the whole of the magnificent park of field artillery. Among the troops thus cut off were the 110th New York, the 161st New York, the 7th Vermont, the 6th Michigan, the 4th Wisconsin, the 1st Indiana Heavy Artillery, the 1st Louisiana, and the 2nd Louisiana Mounted Infantry. Reynolds with the corps headquarters and the new Third division remained in Louisiana. Since this came from the old Thirteenth Corps, was afterward incorporated in the new Thirteenth Corps, formed for the siege of Mobile, never saw service in the Nineteenth Corps and nominally belonged to it but a few days, and since the detachment now sent north was presently constituted the Nineteenth Corps, the title of the corps will hereafter be used in this narrative when speaking of the services of the First and Second divisions.

On the 14th of June Major William H. Sentell, of the 160th New York, was detailed by Emory as acting assistant inspector-general of the corps, and Captain Henry C. Inwood, of the 165th New York,[5] as provost marshal.

To regret leaving the lowlands of Louisiana at the sickly season, the poisonous swamps, the filthy water, the overpowering heat, and the intolerable mosquitoes, was impossible; yet there can have been no man in all that host that did not feel, as the light, cool breezes of the Gulf fanned his brow, a swelling of the heart and a tightness of the throat at the thought of all that he had seen and suffered, and the remembrance of the many thousands of his less fortunate comrades who had succumbed to the dangers and trials on which he himself was now turning his back for the last time.

---

5. In the official records wrongly printed as the 160th.

Chapter 30

On the Potomac

Grant had meant to send the troops to join the Army of the James under Butler at Bermuda Hundred, but already the dust of Early's columns was in sight from the hills behind Washington, and the capital, though fully fortified, being practically without defenders, until the Sixth Corps should come to the rescue, in the stress of the moment the detachments of the Nineteenth Corps were hurried up the Potomac as fast as the transports entered the roads. It was noon on the 11th when Davis landed the fourteen companies from the *Crescent* at the wharves of Washington, where he found orders to occupy and hold Fort Saratoga.[1]

At the hour when Davis was disembarking at the southern end of Sixth Street wharf, Early's headquarters were at Silver Spring, barely five miles away to the northward, and his skirmishers were drawing within range of the guns of Fort Stevens. Behind the defences of Washington there were but twenty thousand soldiers of all arms. Of these less than half formed the garrison of the works, and even of this fraction nearly all were raw, undisciplined, uninstructed, and lacking the simplest knowledge of the ground they were to defend. But five days before this, Grant had taken Ricketts from the lines of the Sixth Corps before Petersburg, and sent him by water to Baltimore, whence his superb veterans were carried by rail to the Monocacy just in time to enable Wallace, with a chance medley of garrison and emergency men, to face Early on the 9th, and compel him to lose a day in crossing. Then, at last, made quite certain of Early's true position and plans, Grant hurried the rest of the Sixth Corps to the

---

1. About three miles N.-N.-E. from the Capitol, overlooking the Baltimore road and railway.

relief of Washington, and thus the steamboat bearing the advance of Wright's men touched the wharf about two hours after the *Crescent* had made fast. The guns of Fort Stevens were already heard shelling the approaches, and thither Wright was at once directed, but in the great heat and dust Early had pressed on so fast that his men arrived before the works parched with thirst and panting with exhaustion. Moreover, evening came before the rear of his column had closed up on the front, and during these critical hours Wright's strong divisions of the veterans of the Army of the Potomac lined the works and stood stiffly across the path, while in supporting distance to the eastward was the little handful from the Gulf. Early, who had seen something of this and imagined more, waited, and so his opportunity, great or little, went. On the afternoon of the next day, the 12th of July, Early still not attacking, Wright sent out a brigade and roughly pushed back the Confederate advance. Then Early, realizing that he had not an hour to lose in extricating his command from its false position, fell back at night on Rockville.

On the 13th of July the *Clinton* arrived at Washington with the 29th Maine and part of the 13th Maine, the *St. Mary* with the 8th Vermont, the *Corinthian* with the remaining six companies of the 114th New York, the *Mississippi* with the 90th and 116th New York and the 30th Massachusetts, the *Creole* with the 47th Pennsylvania. As the detachments landed they were hurried, in most instances by long and needless circuits to Tennallytown, where they found themselves at night without supplies or wagons, without orders, and without much organization.

Now that the enemy had gone and there were enough troops in Washington, the capital was once more a wild confusion of commands and commanders, such as seems to have prevailed at every important crisis during the war. Out of this Grant brought order by assigning Wright to conduct the pursuit of Early. When, therefore, on the morning of the 13th, Wright found Early gone from his front, he marched after him with the Sixth Corps, and ordered the detachment of the Nineteenth Corps to follow. Grant wished Wright to push on to Edwards Ferry to cut off Early's retreat across the Potomac. At nightfall Wright was at Offutt's Cross-Roads, with Russell and Getty of the Sixth corps, the handful of the Nineteenth Corps, and the cavalry.

About 3,600 men of Emory's division had landed at Washington during the 12th and 13th of July, increasing the effective force of the Nineteenth Corps to about 4,200, most of whom spent the night in following the windings of the road that marks the long outline of the northern fortifications. On the morning of the 14th, the roll-call accounted for 192 officers and 2,987 men of the corps, representing ten regiments, in the bivouacs that lay loosely scattered about Tennallytown. On the 14th these detachments marched ten miles and encamped beyond Offutt's Cross-Roads, where they were joined by Battery L of the 1st Ohio, temporarily lent to the division from the artillery reserve of the defences of Washington. Emory himself arrived during the day and assumed command of the division, and Dwight, relieved from duty as Banks's chief of staff, came in the evening to rejoin the 1st brigade. Gilmore, who found himself in Washington without assignment, had been given command of the Nineteenth Corps, but happening to sprain his foot badly he was obliged to go off duty after having held the assignment nominally for less than a day. Thereupon Emory once more took command of the corps, and the First division fell to Dwight.

Moving by the river road, Wright, with Getty's division, was at Poolesville on the night of the 14th, with the last of the Nineteenth Corps eleven miles in the rear. But Early had already made good his escape, having crossed the Potomac that morning at White's Ford, with all his trains and captures intact, while Wright was still south of Seneca Creek.

The next day Emory closed up on Getty at Poolesville, and Halleck began sending the rest of the Sixth Corps there to join Wright.

In the Union army the impression now prevailed that Early, having accomplished the main object of his diversion, would, as usual, hasten to rejoin Lee at Richmond. Wright, therefore, got ready to go back to Washington, but Early was in fact at Leesburg, and word came that Hunter, whose forces were beginning to arrive at Harper's Ferry, after their long and wide excursion over the Alleghenies and through West Virginia, had sent Sullivan's division across the Potomac at Berlin to Hillsborough, where it threatened Early's flank and rear while exposing its own. Therefore Wright felt obliged to cross to the support of Hunter, and on the morning of the 16th of July the Sixth Corps, followed by Emory's detachment of the Nineteenth, waded the Potomac at White's Ford and encamped at Clark's Gap, three miles beyond Leesburg. But Early, by turns bold and wary, slipped away between Wright and Hunter, marched through Snicker's Gap, and put the Shenandoah between him and his enemies. Caution had been enjoined on the pursuit, and the 17th was spend in closing up and reconnoitring. On the 18th the combined forces of Wright and Hunter marched through Snicker's Gap, and in the afternoon Crook, who, having brought up his own division, found himself in command of Hunter's troops, sent Thoburn across the Shenandoah below Snicker's Ferry to seize and hold the ferry for the passage of the army; but when Thoburn had gained the north bank Early fell upon him with three divisions and drove him back across the river with heavy loss. Instead of risking anything more in the attempt to force the crossing in the face of Early's whole force in position, Wright was mediating a turning movement by way of Keyes's Gap, but Duffié, after riding hard through Ashby's Gap and crossing the Shenandoah at Berry's Ferry, likewise came to grief on the north bank, and so the day of the 19th of July was lost.

Meanwhile Hunter, having seen nearly all the rest of his army arrive at Harper's Ferry, sent a brigade and a half under Hayes to march straight up the Shenandoah to Snicker's Ferry, while Averell with a mixed force of cavalry and infantry was sweeping down from Martinsburg on Winchester. Thus menaced in front, flank, and rear, Early, on the night of the 19th of July, retreated on Strasburg.

The next morning Wright crossed the Shenandoah, meaning to move toward Winchester, but when he learned where Early had gone he recrossed the river in the evening, marched by night to Leesburg, and encamped on Goose Creek, presently crossing to the south bank. On the morning of the 22nd Wright marched on Washington, the Sixth Corps leading, followed by the Nineteenth. On the afternoon of the 23rd Emory crossed the chain bridge and went into bivouac on the high ground overlooking the Potomac near Battery Vermont. So ended the "Snicker's Gap war."

During this expedition Kenly's brigade of the Eighth Corps served with the Nineteenth.

As soon as Early's withdrawal from Maryland had quieted all

apprehensions for the safety of Washington, the orders that had met the advance of the Nineteenth Corps at Hampton Roads were recalled, and, reverting to his original intention, Grant sent the detachments of the corps as they arrived up the James River to Bermuda Hundred to join the right wing of his armies under Butler. Indeed, at the moment of its arrival at Poolesville, the First division had been ordered to take the same destination, but this the movements of the contending armies prevented. The first of the troops to land at Bermuda Hundred was the 15th Maine on the 17th of July. It was at once sent to the right of the lines before Petersburg, and within the next ten days there were assembled there parts of four brigades—McMillan's and Currie's of the First division, and Birge's and Molineux's of Grover's. Part of Currie's brigade was engaged, under Hancock, in the affair at Deep Bottom on the north bank of the James on the 25th of July, losing eighteen killed and wounded and twenty-four prisoners. The work and duty in the trenches and on the skirmishing line were hard and constant, reminding the men of their days and nights before Port Hudson, but this was not to last long, and the loss was light.[2]

On the 20th of July at Carter's Farm, three miles north of Winchester, Averell, who was following Early, met and routed Ramseur, who had been sent back to check the pursuit. Early continued his retreat to Strasburg on the 22nd, but when the next day he learned that Wright was gone, he turned back to punish the weak force under Hunter, and on the 24th overwhelmed Crook at Kernstown. Crook retreated through Martinsburg into Maryland, and marching by Williamsport and Boonsborough, took post at Sharpsburg, while Averell stayed at Hagerstown to watch the upper fords of the Potomac.

To break up the Baltimore and Ohio railway and to ravage the

---

2. In Major William F. Tiemann's truly admirable *History of the 159th New York*, he says: "July 26th we were camped near Major-General Birney's headquarters, not far from Hatcher's house between batteries 'five' and 'six,' one of which enjoyed the euphonious title of 'Fort Slaughter.' . . . The works were built more strongly and with more art than at Port Hudson, but were not nearly as strong in reality, as Port Hudson was fortified naturally and the obstructions were much harder to overcome." (P. 87.) I think this book a model of everything that a regimental history ought to be; above all, for the rare gifts of modesty and accuracy.

borders of Pennsylvania were favourite ideas with Early. He now entered with zest on the unopposed gratification of both desires, and while he himself bestrode the railway at Martinsburg with his army engaged in its destruction, he sent McCausland with his own brigade of cavalry and Bradley Johnson's on the famous marauding expedition that culminated in the wanton burning of Chambersburg in default of an impossible ransom, and at last resulted in the flight of McCausland's whole force, with Averell at his heels, and its ultimate destruction or dispersion by Averell, after a long chase, at Moorefield far up the south branch of the Potomac.

When on the 23rd of July he saw Wright back at Washington and Early at Strasburg in retreat, as was imagined, up the valley, Grant partly changed his mind about recalling the troops he had spared for the defence of Washington, and determining to content himself with Wright's corps, directed Emory to stay where he was. Emory now had 253 officers and 5,320 men for duty.

As one turn of the wheel had given the Nineteenth Corps to Butler, restoring to his command some of the regiments that had gone with him to the capture of New Orleans, so the next turn was to bring the corps under Augur, who since leaving Louisiana had been in command of the department of Washington. So at least run the orders of the 23rd of July, yet hardly had Emory reported his division to Augur, when the whole arrangement was suddenly broken up, and the army that had just marched back to Washington with Wright was once more hurried off to meet what was supposed to be a fresh invasion by Early. In fact Early was quietly reposing at Bunker Hill, where he easily commanded the approaches and debouches of the Shenandoah valley, the fords of the Potomac, from Harper's Ferry to Williamsport, and the whole line of the railway across the great bend of the Potomac.

By this time Grant had found out that it often took twenty-four hours to communicate with Washington by telegraph, and that it was consequently impossible to control from the James the movements of his forces on the upper Potomac. On his suggesting this, the government confided to Halleck the direction of Wright's operations against Early. The Sixth Corps marched from Tennallytown on the morning of the 26th of July, and immediately afterwards the Nineteenth Corps broke up its camp near the chain bridge and followed the Sixth. The line of march followed the road to Rockville, where Wright divided the column, sending a detachment to the left by way of Poolesville, while the main body pursued the direct road towards Frederick. Emory encamped that night on the Frederick road, four miles north of Rockville, after a march of nineteen miles. The next day, the 27th of July, Emory, leading the column, marched at three in the morning, moved fifteen miles, and encamped beyond Hyattstown. On the 28th Emory took the road at five, marched to Monocacy Junction, where the Sixth Corps crossed the Monocacy, then filed to the right, and crossed at the upper ford, and passing through Frederick went into bivouac four miles beyond. The distance made was thirteen miles. On the 29th, an intensely hot day, Emory marched at eight, following the Sixth Corps, crossed the Potomac at Harper's Ferry, marched nineteen miles, and went into bivouac at Halltown. Here Wright was joined by Crook, who came from Sharpsburg by way of Shepherdstown.

It was on the 30th of July that McCausland burned Chambersburg. In the confusion caused by his rapid movements, Halleck imagined that Early's whole force was in Pennsylvania. Therefore he ordered Wright back into Maryland, first to Frederick and them to Emmettsburg, to hold the passes of the South Mountain against the supposed invader. About noon Wright faced about, taking Crook with him, and recrossed the Potomac. Toward evening Crook and Wright covered the passes, while Emory crossed the Catoctin and at one in the morning of the 31st halted near Jefferson after a hard day's march of thirteen miles, during which the men and animals of all the corps suffered terribly from the heat and dust, added to the accumulated fatigue they had already undergone from a succession of long days and short nights. Reveille was sounded at five o'clock, and at six the march was resumed. Emory passed through Frederick, moved about two miles on the Emmettsburg road and went into bivouac, having made thirteen miles during the day. The army was now concentrated at Frederick, holding the line of the Monocacy and observing the passes of the South Mountain. Fortunately for the men and horses, Halleck now learned from Couch, who commanded in Pennsylvania, with rather less than a handful of troops, the exact dimensions of McCausland's raid. Accordingly Wright's troops were allowed to rest where they were.

Grant ordered up a division of cavalry from the Army of the Potomac, and on the 4th of August set out in person for Frederick, avoiding Washington, to see for himself just what the situation was, and to make better arrangements for the future. On the 5th of August he joined Hunter on the Monocacy, and at once ordered him to take Wright, Emory, and Crook across the Potomac, to find the enemy, and to attack him.

Grover's division and the parts of Emory's that had been at Bermuda Hundred embarked on the James on the 31st of July, and passed up the Potomac to Washington, but too late to join Emory on the Monocacy. Thus, before beginning the new movement, Emory had of his own division 4,600 effective and eight regiments of Grover's, numbering 2,750. These, being part of four brigades, were temporarily organized into two, and as Grover himself had not yet joined, their command was given to Molineux.

About this time, Battery L, 1st Ohio, was relieved from duty with the Nineteenth Corps, and four other batteries joined it from the reserve park at Washington. Of these Taft's 5th New York was assigned to the First division, Bradbury's 1st Maine, an old friend, to the Second division, Lieutenant Chase's D, 1st Rhode Island and Miner's 17th Indiana to the Artillery Reserve, commanded at first by Captain Taft, afterward by Major Bradbury.

Crook led the way across the Potomac at Harper's Ferry on the evening of the 5th of August, Emory followed the next morning, and Ricketts with the Sixth Corps brought up the rear. Averell with the cavalry, as will be remembered, was still far away, engaged in the long chase after McCausland. Hunter took up his position covering Halltown and proceeded to strengthen it by entrenchments. Crook's left rested on the Shenandoah, Emory extended the line to the turnpike road, and Wright carried it to the Potomac.

On the very day Grant left City Point, Early marched north from Bunker Hill, meaning to cover McCausland's retreat and to destroy Hunter, and so, curiously enough, it happened that Early's whole army actually crossed the Potomac into Maryland at Martinsburg and Shepherdstown a few hours before Crook passed over the ford at Harper's Ferry into Virginia; and, still more curiously, while, ten days before, the groundless apprehension of another invasion by Early had thrown the North into a fever and the government into a fright, here was Early actually in Maryland on the battle-field of Antietam without producing so much as a sensation. As soon as Early got the first inkling of what was going on behind him, he tripped briskly back to Martinsburg, and finding Hunter at Halltown resumed his old position at Bunker Hill.

Grant had already proposed to unite in a single command the four distinct departments covering the theatre of war on the Shenandoah and on the upper Potomac; as the commander he had first suggested Franklin and afterward Meade. Now, since no action had followed either suggestion, he sent up Sheridan, meaning to place him in command of all the active forces of these four departments, for the purpose of overthrowing Early or expelling him from the Shenandoah. Upon learning this, Hunter, to remove the difficulty, asked to be relieved; and thus, on the 7th of August, Grant gained his wish, and an order was issued by the War Department, creating the Middle Military Division, to include Washington, Virginia, West Virginia, Maryland, Pennsylvania, and part of Ohio, and Sheridan was assigned to the command.

Amusing though it may have been to Early and his followers to note the panic and confusion into which McCausland's predatory riders once more threw the capital and the border States, this absurd freak produced far-reaching consequences that were not in the thoughts of any one on either side. Its first effect was to stop the withdrawal of the Sixth Corps, and to put Wright and Emory once more in march toward the Shenandoah. It determined Lee to keep Early in the valley, where his presence seemed so effective; and this shortly led to the concentration there, under a single commander, and that commander Sheridan, of the largest and best appointed Union army that had ever occupied that theatre of war, and thus at last in one short campaign worked the destruction of Early's army and the elimination of the valley as a feature in the war.

Upon the officers and men of the Nineteenth Corps the change from the enervating climate of Louisiana to the bracing air, the crystal waters, the rolling wheat fields, and the beautiful blue mountains of the Shenandoah acted like a tonic. Daily their spirits rose and their numbers for duty increased. The excellence of the roads and the openness of the country on either side enabled them to achieve long marches with ease and comfort. Nor were they slow in remarking that they had never had a commissary and quartermaster so good as Sheridan.

Chapter 31

In the Shenandoah

The fourth year of the war was now well advanced, and the very name of the Shenandoah valley had long since passed into a byword as the Valley of Humiliation, so often had those fair and fertile fields witnessed the rout of the national forces; so often had the armies of the Union marched proudly up the white and dusty turnpike, only to come flying back in disorder and disgrace. With the same rough humour of the soldier, half in grim jest, half in sad earnest, yet always with a grain of hard sense lying at the bottom, the Union veterans had re-named as *Harper's Weekly* the picturesque landscape that appeared to them so regularly; and Lee's annual invasion of the country beyond the Potomac had come to be known among them as the Summer Excursion and Picnic into Maryland.

To mete out the blame for this state of things; to apportion the precise share of the mortifying result due to each one of several contributing causes; to show how much should be ascribed to division and subdivision of councils; how much to the unfitness of commanders, too often disqualified alike by nature and training, for the leadership of men in emergencies, or even for their temporary profession, and in truth owing their commissions, in Halleck's phrase, to "reasons other than military;" and how much finally to a dense ignorance or a fine disregard of the very elements and first principles of the art of war; all this lies outside the scope of this history, curious, entertaining, and instructive though the inquiry would be. Certain it is that at no period was the problem at once comprehended and controlled until Grant took it in hand, and equally so that the work was never done until he confided it to Sheridan. To this, in fairness, must be added three considerations

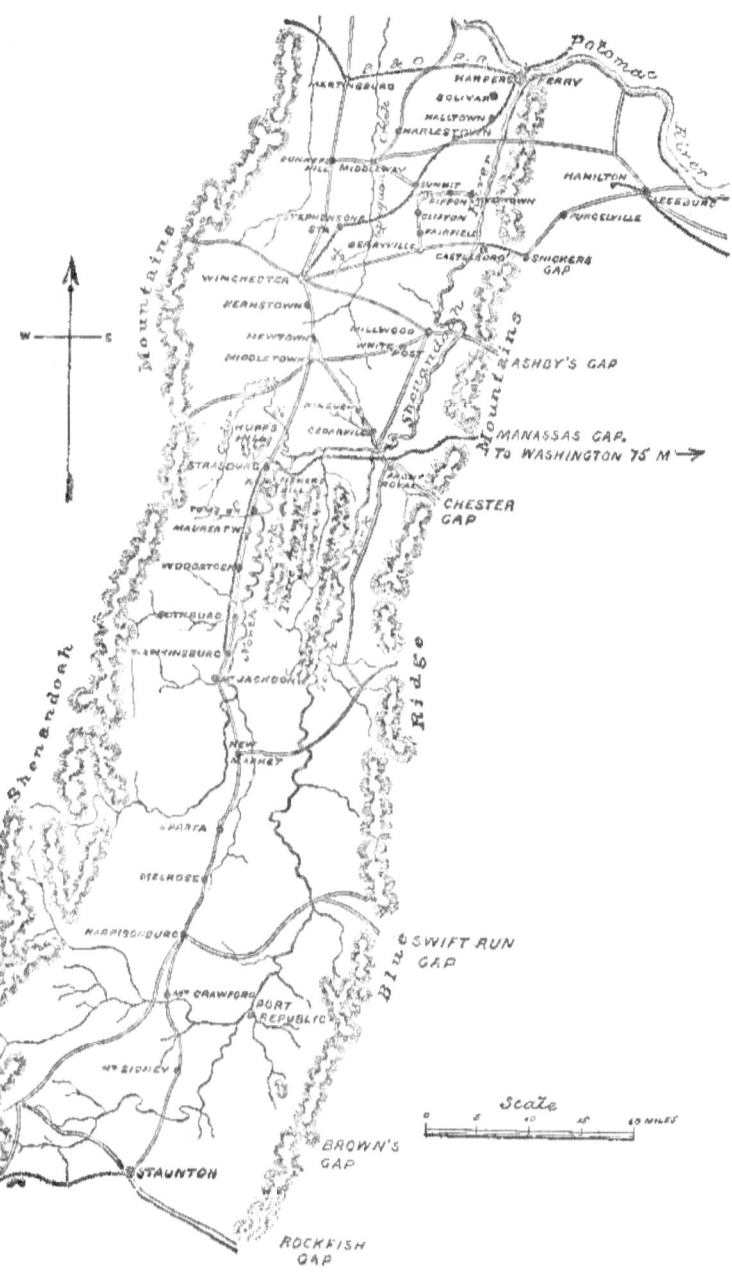

SHENANDOAH VALLEY CAMPAIGN.
FROM MAJOR W. F. TIEMANN'S "HISTORY OF THE 159TH NEW YORK."

of great moment. No commander had previously enjoyed the undivided confidence of the government as Grant did at this period; the relations between Grant and Sheridan were those of perfect trust and harmony; and the Army of the Shenandoah was for the first time made strong enough for its work. Moreover, though Early was a good and useful general, and was soon to prove himself the master of resources and resolution equal to the occasion, he was not Jackson; and even had he been, no second Jackson could ever have fallen heir to the prestige of the first.

The parallel ranges of the Blue Ridge, extending from the headwaters of the James to the Susquehanna in mid-course, presented peculiar strategic conditions of which the Confederates were as quick as the government of the United States was slow to take advantage. Rising in the southwest, the twin forks of the Shenandoah, wedged apart by the long and narrow range, or rather ranges, known as the Massanutten, unite near Front Royal, where the valley begins to widen to a plain, and pour their waters into the Potomac at Harper's Ferry. Of the two valleys thus formed, the easternmost, through which runs the South Fork, takes the name of Luray, or, in local usage, Page, from its chief county, while the more western and more important, in the lap of which lies the North Fork, preserves the name of Shenandoah, as well for the river as the county. Through this valley lies the course of the great macadamized highway that before the days of steam formed the chief avenue of communication between Pennsylvania and Virginia. Soon after the valley begins to widen, beyond Strasburg and Front Royal, the Opequon takes its rise in the western range, here known as Little North Mountain, and, flowing northeast, falls into the Potomac below Williamsport. The Cumberland valley continues the valley of Virginia into Pennsylvania, the two being separated by the Potomac, which in this part of its course is usually fordable at many points. Topography was by no means Grant's strong suit, yet he was not long in perceiving that the south-westerly trend of this great valley led and must always lead an invading column at every step farther away, not only from its base on the Potomac, but practically also from its objective at Richmond. Wherefore this zone was useless to the armies of the Union, while for the Confederates it had the triple advantage of a granary, an easy and secure way into Maryland and Pennsylvania, and on the flank toward Washington a mountain wall, cut by numerous gaps, of equal convenience in advance or retreat, besides being a constant menace to Washington as well as to the Union army operating between the Blue Ridge and the Potomac. Thus it was that the Confederate force was able to move speedily and unobserved to the north bank of the Potomac at Williamsport, and there, ninety miles north of Washington, equally distant from Baltimore and from Washington, and actually nearer to the Susquehanna than the capital is, held the whole country at its mercy until the Army of the Potomac could be hurried to the rescue.

Grant's first orders to Sheridan were twofold: he was to move south by the valley, no matter where Early might be, or what he might be doing, in full confidence that Early would surely be found in his front; and he was to devastate the valley so far as to destroy its future usefulness as a granary and a storehouse of the Confederate army of Northern Virginia.

Following the instructions turned over to him by Hunter, Sheridan moved out from Halltown on the 10th of August, and marching through Charlestown, took up a position threatening the crossing of the Opequon and Early's communications at Winchester. Crook, on the left, rested on Berryville, Emory held the centre, and Wright prolonged the line to Clifton. Torbert covered the right flank at Summit Point, which lies eleven miles east-northeast from Winchester, and the left, with the main body of the cavalry, nine miles south by east from Winchester, at White Post, where his presence strongly emphasized the menace to Early's rear. The position thus held presently became known as the Clifton-Berryville line. While worthless for defence, it had the double advantage of covering the short roads to Washington through Snicker's Gap and Ashby's Gap, and of elbowing Early out of his favourite position at Bunker Hill, at the same time that by throwing back the right flank toward Clifton, Sheridan's road to Charlestown and Harper's Ferry was made safe. Early quietly let go his hold on the Baltimore and Ohio railway, and, just as Grant had anticipated, hastened to place himself across Sheridan's path at Winchester.

On the morning of the 11th of August, Sheridan took ground to the left, meaning to seize and hold the fords of the Opequon, Wright at the turnpike road between Berryville and Winchester,

Emory farther up the creek at the Senseny road, and Crook on Emory's left, probably at the Millwood pike. The cavalry covered the right of the Sixth Corps, and on both flanks threatened Winchester. Early, who had moved on the previous day from Bunker Hill to a position covering Winchester from the south, was in the act of retiring on Strasburg when Torbert ran into his cavalry. Sharp skirmishing resulted without bringing on a general engagement. At night Early held and covered the valley turnpike between Newtown and Middletown, while Sheridan, who before crossing the Opequon had heard of Early's movement, and had simply continued his own march up the right or east bank, rested between the Millwood crossing of the Opequon and Stony Point on the road to Front Royal.

The melancholy failure attending the explosion of the mine before Petersburg and the continued reduction of Grant's forces, brought about by Early's diversions, coming on top of the losses since crossing the Rapidan, had brought affairs on the James to a dead-lock. While Grant in this situation was willing to spare the Sixth corps and the Nineteenth and even to strengthen them by two divisions of cavalry from the Army of the Potomac, Lee on his part not only gave up all present thought of recalling Early, as had been the custom in former years, but even sent Anderson with Kershaw's division of infantry, Fitzhugh Lee's division of cavalry, and Cutshaw's battalion of artillery, to strengthen Early, so as to enable him to hold his ground, and thus to cover the gathering of the crops in the valley, and perhaps to encourage still further detachments from the investing forces before Richmond and Petersburg. The first week of August found Anderson on the march and he was now moving down the valley. Therefore Early very properly drew back through Strasburg to wait for Anderson, and on the night of the 12th of August took up a strong position at Fisher's Hill. Its natural advantages he proceeded to increase by entrenchments.

Sheridan, following, encamped in the same order as before on the left bank of Cedar Creek. On the 13th Wright crossed Cedar Creek and occupied Hupp's Hill, and sending his skirmishers into Strasburg, discovered Early in position as described; but at nightfall Sheridan, who now had information that caused him to suspect Anderson's movement, drew back and set the cavalry to guard the

Front Royal road. Then Early advanced his outposts to Hupp's Hill, and so for the next three days both armies rested.

On the 14th of August, Sheridan received from Grant authentic, rather than exact, information of Anderson's movement, for this was supposed to include two infantry divisions, instead of one. Coupled with this was Grant's renewed order to be cautious.

With his quick eye for country, Sheridan soon saw that he had but one even tolerable position for defence, and that this was at Halltown. The Confederate defence, on the other hand, rested on Fisher's Hill, and between these two positions the wide plain lay like a chess-board between the players. And now began a series of moves, during which each side watched and waited for the adversary to weaken himself, or to make a mistake, or for some chance encounter to bring about an unlooked-for advantage. Finding his position at Cedar Creek, to use his own words, "a very bad one," Sheridan was about to retire to the extreme limit of the valley at the confluence of the Potomac and the Shenandoah; and this was but to be the beginning of a series of seesaw movements, in which, as often as Sheridan went back to Halltown, Early would advance to Bunker Hill. Early, having taken the offensive, was bound to keep it, or lose his venture. Now, at this time, Early's objective was the Baltimore and Ohio railway; but Sheridan's was Early. Thus, whenever he found Early at Bunker Hill, wreaking his pleasure on the railway and the canal, Sheridan had only to take a step forward to the Clifton-Berryville line in order to force Early to hasten back to Winchester, and to lay hold of the Opequon; and so this alternating play might have continued as long as the war lasted, if other causes and events had not intervened.

At eleven o'clock on the night of the 15th of August, Sheridan's retreat began, Emory moving to Winchester, where he went into bivouac at six o'clock on the morning of the 16th. At eight o'clock on the evening of the 16th, Wright and Crook followed, and on the 17th Early, who had now been joined by Anderson, marched in pursuit. The same evening Sheridan took up the Clifton-Berryville position in the old order; the cavalry, now strengthened by the arrival of Wilson's division, covering the rear and flanks. At Berryville, at midnight, Grover joined Emory, from Washington by Leesburg and Snicker's Gap, with the remainder of the Nineteenth

Corps from the James;[1] and since the receipt of these reinforcements formed Sheridan's only reason for staying at Berryville, on the 18th he fell back to Charlestown, holding the roads leading thence to Berryville and to Bunker Hill.

On the 19th and 20th of August, Sheridan stood still while Early occupied Bunker Hill and Winchester; but, on the 21st, Early from Bunker Hill and Anderson from Winchester moved together to the attack. Rodes and Ramseur had a sharp fight with Wright, which caused Sheridan to bring up Crook on the left and Emory on the right; but neither came into action, because Merritt and Wilson stood so stiffly that Anderson got no farther than Summit Point. During the night Sheridan fell back to Halltown.

In retreating from Cedar Creek Sheridan began to put in force Grant's new policy of making the valley useless to the Confederate armies by burning all the grain and carrying off all the animals above Winchester. "I have destroyed everything eatable," are Sheridan's words.

On the 25th of August, after three days spent in skirmishing, Early left Anderson to mask Halltown, and sent Fitzhugh Lee by Martinsburg to Williamsport, marching himself to Shepherdstown. A rough fight with Torbert's cavalry resulted near Kearneysville, in which Custer narrowly avoided the loss of his brigade by a rapid flight across the Potomac at Shepherdstown. Sheridan sent two divisions of cavalry under Averell and Wilson over the Potomac to watch the fords and to hold the gaps of the South Mountain. Thus when Fitzhugh Lee got to the Potomac, he found Averell waiting for him, and Anderson being pressed back by Crook on the 26th, Early fell back behind the Opequon to Bunker Hill and Stephenson's Depot. On the 28th of August Sheridan advanced to Charlestown, and waiting there five days while his cavalry was concentrating and feeling the enemy, he again moved forward to the Clifton-Berryville line on the 3rd of September, and encamped in the usual order.

Two marked features had now become regularly established: as often as the troops halted, no matter for how short a time, of their own accord they instantly set about protecting their front with

---

1. Grover's men made the hard march of 69 miles from Washington in three days; the last 33 miles in 13½ hours, actual time. See Major Tiemann's *History of the 159th New York*, pp. 91, 92.

the spade and the axe; and, secondly, the depots of the army were fixed behind the strong lines of Halltown with a sufficient force to guard them, and thence, as needed, supplies were sent forward to the troops in the field by strongly guarded trains, and these, as soon as unloaded, were returned to Halltown, thus reducing to a minimum the impedimenta of the army as well as the detachments usually demanded for their care. For the Nineteenth Corps, Currie's brigade of Dwight's division performed this service during the campaign.

The contingency for which Grant and Sheridan were waiting was now close at hand. Anderson had been nearly a month away from Lee, and meanwhile Grant had not only kept Lee on the watch on both banks of the James, as well as for Richmond as for Petersburg, but had taken a fast hold on the Weldon railway. Unable to shake off Grant's clutch either on the James or on the Shenandoah, Lee greatly needed Anderson back with him. Accordingly, on the very day when Sheridan went back to Berryville, Anderson, seeking the shortest way to Richmond, ran into Crook in the act of going into camp, and darkness shortly put an end to a sharp fight that might otherwise have proved a pitched battle. This brought Early in haste from Stephenson's to Anderson's help, but when the next day Early saw how strongly posted Sheridan was, he fell back across the Opequon to cover Winchester, and finally, on the 14th of September, sent off Anderson by Front Royal and Chester Gap, but this time without Fitzhugh Lee.

The interval was occupied in continual skirmishes and reconnoissances. Meanwhile Crook changed over from the left flank to the right at Summit Point, the cavalry covering the front and flanks from Snicker's Gap by way of Smithfield and Martinsburg to the Potomac. On the 16th of September, Grant, pressed by the government in behalf of the business interests disturbed by the enemy's control of the railway and the canal, went to Charlestown to confer with Sheridan. In the breast-pocket of his coat Grant carried a complete plan of the campaign he meant Sheridan to carry out; but when, having asked Sheridan if he could be ready to move on Tuesday, Sheridan promptly answered he should be ready whenever the General should say "Go in"—at daylight on Monday, if necessary,—so delighted was Grant that he said not a word about the plan, but contented himself with echoing the words, "Go in!"

CHAPTER 32

The Opequon[1]

Grant's approval of Sheridan's attack was founded on the withdrawal of Kershaw; but on the 18th of September, just as Sheridan was about to move on Newtown, meaning to offer Early the choice of being turned out of Winchester, or being overwhelmed if he should stay, news came from Averell that he had been driven out of Martinsburg by two divisions of infantry. These were the divisions of Rodes and Gordon, with which, enticed at last into a grave error by the temptation of hearing that the railway was being repaired, Early had marched on the 17th to Bunker Hill and Martinsburg. When Sheridan heard of this, and perceived that Early's forces, already diminished, were strung along all the way from Winchester to Martinsburg, he stopped the execution of the orders he had already issued for the movement at four o'clock in the afternoon of that day, the 18th of September, and replaced them by fresh arrangements which led to the battle of the Opequon on the 19th. Since last moving to the Clifton-Berryville line, Sheridan had used his cavalry to preserve in his front an open space fully six miles in depth, extending to the banks of the Opequon, meaning not only to have the first tidings of any offensive movement by the enemy, but also that when himself ready to move he might be able to take the enemy by surprise.

On the evening of the 18th of September, part of Early's cavalry was at Martinsburg, Gordon occupied Bunker Hill, Wharton was at Stephenson's, with Rodes closing back on him, while Ramseur alone covered Winchester in the path of Sheridan's advance. Sheridan naturally supposed that in a quick movement he would have two divisions to deal with after crossing the Opequon.

---
1. Also spelled "Opequan." Pronounced O-peck'-an.

At two o'clock on the morning of Monday, the 19th of September, on the very day when Sheridan had told Grant he would be ready to move, but just three hours earlier, Sheridan put his army in motion toward the Opequon, covering his flank by directing Merritt and Averell on Stephenson's. He sent Wilson rapidly ahead on the Berryville road to carry the ford and to seize the long and deep defile on the left or east bank through which the main column would have to advance. Wright was to lead the infantry, closely followed by Emory, who, in order to solidify the movement, was instructed to take his orders from Wright after reaching the ford. Crook, coming in from his more distant position, would naturally fall in the rear of the others, and he was to mass his men in reserve, covering the ford. Wright had to move partly across country, and had farther to go than Emory. Although both started punctually at the appointed hour, it happened that, about five o'clock, the head of Wright's column ran into Emory's in march near the crest, whence the road sweeps down to the Opequon. There Emory halted, by Wright's orders, to let the Sixth Corps pass. Unfortunately, minute and thorough as Sheridan's plans and instructions were, he appears to have underrated the double difficulty of crossing the ford and threading the long defile, for to this cause must be attributed the presence of Wright's entire wagon-train in the rear of his corps, as well as the excess of artillery for the work and the field. The head of the column could move but slowly; thus the rear was so long retarded, that, although the crossing began about six o'clock, and the whole movement was urged on by Sheridan, Wright, and Emory, and indeed by every one, it wanted but twenty minutes of noon when the line of battle was finally formed on the rolling ground overlooking the vale of the Opequon to the rear and Winchester to the front. Even as it was, Sheridan's eagerness being great, and the delay seeming interminable, Emory felt obliged to take upon himself the responsibility of departing from the strict order of march, and directed Dwight to move his men to the right of the road and pass the train. Thus it had taken six hours to advance three miles and to form in order of battle, and the immediate effect of this delay was that Sheridan had now to deal, not only with Ramseur, or with the two divisions counted on, but with the whole of Early's army; for between five and six o'clock in the morning Gordon, Rodes, and Wharton were all at Stephenson's, distant only five miles from Winchester or from the field of battle, toward which they all moved rapidly at the sound of the first firing, due to Wilson's advance.

Opequon Creek flows at the foot of a broad and thickly wooded gorge, with high and steep banks. The ravine through which the Berryville road rises to the level of the rolling plain, in the middle of whose western edge stands Winchester, is nearly three miles long. Here and there the high ground is covered with large oaks, pines, and undergrowth, and is intersected by many brooks, called runs. Of these the largest is Red Bud Run, which forms a smaller parallel ravine flanking the defile on the north, while a still larger stream, called Abraham's Creek, after pursuing a nearly parallel course on the south side of the defile, crosses the road not far from the ford, and just below it falls into the Opequon.

Wilson, after crossing the Opequon and completing his task of covering the advance of the infantry through the defile, had turned to the left on the high ground and taken post to cover the flank on the Senseny road, which, after crossing the Opequon about a mile and a quarter above the main ford, reaches the outskirts of Winchester at a point little more than three hundred yards from the Berryville road. The Sixth Corps formed across the Berryville road, Getty on its left, Ricketts on its right. Getty rested his left on Abraham's Creek. Behind him Russell stood in column in support. Emory prolonged the line of battle to the Red Bud on the right by posting Sharpe's and Birge's brigades of Grover, with Molineux and Shunk in the second line, the 9th Connecticut deployed as skirmishers to cover the right flank of Birge. Dwight's two brigades formed on the right and rear of Grover in echelon of regiments on the right, in order not only to support Grover's line, but to cover the flank against any turning movement by the Confederates or an attack by their reinforcements coming straight from Stephenson's. Beal's brigade held the right of Dwight's line, and the brigade line from right to left was formed in order of the 114th New York, 153rd New York, 116th New York, 29th Maine, and 30th Massachusetts. Beal covered his right flank by a detail of skirmishers taken from all his regiments and commanded by Lieutenant-Colonel Strain, of the 153rd New York. McMillan, on the left and rear of Beal, formed in order of the 47th

Pennsylvania, 8th Vermont, 160th New York, and 12th Connecticut, with five companies of the 47th Pennsylvania deployed to cover the whole right flank of his brigade and to move forward with it by the flank left in front. Crook had by this time crossed the ford and was massed on the left or west bank.

In climbing the hill the Berryville road follows nearly a northwesterly course, but soon after reaching the high ground bends rather sharply toward the left, crosses the ravine called Ash Hollow forming the head of Berryville Cañon, and runs for nearly a mile almost westerly. Wright was following the road, but as Emory guided upon Wright, the alignment was to be preserved by Sharpe's keeping his left in touch with the right of Ricketts. While the ground in Wright's front was for the most part open, Emory was chiefly in the dense wood, where the heavy leafage and undergrowth prevented him from seeing not only the enemy before him, but also the full extent of his own line. It should be observed with care that Ricketts was between Sharpe and the Berryville road, while the road was between Getty and Ricketts, and formed the guide for both; for these facts, of slight importance though they may seem, were destined presently to exert an influence well-nigh fatal on the fortunes of the day.

During the early hours of the morning Ramseur, on the Berryville road, and the cavalry of Lomax on the Senseny road, had been the only Confederate force between Sheridan and Winchester. But first Gordon came up at nine o'clock, and placed himself opposite Emory's right, his own left resting on the line of the Red Bud; then Rodes, closely following Gordon, formed between him and Ramseur against the right of Emory and the left of Wright.

About a quarter before twelve o'clock, at the sound of Sheridan's bugle, repeated from corps, division, and brigade headquarters, the whole line moved forward with great spirit, and instantly became engaged. Wilson pushed back Lomax, Wright drove in Ramseur, while Emory, advancing his infantry rapidly through the wood, where he was unable to use his artillery, attacked Gordon with great vigour. Birge, charging with bayonets fixed, fell upon the brigade of Evans, forming the extreme left of Gordon, and without a halt drove it in confusion through the wood and across the open ground beyond to the support of Braxton's artillery, posted by

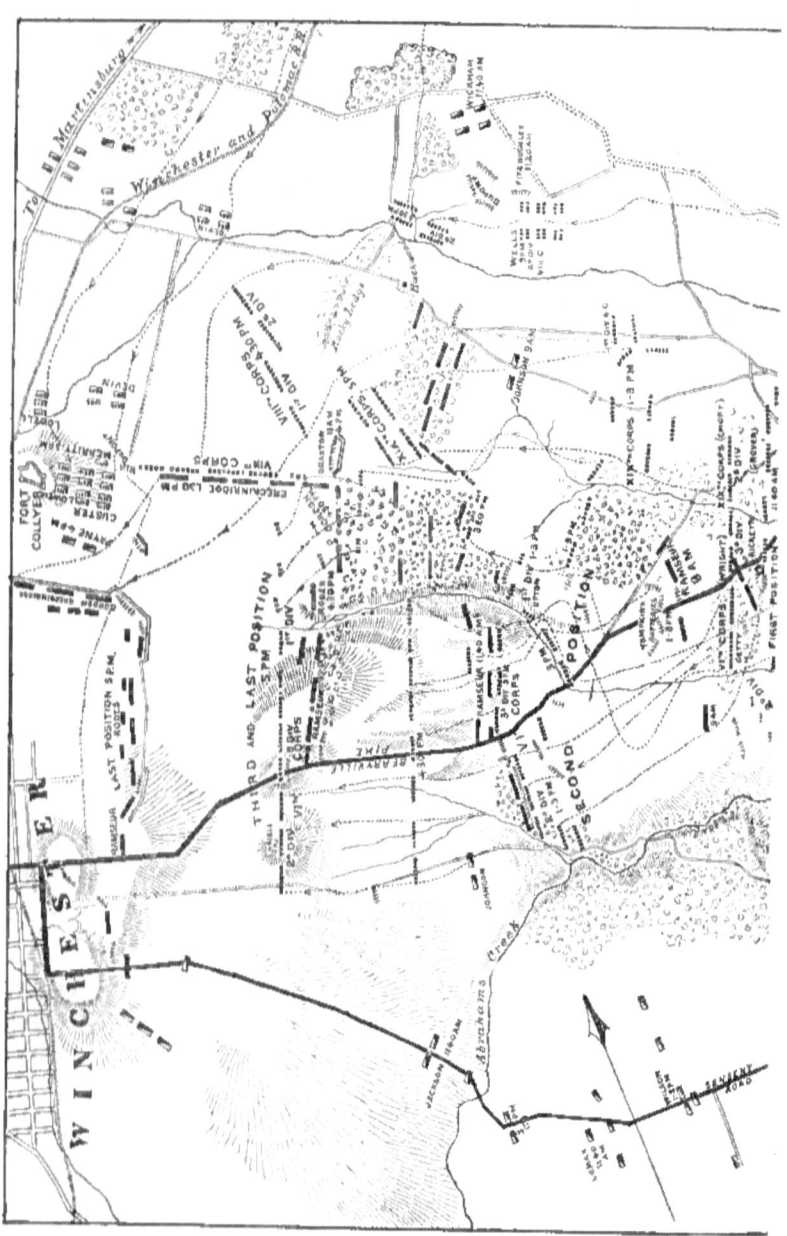

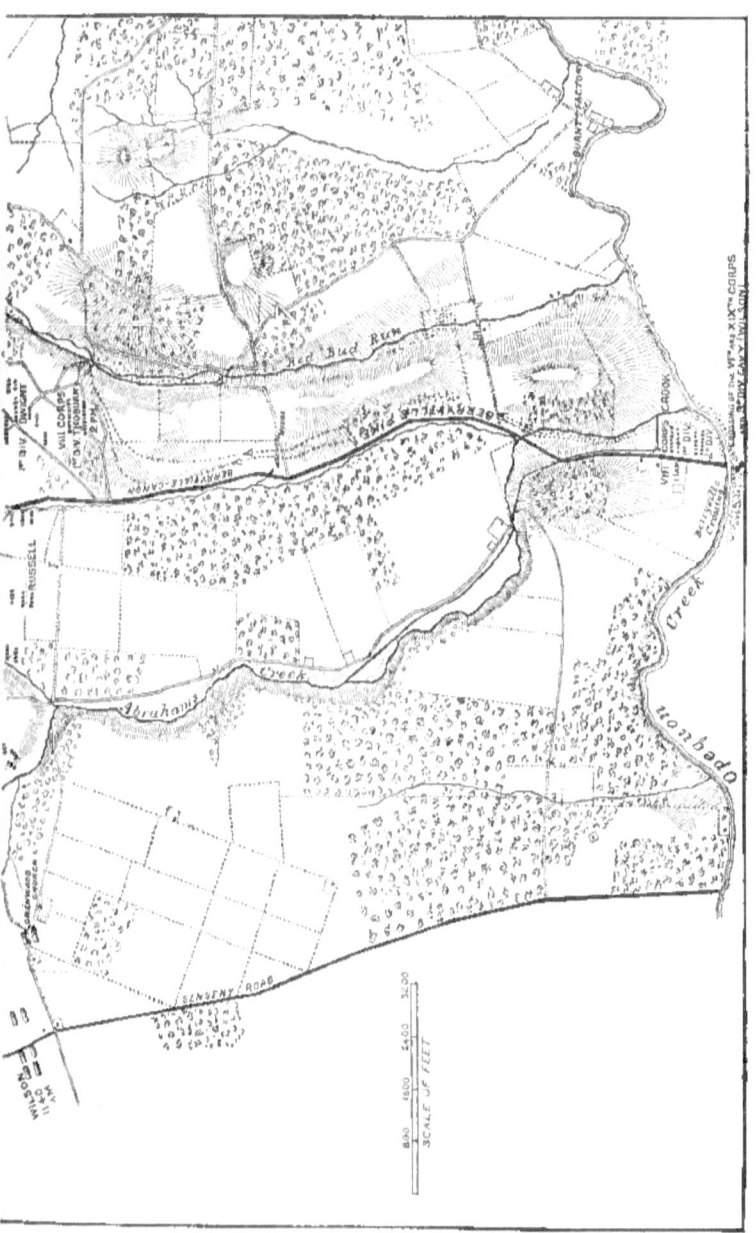

OPEQUON.

SEPTEMBER 19, 1864. FROM THE OFFICIAL MAP, 1873.

Gordon to secure his flank on the Red Bud road. In this brilliant charge, led by Birge in person, his lines naturally became disordered, and Grover, foreseeing the effect of an advance so swift and tumultuous, ordered Birge to halt and re-form in the wood. This order Birge tried to execute; but whether the words of command were not heard or were misunderstood, or in the wild excitement of the moment were wilfully disregarded by the men, certain it is that their officers found it impossible to restrain their ardour until they had followed on the run the broken fragments of Evans quite through the wood and beyond its farther skirt, where Braxton, using his guns with energy and skill, brought them to a stand.

Sharpe, advancing simultaneously on Birge's left, tried in vain to keep the alignment with Ricketts and with Birge; for now the peculiar feature of the long alignment across the swerving road began to work, yet, by reason of the screen of timber, without the cause being immediately observed by any one. At first the order of battle formed a right angle with the road, but the bend once reached, in the effort to keep closed upon it, at every step Ricketts was taking ground more and more to the left, while the point of direction for Birge, and equally for Sharpe, was the enemy in their front, standing almost in the exact prolongation of the defile, from which line, still plainly marked by Ash Hollow, the road, as we have seen, was steadily diverging. In short, to continue the march parallel with the road compelled a left half-wheel, while the battle was with the enemy straight in front, so that even had it been possible for Emory to execute his orders literally he must have offered his wheeling flank fairly to Rodes and to Gordon.

Sharpe, seeing that the gap between himself and Ricketts was growing every moment wider, in vain tried to cover it by more than one oblique movement to the left, and Keifer, whose brigade formed the right of Ricketts, being also among the first to perceive the fault, tried to make it good by deploying three of his regiments across the interval.

Birge's advance had borne him far to the right, and as Sharpe, in the vain attempt to keep his alignment with Ricketts, was always drifting to the left, there came a second and smaller gap between the two leading brigades of Grover. Into this Molineux was quickly thrust, and, deploying in parade order, under a heavy fire of cannon and musketry, at once began firing in return with great effect on the advancing columns of the enemy. But, shortly before this happened, the interval between Ricketts and Sharpe had grown to be nearly four hundred yards wide, and Birge's advance being stayed at nearly the same instant, Early saw his opportunity and seized it by throwing against the diverging flanks of Sharpe and Ricketts the fresh brigade that Battle had that moment brought up from Stephenson's. This new impulse once more carried forward the rest of Rodes's division; Ramseur rallied; Early restored his formation; and the whole Confederate line swept forward with renewed impetuosity, broke in the whole right of Ricketts and the left of Sharpe, surged around both flanks of Molineux, and swept back Birge. Sharpe's line, thus taken fairly in flank, was quickly rolled up. By this, the left regiment of Molineux, the gallant 22nd Iowa, being in quite open ground, was greatly exposed, so that it, too, was presently swept back. The 159th New York and the 13th Connecticut, after holding on stiffly for a time under the partial cover of a sort of gully, were in like manner swept away, and on the right Birge's men paid the penalty of their own impetuosity. The left of Ricketts, less exposed to the shock, stood firm, and the right of Molineux, isolated as it was, held its ground; but otherwise the whole front of the battle, from the road to the Red Bud, was gone. As the Confederates charged down upon a section of Bradbury's 1st Maine Battery, posted about the centre of the division, Day, who under many drawbacks had brought up his regiment, the 131st New York, to a high standard of discipline and efficiency, took prompt and full advantage of the slight cover afforded by the little wooded ravine in which he happened to be. With equal coolness and readiness he changed front forward on his tenth company, yet held his fire until he could see the shoulders and almost the backs of the enemy; then, pouring in a hot fire, and being immediately supported by the 11th Indiana, part of the 3rd Massachusetts, and the 176th New York, which had quickly rallied from Sharpe's reverse, the attacking force was driven back in disorder; but unfortunately, in retiring it swept across the remains of Molineux's left centre, which had been cut off in the gully, and took many prisoners, especially from among the officers who had stood to their posts through everything.

Just as when victory had seemed about to alight on the standard of the Union, the very perch itself had been suddenly and rudely shaken by the tread of Early's charging columns; so now, at the precise moment when defeat—bitter, perhaps disastrous defeat—seemed inevitable, the fortunes of the battle were once more reversed, and the day was suddenly saved by the prompt and orderly advance of Russell into the fatal gap. As he changed front from the wood to the right and swept on in splendid array, it happened that the charging line of Early, already disarranged by its own success, offered its right flank to Russell's front. Russell himself, bravely leading his division, fell, yet not until he had struck the blow that gave the victory to the defenders of his country,—a noble sacrifice in a noble cause.

But on the right a danger almost equally serious menaced the flank of Emory, for when Birge's men came streaming back, Shunk, who had been supporting Birge without having men enough to cover the whole ground, found his left uncovered to Gordon by the giving way of Sharpe, while at the same time his line was nearly enfiladed from the right by a section or battery of Fitzhugh Lee's horse artillery on the north bank of the Red Bud. Seeing all this, Emory instantly ordered his own old division to deploy at the top of its speed, and to make good the broken line. "Have this thing stopped at once," were the terse words of his command to Dwight. Once more, as at the Sabine Cross-Roads, the 1st brigade was called upon the yield up its leading regiment for a sacrifice, and again the lot fell to New York, yet this time upon the 114th, and upon not one of all the good veteran battalions that held the field on that 19th of September—if indeed upon any in all the armies of the Union—could the choice have rested more securely. To the left and front, far into the open field, through the wreck of Grover's right, into the teeth of the pursuing lines of Gordon, Per Lee led his regiment. No sooner had his men emerged from the cover of the wood than they came under the fire of Gordon's infantry and artillery, crossed with the fire of Fitzhugh Lee's guns beyond the Red Bud; yet they were not able to fire a musket in return until their own defeated comrades had passed to the rear. Cruel as the situation was, the 114th marched steadily forward nearly two hundred yards in front of the forest; then, finding itself quite alone and unsupported, confronted by the line of battle of the enemy at the skirt of the timber opposite, Per Lee made his men lie down without other cover than the high grass, and there, loading on their backs and at every moment losing heavily, without yielding an inch, they held off the enemy until support came. That this was longer than usual in coming was no fault of their comrades, but a mere accident of the situation; for Dwight's division being formed in echelon of battalions on the right, just as it had in the first instance been necessary to bring the 114th into action obliquely to the left, so now Beal was forced to form the line of battle of his brigade by inversion, and this, moreover, in the woods, with the steep bank of the Red Bud hampering his right. Slow though it must have seemed to Per Lee, standing out there alone, this difficult movement was in reality executed by Beal with great promptness and rapidity and in admirable order. As regiment after regiment, beginning with the 153rd, came into the new line at the double-quick by the shortest path, each advanced with a shout to the rail fence on Per Lee's right and somewhat toward his rear, and, throwing down the rails, opened a rapid fire. This checked the enemy. Finding Beal unable to cover all the ground he was now trying to hold, Emory made Dwight take the 160th New York from McMillan's brigade and posted it on the right of Beal's.

McMillan had been ordered to move forward at the same time as Beal, and to form on his left. The five companies of the 47th Pennsylvania that had been detached to form a skirmish line on Red Bud Run, to cover McMillan's right flank, had somehow lost their way on the broken ground among the thickets, and, not finding them in place, McMillan had been obliged to send the remaining companies of the regiment to do the same duty. This detail and the employment of the 160th New York in Beal's line left McMillan but two of his battalions, the 8th Vermont and the 12th Connecticut; but although McMillan, holding the left of the formation in echelon, had farther to go to reach his position, it was only necessary for him to move straight to the front, and thus the 8th Vermont formed the right of his line and the 12th Connecticut the left. Not a moment too soon did Thomas and Peck bring their good regiments to the support of Molineux's diminished and almost exhausted brigade, and thus complete the restoration of Emory's line of battle. Almost at the first fire

Lieutenant-Colonel Peck, the brave, accomplished, and spirited soldier who had led the 12th Connecticut in every action, fell mortally wounded by the fragment of a shell.

The shaken regiments of Grover quickly rallied and re-formed in good order behind the lines of Dwight, and all pressing forward once more, took part in the counter-charge begun by Russell, by which the whole Confederate line was driven back in confusion quite beyond the positions from which they had advanced to the attack. To this line, substantially, Wright and Emory followed, and, correcting their position and alignment, waited for events or for orders. By one o'clock the morning's fight was over. Fierce and eventful as it had been, it had lasted barely an hour.

The Confederates, greatly outnumbered from the first, were now, after their losses and the rough handling they had received, no longer in condition for the offensive, and from the defensive they had, as things stood, little to hope. Sheridan, on his part, with some reluctance, made up his mind that it would be better to give up his original plan of putting in Crook to the left to cut off Early's retreat by moving against the valley turnpike near Newtown, and instead of this to use Crook and the cavalry on the Red Bud line against Early's left. The time needed for this movement caused a comparative lull in the battle of about two hours' duration. It was not so much that the battle died away, for the fire of artillery and even of musketry was still kept up, as that neither side moved in force against the other. While waiting for Crook to come into position on the right, Emory's restored line was formed by Beal on the right, prolonged toward the left by Shunk, Birge supported by Molineux, Day with the 131st New York, Allen with the battalion of the 38th Massachusetts, the 8th Vermont, and the 12th Connecticut of McMillan supported by the 160th New York, now withdrawn from the right, and finally Neafie, leading Grover's 3rd brigade in place of Sharpe, who had been carried off the field severely wounded.

From his position in reserve, covering the Opequon ford, Crook moved up the right bank of the Red Bud to the rear of Dwight's first position, and then, dividing his command, posted Thoburn on the right of Dwight, and sent Duval across the Red Bud to his point of attack. Then Thoburn, at Emory's request, relieved Beal's front line of battle, while Emory drew out the 114th, the 116th, and the 153rd New York and placed them under Davis to strengthen the centre. Beal himself was looking to his flank, held by the 47th Pennsylvania and the 30th Massachusetts.

Meanwhile Wharton had gone back from the desperate task of covering the flank at Stephenson's against Merritt's advance and had taken position in the rear of Rodes.

As soon as Crook was fairly across the Red Bud, his movement silenced the battery on the left bank that had been enfilading Emory's line, and this served to tell Emory that Crook was in place and at work. Averell and Merritt could be plainly seen surging up the valley road far in Gordon's left and rear, furiously driving before them the main body of Fitzhugh Lee's cavalry. About four o'clock the cheers of Duval's men beyond the Red Bud served as the signal for Thoburn, and now as Crook moved forward, sweeping everything before him, from right to left the whole army responded to the impulse. To meet Thoburn, Breckinridge placed Wharton in position at right angles with Gordon and with the valley road. Duval, having easily driven before him everything on the left bank of the Red Bud, waded through the marsh on his left, crossed the run, and united with Thoburn. Then Crook, with a sudden and irregular but curiously effective half-wheel to the left, fell vigorously upon Gordon, and Torbert coming on with great impetuosity at the same instant, the weight was heavier than the attenuated lines of Breckinridge and Gordon could bear. Early saw his whole left wing give back in disorder, and as Emory and Wright pressed hard, Rodes and Ramseur gave way, and the battle was over.

All that remained to Early was to make good his retreat, now seriously compromised by the steady progress of Wilson toward and at last upon the Millwood road. Early vainly endeavoured to reunite his shattered fragments behind the lines constructed in the former campaigns for the defence of Winchester on the east. About five o'clock Torbert and Crook, fairly at right angles to the first line of battle, covered Winchester on the north from the rocky ledges that lie to the eastward of the town nearly to the first position of Braxton's guns. Thence Wright extended the line at right angles with Crook and parallel with the valley road, while Sheridan drew out Emory, who was naturally displaced by these converging movement, and sent him to extend Wright's line toward the south.

The disorderly retreat of Early's men once begun, there was no staying it. Torbert pursued the fugitives to Kernstown, where Ramseur faced about, but Sheridan, mindful that his men had been on their feet since two o'clock in the morning, many of them since one, and had in the meantime fought with varying success a long and hard fight ending in a great victory, made no attempt to send his infantry after the flying enemy.

For what was probably the first time in their lives, his men had seen every musket, every cannon, and every sabre put in use, and to good use, by their young and vigorous commander. They had looked upon a decisive victory ending with the rout of their enemy. Sheridan himself openly rejoiced, and catching the enthusiasm of their leader, his men went wild with excitement when, accompanied by his corps commanders, Wright and Emory and Crook, Sheridan rode down the front of his lines. Then went up a mighty cheer that gave new life to the wounded and consoled the last moments of the dying, for in every breast was firmly implanted the conviction that now at last the end was in sight, and that deep-toned shout that shook the hills and the heavens was not the brutal roar of a rude and barbarous soldiery, coarsely exulting over the distress and slaughter of the vanquished, but the glad voice of the American people[2] rejoicing from the hill-top at the first sure glimpse of the final victory that meant to them peace, home, and a nation saved.

When the President heard the news his first act was to write with his own hand a warm message of congratulation, and this he followed up by making Sheridan a brigadier-general in the regular army, and assigning him permanently to the high command he had been exercising under temporary orders.

The losses of the Army of the Shenandoah, according to the revised statements compiled in the War Department were 5,018, including 697 killed, 3,983 wounded, 338 missing. Of the three infantry corps, the Nineteenth, though in numbers smaller than the Sixth, suffered the heaviest loss, the aggregate being 2,074, while the total casualties of the Sixth Corps were 1,699, and those of the

---

2. "Hear that! That's the voice of the American people!" Thomas is said to have exclaimed on hearing the tremendous cheers of his men for their decisive victory of Nashville.

West Virginia forces, 794. The total loss of the cavalry was 451. The loss of the Nineteenth Corps was divided into 314 killed, 1,554 wounded, 206 missing. Of this, far the heaviest share fell upon Grover's division, which reported 1,527 against 542 in Dwight's division. Dwight reports 80 killed, 460 wounded, 2 missing; Grover, 234 killed, 1,089 wounded, 204 missing; but Grover had four brigades in the action while Dwight had two, and this nearly represents the relative strength of the two divisions. Of the brigades, Birge's suffered the most, having 107 killed, 349 wounded, 69 missing—together, 525; while Molineux, who came next, had 58 killed, 362 wounded, 87 missing—together, 507; yet in proportion Sharpe fared the worst, for his brigade, though but half as strong as Birge's, lost 39 killed, 222 wounded, 17 missing—together, 278. The 114th New York heads the fatal record for the day with 44 killed and mortally wounded, and 141 wounded—together, 185 out of about 270 in action—nearly sixty-five per cent.

Dwight's report having been sent back to him by Emory for correction, and not again presented, no report is to be found from the First division or any portion of it, except McMillan's brigade and the 12th Connecticut. The most useful detailed accounts of the part taken by the division are to be found in the admirable histories of the "First-Tenth-Twenty-Ninth Maine" by Major John M. Gould, and of the 114th New York by Assistant-Surgeon Harris H. Beecher.

Prominent among the slain of the Nineteenth Corps, besides Lieutenant-Colonel Peck, already spoke of, were Colonel Alexander Gardiner, 14th New Hampshire, Lieutenant-Colonel Willoughby Babcock, 75th New York, Major William Knowlton, 29th Maine and Major Eusebius S. Clark, 26th Massachusetts. These were fine officers, and their loss was deeply deplored.

Early lost nearly 4,000 in all, including about 200 prisoners. Rodes was killed, Fitzhugh Lee severely wounded. Early was forced to leave his dead and most of his wounded to be cared for by the victors, into whose hands also fell five guns and nine battle-flags.

Severe military critics have sometimes been disposed to find fault with Early, not merely for scattering his army—which, though certainly a fault, was handsomely made good by the rapid concentration,—but even for fighting his battle at Winchester at all. Weakened by the loss of Kershaw, Early should, these critics think, have fallen back to Fisher's Hill at the first sign of Sheridan's advance; yet upon a broad view it is difficult to concede this. The odds against Early were the same that the Confederates had necessarily assumed from the beginning. They were desperate; they could not possibly be otherwise than desperate; they called for desperate campaigns, and these for desperate battles. Standing on the defensive at Fisher's Hill, Early would not only have given up the main object of his campaign and of his presence in the valley, but would have exposed himself to the risk of being cut off by a turning column gaining his rear by way of the Luray valley. Indeed, this would have been more than a risk; sooner or later it would have been a certainty.

CHAPTER 33

Fisher's Hill

The frowning heights of Fisher's Hill had long been the bugbear of the valley. The position was, in truth, a purely defensive one, its chief value being that there was no other. Except for defence it was worthless, because it was as hard to get out of as to get at; and even for defence it was subject to the drawback that it could be easily and secretly turned upon either flank. In a word, its strength resided mainly in the fact that between the peaks of Massanutten and the North Mountain the jaws of the valley were contracted to a width of not more than four miles. The right flank of the shortened front rests securely upon the north fork of the Shenandoah, where it winds about the base of Three Top Mountain before bending widely toward the east to join the south fork and form the Shenandoah River. Across the front, among rocks, between steep and broken cliffs, winds the brawling brook called Tumbling Run, and above it, from its southern edge, rises the rugged crag called Fisher's Hill. Here, behind his old entrenchments, Early gathered the remnants of his army for another stand, and began to strengthen himself by fresh works. The danger of a turning movement through the twin valley of Luray was in his mind, and to guard against it he sent his cavalry to Milford, while Sheridan, who was thinking of the same thing, ordered Torbert to ride up the Luray valley from Front Royal.

On the morning of the 20th of September Sheridan set out to follow Early, and in the afternoon took up a position before Strasburg, the Sixth Corps on the right, Emory on the left, and Crook behind Cedar Creek in support. The next morning, the 21st, Sheridan pushed and followed Early's skirmishers over the high hill that stands between Strasburg and Fisher's Hill, overlooking both, drove them behind the defences of Fisher's Hill, and took up a position covering the front from the banks of the North Fork on the left, where Emory's left rested lightly, to the crown of the hill just mentioned, which commanded the approach by what is called the back road, or Cedar Creek grade, and was but slightly commanded by Fisher's Hill itself. This strong vantage-ground Wright wrested from the enemy after a struggle, and felling the trees for protection and for range, planted his batteries there. The ground was very difficult, broken and rocky, and to hold it the Sixth corps had to be drawn toward the right, while Emory, following the movement, in the dark hours of the early morning of the 22nd of September, extended his front so as to cover the ground thus given up by Wright.

Sheridan now thought of nothing short of the capture of Early's army. Torbert was to drive the Confederate cavalry through Luray, and thence, crossing the Massanutten range, was to lay hold of the valley pike at New Market, and plant himself firmly in Early's rear on his only line of retreat. Crook, by a wide sweep to the right, his march hidden by the hills and woods, was to gain the back road, so as to come up secretly on Early's left flank and rear, and the first sounds of battle that were certain to follow the discovery of his unexpected approach in this quarter were to serve as a signal for Wright and Emory to fall on with everything they had.

During the forenoon of the 22nd, Grover held the left of the position of the Nineteenth Corps, his division formed in two lines in the order of Macauley,[1] Birge; Shunk, Molineux. Dwight, in the order of Beal, McMillan, held the right, and connected with Wheaton. In taking ground towards the right, as already described, this line had become too extended, and, as it was necessary that the left of the skirmishers, at least, should rest upon the river, Grover shortened his front by moving forward Foster with the 128th and Lewis with the 176th New York to drive in the enemy's skirmishers opposite, and to occupy the ground that they had been holding. This was handsomely done under cover of a brisk shelling from

---

1. As the wounding of Sharpe left no officer present with his brigade of higher rank than lieutenant-colonel, Emory took Colonel Daniel Macauley, 11th Indiana, from the 4th brigade and placed him in command of the 3rd.

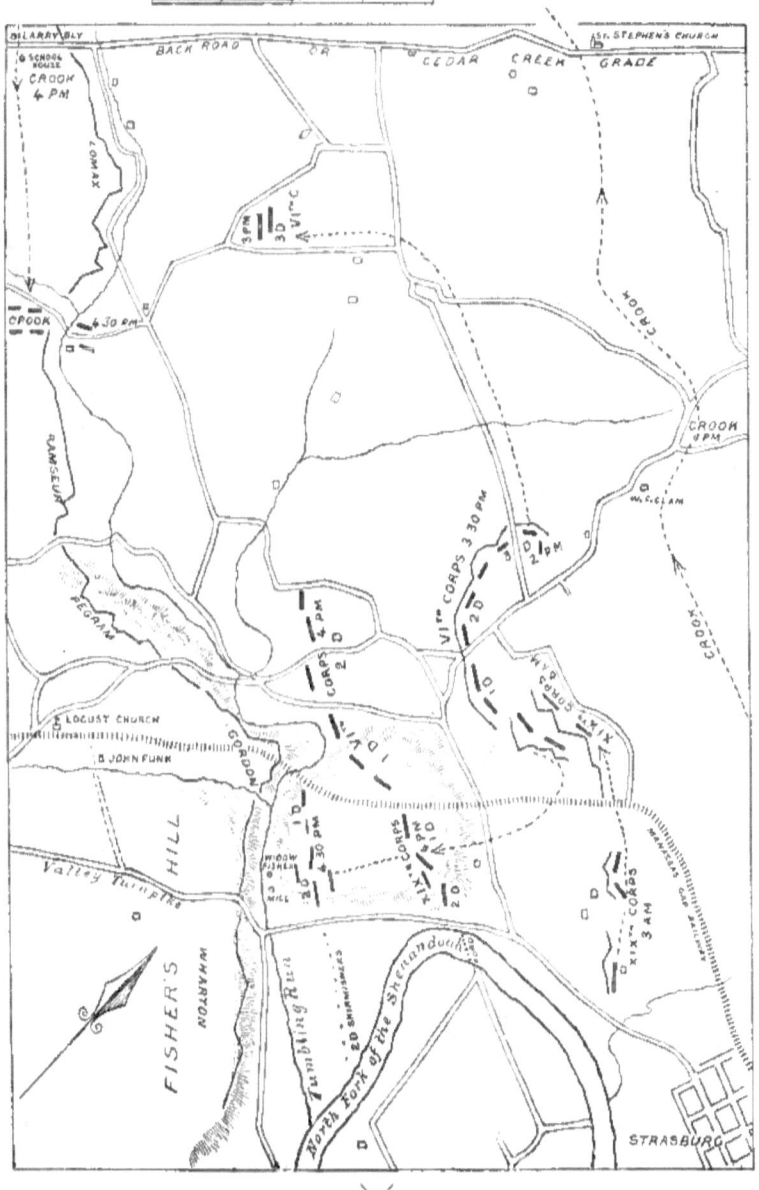

FISHER'S HILL.
SEPTEMBER 22, 1864. FROM THE OFFICIAL MAP.

Taft's and Bradbury's guns. As on the rest of the line, the whole front of the corps was covered as usual by hasty entrenchments. In the afternoon Ricketts moved far to the right, and seized a wooded knoll commanding Ramseur's position on Fisher's Hill. In preparation for the attack Sheridan gave Emory the ground on the left of the railway, and Wright that beyond it, and Molineux moved forward to lead the advance of Grover. The sun was low when the noise of battle was heard far away on the right. This was Crook, sweeping everything before him as he charged suddenly out of the forest full upon the left flank and rear of Lomax and Ramseur, taking the whole Confederate line completely in reverse. The surprise was absolute. Instantly Wright and Emory took up the movement, and, inspired by the presence and the impetuous commands of Sheridan, descended rapidly the steep and broken sides of the ravine, at the bottom of which lies Tumbling Run, and then rather scrambling than charging up the rocky and almost inaccessible sides of Fisher's Hill, swarmed over the strong entrenchments, line after line, and planting their colours upon the parapets, saw the whole army of Early in disorderly flight. Foremost to mount the parapet was Entwistle with his company of the 176th New York. To them the good fortune fell of being the first to lay hands on four pieces of artillery in battery, abandoned in the panic caused by the appearance of Crook, but almost at the same instant Wilson, gallantly leading the 28th Iowa, planted the colours of his regiment on the works. That nothing might be wanting to the completeness of the victory, the Confederates, who, until that moment had felt their position so secure that they had even taken the ammunition boxes from the caissons, abandoned sixteen pieces of artillery where they stood. Early was unable to arrest the retreat of his army until he found himself near Edenburg, four miles beyond Woodstock.

Sheridan's loss in this battle was 52 killed, 457 wounded, 19 missing, in all, 528. Of this the Sixth Corps suffered nearly half, namely, 27 killed, 208 wounded, 3 missing, in all, 238. Crook's loss was 8 killed, 152 wounded, 2 missing, total 162, and Emory accounts for 15 killed, 86 wounded, 13 missing, together 114. All the casualties of the cavalry numbered but 14. Early reports his loss in the infantry and artillery alone as 30 killed, 210 wounded, 995 missing, total 1,235; but Sheridan claims 1,100 prisoners.

Now came Torbert's opportunity, but unfortunately, after suffering a check from the two brigades of Fitzhugh Lee under Wickham, Torbert had on the 22nd fallen back down the Luray valley toward his starting-point, and when on the afternoon of the 23rd word came to him of what had happened at Fisher's Hill, although he again advanced, he was then too late. Thus for once the cavalry column completely failed. Sheridan, from the tenor of his despatches to Torbert, must have felt that this result was probable, but he did not let it disturb his own movements, and without a halt he pushed forward his whole force in pursuit, with slight regard to organization, each regiment or brigade nearly in the order in which it chanced to file into the road. Devin's cavalry brigade trod closely on the heels of what was left of Lomax, and Emory, whose line had crossed the valley road, pushed up it as fast as the men could move over the ground. Wright moved in close support of Emory and personally directed the operations of both corps, the Nineteenth as well as the Sixth. So fast did the infantry march that it was ten o'clock at night before Devin, from his place in line on the right of the Sixth Corps, was able to take the road abreast with the Nineteenth, and broad daylight before his or any other horsemen passed the hardy yet toil-worn soldiers of Molineux, who were left all night to lead the swift pursuit. Molineux caused Day to deploy the 131st New York as skirmishers on the right of the road, while the 11th Indiana, led by Macauley, performed the same service on the left. About half-past eight the head of the column first came in contact with the rear-guard of the enemy, but this was soon driven in, and no further resistance was offered until about an hour later, at the crossing of a creek near Woodstock, a brisk fire of musketry, aided by two guns in the road, was opened on Molineux's front, but was quickly silenced. At dawn on the 23rd of September Sheridan went into bivouac covering Woodstock, and let the infantry rest until early in the afternoon, when he again took up the pursuit with Wright and Emory, leaving Crook to care for the dead and wounded. Early fell back to Mount Jackson, and was preparing to make a stand when Averell coming up, he and Devin made so vigorous a demonstration with the cavalry alone that Early thought it best to continue his retreat beyond the North Fork to Rude's Hill, which stands between Mount Jackson and New Market.

Sheridan advanced to Mount Jackson on the morning of the 24th of September, and before nightfall had concentrated his whole army there. He was moving his cavalry to envelop both of Early's flanks and the infantry, Wright leading, to attack in front. However, Early did not wait for this, but retreated rapidly in order of battle, pursued by Sheridan in the same order, that is by the right of regiments with an attempt at deploying intervals, through New Market and six miles beyond to a point where a country road diverges through Keezeltown and Cross Keys to Port Republic, at the head of the South Fork. Here both armies halted face to face, Sheridan for the night; but Early, as soon as it was fairly dark, fell back about five miles on the Port Republic road, and again halted at a point about fourteen miles short of that town.

Early's object in quitting the main valley road, which would have conducted him to Harrisonburg, covering Staunton, was to receive once more the reinforcements that Lee, at the first tidings from Winchester, had again hurried forward under Kershaw. On the 25th of September, therefore, Early retreated through Port Republic towards Brown's Gap, where Kershaw, marching from Culpeper through Swift Run Gap, joined him on the 26th. Here also Early's cavalry rejoined him, Wickham from the Luray valley, and Lomax, pressed by Powell, from Harrisonburg.

Sheridan, keeping to the main road, advanced to Harrisonburg with Wright and Emory, leaving Crook to hold the fork of the roads where Early had turned off. At Harrisonburg Torbert rejoined with Merritt and Wilson. Then Sheridan sent Torbert with Wilson and Lowell by Staunton to Waynesboro', where, before quitting the valley by Rockfish Gap, the major road, as well as the railway to Charlottesville, crossed the affluent of the Shenandoah known as the South River. To divert attention from this raid Sheridan reinforced Devin, who, in the absence of Torbert's main body, had been following and observing Early near Port Republic without other cavalry support, and thus Merritt presently ran into Kershaw marching to join Early at Brown's Gap. Early, having gone as far as he wished, turned upon Merritt and drove him across the South Fork, but just then getting the first inkling of Torbert's movements, divined their purpose, and, to check them, marched with all speed, in compact order and with the greatest watchfulness in every direction, on Rockfish Gap. But Torbert, having a good start, won the race, and had accomplished his object when the advance of Early's column came up, and caused him to draw off.

Sheridan, on his part, had gone nearly as far as he intended, but as he meant presently to begin with his cavalry above Staunton the work of destroying the value of the whole valley to the Confederate army, on the 29th he ordered Wright and Emory to Mount Crawford to support Torbert in this work.

Grant, who, ever since he reached the James, had cast longing eyes upon the Virginia Central railway, as well as upon the great junction at Gordonsville, now strongly desired Sheridan to go to Staunton or Charlottesville, but Sheridan set himself firmly against the plan on account of the daily increasing difficulty of supplying his army and the great force that must be wasted in any attempt to keep open a line of communication longer or more exposed than that he already had to maintain. As an alternative, Sheridan, who seems to have thought Early had quitted the valley for good, proposed to bring the Valley campaign to an end with the destruction of the crops, and then to move with his main force to join Grant on the James. Grant, at once agreeing to this, directed Sheridan to keep Crook in the valley and to transfer the rest of his force to the armies before Richmond.

On the morning of the 6th of October Sheridan faced about and began moving down the valley, the infantry leading in the inverse order of its advance, and the cavalry bringing up the rear in one long line that reached from mountain to mountain, busied in burning as it marched the mills, the barns, and everything edible by man or beast. From the Blue Ridge to the Shenandoah Mountains, nothing was spared that might be of use to the Confederates in prolonging the war.

When Early discovered this he followed on the morning of the 7th of October, with his whole force, including Kershaw, as well as the cavalry brigade of Rosser, sent by Lee from Petersburg. The command of all the cavalry being given to Rosser, he at once began treading on the heels of Torbert. On the 9th, at Tom's Brook, Torbert, under the energetic orders of Sheridan to whip the Confederate cavalry or get whipped himself, turned on Rosser, and, after a sharp fight, completely overwhelmed him and hotly pursued his flying columns more than twenty miles up the valley. Several hundred prisoners, eleven guns with their caissons, and many wagons—tersely described by Sheridan "as almost everything on wheels"—fell into the hands of the captors. But more important even than these trophies, confidence in Rosser's cavalry was destroyed at a blow, and its early prestige wiped out forever.

On the 10th of October Sheridan once more crossed Cedar Creek and went into camp, Emory holding the right or west of the valley road, Crook on the left or east of the road, and the cavalry covering the flanks. Wright took up the line of march by Front Royal on Washington.

The first intention of the government was that he should take advantage of the Manassas Gap railway, which was again being restored under the protection of Augur's troops; but this work was not yet completed, and while Wright waited at Front Royal, Grant once more fell back on his first and favourite plan of a movement on Charlottesville and Gordonsville. To effect this he wished Sheridan to take up an advanced position toward the head of the valley, and to this the government added its favourite notion of rebuilding the railways in the rear. Halleck even went so far as to instruct Sheridan to fortify and provision heavily the position Grant had directed him to occupy. All these ideas Sheridan combated with such earnestness that he was summoned to Washington for consultation. Grant at the same time reduced his call on Sheridan for troops for service on the James to the Sixth Corps, and Sheridan, having on his own motion stopped the work on the Manassas Gap railway, ordered Wright to march on Alexandria by Ashby's Gap. Wright set out on the 12th.

Sheridan having lost touch with the main body of the Confederates in returning down the valley, he, in common with Grant and with the government, now thought that Early had quitted the region for good. Sheridan's information placed Early variously at Gordonsville, Charlottesville, and in the neighbourhood of Brown's Gap; but in truth, though nothing had been seen of Early's troops for some days, they had never gone out of the valley, but had slowly and at a long and safe interval been following Sheridan's footsteps, so that on the 13th, while Wright was well on his way towards Alexandria, and Sheridan himself was getting ready to go to Washington, Early once more took post at Fisher's Hill, and sent his advance guard directly on to Hupp's Hill to look down into the Union camps on the farther bank of Cedar Creek and see what was going on there. The first news of Early's presence, within two miles of the Union camp, at the very moment when he was thought to be sixty miles away on the line of the Virginia Central railway, was brought by the shells his artillery suddenly dropped among the tents of Crook. Thoburn at once moved out to capture the battery whose missiles had presented themselves as uninvited guests at his dinner-table, but was met by Kershaw and driven back after a sharp fight. Custer, who was covering the right flank of the army, was assailed at the same time by the Confederate cavalry, but easily threw off the attack. At the first sound Torbert sent Merritt from the left to the support of Custer, and afterward Sheridan kept him there.

When on the 12th of October Sheridan received Grant's definite instructions for the movement on Gordonsville and Charlottesville, he ceased to offer any further opposition, yet, realizing that he would need his whole force, he withdrew the order for Wright's movement to Alexandria and sent him word to come back to Cedar Creek. The head of Wright's column was wading the Shenandoah when these orders overtook it. Wright at once faced about, and on the next day, the 14th of October, went into camp behind the lines of Cedar Creek on the right and rear of Emory. No change was made in the positions of the other troops, because, until Sheridan's return from Washington, the policy and plan of the campaign must remain unsettled, and Wright might at any moment be called upon to resume his march.

On the 15th of October Sheridan received formal instructions from Grant, limiting the proposed movement on Charlottesville and Gordonsville to a serious menace, instead of an occupation, and again reducing the call for troops to a single division of cavalry. Sheridan at once sent Merritt in motion toward Chester Gap, directing Powell to follow, and he himself rode with Merritt to Front Royal, meaning to pay his postponed visit to the Secretary of War at Washington; but on the 16th, before quitting Front Royal, he was overtaken by an officer from Wright bringing the words of the strange message read off by our signal officers from the waving flags of the Confederates in plain sight on the crest of Three Top Mountain.[2] This message purported to have been sent by Longstreet to Early. "Be ready," it said, "to move as soon as my forces join you, and we will crush Sheridan." The true story of this despatch has not until now been made public,[3] and many are the surmises, clever or stupid, that have been wasted upon the mystery. In fact, the message was, as both Sheridan and Wright naturally inferred, a trick intended to deceive them; Early thought to induce them to move back without waiting for the attack which, with his reduced strength, he wished to avoid. The effect was to put the Union commanders on their guard against what was actually about to happen. Therefore Sheridan instantly turned back all the cavalry save one regiment, which he kept for an escort, and rode on to Rectortown, and so went by rail to Washington—first, however, taking the precaution to warn Wright to strengthen his position, to close in Powell from Front Royal, to look well to the ground, and to be prepared. In his official report of the campaign, Sheridan, speaking of the events now to be related, said:

> This surprise was owing probably to not closing in Powell or that the cavalry divisions of Merritt and Custer were placed at the right of our line, where it had always occurred to me there was but little danger of attack.

---

2. According to Sheridan, agreeing with the general recollection of the survivors; but Wright and Early both say Round Top, which is behind Fisher's Hill. Might not the message sent from Round Top have been repeated from Three Top?
3. To the courtesy and kindness of General Early, the author is greatly indebted for the key to the riddle. Under date of Lynchburg, Virginia, November 6, 1890, he writes: "The signal message ... was altogether fictitious. As Sheridan's troops occupied the north bank of Cedar Creek in such a strong position as to render it impracticable for me to attack them in front, I went to the signal station just in my rear for the purpose of examining the position, and I found the officer in charge of the station reading some signals that were being sent by the Federal signal agents. I then asked him if the other side could read his signals and he told me that they had discovered the key to the signals formerly used, but that a change had been made. I then wrote the message purporting to be from Longstreet and had it signalled in full view of the Federal signal men whom we saw on the hill in front of my position, so that it might be read by them. My object was to induce Sheridan to move back his troops from the position they then occupied, and I am inclined to think that if he had then been present with his command he would have done so. However, the movement was not made, and I then determined to make the attack which was made on the 19th of October. The object of that attack was to prevent any troops from being returned to Grant's army."

But it is important to observe and remember that although Wright, in sending Longstreet's message, had remarked—

"If the enemy should be strongly reinforced in cavalry he might, by turning my right, give us a great deal of trouble.... I shall only fear an attack on my right."

Yet Sheridan in his reply made no allusion to any difference of opinion on his part as to the place of danger. His instructions to close in Powell, Torbert, under Wright's direction, executed by calling in Moore's brigade to cover Buckton's Ford, on the left and rear of Crook. Powell, with the rest of his division, was left at Front Royal to hold off Lomax.

Sheridan went on to Washington. Arriving there on the morning of the 17th, he at once asked for a special train to take him to Martinsburg at noon, and having, between a late breakfast and an early luncheon, transacted all his business at the War Office, including the conversion of the government to his views, set out to rejoin his command. With him went two engineer officers, Alexander and Thom, with whom he was to consult as to the best point, if any, in the lower valley to be fortified and held; for this venerable error was not dead, merely sleeping.

Torbert rejoined the army at Cedar Creek on the 16th, and Merritt took up his old position on the right. On the same night Rosser took one of his brigades with a brigade of infantry mounted behind the horsemen, and, supported by the whole of Early's army, set out to capture the outlying brigade of Custer's division, but found instead a single troop on picket duty. This he took, but it was a rather mortifying issue to his heavy preparations and great expectations, and a long price to pay for putting Torbert on the alert.

For the next two days nothing was seen of Early, although the cavalry and both of the infantry corps of the main line kept a good watch toward the front. There was some probability that Early would attack, especially if he should have heard of Wright's departure and not of his return. That Early must either attack soon or withdraw to the head of the valley was certain, for Sheridan had stripped the country of the supplies on which the Confederates had been accustomed to rely, and Early had now to feed his men and animals by the long haul of seventy-five miles from Staunton. It was thus that Wright viewed the situation, and in fact the same things were passing through the mind of Early. On the 18th of October, Crook, by Wright's orders, sent Harris with his brigade of Thoburn's division, to find out where Early really was and what he was doing. How far Harris went is not certainly known, but when he returned at nightfall he reported that he had been to Early's old camps and found them evacuated. In reality Early was at Fisher's Hill with his whole force, engaged in his last preparations for the surprise of the morrow, but the report brought back by Harris soon spread as a camp rumour among the officers and men of Crook, so that they may have slept that night without thought of danger near, and even the vigilance of their picket line, as well as that of the cavalry to whom they largely looked for protection against a surprise, may or may not have been inopportunely relaxed.

For Early, warned of the strength of Sheridan's right, by the failure of Rosser's adventure, had since been studying the chances of an attack on the opposite flank. To this indeed the very difficulty of the approach invited, for in all wars enterprises apparently impracticable have been carelessly guarded against and positions apparently impregnable have been loosely watched and lightly defended, so that it might not be too much to say that every insurmountable difficulty has been surmounted and every impregnable stronghold taken. Such apprehensions as the commander of the Union army may be supposed to have entertained were directed toward his right, where Torbert was, and where the back road to Winchester gave easy access to his rear.

While Early was engaged in considering this plan, he sent Gordon, accompanied by Major Hotchkiss of the engineers, to the signal station on the crest of Three Top Mountain to examine the position of the Union army and to study the details of the proposed movement. From this height these officers looked down upon the country about Cedar Creek as upon an amphitheatre and saw the Union camps as in a panorama. Every feature was in plain view; they counted the tents; they noted the dispositions for attack; they made out the exact situation of the various headquarters; and casting careful glances into the shadowy depths of the Shenandoah, winding about the foot of the mountain far below them, they perceived that the flank of Three Top afforded a footing for the passage of the infantry at least. Upon this information Early was not long in deciding upon his course. Under cover of the night he would send the divisions of Gordon, Ramseur, and Pegram,[4] all under the command of Gordon, over the Shenandoah near Fisher's Hill, across the ox-bow, to the foot of Three Top. Thence picking his way over the foot of the mountain, Gordon in two columns was to cross the river a second time at McInturff's Ford, just below the mouth of Cedar Creek and at Bowman's Ford, several hundred yards below. There he would find himself on the flank and in easy reach of the rear of Crook, and indeed of the whole Union army, with nothing but a thin line of pickets to hinder the rush. While Gordon was thus stealthily creeping into position for his spring, Early meant to take Kershaw and Wharton upon the valley road and quietly to gain a good position for assailing Crook and Emory in front, as soon as the rifles of Gordon should be heard toward the rear. Rosser was to drive in the cavalry on the right of the Union army, while Lomax, from the Luray, was expected to gain the valley road somewhere near Newtown, so as to cut off the retreat. Everything that could jingle or rattle was to be left behind, and the march was to be made in dead silence, while, as the rumble of the guns would be sure to reveal the movement, the whole of the artillery was massed at Strasburg, all ready to gallop to the front as soon as the battle should begin.

A closer study of the trail showed Gordon that it would be possible, however difficult and risky, for dismounted troopers to lead their horses over the path already marked out for his infantry. Accordingly the cavalry brigade of Payne was added to Gordon's column, and after surprising and making good the passage of the fords, the first duty of these horsemen was to ride straight to Belle Grove House and capture Sheridan. Early supposed Sheridan to be still present in command.

Bold as was Early's design of surprising and attacking the vastly superior forces of Sheridan, under conditions that must inevitably stake everything upon the hazard of complete success, it may well be doubted whether in the whole history of war an instance can be found of any similar plan so carefully and successfully arranged and so completely carried out in every detail, up to the moment that must be looked for in the execution of every operation of war, when the shock of battle comes and puts even the wisest prevision in suspense.

---

4. Observe that Ramseur was now commanding the division that had been Rodes's; Pegram having succeeded to Ramseur's old division.

CHAPTER 34

Cedar Creek

The ground whereon the Army of the Shenandoah now found itself was the same on which Sheridan had left it, the troops were the same, and the formations were in all important particulars the same as when he had been present in command, strengthened, however, by additional entrenchments. Twice before the army had occupied the same line, and on both occasions Sheridan had emphatically condemned it as a very bad one. Briefly, the position was formed by the last great outward bend of Cedar Creek before its waters mingle with those of the Shenandoah, the left flank resting lightly on the river, the centre strongly across the valley road, and the extreme right on the creek near the end of the bow.

Crook held a high and partly wooded height or range of heights on the left or east[1] of the valley road, and nearly parallel with it. Thoburn occupied the most advanced spur overlooking the mouth of the creek, while on his left and rear Hayes and Kitching faced toward the Shenandoah with their backs to the road. As the road descended to cross Cedar Creek by the bridge[2] and ford, it followed the course of a rivulet on its left, and three quarters of a mile from Crook, on the opposite side of this ravine and of the road, Emory was posted on a hill whose crest rose steeply a hundred and fifty feet above the bed of the creek. Here Emory planted nearly the whole of his artillery to command the bridge and the neighbouring ford and the approaches on the op-

---

1. Strictly southeast, for the course of the turnpike toward Winchester is about northeast.
2. The present bridge is a short distance above where the old one was.

posite bank, but the slope and crest of this hill were completely and easily commanded from the higher ground held by Thoburn and by Hayes. From the valley road on the left, Emory's line stretched crescent-wise, until its right rested upon a natural bastion formed by the highest part of the hill, whence the descent is precipitous, not only to the creek in front, but on the flank to the gorge of Meadow Brook. This little stream rising some miles farther north near Newtown, and flowing now between high banks and again through marshy borders in a general direction nearly parallel to the road, empties into Cedar Creek about three quarters of a mile above the bridge. Just below the mouth of the brook Cedar Creek can be crossed by a ford lying nearly in a direct prolongation of the line of the valley road from the point where in descending it swerves to the east to pass the bridge, and midway between the bridge and the Meadow Brook ford is still another ford overlooked by Emory's right wing and commanded by the guns of his artillery. Dwight's division formed the right of Emory's line and Grover's the left. From right to left the front line was composed of the brigades of Thomas, Molineux, Birge, and Macauley, with Davis in reserve supporting Thomas, and Shunk, likewise in reserve, supporting Macauley and Birge.[3]

The fronts of Emory and Crook overlooking the creek were strongly entrenched, and Crook was engaged in extending his line of works toward the left and rear of Thoburn to cover the front of Hayes, but this fresh line was as yet unoccupied. Wright's corps, commanded by Ricketts during the absence of Sheridan, while Wright himself commanded the army, was held in reserve on the high ground known as Red Hill overlooking Meadow Brook from the eastward, the divisions encamped for convenience in a sort of irregular echelon, with Ricketts's, under Keifer, in front, Upton's, commanded by Wheaton, on the right and rear in close support, and Getty's on the left and rear of both, and thus nearer to the valley road than either. Behind the Sixth Corps, opposite Middletown, on the high ground on both sides of Marsh Run,

---
3. Dwight having been in arrest during the past fortnight by Emory's orders under charges growing out of criticisms and statements made in his report of the battle of the Opequon, McMillan commanded the First division, leaving his brigade to Thomas. Beal had gone home on leave of absence when the campaign seemed ended, and Davis commanded his brigade.

was Merritt, and far away on his right, watching the approaches and the crossing by the back road, stood Custer.

As the Sixth Corps held no part of the front, but formed a general reserve, its position was not entrenched. Torbert, Emory, and Crook each picketed and watched his own front, and there was not a horseman between the infantry and the supposed position of the enemy at or beyond Fisher's Hill.

Emory had for some days been distrustful of the excessive tranquillity, and on the previous evening his uneasiness had rather been augmented by a report that came to him from Thomas of a little group of men in citizens' dress that had been seen during the day moving about on the edge of Hupp's Hill, as if engaged in noting with more intentness than is usual among civilians the arrangement of the Union camps. This incident Emory reported to Wright for what it might be worth, and Wright, on his part, being already doubtful of the exactness of the information brought in by Harris, ordered Emory and Torbert each to send out a strong reconnoitring party in the early morning, to move in parallel columns on the valley road and on the back road, with the significant caution that they were to go far enough to find out whether Early was still at Fisher's Hill or not.

After crossing the Shenandoah and reaching the foot of Three Top, Gordon halted his men for a few hours' rest before the hard work awaiting them. At one o'clock he silently took up the line of march over the rugged trail toward McInturff's and Bowman's fords, and at five o'clock seized both crossings, with the merest show of resistance from Moore's outlying brigade, and pressed on to Cooley's house, the white house he had noted from Three Top. This landmark, as he knew, was barely thirteen hundred yards from the nearest flank of his enemy. He passed nearly half that distance beyond the house and, as pre-arranged, silently formed his three divisions for the attack. Within five minutes he could be in Kitching's camp.

At the last moment, hearing that Crook was strengthening his entrenchments, Early so far changed his plan as to part company with Wharton at Strasburg, and then, bearing off to the right, to conduct Kershaw to the banks of Cedar Creek at the ford that now bears the name of Roberts. This is about twelve hundred yards above the mouth of the creek; and there, at half-past three in the morning, in the long shadows of the full moon,[4] Early stood with Kershaw at his back and the sleeping ranks of Thoburn directly in his front, and waited only for the appointed hour. At half-past four, Early again set Kershaw in motion. The crossing of Cedar Creek was unobserved and unopposed. Once on the north bank, Kershaw deployed to the right and left, and stood to arms listening for Gordon.

Wharton, who had already formed under cover of the tress, on the edge of Hupp's Hill, crept down the slope to the front of the wood, and there, likewise in shadow, hardly a thousand feet from the bridge and the middle ford, he too watched for the signal.

To crown all, as the dawn drew near a light fog descended upon the river bottom and covered all objects as with a veil.

Almost from the beginning it had been the custom of the Nineteenth Army Corps, at all times when in the presence of the enemy, to stand to arms at daybreak. Moreover as Molineux was to go out on a reconnaissance by half-past five, his men had breakfasted and were lying on their arms waiting for the order to march. Birge and Macauley were to be ready to follow in support after a proper interval, and Shunk was to cover the front of all three during their absence. McMillan had also been notified to support the movement of Grover's brigades. Emory himself was up and dressed, the horses of his staff were saddled, and his own horses were being saddled, when from the left a startling sound broke the stillness of the morning air.

This was the roar of the one tremendous volley by which Kershaw made known his presence before the sleeping camp of Thoburn. In an instant, before a single shot could be fired in return, before the muskets could be taken from the stacks, before the cannoneers could reach their pieces, Kershaw's men, with loud and continuous yells, swarmed over the parapet in Thoburn's front, seized the guns, and sent his half-clad soldiers flying to the rear. Thus Kershaw, who a moment before had been without artillery, suddenly found himself in possession of the seven guns that had

---

4. Being actually three days past the full, the moon rose October 18-19, 1864 at 8.5 p.m., southed at 2.25 a.m., and set at 8.45 a.m. Daylight on the 19th was at 5.40 a.m.; the sun rose at 6.14, set at 5.16; twilight ended 5.50 p.m.

been planted to secure Thoburn's ground. Then upon Emory and upon Hayes, as well as against the flying fugitives, he turned the cannon thus snatched from their own comrades.

At the first sound Molineux moved his men back into the rifle-pits they had left an hour before, and Emory, ordering his corps to stand to arms, rode at once to the left of his line at the valley road to find out the meaning of this strange outbreak. Knowing that Molineux was near and ready, Emory drew from him two regiments, the 22nd Iowa and the 3rd Massachusetts, to support the artillery planted on the left to command the bridge. Hardly had this been done when the shells began to fall among the guns and to enfilade the lines of the infantry. What could this mean but the thing that had actually happened to Thoburn? Grover joined Emory, Crook came from Belle Grove, and Wright from his camp beyond Meadow Brook. The fugitives from Thoburn's unfortunate division went streaming by.

Then suddenly from the left and rear came the startling rattle of the rifles that told of Gordon's attack on the exposed flank of Hayes and Kitching. While all eyes were directed toward Kershaw, Gordon, still further favoured by the fog, the outcry, and the noise of the cannonade, was not perceived by the troops of Hayes and Kitching until the instant when his solid lines of battle, unheralded by a single skirmisher of his own, and unannounced by those set to watch against him, fell upon the ranks of Crook. He tried in vain to form on the road. Startled from their sleep by the surprise of their comrades on their right, and naturally shaken by the disordered rush of the fugitives through their ranks, his men, old soldiers and good soldiers as they were, gave way at the first onset, before the fire of Gordon had become heavy and almost without stopping to return it.

Then swiftly Gordon and Kershaw moved together against the uncovered left and rear of Emory, while at the same time Early, who after seeing Kershaw launched, had ridden back for Wharton and the artillery, was bringing them into position for a front attack. Besides the sounds that had aroused Emory and Crook, Wright, from his more remote position, had listened to the rattle of Rosser's carbines,[5] but after a moment of natural doubt had perceived that the true attack was on the left, and accordingly he

---

5. This was probably the first sound heard that morning.

had ordered Ricketts to advance with Getty and Keifer to the valley road toward the sound of the battle. If this was to be of the least advantage, the valley road must be somehow held by somebody until Ricketts should come. Emory sent Thomas across the road into the ravine and the wood beyond, and bade him stand fast at all hazards. But the time was too short. Thomas, after a desperate resistance, was forced back by the overwhelming masses of Kershaw, yet not until this tried brigade had left a third of its number on the ground to attest its valour. About the colours of the 8th Vermont the fight was furious. Again and again the colours were down; three bearers were slain; before the sun rose two men out of three had fallen, that the precious emblems might be saved.[6] Thus were many priceless minutes won. Then, as there was no longer anything to hinder the advance of Kershaw on the left, and of Gordon on the rear, while Wharton and the forty guns of Early's artillery were beginning their work in front, from the left toward the right, successively the brigades of the Nineteenth Corps began to give way; yet as they drifted toward the right and rear, in that stress the men held well to their colours, and although there may and must have been many that fell out, not a brigade or a regiment lost its organization for a moment.

When the pressure reached Molineux and Davis on the reverse side of the entrenchments, both brigades began moving off, under Emory's orders, by the right flank to take position near Belle Grove on the right of Ricketts's division of the Sixth Corps, which had come up and was trying to extend its line diagonally to reach the valley road. To cover this position and to hold off the onward rush of Gordon, Emory had already posted the 114th and the 153rd New York on the commanding knoll five hundred yards to the southward overlooking the road. When driven off these regiments rejoined their brigade before Belle Grove. Thither also came the detached regiments of Molineux, and there Neafie joined them with the 3rd brigade, after a strong stand at their breastworks, wherein Macauley fell severely wounded, and

---

6. According to the regimental history (p. 218) over 100 were lost out of 159 engaged; of 16 officers 13 were killed or wounded. The monument erected September 21, 1885, says 110 were killed and wounded out of 164 engaged. The revised official figures are 17 killed, 66 wounded—together 83 (including 12 officers); besides these there were 23 missing; in all, 106.

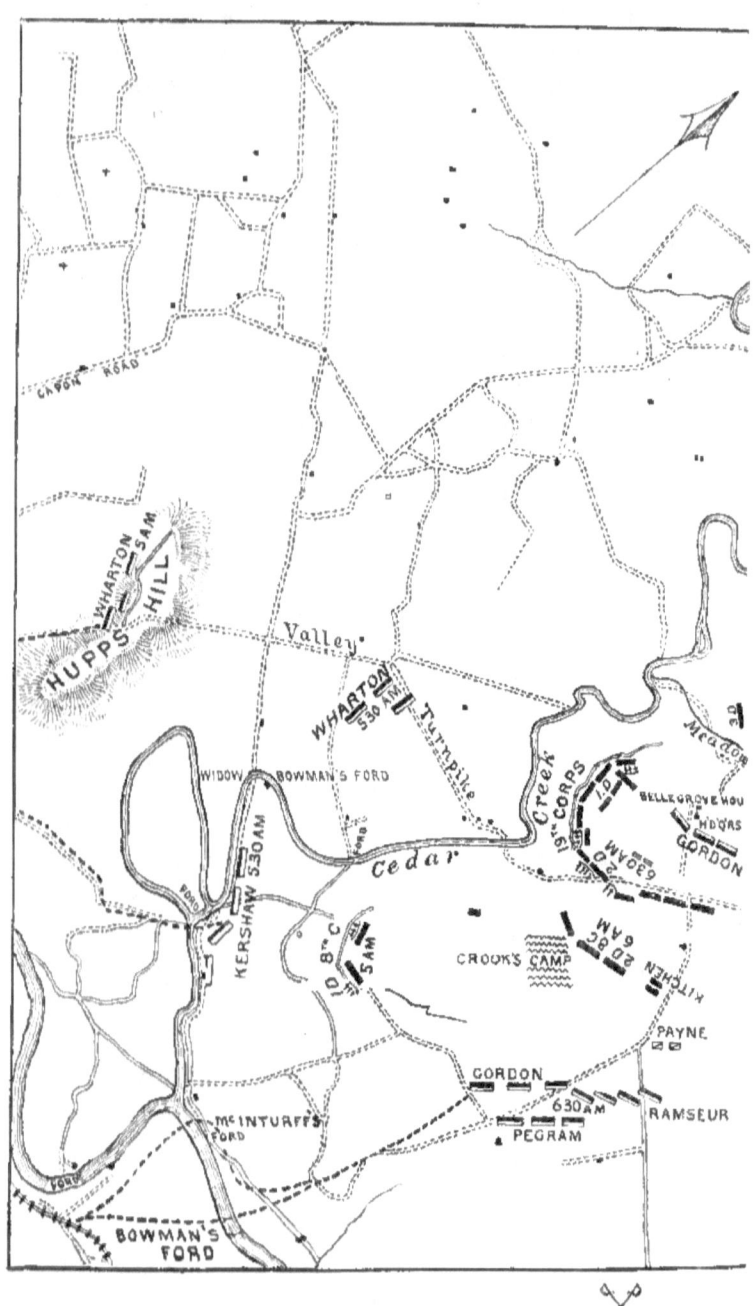

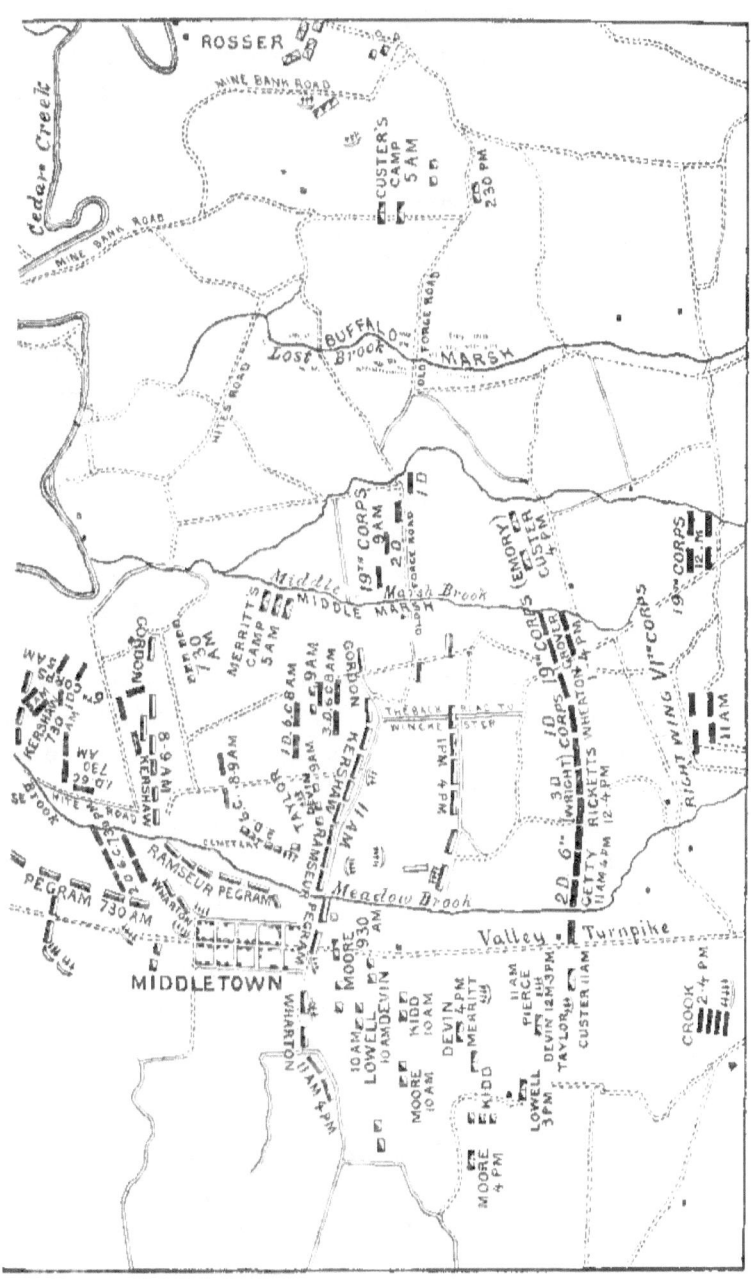

OCTOBER 19, 1864.

MAP OF 1873.

the 156th and 176th had hard fighting hand-to-hand to keep their colours, at the cost of the staves. Birge retired along the line of works to the open ground beyond Meadow Brook, where Shunk joined him.

In quitting their posts at the breastworks Haley, having lost forty-nine horses killed in harness, had to abandon three guns of his 1st Maine battery, and Taft lost three pieces of his 5th New York battery at the difficult crossing of Meadow Brook. There, too, from the same cause, three guns of the 17th Indiana and two of the Rhode Island battery were abandoned. The losses of the infantry were to be counted in thousands. Grover was slightly wounded; Macauley, as has been said, severely. Emory had lost both his horses, and was for a time commanding the corps afoot. Birge rode a mule. Thus the Nineteenth Corps lost eleven guns. Crook had already lost seven, and the Sixth Corps was presently to lose six.

With Gordon on his flank and rear, every moment drawing nearer to the mastery of the valley road, Wright had to think, and to think quickly, of the safety and the success of the army he commanded. For it there was no longer a position south of Middletown. What security was there that Custer and Powell would be able all day long to hold off, as in the event they did, the flank and rear attacks of Rosser and of Lomax? What if the Longstreet message were true and yet a third surprise in store? Time, time was needed, whether to bring up the troops or to change front, to march to the rear past the faces of the advancing enemy, to hold him in check, and to re-form. Whatever was to be done was to be done quickly; and Wright, throwing prudence into the balance, made up his mind for a retreat to a fresh position, where his line of communications would be preserved and its flanks protected. Middletown and the cavalry camp pointed out the ground. Accordingly he gave the word to Getty, Ricketts being wounded, to retire on Middletown, guiding on the valley road, and to Emory to form on Getty's right—that is, on the left of the Sixth Corps in retreat. The battle had been raging for nearly an hour when Wright gave this order to abandon Belle Grove. The retreat threw upon Getty's division, now under Grant, the severe task of covering the exposed right flank of the army in retreat, while the left was gradually swinging into the direction of the new line. Getty, having handsomely performed this service, crossed Meadow Brook abreast with Middletown and took position on the high and partly wooded ground that rises beyond the brook to the west of the village and on a line with Merritt's camp. Here, on the southern edge of the village cemetery and on the crest behind it, Getty planted his artillery, posted Grant to hold the immediate front, and somewhat in his rear, under the trees, following the contour of the hill, as it rises toward the west, he placed Wheaton and Keifer.

To reach his position on the left of Getty in retreat, Emory had to gain ground to the westward, to descend the hill from Belle Grove, to cross Meadow Brook, and climbing the opposite slope to face about and re-form his line in good order on the crest of Red Hill. Here, before Dr. Shipley's house, nearly across the ground where the men of Wheaton and of Getty had slept the night before, for the best part of an hour Emory stood at bay. Kershaw followed over the Belle Grove Hill, across Meadow Brook, up the slope of Red Hill, and formed line facing north; but then, seeing the fighting part of Emory's infantry before him and the formidable array of Merritt's cavalry in close support, he refrained from renewing the attack until Early could send Gordon to his aid. Thus the bold stand at Red Hill gave the time the situation craved, and while Kershaw waited, Emory, following his orders from Wright, crossed over to the cemetery[7] and placed himself on the west of Getty. Thomas rejoined McMillan. Torbert meanwhile had moved over with Merritt to the left flank. Thus around the cemetery, about half-past seven, the unshaken strength of the Army of the Shenandoah was gathered, every eye looking once more toward the south.

While awaiting the general attack for which Early was plainly preparing, Wright deployed his lines, according to the ground, from the south wall of the cemetery overlooking Meadow Brook on the left, in a rough echelon of divisions to Marsh Brook on the right, in order of Grant, Keifer, Wheaton, Grover, McMillan. Between the arms of Marsh Brook, in front and behind the Old Forge road, on open ground nearly as high as Getty's, Emory formed his corps in

---

7. The official map, accurate as it is in general, errs in some important particulars; for one, in representing Emory as retreating in a direct line toward the north from Red Hill to the Old Forge line. This would actually have carried his force through the ranks of the cavalry.

echelon of brigades. Here, not doubting that the decisive combat of the day was to be fought, Emory began fortifying his front with the help of loose rails and stones.

To protect himself against the menacing movement of the cavalry on his right in front of Middletown, Early posted Ramseur with two batteries directly across the valley road, and when he saw Getty's stand near the cemetery, he brought Wharton directly down the road and sent him to the attack, but this Getty easily threw off and drove back Wharton in such confusion that before renewing the attempt Early waited to complete a new line of battle almost perpendicular to his first and therefore to the road. From the right at Middletown to the left at Red Hill the new line was formed by Pegram, Ramseur, Kershaw, and Gordon, with Wharton behind Pegram. On the right of this line also Early massed the forty guns of his artillery augmented by some of the twenty-four pieces taken from the Union army.

And now the increasing heat of the sun dissolved the fog, and revealed to the combatants the true situation of affairs. To Early the position of the Union army, its salient, as it were, lying directly before him where he stood, seemed so strong that he hesitated to hazard another attack until the concentrated fire of his artillery should have produced an impression, while to Wright, not only was the menace of Early's artillery very obvious, but the weakness of his own left flank, broken by Meadow Brook and adhering lightly to the valley road, was still present.

The force of Early's first onset was spent; his one chance of seizing and holding the valley road in the rear of the Union army had slipped away, while his cavalry had utterly failed to accomplish any part of the task confided to it. Time and strength had both been lost to the Confederates by the uncontrollable plunder of the camps and the sutlers' stores.

The Old Forge road is but a country lane that crosses the field from the north end of Middletown. It afforded no position, its chief value being as uniting the wings of the army, and Wright's object in taking up this line was simply to gain time to develop a better fighting line still farther to the rear. Now, seeing that Getty had accomplished his purpose in holding on at the cemetery, Wright ordered him to move slowly, in line of battle, toward the north, guiding on the valley road, with Merritt's cavalry beyond it following and covering the operation, while Emory, taking up the movement in his turn, was to look to Wheaton for his guide. Wright's order found Emory's men in the act of completing their hasty defences, while Emory was moving about among them strongly declaring his purpose not to go back another inch.

Getty began by withdrawing Grant, and when Grant had passed for some distance beyond the left of Keifer, his right in retreat, Keifer followed, while on his left, in retreat, Wheaton, and on Wheaton's left Emory marched, as nearly as may be, shoulder to shoulder in a solid line. Thus Keifer formed the centre of the retreating line of battle, with Ball on his right and Emerson on his left. Having to pass over rough ground and among trees, the line was broken to the reversed front by the right of regiments, the head of each guiding on its right-hand neighbour. Thus it happened[8] that in passing through a thick wood, Keifer's division was split in two, his brigades losing sight of one another, so that on coming once more into the open field, Ball found himself alone with no other troops in sight on either hand; but soon hearing the sound of Getty's guns over the right shoulder, he faced about and marched back to a stone wall upon a lane, where he found Getty already in position. Emerson, however, moving more quickly through the wood, because the ground was easier, continued his march toward the north, continually bearing to the right as he went, in order to regain the lost touch with Ball, while on the left Wheaton and Emory, knowing nothing of the break, naturally and gradually conformed to the movement of Emerson. Finally, when the left of the line once more entered the woods, Emerson, gradually changing the direction toward the right, drifted Wheaton away from Emory, and when this was perceived by the commanders, each began to look for his neighbour. It is also probable that when the separation took place the interval was gradually widened by Emory's movement with his right resting on a road that, while apparently following the true line of direction, really carried him every mo-

---

8. "The Battle of Cedar Creek," by Col. Moses M. Granger, 122nd Ohio, printed in the valuable collection of *Sketches of War History*, published by the Ohio Commandery of the Loyal Legion, vol. iii., pp. 122-125. The author is likewise indebted to General Keifer for the opportunity to use in this manuscript his paper on Cedar Creek, prepared for the same series.

ment a little farther toward the left. However that may be, when almost at the same instant Wheaton and Emory halted and faced about, they found themselves about eight hundred yards apart, a thousand yards behind the line that Getty had just taken up, on the westward prolongation of which Keifer had joined him with the brigade of Ball.

The affair had now lasted five hours; the retreat was at an end; a tactical accident had carried it half a mile farther than was intended; as it was, from the extreme front of Emory at daybreak to his extreme rear at eleven o'clock, the measured distance was but four miles. Every step of the way had been traversed under orders—under orders that had carried the Nineteenth Corps three times across the field of battle, so that its march, from Belle Grove to the Old Forge road, might be represented by the letter N.

When Early saw the Union line retreating, he moved forward to the cross-road beyond the cemetery, and posted his troops behind the stone walls. Wharton extended the line on the east side of the turnpike, with three batteries massed between him and the road. Pegram covered the turnpike, his left resting on Meadow Brook, and beyond it Ramseur, Kershaw, and Gordon carried the line to the east bank of Middle Marsh Brook. Early had now two courses open to him: one was to extricate his army from its position, with its enemy directly in front and Cedar Creek in rear, before the Union commander could take the initiative; the other was to attack vigorously with all his force before the Union infantry should be able to complete the new line of battle now plainly in the act of formation. In either case, although he could easily see than on both flanks the line of his infantry far overlapped that of his antagonist, Early must have perceived that he had to reckon with the whole mass of the Union cavalry, unshaken and as yet untouched. Moreover, his men had already done a long and hard day's work after a short night.

Depleted as were the ranks of the Union infantry by the heavy battle losses of the early morning, and the still heavier losses by the misconduct of the stragglers of all the corps except the cavalry, it was not to be doubted that the men who stood by the colours on the Old Forge road meant to abide to the end. As all old soldiers know, the fighting line, granting that enough remain to make a fighting line, is never so strong as the moment after the first shock of battle has shaken out the men that always straggle on the march and skulk on the field. When, therefore, the first compact line faced about, it was with determination and with hope; yet scarcely had the fires of resolution been relit and begun to kindle to a glow than they were suddenly extinguished and all was plunged in gloom by the unlooked-for order to retreat. Upon the whole army a lethargy fell, and though every man expected and stood ready to do his duty, it was with a certain listlessness amounting almost to indifference that he waited for what was to come next. In the sensations of most, hunger was perhaps uppermost, and while some munched the bread and meat from their haversacks and other waited to make coffee, many threw themselves upon the ground where they stood and fell asleep.

Far down the road from among the crowd of fugitives, where no man on that field cared to look, came a murmur like the breaking of the surf on a far-off shore. Nearer it drew, grew louder, and swelled to a tumult. Cheers! The cheers of the stragglers. As the men instinctively turned toward the sound, they were seized with amazement to see the tide of stragglers setting strongly toward the south. Then out from among them, into the field by the roadside, cantered a little man on a black horse, and from the ranks of his own cavalry arose a cry of "Sheridan!" Through all the ranks the message flashed, and, as if it had been charged by the electric spark, set every man on his feet and made his heart once more beat high within him.

This was Wednesday, and Sheridan, before finally setting out for Washington, had told Wright to look for him on Tuesday. Rapidly despatching, as has been seen, his business at the War Office, Sheridan left Washington by the special train he had asked for at noon on the 17th, accompanied by the engineers charged with the duty of selecting the position that Halleck wished to fortify. They slept that night at Martinsburg, and rode the next day, the 18th of October, to Winchester. There Sheridan learned that all was well with his army and was also told of the reconnoissances projected for the next morning. He determined to remain at Winchester in order to go over the ground the next morning with the engineers. Aroused about six o'clock by the report of heavy firing, he ascribed it to the reconnoitring column, and thought but little of it until, between half-past eight and nine, having finished his breakfast, he became uneasy at the continued sound of the cannon. Then mounting "Rienzi," accompanied by his staff and followed by his escort, he rode out to join his army where he had left it, fourteen miles away, on the banks of Cedar Creek. The fight of the morning had come to an end an hour ago. Riding at an easy trot half a mile out on the hill beyond Abraham's Creek,[9] he was shocked to see the tattered and dishevelled head of the column of stragglers, every man making the best of his way toward the Potomac, without his arms, his equipments, or his knapsack, carrying, in short, nothing but what he wore. Most of these must have been shaken out of the ranks when Kershaw surprised the camp of Thoburn. If this be so, they had travelled more than thirteen miles in little more than three hours.

This appalling sight brought to Sheridan's mind the Longstreet message, "Be ready when I join you, and we will crush Sheridan." Should he stop his routed army at Winchester and fight there? No, he must go to his men, restore their broken ranks, or share their fate. How he rode on has been made famous in song and story, yet never so well told as in the modest narrative, stamped in every line with the impress of the soldier's truthful frankness, than in the entertaining volumes that were the last work of the great leader's life.[10]

Once arrived on the field, about half-past ten or perhaps eleven o'clock, Sheridan lost no time in assuming personal command of the army. Establishing his headquarters on the hill behind Getty, he proceeded to complete the dispositions he found already in progress. He saw at a glance that the line on which Wright had placed Getty was well chosen; and though knowing nothing of the break that had taken place during the accidental loss of direction by the left wing of Getty's corps, and so wrongly inferring from what he saw that Getty was a mere rear-guard, he yet adopted the position for his fighting line, sent his staff officers with orders for the rest of the troops to form on that line, and thus actually completed the arrangements begun by Wright. It sufficed that Emerson, Wheaton,

---

9. Called Mill Creek in Sheridan's report and *Memoirs*. There is a mill on the north bank.
10. *Personal Memoirs of P. H. Sheridan*, vol. ii., pp. 75-83. The distance from Winchester to Getty's position is ten and three quarter miles.

and Emory should face about, as they were already about to do, and should form on the prolongation of Getty's line. This they did promptly and in perfect order. Wright resumed the command of the Sixth Corps and Getty of his own division. Then feeling his left quite strong enough under Merritt's care, Sheridan sent Custer, for whom he had other designs, back to the right flank.

It was past noon before all this was accomplished. Then Sheridan, content with the position and appearance of his own army, and perceiving that Early was getting ready to attack him, acted on the suggestion of Major George Forsyth, his aide-de-camp, and rode the length of the line of battle in order to show himself to his men. A tumult of cheers greeted him and followed him as, hat in hand, he passed in front of regiment after regiment, speaking a few words of encouragement to each. Sheridan possessed in a degree unequalled the power of raising in the hearts of his soldiers the sort of enthusiasm that, transmuting itself into action, causes men to attempt impossibilities, and to disregard and overcome obstacles. Almost from the moment of entering the valley he had gained the confidence of the infantry, to whom he had been a stranger. By the cavalry he had long been idolized. The feeling of an army for its general is a thing not to be reasoned with or explained away; once aroused, it belongs to him as exclusively as the expression of his face, the manner of his gait, or the form of his signature, and is not to be transferred to his successor or delegated even to the ablest of his lieutenants, whatever the skill, the merit, or the reputation of either. The mere presence of Sheridan in the ranks of the Army of the Shenandoah that day brought with it the assurance of victory.

Emory at first formed his corps in two lines, the First division under Dwight, whom Sheridan had released from arrest, on the right, and Grover on the left; but soon the whole corps was deployed in one line in the order from right to left by brigades of McMillan, Davis, Birge, Molineux, Neafie, Shunk.

When the line of the Old Forge road was abandoned by Wright, Early moved forward and occupied it. Between one and two o'clock he advanced Gordon and Kershaw to attack Wheaton and Emory. Seeing that the weight of the attack was about to fall on the right, Sheridan sent Wheaton to the support of Emory.

However, Gordon's onset proved so light that no assistance was needed, for, after three or four volleys had been exchanged, the attack was easily and completely thrown off. Kershaw's movement was even more feeble.

Several causes now delayed the counter attack of Sheridan. Crook was endeavouring to re-form the stragglers on his colours behind Merritt. Apprehension of the coming of Longstreet was only dissipated by the information gained from prisoners during the afternoon, and finally arose a false rumour of the appearance of a column of Confederate cavalry in the rear toward Winchester; and this seemed plausible enough until at last word came from Powell that he was still holding off Lomax. Then Sheridan gave the signal for the whole line to go forward against the enemy, beginning with Getty on the left, as a pivot, while the whole right was to sweep onward, and, driving the enemy before it, to swing toward the valley road near the camps of the morning.

About four Getty started, and the movement being taken up in succession toward the right, in a few minutes the whole line was advancing steadily. From that moment to the end the men hardly stopped an instant for anything. The resistance of the Confederates, though at first steady, and here and there even spirited, was of short duration. For a few moments, indeed, the attack seemed to hang on the extreme right as McMillan, rushing on even more rapidly than the order of the combat demanded, found himself suddenly enveloped by the right wheel of the brigade of Evans, forming the extreme left of the division of Gordon and of the Confederate army. But while McMillan was thus attacked and his leading troops were called to meet the danger, this, as suddenly as it had come, was swept away by the swift onset of Davis directly upon the front and flank of Evans. To do this Davis had not only to act instantly, but also to change front under a double fire; yet he and his brigade were equal to the emergency, and McMillan joining in, together they not only threw off the attack of Evans, but bursting through the re-entrant angle of Gordon's line, quickly swept Evans off the field. Knowing this to be the critical point of his line, because the wheeling flank, Sheridan was there. "Stay where you are," was his order, "till you see my boy Custer over there."

Then upon the high ground appeared Custer at the head of his bold troopers, making ready to swoop down upon the broken wing of Gordon. Almost at the same instant, the whole right of the line rushed to the charge, and while Custer rode down Gordon's left flank, Dwight, with McMillan and Davis, began rolling up the whole Confederate line. Meanwhile, on the left centre the Union attack likewise hung for a moment, where Molineux, on the southerly slope of a wooded hollow, saw himself confronted by Kershaw on the opposite crest, only to be reached by climbing the steep bare side of the "dirt hill." But the keen eye of Molineux easily saw through the difficulties of the ground, and when he was ready his men and Birge's, rising up and together charging boldly out of the hollow, up the hill, across the open ground, and over the stone wall, in the face of a fierce fire, settled the overthrow of Kershaw and sent a panic running down the line of Ramseur. Wright attacking with equal vigour, soon the disorder spread through every part of Early's force, and in rout and ruin the exultant victors of the morning were flying up the valley.

"Back to your camps!" had been the watchword ever since Sheridan showed himself on the field. Dwight's men were the first to stand once more upon their own ground, but by that time Sheridan's army had executed, though without much regard to order, a complete left wheel. While the infantry took up its original positions, the cavalry pursued the flying enemy with such vigour that an accidental displacement of a single plank on a little bridge near Strasburg caused the whole of Early's artillery that had not yet passed on, to fall into the hands of Sheridan. Thus were taken 48 cannon, 52 caissons, all the ambulances that had been lost in the morning, many wagons, and seven battle flags; of the artillery 24 pieces were the same that had been lost in the early morning. From every part of the abandoned field great stacks of rifles were gathered. The prisoners taken were about 1,200, according to the reports of Sheridan's officers, or something over 1,000 by Early's account. Early also gives his loss in killed and wounded, without distinguishing between the two, as 1,860, and reports the capture of 1,429 prisoners from the Union army in the early hours of the day. Of these he had made sure by sending them promptly to the rear. Ramseur was mortally wounded in the last stand made by his division, and died a few days later in the hands and under the care of his former comrades of Sheridan's army.

Sheridan's loss was 644 killed, 3,430 wounded, and 1,591 captured or missing; in all, 5,665. Of these the Sixth Corps had 298 killed, 1,628 wounded—together, 1,926; the Nineteenth Corps 257 killed, 1,336 wounded—together, 1,593. Crook lost 60 killed, 342 wounded—together, 402; the cavalry 29 killed, 224 wounded—together, 253. The missing were thus divided: Wright 194, Emory 776, Crook 548, Torbert 43. The greatest proportionate loss of the day was suffered by the 114th New York, which had 21 killed, 86 wounded, including 17 mortally, and 8 missing—in all, 115 out of 250 engaged. Its fatal casualties reached 15.2, and the killed and wounded 42.8 per cent. of the number engaged. These figures are from the corrected reports of the War Department. The missing exceed the captured, as set down in Early's report, by only 132. Among the killed and mortally wounded were Bidwell, Thoburn, Kitching, and that superb soldier and accomplished gentleman, General Charles Russell Lowell, who, although severely wounded in the morning, at the head of his brigade held fast to the stone wall until, in the last decisive charge, his death-blow came. Grover received a second severe wound early in the final charge that broke the Confederate left. Birge then took his division.

Without a halt and with scarcely a show of organized resistance, Early retreated to Fisher's Hill. Merritt and Custer, uniting on the south bank of Cedar Creek, kept up the pursuit until the night was well advanced, but soon their captures became so heavy in men and material, that help was needed to take care of them, so, barely an hour after going into camp the jaded infantry of Dwight once more turned out and marched with alacrity to Strasburg.

Toward morning Early withdrew his infantry from the lines of Fisher's Hill, and marched on New Market, leaving Rosser to cover the movement. In the morning, upon Torbert's approach, Rosser retired, closely pursued to Edenburg, sending Lomax to the Luray to guard the right flank of the retreating Confederates.

The strength of the contending forces in this remarkable battle may always give ground for dispute. No official figures exist to determine the question directly; therefore on either side the numbers are a matter of opinion. The author's, formed after a careful consideration of all the authorities, is that when the battle began, Wright commanded an effective force of not more than 31,000 officers and men of all arms, made up of 9,000 in the Sixth Corps, 9,500 in the Nineteenth Corps, 6,000 in Crook's command, and 6,500 cavalry. The infantry probably numbered 23,000: Ricketts 8,500, Emory 9,000, Crook 5,500. Of these, therefore, the hard fighting fell on 17,500. The losses in the Sixth and Nineteenth Corps, nearly all incurred in the early morning, being about 4,500, the two corps should have mustered 13,500 for the counter-attack of the afternoon, yet the ground they then stood upon, from the road to the brook, measures barely 7,400 feet. With all allowances, therefore, Sheridan cannot have taken more than 8,000 of his infantry into this attack. This leaves out Crook's men bodily, and calls for 5,500 unrepentant stragglers from the ranks of Emory and Wright—one man in three. After all is said, unhappily there is nothing so extraordinary in this, but strange indeed would it have been if many of these skulkers had come back into the fight, as Sheridan considerately declares they did.

As to Early's force, the difficulty of coming to a positive conclusion is even greater. General Early himself says he went into the battle with but 8,800 muskets. General Dawes, perhaps the most accomplished statistician of the war, makes the total present for duty 22,000; of these 15,000 would be infantry. The figures presented by the unprejudiced statistician of the *Century War Book*[11] call for 15,000 of all arms. Of these 10,000 would be infantry.

Early may be said to have accomplished the ultimate object of his attack at Cedar Creek, yet at a fearful cost, for although all thought of transferring any part of Sheridan's force to the James was for the moment given up, on the other hand Early had completed the destruction[12] of his prestige, had suffered an irreparable diminution of numbers, and had seen his army almost shaken to pieces.

Grant once more returned to his favourite project of a movement in force on Charlottesville and Gordonsville, but Sheridan continuing to oppose the scheme tenaciously, it came to nothing.

---

11. Vol. iv., pp. 524, 532. And see appendix for the valuable memorandum kindly prepared expressly for this work by General E. C. Dawes.
12. Justly or unjustly; unjustly I think, being unable to see how any one could have done better.

His own plan, eventually carried out, was to hold the lower valley in sufficient strength, and to move against the line of the Virginia Central railway with all his cavalry. The rails of the Manassas Gap line, so often re-laid, were once more and for the last time taken up from the Blue Ridge back to Augur's outposts at Bull Run, and so this will-o'-the-wisp, that had danced before the eyes of the government ever since 1861, was at last extinguished, while from Winchester to the Potomac the railway, abandoned by Johnston when he marched to Bull Run, was re-constructed to simplify the question of supplies.

CHAPTER 35

Victory and Home

On the 7th of November, on the battle-field of Cedar Creek, Emory passed his corps in review before Sheridan. Sheridan spoke freely and in the highest terms of the soldierly bearing and good conduct of the officers and men. On the same day the President broke up the organization of the remnant of the various detachments, still known as the Nineteenth Corps, left under the command of Canby in Louisiana and Mississippi, and appointed Emory to the permanent command of the Nineteenth Army Corps in the field in Virginia.

The corps staff, mainly composed of the same officers who with lower rank had been serving at the headquarters of the Detachment, so called, since quitting Louisiana, included Lieutenant-Colonel Duncan S. Walker, Assistant Adjutant-General; Lieutenant-Colonel John M. Sizer, Acting-Assistant Inspector-General; Captain O. O. Potter, Chief Quartermaster; Captain H. R. Sibley, Chief Commissary of Subsistence; Captain Robert F. Wilkinson, Judge Advocate; Surgeon W. R. Brownell, Medical Director; Captain Henry C. Inwood, Provost-Marshal; Major Peter French, Captain James C. Cooley, and Captain James W. De Forest, aides-de-camp.

On the 17th of November Emory adopted a corps badge and a new system of headquarters flags. The badge was to be a fan-leaved cross with an octagonal centre; for officers, of gold suspended from the left breast by a ribbon, the colour red, white, and blue for the corps headquarters, red for the First division, blue for the Second. Enlisted men were to wear on the hat or cap a similar badge of cloth, two inches square, in colours like the ribbon. The flags were to have a similar cross, of white on a blue swallowtail for corps headquarters;

for divisions, a white cross on a triangular flag, the ground red for the First division, blue for the Second; the brigade flags rectangular in various combinations of red, blue, and white cross and ground, the ground divided horizontally for the brigades of the First division, and perpendicularly for those of the Second division.

On the 9th of November Sheridan drew back to Kernstown, meaning to go into winter quarters. Early eagerly followed as far as Middletown, intent on discovering what this might mean; but when, on the 12th, Torbert once more fell upon the unfortunate cavalry of Rosser, on both flanks of the Confederate position, and completely routed it, while Dudley, advancing with his brigade[1] in support of the cavalry, showed that Sheridan was ready to give battle, the Confederate commander became satisfied that Sheridan had sent no troops to Petersburg. Sheridan made all his arrangements to attack Early on the morning of the 13th, but Early did not wait for this, and when the sun rose he was again far on the way to New Market. It was during Dudley's movement that the Nineteenth Corps suffered its last loss in battle, the 29th Maine having one man wounded, by name Barton H. Ross.

When the approach of winter made active operations in the valley impossible, Lee, who had already detached Kershaw, called back to the defence of Richmond and Petersburg the whole of Early's corps, and at the same time, almost to the very day, Grant called on Sheridan for the Sixth Corps. Thus in the second week of December Wright rejoined the Army of the Potomac. Soon afterward Crook's command was divided and detached to Petersburg and West Virginia, leaving only Torbert and Emory with Sheridan in the valley. Early, his force reduced to Wharton and Rosser, went into winter quarters at Staunton, with his outposts at New Market and a signal party on watch at the station on Massanutten.

These reductions of force, together with the increasing severity of the winter, made it desirable to occupy a line nearer the base of supplies at Harper's Ferry, and, accordingly, on the 30th of December, after living for six weeks in improvised huts or "shebangs,"

---

1. Beal's, of Dwight's division. Dudley, having rejoined November 2nd, commanded it till November 14th, when Beal came back and relieved him; again from November 18th to December 7th, when a dispute as to relative and brevet rank was ended by Beal's receiving his commission as a full brigadier-general.

as they were called, roughly put together of rails, stones, and any other material to be found, the Nineteenth Corps broke up its cantonment before Kernstown, called Camp Russell, and marching over the frozen ground, took up a position to cover the railway and the roads near Stephenson's. Here, at Camp Sheridan, it was intended to build regular huts, but on the last day of the year, when the men were as yet without shelter of any kind, a heavy snow storm set in, during which they suffered severely. As soon as this was over, the men fell to work in earnest, and with lumber from the quartermaster's department and timber from the forest, soon had the whole command comfortably housed. Meanwhile Currie's brigade, which had been so long detached, engaged in the arduous and thankless duty of guarding the wagon-trains, rejoined Dwight's division. Brigadier-General James D. Fessenden having succeeded Currie in command the 5th of January, 1865, the brigade was again detached to Winchester; McMillan was at Summit Point; and Beal, as well as the headquarters of Dwight and Emory, at Stephenson's.

On the 6th of January Grover's division bade farewell to the Nineteenth Corps, and, embarking upon the cars of the Baltimore and Ohio railway, set out by way of Baltimore for some unknown destination. This presently proved to be Savannah, whither Grover was ordered to hold the ground seized by the armies under Sherman, while Sherman went on his way through the Carolinas. On the 27th of February, Sheridan broke up what remained of his Army of the Shenandoah, and placing himself at the head of his superb column of 10,000 troopers, marched to achieve Grant's longing for Lynchburg, Charlottesville, and Gordonsville, and to rejoin the Army of the Potomac.

Hancock now took command of the Middle Military Division. Of the Army of the Shenandoah there remained only the fragment of the Nineteenth Corps. On the 14th of March the men of Emory's old division passed for the last time before their favourite commander. A week later was published to the command the order of the President, dated March 20, 1865, by which the Nineteenth Army Corps was dissolved. Then bidding them a tender and touching farewell, on the 30th of March Emory quitted the cantonment at Stephenson's, and went to Cumberland to take command of the Military Department of that name.

In the early days of April the tedium of winter quarters was relieved by the good news of Grant's successes before Petersburg. It was evident that Lee's army was breaking up, and to guard against the possible escape of any fragment of it by the valley highway, on the 4th of April Hancock sent Dwight's division back to Camp Russell, but on the 7th the troops were drawn in to Winchester and encamped on the bank of Abraham's Creek. Here, at midnight on the 9th of April, the whole command turned out to hear the official announcement of Lee's surrender. The next morning, in a drenching rain, Dwight marched eighteen miles to Summit Point. On the 20th of April the division moved by railway to Washington, where it arrived on the morning of the 21st, and with colours shrouded in black for the memory of Lincoln, marched past the President's house and encamped at Tennallytown on the same ground the detachments of the corps had occupied on the night of the 13th of July the year before. Here the duty devolved upon the division of guarding all the ways out of Washington toward the northwest, from Rock Creek to the Potomac, in order to prevent the escape of such of the assassins of the President as might still be lurking within the city. This was but a part of the heavy and continuous line of sentries that stretched for thirty-five miles around the capital. A week later Dwight moved to the neighbourhood of Bladensburg and encamped on the line the division had been ordered to defend on the afternoon of its arrival from New Orleans. In the first week of May heavy details were furnished to guard the prison on the grounds of the arsenal where the assassins were confined.

The armies of Meade and Sherman were now concentrating on the hills about Washington, preparatory to passing in review before President Johnson; and Dwight being ordered to report to Willcox, then commanding the Ninth Army Corps, and to follow that corps on the occasion of the review. Willcox inspected the division on the 12th of May on the parade ground of Fort Bunker Hill.

Sheridan, although he had brought up his cavalry for the great review, had been ordered to take command in the Southwest, and as Grant deemed the matter urgent, because of French and Mexican complications, Sheridan was destined to have no part in the approaching ceremonies, yet he could not resist the chance of once more looking at what was left of the infantry that had followed him in triumph through the Shenandoah. When the men saw him riding at the side of Willcox, mounted once more upon "Rienzi" and wearing the same animated smile that had cheered and encouraged them in the evil hour at Winchester, before the cliffs of Fisher's Hill, and in the gloom of Cedar Creek, they were not to be restrained from violating all the solemn proprieties of the occasion, but broke out into a tumult of cheers.

On the 22nd of May, Dwight broke camp near Bladensburg, and, marching to the plain east of the Capitol, near the Congressional Cemetery, went into bivouac with the Ninth Corps. Here the men, after their long and hard field service, gave way to open disgust at hearing the order read on parade requiring them to appear in white gloves at the great review. On Tuesday, the 23rd of May, the review took place. The men were up at three, and were inspected at half-past seven, but it was half-past ten before Dwight took up the line of march in the rear of the Ninth Corps, followed by the Fifth.

On the 1st of June, 1865, the breaking up began. The 114th and 116th New York were taken from Beal's brigade, and the 133rd from Fessenden's, and ordered to be mustered out of the service of the United States. The 8th Vermont had already gone to the Sixth Corps to join the old Vermont brigade. The rest of Dwight's division embarked on transport steamers, under orders for Savannah, where they landed on the 4th of June. There they found many of their comrades of Grover's division.

To return to Grover. Embarking at Baltimore about the 11th of January, after some detention, the advance of his division landed at Savannah on the 19th of January. The rest of the division gradually followed, and at Savannah the troops remained doing garrison and police duty until about the 4th of March, when Grover was ordered to take transports and join Schofield in North Carolina, in order to open communication with Sherman's army, then advancing once more toward the sea-coast. Wilmington had fallen on the 22nd of February. Then Schofield sent a force, under Cox, to open the railway from Newbern to Goldsboro, on the south bank of the Neuse. D. H. Hill met and fought him on the 8th, 9th, and 10th, on the south side of the river; but, the Confederates retreating to Goldsboro to oppose Sherman's march, Schofield occupied Kinston on the 14th and Goldsboro on the 21st. In these movements the 3rd brigade, formerly Sharpe's, now commanded by Day, took part, while Birge's brigade was posted at Morehead City, and Molineux's at Wilmington.

On the 1st of April, Schofield's force, composed of the Tenth Corps, under Terry, and the Twenty-third Corps, under Cox, was reconstructed by Sherman as the centre of his armies, and designated as the Army of the Ohio. The next day the troops of Grover's division, then in North Carolina, were attached to the Tenth Corps, reorganized into three brigades, and designated as the First division; the command being given to Birge, and the brigades being commanded by the three senior colonels, Washburn, Graham, and Day. Some time before this, Shunk's 4th brigade of Grover's division had been broken up and its regiments distributed; the 8th and 18th Indiana to Washburn, the 28th Iowa to Graham, and the 24th Iowa to Day. The 22nd Indiana battery formed the artillery of the division. All active operations coming to an end with the final surrender of Johnston on the 26th of April, about the 4th of May the division went back to Savannah. On the 11th of May it marched to Augusta, leaving Day with all his regiments except the 24th Iowa and the 128th New York to take care of Savannah.

Meanwhile, orders being issued by the government for disbanding the regiments whose time was to expire before the 1st of November, and the re-enlisted veterans of Dwight's division beginning to arrive in Savannah on the 5th of June, Birge's brigade came down from Augusta on the 7th and Day marched on the 9th to replace it.

From this time the work of disintegration went on rapidly, yet all too slowly for the impatience of the soldiers, now thinking only of home, and soon sickened by the weary routine of provost duty in the first dull days of peace. What was left of the divisions of Dwight and Grover continued to occupy Charleston, Savannah, and Augusta, and the chief towns of Georgia and South Carolina.

When at last the final separation came, and little by little the old corps fell apart, every man, as with inexpressible yearning he turned his face homeward, bore with him, as the richest heritage of his children and his children's children, the proud consciousness of duty done.

Appendices

ROSTERS.

I.

DEPARTMENT OF THE GULF.

As of March 22, 1862.

FIRST BRIGADE :
    Brigadier-General JOHN W. PHELPS

8th New Hampshire	Colonel HAWKES FEARING, Jr.
9th Connecticut	Colonel THOMAS W. CAHILL
7th Vermont	Colonel GEORGE T. ROBERTS
8th Vermont	Colonel STEPHEN THOMAS
12th Connecticut	Colonel HENRY C. DEMING
13th Connecticut	Colonel HENRY W. BIRGE
1st Vermont Battery	Captain GEORGE W. DUNCAN
2d Vermont Battery	Captain PYTHAGORAS E. HOLCOMB
4th Massachusetts Battery	Captain CHARLES H. MANNING [1]
	Captain GEORGE G. TRULL
A 2d Battalion Massachusetts Cavalry,	Captain S. TYLER READ

SECOND BRIGADE :
    Brigadier-General THOMAS WILLIAMS

26th Massachusetts	Colonel ALPHA B. FARR
31st Massachusetts	Colonel OLIVER P. GOODING
21st Indiana	Colonel JAMES W. McMILLAN
6th Michigan	Colonel THOMAS S. CLARK
4th Wisconsin	Colonel HALBERT E. PAINE
6th Massachusetts Battery	Captain CHARLES EVERETT
2d Massachusetts Battery	Captain ORMAND F. NIMS
C 2d Battalion Massachusetts Cavalry	Captain HENRY A. DURIVAGE [2]
	Captain JONATHAN E. COWAN

THIRD BRIGADE :
    Colonel GEORGE F. SHEPLEY

12th Maine	Lieutenant-Colonel W. K. KIMBALL
13th Maine	Colonel NEAL DOW
	Colonel HENRY RUST, Jr.

[1] *Resigned October* 20, 1862.   [2] *Drowned April* 23, 1862.

14th Maine	Colonel FRANK S. NICKERSON
15th Maine	Colonel JOHN MCCLUSKY
	Colonel ISAAC DYER
30th Massachusetts	Colonel N. A. M. DUDLEY
1st Maine Battery	Captain E. W. THOMPSON
B 2d Battalion Massachusetts Cavalry	Captain JAMES M. MAGEE

II.

TECHE AND PORT HUDSON.

As of April 30, 1863.

FIRST DIVISION.

Major-General CHRISTOPHER C. AUGUR

FIRST BRIGADE:
   Colonel EDWARD P. CHAPIN

116th New York	Lieutenant-Colonel JOHN HIGGINS
21st Maine [1]	Colonel ELIJAH D. JOHNSON
48th Massachusetts [1]	Colonel EBEN F. STONE
49th Massachusetts [1]	Colonel WILLIAM F. BARTLETT

SECOND BRIGADE:
   Brigadier-General GODFREY WEITZEL

8th Vermont	Colonel STEPHEN THOMAS
75th New York	Colonel ROBERT B. MERRITT
160th New York	Colonel CHARLES C. DWIGHT
12th Connecticut	Colonel LEDYARD COLBURN
	Lieutenant-Colonel FRANK H. PECK
114th New York	Colonel ELISHA B. SMITH

THIRD BRIGADE:
   Colonel NATHAN A. M. DUDLEY

30th Massachusetts	Lieutenant-Colonel WILLIAM W. BULLOCK
2d Louisiana	Colonel CHARLES J. PAINE
50th Massachusetts [1]	Colonel CARLOS P. MESSER
161st New York	Colonel GABRIEL T. HARROWER
174th New York	Colonel THEODORE W. PARMELE

ARTILLERY:

1st Maine	Captain ALBERT W. BRADBURY
	Lieutenant JOHN E. MORTON
6th Massachusetts	Captain WILLIAM W. CARRUTH
	Lieutenant JOHN F. PHELPS
A 1st United States	Captain E. C. BAINBRIDGE

[1] *Nine-months' men.*

SECOND DIVISION.

Brigadier-General T. W. SHERMAN

FIRST BRIGADE :
    Brigadier-General NEAL DOW

6th Michigan	Colonel THOMAS S. CLARK
128th New York	Colonel DAVID S. COWLES
26th Connecticut [1]	Colonel THOMAS G. KINGSLEY
15th New Hampshire [1]	Colonel JOHN W. KINGMAN

SECOND BRIGADE :
    Colonel ALPHA B. FARR

26th Massachusetts	Lieutenant-Colonel JOSIAH A. SAWTELL
9th Connecticut	Colonel THOMAS W. CAHILL
47th Massachusetts [1]	Colonel LUCIUS B. MARSH
42d Massachusetts [1]	Lieutenant-Colonel JOSEPH STEDMAN
28th Maine [1]	Colonel EPHRAIM W. WOODMAN

THIRD BRIGADE :
    Colonel FRANK S. NICKERSON

14th Maine	Lieutenant-Colonel THOMAS W. PORTER
177th New York [1]	Colonel IRA W. AINSWORTH
165th New York	Lieutenant-Colonel ABEL SMITH, Jr.
24th Maine [1]	Colonel GEORGE M. ATWOOD

ARTILLERY :

18th New York	Captain ALBERT G. MACK
G 5th United States	Lieutenant JACOB B. RAWLES
1st Vermont	Captain George T. HEBARD

THIRD DIVISION.

Brigadier-General WILLIAM H. EMORY

FIRST BRIGADE :
    Colonel TIMOTHY INGRAHAM, 38th Massachusetts

162d New York	Colonel LEWIS BENEDICT
110th New York	Colonel CLINTON H. SAGE
16th New Hampshire [1]	Colonel JAMES PIKE
4th Massachusetts [1]	Colonel HENRY WALKER

SECOND BRIGADE :
    Colonel HALBERT E. PAINE

4th Wisconsin	Lieutenant-Colonel SIDNEY A. BEAN
133d New York	Colonel LEONARD D. H. CURRIE

[1] *Nine-months' men.*

173d New York   Colonel LEWIS M. PECK
8th New Hampshire   Colonel HAWKES FEARING, Jr.

THIRD BRIGADE :
    Colonel OLIVER P. GOODING

31st Massachusetts   Lieutenant-Colonel W. S. B. HOPKINS
38th Massachusetts   Lieutenant-Colonel WILLIAM L. RODMAN
156th New York   Colonel JACOB SHARPE
175th New York   Colonel MICHAEL K. BRYAN
53d Massachusetts [1]   Colonel JOHN W. KIMBALL

ARTILLERY :

4th Massachusetts   Captain GEORGE G. TRULL
F 1st United States   Captain RICHARD C. DURYEA
2d Vermont   Captain PYTHAGORAS E. HOLCOMB

FOURTH DIVISION.

Brigadier-General CUVIER GROVER

FIRST BRIGADE :
    Brigadier-General WILLIAM DWIGHT, Jr.

6th New York [2]   Colonel WILLIAM WILSON
91st New York   Colonel JACOB VAN ZANDT
131st New York   Lieutenant-Colonel NICHOLAS W. DAY
22d Maine [1]   Colonel SIMON G. JERRARD
1st Louisiana   Colonel RICHARD E. HOLCOMB

SECOND BRIGADE :
    Colonel WILLIAM K. KIMBALL

12th Maine   Lieutenant-Colonel EDWARD ILLSLEY
41st Massachusetts   Colonel THOMAS E. CHICKERING
52d Massachusetts [1]   Colonel HALBERT S. GREENLEAF
24th Connecticut [1]   Colonel SAMUEL M. MANSFIELD

THIRD BRIGADE :
    Colonel HENRY W. BIRGE

25th Connecticut [1]   Colonel GEORGE P. BISSELL
26th Maine [1]   Colonel NATHANIEL H. HUBBARD
159th New York   Colonel EDWARD L. MOLINEUX
13th Connecticut   Lieutenant-Colonel ALEXANDER WARNER

[1] *Nine-months' men.*
[2] *Detached for muster out May 20, 1863.*

ARTILLERY.

    2d Massachusetts   Captain ORMAND F. NIMS
    L 1st United States   Captain HENRY W. CLOSSON
    C 2d United States   Lieutenant JOHN I. RODGERS

OUTSIDE OF THE DIVISIONS.

    1st Louisiana Native Guards [1]   Colonel SPENCER H. STAFFORD
    2d Louisiana Native Guards [2]   Colonel NATHAN W. DANIELS
    3d Louisiana Native Guards [1]   Colonel JOHN A. NELSON
    4th Louisiana Native Guards [1]   Colonel CHARLES W. DREW
    13th Maine [2]   Colonel HENRY RUST, Jr.
    23d Connecticut [3,7]   Colonel CHARLES E. L. HOLMES
    176th New York [2,8]   Colonel CHARLES C. NOTT
    90th New York [4]   Colonel JOSEPH S. MORGAN
    47th Pennsylvania [4]   Colonel TILGHMAN H. GOOD
    28th Connecticut [5,7]   Colonel SAMUEL P. FERRIS
    15th Maine [5]   Colonel ISAAC DYER
    7th Vermont [5]   Colonel WILLIAM C. HOLBROOK

ARTILLERY:

    H 2d United States [6]   Captain FRANK H. LARNED
    K 2d United States [5]   Captain HARVEY A. ALLEN
    1st Indiana Heavy [1]   Colonel JOHN A. Keith
    12th Massachusetts [1]   Lieutenant EDWIN M. CHAMBERLIN
    B 1st Louisiana N. G. Heavy [2] Captain LOREN RYGAARD
    13th Massachusetts [9]   Captain CHARLES H. J. HAMLEN
    21st New York [9]   Captain JAMES BARNES
    25th New York [9]   Captain JOHN A. GROW
    26th New York [2]   Captain GEORGE W. FOX

CAVALRY:

    1st Louisiana C and E [1]   Captain J. F. GODFREY
    1st Louisiana A and B [6]   Captain HENRY F. WILLIAMSON
    2d Rhode Island Battalion [6]   Lieutenant-Colonel A. W. CORLISS
    2d Massachusetts Cavalry Battalion A [2]   Captain S. TYLER READ
                  B [1]   Captain JAMES M. MAGEE
                  C [6]   Captain JONATHAN E. COWAN
                                          Lieutenant SOLON A. PERKINS
    14th New York Cavalry   Colonel THADDEUS P. MOTT
    1st Texas [2]   Colonel EDMUND J. DAVIS

        [1] *With Augur.*   [6] *Pensacola.*
        [2] *Defences of New Orleans.*   [8] *With Weitzel.*
        [3] *La Fourche District.*   [7] *Nine-months' men.*
        [4] *Key West.*   [9] *Partly nine-months' men.*

III.

AFTER PORT HUDSON.

August, 1863.

FIRST DIVISION.

Brigadier-General GODFREY WEITZEL.[1]
Brigadier-General WILLIAM H. EMORY.[2]

FIRST BRIGADE :
    Colonel N. A. M. DUDLEY
    Colonel GEORGE M. LOVE

30th Massachusetts	Lieutenant-Colonel W. W. BULLOCK
2d Louisiana	Colonel CHARLES J. PAINE
161st New York	Lieutenant-Colonel W. B. KINSEY
174th New York	Colonel BENJAMIN F. GOTT
116th New York	Colonel GEORGE M. LOVE

SECOND BRIGADE :
    Colonel OLIVER P. GOODING
    Colonel JACOB SHARPE

31st Massachusetts	Colonel OLIVER P. GOODING
	Lieutenant-Colonel W. S. B. HOPKINS
38th Massachusetts	Lieutenant-Colonel JAS. P. RICHARDSON
128th New York	Colonel JAMES SMITH
156th New York	Colonel JACOB SHARPE
175th New York	Lieutenant-Colonel JOHN A. FOSTER

THIRD BRIGADE :
    Colonel ROBERT B. MERRITT

12th Connecticut	Colonel LEDYARD COLBURN
	Lieutenant-Colonel FRANK H. PECK
75th New York	Captain HENRY B. FITCH
114th New York	Colonel SAMUEL R. PER LEE
160th New York	Colonel CHARLES C. DWIGHT
	Lieutenant-Colonel JOHN B. VAN PETTEN
8th Vermont	Colonel STEPHEN THOMAS

ARTILLERY :
    Captain E. C. BAINBRIDGE

1st Maine	Captain ALBERT W. BRADBURY
18th New York	Captain ALBERT G. MACK
A 1st United States	Captain EDMUND C. BAINBRIDGE
6th Massachusetts [3]	Captain WILLIAM W. CARRUTH

[1] *To December 9th.*   [2] *From December 13th.*
[3] *From Artillery Reserve, in December.*

SECOND DIVISION.

Broken up July 10th.

THIRD DIVISION.

Brigadier-General WILLIAM H. EMORY.
Brigadier-General CUVIER GROVER.

FIRST BRIGADE:
    Brigadier-General FRANK S. NICKERSON

14th Maine	Colonel THOMAS W. PORTER
110th New York	Colonel CLINTON H. SAGE
162d New York	Colonel LEWIS BENEDICT
165th New York	Lieutenant-Colonel GOUVERNEUR CARR
	Captain FELIX AGNUS

SECOND BRIGADE:
    Brigadier-General JAMES W. MCMILLAN

26th Massachusetts	Colonel ALPHA B. FARR
	Major EUSEBIUS S. CLARK
8th New Hampshire	Colonel HAWKES FEARING, Jr.
	Captain JAMES J. LADD
133d New York	Colonel L. D. H. CURRIE
	Captain JAMES K. FULLER
173d New York	Colonel LEWIS M. PECK

ARTILLERY:

4th Massachusetts	Captain GEORGE G. TRULL
	Lieutenant GEORGE W. TAYLOR
F 1st United States	Captain RICHARD G. DURYEA
	Lieutenant HARDMAN P. NORRIS
1st Vermont	Captain GEORGE T. HEBARD
	Lieutenant EDWARD RICE

FOURTH DIVISION.

Brigadier-General CUVIER GROVER.
Colonel EDWARD G. BECKWITH.

FIRST BRIGADE:
    Colonel HENRY W. BIRGE

13th Connecticut	Captain APOLLOS COMSTOCK
90th New York	Colonel JOSEPH S. MORGAN
	Lieutenant-Colonel NELSON SHAURMAN
131st New York	Colonel NICHOLAS W. DAY
159th New York	Colonel EDWARD L. MOLINEUX

SECOND BRIGADE:
    Colonel THOMAS W. CAHILL

9th Connecticut	Lieutenant-Colonel RICHARD FITZ GIBBONS
1st Louisiana	Colonel WILLIAM O. FISKE
12th Maine	Colonel WILLIAM K. KIMBALL
13th Maine [1]	Colonel HENRY RUST, Jr.
15th Maine [1]	Colonel ISAAC DYER
97th Illinois [2]	Colonel FRIEND S. RUTHERFORD

ARTILLERY:

25th New York	Captain JOHN A. GROW
26th New York	Captain GEORGE W. FOX
C 2d United States	Lieutenant THEODORE BRADLEY
L 1st United States [3]	Captain HENRY W. CLOSSON
	Lieutenant JAMES A. SANDERSON

CAVALRY:

3d Massachusetts [4]	Colonel T. E. CHICKERING
	Lieutenant-Colonel LORENZO D. SARGENT
1st Texas [5]	Colonel EDMUND J. DAVIS
4th Wisconsin [5]	Colonel FREDERICK A. BOARDMAN
	Major GEORGE W. MOORE

RESERVE ARTILLERY [6]:
    Captain HENRY W. CLOSSON

2d Massachusetts	Captain ORMAND F. NIMS
6th Massachusetts [7]	Captain WILLIAM W. CARRUTH
L 1st United States [8]	Captain HENRY W. CLOSSON
	Lieutenant FRANCK E. TAYLOR

OUTSIDE OF THE DIVISIONS.

Headquarters Troops Companies A and B [9]	Captain RICHARD W. FRANCIS
Troop C	Captain FRANK SAYLES

DEFENCES OF NEW ORLEANS.

    Colonel E. G. BECKWITH

24th Connecticut [10]	Colonel SAMUEL M. MANSFIELD
31st Massachusetts	Captain ELIOT BRIDGMAN

[1] *In 3d Brigade, 2d Division, Thirteenth Corps, December 31st.*
[2] *December 31st, from 2d Brigade, 4th Division, Thirteenth Corps.*
[3] *From Artillery Reserve, in December.*
[4] *At Port Hudson.*
[5] *At New Orleans.*
[6] *At Baton Rouge.*
[7] *In First Division, December 31st.*
[8] *In Fourth Division, December 31st.*
[9] *Raised in Louisiana; re-enlisted nine-months' men.*
[10] *Nine-months' men.*

176th New York	Colonel CHARLES C. NOTT
	Major MORGAN MORGAN, Jr.
1st Louisiana Cavalry	Lieutenant-Colonel HARAI ROBINSON
A 3d Massachusetts Cavalry	Lieutenant HENRY D. POPE
14th New York Cavalry	Lieutenant-Colonel ABRAHAM BASSFORD
12th Massachusetts Battery	Captain JACOB MILLER
13th Massachusetts Battery	Captain CHARLES H. J. HAMLEN
15th Massachusetts Battery	Captain TIMOTHY PEARSON
91st New York [1]	Colonel JACOB VAN ZANDT

PORT HUDSON.

Brigadier-General GEORGE L. ANDREWS

1st Michigan Heavy Artillery	Colonel THOMAS S. CLARK
21st New York Battery	Captain JAMES BARNES
Battery G 5th United States	Lieutenant JACOB B. RAWLES
2d Vermont Battery	Captain P. E. HOLCOMB

IV.

RED RIVER.

As of March 13, 1864.

FIRST DIVISION.

Brigadier-General WILLIAM H. EMORY

FIRST BRIGADE :

Brigadier-General WILLIAM DWIGHT, Jr.

29th Maine	Colonel GEORGE L. BEAL
114th New York	Colonel SAMUEL R. PER LEE
	Lieutenant-Colonel HENRY B. MORSE
116th New York	Colonel GEORGE M. LOVE
153d New York	Colonel EDWIN P. DAVIS
161st New York	Lieutenant-Colonel W. B. KINSEY
30th Massachusetts [2]	Colonel N. A. M. DUDLEY

SECOND BRIGADE :

Brigadier-General JAMES W. MCMILLAN

12th Connecticut [2]	Lieutenant-Colonel FRANK H. PECK
13th Maine	Colonel HENRY RUST, Jr.
15th Maine	Colonel ISAAC DYER
160th New York	Colonel CHARLES C. DWIGHT
	Lieutenant-Colonel JOHN B. VAN PETTEN
47th Pennsylvania	Colonel TILGHMAN H. GOOD
8th Vermont	Colonel STEPHEN THOMAS

[1] *Heavy Artillery.* [2] *On veteran furlough.*

THIRD BRIGADE:
    Colonel LEWIS BENEDICT

30th Maine	Colonel FRANCIS FESSENDEN
162d New York	Lieutenant-Colonel JUSTUS W. BLANCHARD
165th New York	Lieutenant-Colonel GOUVERNEUR CARR
173d New York [1]	Colonel LEWIS M. PECK
	Captain HOWARD C. CONRADY

ARTILLERY:
    Captain GEORGE T. HEBARD

25th New York	Captain JOHN A. GROW
	Lieutenant IRVING D. SOUTHWORTH
L 1st United States	Lieutenant FRANCK E. TAYLOR
1st Vermont [2]	Lieutenant EDWARD RICE
1st Delaware [3]	BENJAMIN NIELDS

SECOND DIVISION.

Brigadier-General CUVIER GROVER

FIRST BRIGADE:
    Brigadier-General FRANK S. NICKERSON

9th Connecticut [4]	Colonel THOMAS W. CAHILL
12th Maine [4]	Colonel WILLIAM K. KIMBALL
14th Maine [4]	Colonel THOMAS W. PORTER
26th Massachusetts [4]	Colonel ALPHA B. FARR
133d New York	Colonel L. D. H. CURRIE
176th New York	Colonel CHARLES C. NOTT
	Major CHARLES LEWIS

SECOND BRIGADE:
    Brigadier-General HENRY W. BIRGE
    Colonel EDWARD L. MOLINEUX

13th Connecticut	Colonel CHARLES D. BLINN
1st Louisiana	Colonel WILLIAM O. FISKE
90th New York [5]	Major JOHN C. SMART
159th New York	Colonel EDWARD L. MOLINEUX
	Lieutenant-Colonel EDWARD L. GAUL
131st New York [6]	Colonel NICHOLAS W. DAY

THIRD BRIGADE:
    Colonel JACOB SHARPE

38th Massachusetts	Lieutenant-Colonel JAMES P. RICHARDSON
128th New York	Colonel JAMES SMITH
156th New York	Captain JAMES J. HOYT
175th New York	Captain CHARLES MCCARTHEY

[1] *The 174th consolidated with the 173d.*
[2] *In Reserve Artillery, April 30th.*
[3] *In Reserve Artillery, March 31st.*
[4] *On veteran furlough.*
[5] *Three companies.*
[6] *In district of La Fourche, Colonel Day commanding the district.*

ARTILLERY:
    Captain GEORGE W. FOX

7th Massachusetts	Captain NEWMAN W. STORER
26th New York	Captain GEORGE W. FOX
F 1st United States [1]	Lieutenant HARDMAN P. NORRIS
	Lieutenant WILLIAM L. HASKIN
C 2d United States	Lieutenant JOHN I. RODGERS

ARTILLERY RESERVE:
    Captain HENRY W. CLOSSON

1st Delaware [2]	Captain BENJAMIN NIELDS
D 1st Indiana Heavy	Captain WILLIAM S. HINKLE

V.

SHENANDOAH.

From June 27, 1864.

FIRST DIVISION.

Brigadier-General WILLIAM DWIGHT

FIRST BRIGADE:
    Colonel GEORGE L. BEAL

29th Maine	Colonel GEORGE L. BEAL
30th Massachusetts	Colonel N. A. M. DUDLEY
90th New York [3]	Lieutenant-Colonel NELSON SHAURMAN
114th New York	Colonel SAMUEL R. PER LEE
116th New York	Colonel GEORGE M. LOVE
153d New York	Colonel EDWIN P. DAVIS

SECOND BRIGADE:
    Brigadier-General JAMES W. McMILLAN

12th Connecticut	Lieutenant-Colonel FRANK H. PECK
	Captain SIDNEY E. CLARKE
	Lieutenant-Colonel GEORGE N. LEWIS
13th Maine [4]	Colonel HENRY RUST, Jr.
15th Maine [4]	Colonel ISAAC DYER
160th New York	Colonel CHARLES C. DWIGHT
	Lieutenant-Colonel JOHN B. VAN PETTEN
47th Pennsylvania	Colonel TILGHMAN H. GOOD
	Major J. P. SHINDEL GOBIN
8th Vermont	Colonel STEPHEN THOMAS

[1] *With the Cavalry, April 30th.*
[2] *In the 1st Division, April 30th.*
[3] *On veteran furlough in August and September.*
[4] *On veteran furlough in August and September, at Martinsburg afterward.*

THIRD BRIGADE :
    Colonel L. D. H. CURRIE

30th Maine	Colonel THOMAS H. HUBBARD
133d New York	Colonel L. D. H. CURRIE
162d New York	Colonel JUSTUS W. BLANCHARD
165th New York	Lieutenant-Colonel GOUVERNEUR CARR
173d New York	Colonel LEWIS M. PECK

ARTILLERY :

5th New York	Captain ELIJAH D. TAFT

SECOND DIVISION.

Brigadier-General CUVIER GROVER

FIRST BRIGADE :
    Brigadier-General HENRY W. BIRGE

9th Connecticut	Colonel THOMAS W. CAHILL
12th Maine	Colonel WILLIAM K. KIMBALL
14th Maine	Colonel THOMAS W. PORTER
26th Massachusetts	Colonel ALPHA B. FARR
14th New Hampshire	Colonel ALEXANDER GARDINER
75th New York	Lieutenant-Colonel WILLOUGHBY BABCOCK

SECOND BRIGADE :
    Colonel EDWARD L. MOLINEUX

13th Connecticut[1]	Colonel CHARLES D. BLINN
3d Massachusetts Cavalry (dismounted)	Lieutenant-Colonel LORENZO D. SARGENT
11th Indiana	Colonel DANIEL MACAULEY
22d Iowa	Colonel HARVEY GRAHAM
131st New York	Colonel NICHOLAS W. DAY
159th New York	Lieutenant-Colonel WILLIAM WALTERMIRE

THIRD BRIGADE :
    Colonel JACOB SHARPE
    Colonel DANIEL MACAULEY

38th Massachusetts	Major CHARLES F. ALLEN
128th New York	Lieutenant-Colonel J. P. FOSTER
156th New York	Lieutenant-Colonel ALFRED NEAFIE
175th New York	Lieutenant-Colonel JOHN A. FOSTER
176th New York	Colonel AMBROSE STEVENS[2]
	Major CHARLES LEWIS

FOURTH BRIGADE :
    Colonel DAVID SHUNK

8th Indiana	Lieutenant-Colonel ALEXANDER J. KENNEY
18th Indiana	Colonel HENRY D. WASHBURN
24th Iowa	Colonel JOHN Q. WILDS

[1] On veteran furlough in August and early September.
[2] From November 19, 1864.

28th Iowa Colonel JOHN CONNELL
  Lieutenant-Colonel BARTHOLOMEW W. WILSON
ARTILLERY:
  A 1st Maine Captain ALBERT W. BRADBURY
RESERVE ARTILLERY:
  Captain ELIJAH D. TAFT
  Major ALBERT W. BRADBURY
  D 1st Rhode Island Lieutenant FREDERICK CHASE
  17th Indiana Captain MILTON L. MINER

DETACHMENTS LEFT IN LOUISIANA.

The following troops served under Canby in the siege of Mobile, March 20–April 12, 1865:

1ST INDIANA HEAVY ARTILLERY.
31ST MASSACHUSETTS, as mounted infantry, from Pensacola, with Steele.
2D MASSACHUSETTS BATTERY. Also engaged at Daniel's Plantation, Alabama, April 11, 1865.
4TH MASSACHUSETTS BATTERY. Afterward at Galveston.
7TH MASSACHUSETTS BATTERY.   "   "
15TH MASSACHUSETTS BATTERY.   "   "
4TH WISCONSIN CAVALRY. Afterward on Rio Grande in Weitzel's corps.
1ST MICHIGAN HEAVY ARTILLERY.
161ST NEW YORK, in Third brigade, First division, new XIIIth Corps, Kinsey commanding the brigade. Loss: 2 killed, 1 wounded. Afterward in Florida.
7TH VERMONT, in First brigade, Third division, new XIIIth Corps. Loss: 18 wounded, 43 captured. Afterward on Rio Grande in Weitzel's Corps of Observation.
18TH NEW YORK BATTERY.
21ST NEW YORK BATTERY.
26TH NEW YORK BATTERY.
BATTERY G, 5TH U. S. ARTILLERY.

8TH NEW HAMPSHIRE, as mounted infantry, served at Natchez and at Vidalia, opposite.
91ST NEW YORK, after returning from veteran furlough, September, 1864, went to Baltimore as part of Second separate brigade, VIIIth Corps. March, 1865, joined First brigade, Third division, Vth Corps, Army of the Potomac. Fought at White Oak Ridge, March 29–31, and Five Forks, April, 1865. Loss: 61 killed and mortally wounded, 152 wounded, 17 captured or missing; total, 230.
110TH NEW YORK, at Key West, Florida, from February 9, 1864.

3D MASSACHUSETTS CAVALRY, detached to remount December 26, 1864; with Chapman's brigade; in cavalry review May 23, 1865; afterward in Kansas, Nebraska, and Colorado.

LOSSES IN BATTLE.

BATON ROUGE.
August 5, 1862.

COMMAND.	Killed.		Wounded.		Captured or missing.		Aggregate.
	Officers.	Enlisted men.	Officers.	Enlisted men.	Officers.	Enlisted men.	
General officers,	1	....	....	....	....	....	1
9th Connecticut	....	1	....	9	....	4	14
21st Indiana	2	22	7	91	....	4	126
14th Maine	....	36	7	64	....	12	119
30th Massachusetts	1	2	3	12	....	....	18
6th Michigan	....	15	4	40	1	5	65
7th Vermont	....	....	1	9	....	5	15
Troop B Massachusetts Cavalry	....	....	....	1	....	....	1
2d Massachusetts Battery	....	....	....	4	....	1	5
4th Massachusetts Battery	....	1	....	5	....	....	6
6th Massachusetts Battery	....	3	1	8	....	1	13
Total	4	80	23	243	1	32	383

GEORGIA LANDING.
October 27, 1862.

COMMAND.	Killed.		Wounded.		Captured or missing.		Aggregate.
	Officers.	Enlisted men.	Officers.	Enlisted men.	Officers.	Enlisted men.	
12th Connecticut	....	3	....	16	1	....	20
13th Connecticut	....	1	....	5	....	1	7
1st Louisiana Cavalry, A, B, and C	....	1	....	18	....	1	20
8th New Hampshire	2	10	1	34	....	1	48
75th New York	....	1	....	....	....	1	2
Total	2	16	1	73	1	4	97

BISLAND.

April 12–13, 1863.

COMMAND.	Killed. Officers.	Killed. Enlisted men.	Wounded. Officers.	Wounded. Enlisted men.	Aggregate.
FIRST DIVISION, SECOND BRIGADE : Brigadier-General GODFREY WEITZEL.					
8th Vermont.	.....	1	.....	7	8
75th New York.	.....	2	2	13	17
160th New York.	.....	2	.....	5	7
114th New York.	.....	.....	.....	11	11
12th Connecticut.	.....	2	1	12	15
Total Weitzel's Brigade.	.....	7	3	48	58
THIRD DIVISION : Brigadier-General WILLIAM H. EMORY.					
SECOND BRIGADE : Colonel HALBERT E. PAINE.					
4th Wisconsin.	.....	5	.....	8	13
133d New York.	.....	4	1	20	25
173d New York.	.....	2	.....	5	7
8th New Hampshire.	.....	2	2	7	11
Total Second Brigade.	.....	13	3	40	56
THIRD BRIGADE : Colonel OLIVER P. GOODING.					
31st Massachusetts.	.....	1	.....	5	6
38th Massachusetts.	1	5	1	28	35
156th New York.	1	3	.....	18	22
175th New York.	.....	1	.....	6	7
53d Massachusetts.	1	2	.....	9	12
Total Third Brigade.	3	12	1	66	82
Total Third Division.	3	25	4	106	138
ARTILLERY :					
A 1st U. S.	.....	4	.....	5	9
F 1st U. S.	.....	.....	.....	5	5
1st Maine Battery.	.....	.....	1	1	2
6th Massachusetts Battery.	.....	1	.....	3	4
18th New York Battery.	.....	.....	.....	2	2
1st Indiana Heavy.	.....	.....	.....	3	3
Total Artillery.	.....	5	1	19	25
1st Louisiana Cavalry.	.....	.....	.....	3	3
Total.	3	37	8	176	224

IRISH BEND.
April 14, 1863.

COMMAND.	Killed.		Wounded.		Captured or missing.		Aggregate.
	Officers.	Enlisted men.	Officers.	Enlisted men.	Officers.	Enlisted men.	
FOURTH DIVISION: Brigadier-General CUVIER GROVER.							
FIRST BRIGADE: Brigadier-General WILLIAM DWIGHT.							
6th New York.....................	.....	.....	.....	.....	.....	.....	.....
91st New York....................	.....	2	1	10	.....	.....	13
131st New York...................	.....	.....	.....	3	.....	.....	3
22d Maine........................	.....	.....	.....	1	.....	.....	1
1st Louisiana....................	.....	.....	.....	.....	.....	.....	.....
Total First Brigade.........	.....	2	1	14	.....	.....	17
THIRD BRIGADE: Colonel HENRY W. BIRGE.							
25th Connecticut................	2	7	5	72	.....	10	96
26th Maine......................	.....	11	2	48	.....	.....	61
159th New York..................	4	15	5	73	.....	20	117
13th Connecticut................	.....	7	4	43	.....	.....	54
Total Third Brigade.......	6	40	16	236	.....	30	328
ARTILLERY:							
Battery C 2d U. S...............	.....	1	.....	.....	.....	.....	8
Total	6	43	17	257	.....	30	353

PLAINS STORE.
May 21, 1863.

COMMAND.	Killed.		Wounded.		Captured or missing.		Aggregate.
	Officers.	Enlisted men.	Officers.	Enlisted men.	Officers.	Enlisted men.	
2d Louisiana.....................	.....	2	.....	11	.....	1	14
30th Massachusetts...............	.....	.....	1	3	.....	.....	4
48th Massachusetts...............	.....	2	.....	7	.....	11	20
49th Massachusetts...............	.....	.....	1	4	.....	1	6
116th New York...................	.....	11	1	43	.....	1	56
Total	.....	15	3	68	.....	14	100

PORT HUDSON.

May 23–July 8, 1863.

	Killed.		Wounded.		Captured or missing.		
NINETEENTH ARMY CORPS: Major-General NATHANIEL P. BANKS.	Officers.	Enlisted men.	Officers.	Enlisted men.	Officers.	Enlisted men.	Aggregate.
FIRST DIVISION: Major-General CHRISTOPHER C. AUGUR.							
FIRST BRIGADE: Colonel EDWARD P. CHAPIN,[1] Colonel CHARLES J. PAINE.							
2d Louisiana	....	32	5	103	....	4	144
21st Maine	1	14	3	60	1	9	88
48th Massachusetts	1	8	7	46	....	....	62
49th Massachusetts	1	17	10	73	....	1	102
116th New York	2	18	4	101	....	5	130
Total First Brigade	5	89	29	383	1	19	526
SECOND BRIGADE: Brigadier-General GODFREY WEITZEL.							
Staff	1	....	....	....	....	....	1
12th Connecticut	....	18	5	78	....	....	101
75th New York	....	10	4	88	1	4	107
114th New York	1	10	4	56	....	2	73
160th New York	....	2	4	35	....	....	41
8th Vermont	1	24	4	128	....	9	166
Total Second Brigade	3	64	21	385	1	15	489
THIRD BRIGADE: Colonel NATHAN A. M. DUDLEY.							
30th Massachusetts	....	....	1	18	....	....	19
50th Massachusetts	....	....	1	4	....	....	5
161st New York	....	3	....	14	....	....	17
174th New York	....	2	....	9	....	3	14
Total Third Brigade	....	5	2	45	....	3	55
ARTILLERY:							
1st Indiana Heavy	....	4	1	10	....	7	22
1st Maine Battery	....	1	....	19	....	....	20
6th Massachusetts Battery	....	....	....	1	....	....	1
18th New York Battery	....	....	....	3	....	....	3
Battery A 1st U. S.	....	3	1	12	....	3	19
Battery G 5th U. S.	....	2	....	2	....	....	4
Total Artillery	....	10	2	47	....	10	69
Total First Division	8	168	54	860	2	47	1139

[1] *Killed May 27th.*

COMMAND.	Killed.		Wounded.		Captured or missing.		Aggregate.
	Officers.	Enlisted men.	Officers.	Enlisted men.	Officers.	Enlisted men.	
SECOND DIVISION: Brigadier-General THOMAS W. SHERMAN.[1] Brigadier-General WILLIAM DWIGHT.							
Staff	....	....	2	....	....	....	2
FIRST BRIGADE: Brigadier-General NEAL DOW.[1] Colonel DAVID S. COWLES.[3] Colonel THOMAS S. CLARK.							
Staff	....	....	1	....	....	....	1
26th Connecticut	1	14	9	151	....	1	176
6th Michigan	1	19	5	124	....	....	149
15th New Hampshire	....	17	3	55	....	2	77
128th New York	2	21	3	97	1	5	129
162d New York	1	5	3	47	....	3	59
Total First Brigade	5	76	24	474	1	11	591
THIRD BRIGADE: Brigadier-General FRANK S. NICKERSON.							
14th Maine	....	5	5	23	....	....	33
24th Maine	....	....	....	13	....	....	13
28th Maine	....	3	1	8	....	....	12
165th New York	1	15	7	80	....	3	106
175th New York	1	5	5	38	....	2	51
177th New York	1	3	2	17	....	....	23
Total Third Brigade	3	31	20	179	....	5	238
ARTILLERY:							
1st Vermont Battery	....	1	....	6	....	....	7
Total Second Division	8	108	46	659	1	16	838
THIRD DIVISION: Brigadier-General HALBERT E. PAINE.[2] Colonel HAWKES FEARING, Jr.							
Staff	....	....	1	....	....	....	1
FIRST BRIGADE: Colonel SAMUEL P. FERRIS.							
28th Connecticut	2	5	1	43	1	10	62
4th Massachusetts	1	7	3	57	....	....	68
110th New York	1	4	2	21	....	9	37
Total First Brigade	4	16	6	121	1	19	168

[1] *Wounded May 27th.*   [2] *Wounded June 14th.*   [3] *Killed May 27th.*

COMMAND.	Killed.		Wounded.		Captured or missing.		Aggregate.
	Officers.	Enlisted men.	Officers.	Enlisted men.	Officers.	Enlisted men.	
SECOND BRIGADE: Colonel HAWKES FEARING, Jr., Major JOHN H. ALLCOT.							
8th New Hampshire	4	26	7	191	2	28	258
133d New York	1	22	5	85	....	2	115
173d New York	2	11	6	72	....	1	92
4th Wisconsin [1]	3	46	9	108	1	52	219
Total Second Brigade	10	105	27	456	3	83	684
THIRD BRIGADE: Colonel OLIVER P. GOODING.							
31st Massachusetts	....	13	2	47	....	....	62
38th Massachusetts	2	13	5	85	....	3	108
53d Massachusetts	2	15	7	92	....	5	121
156th New York	....	3	2	25	....	....	30
Total Third Brigade	4	44	16	249	....	8	321
ARTILLERY:							
4th Massachusetts Battery	....	....	....	2	....	....	2
Battery F 1st U. S.	....	1	....	....	....	2	3
2d Vermont Battery	....	....	....	2	....	....	2
Total Third Division	18	166	50	830	4	112	1180
FOURTH DIVISION: Brigadier-General CUVIER GROVER.							
FIRST BRIGADE: Brigadier-General WILLIAM DWIGHT. Colonel JOSEPH S. MORGAN							
1st Louisiana	1	30	3	86	....	3	123
22d Maine	....	4	2	17	1	5	29
90th New York	....	7	1	42	....	....	50
91st New York	2	19	8	112	....	8	149
131st New York	1	20	2	86	2	8	119
Total First Brigade	4	80	16	343	3	24	470
SECOND BRIGADE: Colonel WILLIAM K. KIMBALL.							
24th Connecticut	....	14	6	46	....	....	66
12th Maine	....	10	2	57	....	1	70
52d Massachusetts	....	8	2	12	....	2	24
Total Second Brigade	....	32	10	115	....	3	160

[1] Includes losses at Clinton, June 3d.

COMMAND.	Killed.		Wounded.		Captured or missing.		Aggregate.
	Officers.	Enlisted men.	Officers.	Enlisted men.	Officers.	Enlisted men.	
THIRD BRIGADE: Colonel HENRY W. BIRGE.							
13th Connecticut.................	1	6	3	20	....	1	31
25th Connecticut.................	....	5	4	35	....	2	46
26th Maine.......................	....	5	1	11	....	5	22
159th New York	....	17	1	53	....	2	73
Total Third Brigade	1	33	9	119	....	10	172
ARTILLERY:							
2d Massachusetts Battery.........	....	....	....	2	....	3	5
Battery L 1st U. S...............	....	....	....	2	....	....	2
Battery C 2d U. S...............	....	....	....	1	....	....	1
Total Artillery.............	....	....	....	5	....	3	8
Total Fourth Division......	5	145	35	582	3	40	810
Total Nineteenth Army Corps	39	587	185	2,931	10	215	3,967
CAVALRY: Colonel BENJAMIN H. GRIERSON							
6th Illinois......................	....	1	....	6	1	5	13
7th Illinois......................	....	....	....	4	....	....	4
1st Louisiana....................	....	5	....	16	....	19	40
3d Massachusetts.................	1	1	....	5	....	2	9
14th New York..................	....	2	....	6	....	20	28
Total Cavalry.............	1	9	....	37	1	46	94
CORPS D'AFRIQUE:							
1st Louisiana Engineers...........	1	7	....	26	....	19	53
1st Louisiana Native Guards......	2	32	3	92	....	....	129
3d Louisiana Native Guards.......	1	9	1	37	1	2	51
6th Infantry.....................	....	1	....	1	....	....	2
7th Infantry.....................	....	2	....	3	....	....	5
8th Infantry.....................	....	5	1	5	....	1	12
9th Infantry.....................	....	2	....	....	....	....	2
10th Infantry	1	4	....	2	....	3	10
Total Corps d'Afrique	5	62	5	166	1	25	264
2d Rhode Island Cavalry..........	....	....	1	5	....	2	8
Total Port Hudson	45	658	191	3,139	12	288	4,333

COX'S PLANTATION, OR KOCH'S PLANTATION, BAYOU LA FOURCHE, July 13, 1863.

COMMAND.	Killed.		Wounded.		Captured or missing.		Aggregate.
	Officers.	Enlisted men.	Officers.	Enlisted men.	Officers.	Enlisted men.	
FIRST DIVISION: Brigadier-General GODFREY WEITZEL.							
FIRST BRIGADE: Colonel CHARLES J. PAINE.							
2d Louisiana	....	7	....	21	....	9	37
116th New York	1	5	....	18	....	20	44
Total First Brigade	1	12	....	39	....	29	81
THIRD BRIGADE: Colonel N. A. M. DUDLEY.							
30th Massachusetts	....	8	2	37	....	1	48
161st New York	....	7	1	38	....	7	53
174th New York	1	17	1	28	....	7	54
Total Third Brigade	1	32	4	103	....	15	155
ARTILLERY:							
1st Maine	....	1	1	14	....	1	17
6th Massachusetts	....	....	....	1	....	....	1
Total Artillery	....	1	1	15	....	1	18
Total First Division	2	45	5	157	....	45	254
FOURTH DIVISION: Brigadier-General CUVIER GROVER							
FIRST BRIGADE: Colonel JOSEPH S. MORGAN.							
1st Louisiana	....	3	....	14	....	13	30
90th New York	....	2	1	20	....	48	71
131st New York	....	2	....	10	1	42	55
Total Brigade and Division	....	7	1	44	1	103	156
Total Nineteenth Army Corps	2	52	6	201	1	148	410

SABINE CROSS-ROADS, April 8, and PLEASANT HILL, April 9, 1864.

Compiled in the War Department from the nominal returns: impossible to separate the losses for each day.

COMMAND.	Killed.		Wounded.		Captured or missing.		Aggregate.
	Officers.	Enlisted men.	Officers.	Enlisted men.	Officers.	Enlisted men.	
THIRTEENTH ARMY CORPS (DETACHMENT): Brigadier-General THOMAS E. G. RANSOM,[1] Brigadier-General ROBERT A. CAMERON.							
Staff....................................	....	....	2	....	....	....	2
THIRD DIVISION: Brigadier-General ROBERT A. CAMERON.....................	....	....	1	4	....	1	6
FIRST BRIGADE. Lieutenant-Colonel AARON M. FLORY[1]......................	1	12	3	21	3	126	166
SECOND BRIGADE: Colonel WILLIAM H. RAYNOR..	....	11	3	66	6	59	145
Total Third Division........	1	23	7	91	9	186	317
FOURTH DIVISION: Colonel WILLIAM J. LANDRAM.							
FIRST BRIGADE: Colonel FRANK EMERSON.[2]	1	18	4	79	28	398	528
SECOND BRIGADE: Colonel JOSEPH W. VANCE.[2]...	2	5	9	50	20	438	524
Artillery	1	1	1	5	2	23	33
Total Fourth Division......	4	24	14	134	50	859	1,085
Total Thirteenth Army Corps	5	47	23	225	59	1,045	1,404
NINETEENTH ARMY CORPS: Major-General WILLIAM B. FRANKLIN.[1]							
Staff....................................	....	....	3	....	....	....	3

[1] *Wounded, April 8th.*   [2] *Wounded and captured April 8th.*

COMMAND.	Killed.		Wounded.		Captured or missing.		Aggregate.
	Officers.	Enlisted men.	Officers.	Enlisted men.	Officers.	Enlisted men.	
FIRST DIVISION: Brigadier-General WILLIAM H. EMORY.							
FIRST BRIGADE: Brigadier-General WILLIAM DWIGHT, Jr.							
29th Maine	.....	1	.....	26	.....	.....	27
114th New York	.....	3	3	10	.....	4	20
116th New York	.....	2	2	27	.....	3	34
153d New York [1]	.....	1	.....	28	.....	4	33
161st New York	1	8	4	39	.....	38	90
Total First Brigade	1	15	9	130	.....	49	204
SECOND BRIGADE: Brigadier-General JAMES W. MCMILLAN.							
13th Maine	.....	5	1	29	.....	20	55
15th Maine	.....	1	3	13	.....	11	28
160th New York	2	6	4	23	.....	9	44
47th Pennsylvania	1	6	.....	34	.....	.....	41
Total Second Brigade	3	18	8	99	.....	40	168
THIRD BRIGADE: Colonel LEWIS BENEDICT,[1] Colonel FRANCIS FESSENDEN.							
30th Maine	1	10	3	55	.....	69	138
162d New York	3	13	3	45	1	46	111
165th New York	.....	3	3	21	.....	70	97
173d New York	.....	4	1	38	2	155	200
Total Third Brigade	4	30	10	159	3	340	546
ARTILLERY.							
New York Light, 25th Battery	.....	2	.....	3	.....	.....	5
1st United States Battery L	.....	2	1	4	.....	.....	7
Vermont Light, 1st Battery	.....	.....	.....	1	.....	.....	1
Total artillery	.....	4	1	8	.....	.....	13
Total First Division	8	67	28	396	3	429	931
Total Nineteenth Army Corps	8	67	31	396	3	429	934

[1] *Killed, April 9th.*

COMMAND.	Killed.		Wounded.		Captured or missing.		Aggregate.
	Officers.	Enlisted men.	Officers.	Enlisted men.	Officers.	Enlisted men.	
CAVALRY DIVISION [1]: Brigadier-General ALBERT L. LEE.							
FIRST BRIGADE: Colonel THOMAS J. LUCAS.							
16th Indiana (mounted infantry)...	1	3	2	17	....	32	55
2d Louisiana (mounted infantry)...	1	....	....	11	....	19	31
6th Missouri....................	....	1	5	10	....	3	19
14th New York	....	4	1	18	2	17	42
Total First Brigade........	2	8	8	56	2	71	147
THIRD BRIGADE: Colonel HARAI ROBINSON.[1]							
87th Illinois (mounted infantry) ...	....	4	2	13	....	2	21
1st Louisiana....................	....	4	4	27	1	13	49
Total Third Brigade........	....	8	6	40	1	15	70
FOURTH BRIGADE: Colonel NATHAN A. M. DUDLEY.							
2d Illinois.......................	....	2	1	39	....	3	45
3d Massachusetts................	....	8	1	51	....	11	71
31st Massachusetts (mounted infantry)........................	....	3	1	38	....	16	58
8th New Hampshire (mounted infantry)	....	2	....	22	1	31	56
Total Fourth Brigade.......	....	15	3	150	1	61	230
FIFTH BRIGADE: Colonel OLIVER P. GOODING.							
2d New York Veteran	....	....	1	5	....	....	6
18th New York..................	1	1	1	9	....	2	14
3d Rhode Island (detachment).....	....	....	....	1	....	....	1
Total Fifth Brigade........	1	1	2	15	....	2	21
ARTILLERY:							
2d Massachusetts Battery.........	....	1	2	16	....	1	20
5th United States, Battery G......	....	4	....	13	....	....	17
Total Artillery	....	5	2	29	....	1	37
Total Cavalry Division	3	37	21	290	4	150	505
Grand total......	16	151	76	911	66	1,624	2,843

[1] *Losses at Wilson's Plantation, April 7th, also included.*

SPECIAL FIELD RETURN AFTER SABINE CROSS-ROADS.

TROOPS.	Killed.		Wounded.		Missing.		Total.	Effective strength next day.		
	Officers.	Men.	Officers.	Men.	Officers.	Men.		Officers.	Men.	Total.
NINETEENTH ARMY CORPS:										
First Division (infantry)........	2	22	10	138	1	174	347	243	4,910	5,153
153d New York Volunteers (guarding train).......	....	....	....	....	....	....	....	31	605	636
First Division (artillery).....	....	....	....	....	....	....	....	9	348	357
THIRTEENTH ARMY CORPS (detachment):										
General and staff...	1	....	1	....	....	....	2	....	....	....
Third Division:										
Infantry.........	1	23	6	78	9	198	315	77	1,475	1,552
Artillery..........	....	....	....	....	....	....	....	2	173	175
Fourth Division:										
Commanding officer and escort..	....	....	....	1	....	....	1	....	....	....
Infantry.........	2	23	6	82	59	929	1,101	56	1,418	1,474
Artillery.........	....	....	1	5	3	24	33	5	204	209
STAFF OF THE MAJOR-GENERAL COMMANDING.......	....	....	3	....	....	....	3	....	....	....
Aggregate...	6	68	27	304	72	1,325	1,802	423	9,133	9,556

SPECIAL FIELD RETURN AFTER PLEASANT HILL.

FIRST DIVISION, NINETEENTH ARMY CORPS.	Killed.		Wounded.		Missing.		Total.	Effective strength next day.		
	Officers.	Men.	Officers.	Men.	Officers.	Men.		Officers.	Men.	Total.
Infantry..........	6	43	18	261	3	369	689	243	4,802	5,045
Artillery.........	....	4	1	14	1	5	25	8	331	339
Aggregate.....	6	47	19	275	4	374	714	251	5,133	5,384

PARTIAL RETURN OF LOSSES AT CANE RIVER CROSSING.
April 23, 1864.

THIRD BRIGADE, 1ST DIVISION : Colonel FRANCIS FESSENDEN. Lieutenant-Colonel J. W. BLANCHARD	Killed.		Wounded.		Missing.		Total.
	Officers.	Men.	Officers.	Men.	Officers.	Men.	
162d New York...................	1	3	1	26	.....	1	32
165th New York..................	.....	.....	.....	3	.....	1	4
173d New York...................	.....	3	2	25	.....	1	31
30th Maine......................	2	11	2	64	.....	7	86
Total.......................	3	17	5	118	.....	10	153

THE OPEQUON,
September 19, 1864.

NINETEENTH ARMY CORPS. Brevet Major-General WILLIAM H. EMORY.	Killed.		Wounded.		Captured or missing.		Aggregate.
	Officers.	Enlisted men.	Officers.	Enlisted men.	Officers.	Enlisted men.	
FIRST DIVISION : Brigadier - General WILLIAM DWIGHT.							
FIRST BRIGADE : Colonel GEORGE L. BEAL.							
29th Maine......................	.....	.....	1	23	.....	.....	24
30th Massachusetts	1	4	.....	17	.....	.....	22
114th New York	1	20	8	156	.....	.....	185
116th New York	.....	9	.....	39	.....	.....	48
153d New York...................	.....	10	4	55	.....	.....	69
Total First Brigade.......	2	43	13	290	.....	.....	348
SECOND BRIGADE : Brigadier - General JAMES W. MCMILLAN.							
12th Connecticut.................	3	7	3	57	.....	1	71
160th New York[1]...............	2	13	3	58	.....	1	77
47th Pennsylvania...............	.....	1	.....	8	.....	.....	9
8th Vermont.....................	.....	9	.....	28	.....	.....	37
Total Second Brigade.......	5	30	6	151	.....	2	194
Total First Division[2].......	7	73	19	441	.....	2	542

[1] *Non-veterans of 90th New York, attached.* [2] *The Third Brigade guarding trains.*

COMMAND.	Killed.		Wounded.		Captured or missing.		Aggregate.
	Officers.	Enlisted men.	Officers.	Enlisted men.	Officers.	Enlisted men.	
SECOND DIVISION: Brigadier-General CUVIER GROVER.							
FIRST BRIGADE: Brigadier-General HENRY W. BIRGE.							
9th Connecticut	....	....	....	1	....	....	1
12th Maine	2	12	6	77	....	15	112
14th Maine	1	6	6	46	....	3	62
26th Massachusetts	....	38	11	69	2	19	139
14th New Hampshire	4	27	9	79	....	19	138
75th New York	....	17	4	41	1	10	73
Total First Brigade	7	100	36	313	3	66	525
SECOND BRIGADE: Colonel EDWARD L. MOLINEUX.							
13th Connecticut	....	6	....	39	2	30	77
11th Indiana	1	7	2	56	1	3	70
22d Iowa	2	9	3	60	....	31	105
3d Massachusetts Cavalry (dismounted)	2	17	3	84	....	....	106
131st New York	....	9	9	56	....	....	74
159th New York	....	5	4	46	1	19	75
Total Second Brigade	5	53	21	341	4	83	507
THIRD BRIGADE: Colonel JACOB SHARPE.[1] Lieutenant-Colonel ALFRED NEAFIE.							
38th Massachusetts	....	8	3	44	....	8	63
128th New York	....	6	5	46	....	....	57
156th New York	....	20	3	88	....	....	111
176th New York	....	5	3	30	....	9	47
Total Third Brigade	....	39	14	208	....	17	278
FOURTH BRIGADE: Colonel DAVID SHUNK.							
8th Indiana	....	2	....	5	....	2	9
18th Indiana	1	5	1	31	....	....	38
24th Iowa	1	9	4	53	....	8	75
28th Iowa	1	9	8	48	....	21	87
Total Fourth Brigade	3	25	13	137	....	31	209

[1] *Wounded.*

COMMAND.	Killed.		Wounded.		Captured or missing.		Aggregate.
	Officers.	Enlisted men.	Officers.	Enlisted men.	Officers.	Enlisted men.	
ARTILLERY :							
1st Maine Battery................	.....	2	1	5	.....	.....	8
Total Second Division.....	15	219	85	1,004	7	197	1,527
RESERVE ARTILLERY : Captain ELIJAH D. TAFT.							
17th Indiana Battery...............	.....	.....	.....	1	.....	.....	1
Battery D 1st Rhode Island.......	.....	.....	.....	4	.....	.....	4
Total Reserve Artillery.....	.....	.....	.....	5	.....	.....	5
Total Nineteenth Army Corps	22	292	104	1,450	7	199	2,074

FISHER'S HILL.

September 22, 1864.[1]

NINETEENTH ARMY CORPS : Brevet-Major General WILLIAM H. EMORY.	Killed.		Wounded.		Captured or missing.		Aggregate.
	Officers.	Enlisted men.	Officers.	Enlisted men.	Officers.	Enlisted men.	
FIRST DIVISION : Brigadier-General WILLIAM DWIGHT.							
FIRST BRIGADE : Colonel GEORGE L. BEAL.							
29th Maine.....................	.....	.....	1	3	.....	.....	4
30th Massachusetts.................	.....	3	.....	6	.....	.....	9
114th New York....................	.....	.....	.....	.....	.....	.....	.....
116th New York...................	.....	1	.....	9	.....	.....	10
153d New York....................	.....	.....	.....	3	.....	.....	3
Total First Brigade........	.....	4	1	21	.....	.....	26
SECOND BRIGADE : Brigadier-General JAMES W. MCMILLAN.							
12th Connecticut...................	.....	.....	.....	.....	.....	.....	.....
160th New York [2].................	.....	.....	.....	.....	.....	.....	.....
47th Pennsylvania.................	.....	.....	.....	2	.....	.....	2
8th Vermont	.....	.....	1	3	.....	.....	4
Total Second Brigade......	.....	.....	1	5	.....	.....	6

[1] Including casualties incurred on the 21st.   [2] Non-veterans of 99th New York attached.

COMMAND.	Killed.		Wounded.		Captured or missing.		Aggregate.
	Officers.	Enlisted men.	Officers.	Enlisted men.	Officers.	Enlisted men.	
ARTILLERY :							
5th New York Battery	....	....	1	....	....	....	1
Total First Division [1].......	....	4	2	27	....	....	33
SECOND DIVISION : Brigadier - General CUVIER GROVER.							
FIRST BRIGADE : Brigadier-General HENRY W. BIRGE.							
9th Connecticut..................	....	3	....	10	....	....	13
12th Maine......................	....	....	....	....	....	....	....
14th Maine......................	....	....	....	....	....	....	....
26th Massachusetts...............	....	....	....	....	....	....	....
14th New Hampshire..............	....	....	....	1	....	1	2
75th New York..................	....	....	....	....	....	....	....
Total First Brigade.........	....	3	....	11	....	1	15
SECOND BRIGADE : Colonel EDWARD L. MOLINEUX.							
13th Connecticut.................	....	....	....	2	....	....	2
11th Indiana.....................	....	2	....	8	....	....	10
22d Iowa........................	....	....	....	4	....	....	4
3d Massachusetts Cavalry (dismounted)	....	2	....	1	....	....	3
131st New York.................	....	....	....	1	....	....	1
159th New York.................	....	....	....	....	....	....	....
Total Second Brigade......	....	4	....	16	....	....	20
THIRD BRIGADE : Colonel DANIEL MACAULEY.							
38th Massachusetts...............	....	1	....	2	....	....	3
128th New York.................	....	2	....	6	....	12	20
156th New York.................	....	....	....	4	....	....	4
175th New York (3 companies)....	....	....	....	....	....	....	....
176th New York.................	....	1	....	1	....	....	2
Total Third Brigade........	....	4	....	13	....	12	29
FOURTH BRIGADE : Colonel DAVID SHUNK.							
8th Indiana......................	....	....	....	1	....	....	1
18th Indiana.....................	....	....	2	4	....	....	6
24th Iowa.......................	....	....	1	4	....	....	5
28th Iowa.......................	....	....	....	5	....	....	5
Total Fourth Brigade	....	....	3	14	....	....	17
ARTILLERY :							
Maine Light, 1st Battery (A)......	....	....	....	....	....	....	....
Total Second Division......	....	11	3	54	....	13	81

[1] Third Brigade guarding trains.

COMMAND.	Killed.		Wounded.		Captured or missing.		Aggregate.
	Officers.	Enlisted men.	Officers.	Enlisted men.	Officers.	Enlisted men.	
RESERVE ARTILLERY: Captain ELIJAH D. TAFT.							
17th Indiana Battery...............	....	....	....	....	....	....	....
Battery D 1st Rhode Island.......	....	....	....	....	....	....	....
Total Nineteenth Army Corps	....	15	5	81	....	13	114

CEDAR CREEK.
October 19, 1864.

	Killed.		Wounded.		Captured or missing.		Aggregate.
NINETEENTH ARMY CORPS: Brevet-Major-General WILLIAM H. EMORY.	Officers.	Enlisted men.	Officers.	Enlisted men.	Officers.	Enlisted men.	
Corps Staff................	....	....	2	....	....	....	2
FIRST DIVISION: Brigadier-General JAMES W. MCMILLAN. Brigadier - General WILLIAM DWIGHT.							
FIRST BRIGADE: Colonel EDWIN P. DAVIS.							
29th Maine....................	1	17	4	105	....	....	127
30th Massachussetts............	1	11	5	91	....	....	108
90th New York.................	2	3	3	43	....	22	73
114th New York................	1	20	6	80	1	7	115
116th New York................	....	7	4	39	....	9	59
153d New York.................	....	8	7	56	....	10	81
Total First Brigade........	5	66	29	414	1	48	563
SECOND BRIGADE: Colonel STEPHEN THOMAS. Brigadier-General JAMES W. MCMILLAN.							
12th Connecticut..............	2	20	5	52	....	93	172
160th New York................	....	9	3	31	....	23	66
47th Pennsylvania.............	1	36	1	88	....	28	154
8th Vermont...................	1	16	11	55	....	23	106
Total Second Brigade......	4	81	20	226	....	167	498
Total First Division [1]......	9	147	49	640	1	215	1,061

[1] *Third Brigade guarding trains.*

COMMAND.	Killed.		Wounded.		Captured or missing.		Aggregate.
	Officers.	Enlisted men.	Officers.	Enlisted men.	Officers.	Enlisted men.	
SECOND DIVISION :							
Brigadier-General CUVIER GROVER.[1]							
Brigadier-General HENRY W. BIRGE.							
Staff....................................	....	....	1	....	....	....	1
FIRST BRIGADE :							
Brigadier-General HENRY W. BIRGE.							
Colonel THOMAS W. PORTER.							
9th Connecticut (battalion)............	....	2	2	13	1	7	25
12th Maine.............................	1	6	3	20	1	50	81
14th Maine.............................	1	4	....	34	1	42	82
26th Massachusetts (battalion).........	....	3	2	8	....	16	29
14th New Hampshire	....	8	3	48	1	17	77
75th New York.........................	....	3	1	18	....	33	55
Total First Brigade.........	2	26	11	141	4	165	349
SECOND BRIGADE :							
Colonel EDWARD L. MOLINEUX.							
13th Connecticut......................	....	2	1	16	....	10	29
11th Indiana...........................	....	4	4	35	....	10	53
22d Iowa...............................	....	1	6	43	2	21	73
3d Massachusetts Cavalry (dismounted)............................	....	6	2	29	....	39	76
131st New York........................	....	2	1	21	....	9	33
159th New York........................	2	2	1	12	....	6	23
Total Second Brigade......	2	17	15	156	2	95	287
THIRD BRIGADE :							
Colonel DANIEL MACAULEY.[1]							
Lieutenant-Colonel ALFRED NEAFIE.							
Staff....................................	....	....	1	....	....	....	1
38th Massachusetts...................	....	....	1	18	....	35	54
128th New York.......................	....	5	....	14	2	74	95
156th New York.......................	1	7	5	31	....	48	92
175th New York (battalion)...........	....	1	....	2	....	....	3
176th New York	1	5	4	11	1	31	53
Total Third Brigade........	2	18	11	76	3	188	298
FOURTH BRIGADE :							
Colonel DAVID SHUNK.							
8th Indiana............................	2	2	4	33	4	21	66
18th Indiana...........................	....	5	6	43	....	27	81
24th Iowa..............................	....	8	6	37	....	41	92
28th Iowa..............................	1	8	2	69	....	10	90
Total Fourth Brigade......	3	23	18	182	4	99	329

[1] Wounded.

COMMAND.	Killed.		Wounded.		Captured or missing.		Aggregate.
	Officers.	Enlisted men.	Officers.	Enlisted men.	Officers.	Enlisted men.	
ARTILLERY:							
1st Maine Battery.............	1	2	1	16	....	8	28
Total Second Division.....	10	86	57	571	13	555	1,292
RESERVE ARTILLERY: Major ALBERT W. BRADBURY.							
17th Indiana Battery............	....	4	1	8	....	3	16
Battery D 1st Rhode Island.......	....	1	....	8	....	3	12
Total Reserve Artillery	....	5	1	16	....	6	28
Total Nineteenth Army Corps	19	238	109	1,227	14	776	2,383

OFFICERS KILLED OR MORTALLY WOUNDED.

BATON ROUGE.
August 5, 1862.
Brigadier-General THOMAS WILLIAMS

Lieutenant MATTHEW A. LATHAM	21st Indiana
Lieutenant CHARLES D. SEELY	" "
Captain EUGENE KELTY	30th Massachusetts

GEORGIA LANDING.
October 27, 1862.

Captain JOHN KELLEHER	8th New Hampshire
Captain Q. A. WARREN	" " "

BISLAND.
April 12-13, 1863.

Captain SAMUEL GAULT	38th Massachusetts
Lieutenant GEORGE G. NUTTING	53d Massachusetts
Lieutenant JOHN T. FREER	156th New York

IRISH BEND.
April 14, 1863

Captain SAMUEL S. HAYDEN	25th Connecticut
Lieutenant DANIEL P. DEWEY	" "
Lieutenant-Colonel GILBERT A. DRAPER	159th New York
Lieutenant ROBERT D. LATHROP	" " "
Lieutenant BYRON F. LOCKWOOD	" " "
Lieutenan JOHN W. MANLEY	" " "

PLAINS STORE.
May 21, 1863.

Lieutenant CHARLES BORUSKY	116th New York

PORT HUDSON.
May 23-July 8, 1863.

Captain JOHN B. HUBBARD,[1] Assistant Adjutant-General	
Lieutenant JOSEPH STRICKLAND [2]	13th Connecticut

[1] *In the Assault of May 27th.*   [2] *In the Assault of June 14th.*

Captain JEDEDIAH RANDALL [1]	26th Connecticut
Captain JOHN L. STANTON [1]	" "
Lieutenant HARVEY F. JACOBS [2]	" "
Lieutenant MARTIN R. KENYON [1]	" "
Captain DAVID D. HOAG [2]	28th Connecticut
Lieutenant CHARLES DURAND [2]	" "
Colonel RICHARD E. HOLCOMB [2]	" "
Lieutenant MARTIN V. B. HILL	1st Louisiana
Lieutenant JAMES E. COBURN	2d Louisiana
Lieutenant J. B. BUTLER	1st Engineers, Corps d'Afrique
Captain ANDREW CAILLOUX [1]	1st Louisiana Native Guards
Lieutenant JOHN H. CROWDER [1]	" " " "
Major ADAM HAFFKILLE	3d Louisiana Native Guards
Lieutenant JOHN C. FULTON [1]	14th Maine
Lieutenant CHARLES L. STEVENS	" "
Lieutenant AARON W. WALLACE [1]	21st Maine
Captain HENRY CROSBY	22d Maine
Lieutenant SOLON A. PERKINS [3]	3d Massachusetts Cavalry
Captain WILLIAM H. BARTLETT [2]	4th Massachusetts
Lieutenant-Colonel WILLIAM L. RODMAN,[1]	38th Massachusetts
Lieutenant FREDERICK HOLMES [2]	" "
Lieutenant-Colonel JAMES O'BRIEN [1]	48th Massachusetts
Lieutenant JAMES MCGINNIS	" "
Lieutenant BURTON D. DEMING [1]	49th Massachusetts
Lieutenant ISAAC E. JUDD [1]	" "
Captain GEORGE S. BLISS [2]	52d Massachusetts
Captain GEORGE H. BAILEY [1]	53d Massachusetts
Captain JEROME K. TAFT [2]	" "
Lieutenant ALFRED R. GLOVER [2]	" "
Lieutenant JOSIAH H. VOSE	" "
Lieutenant FREDERICK J. CLARK [1]	6th Michigan
Lieutenant-Colonel OLIVER W. LULL [1]	8th New Hampshire
Lieutenant LUTHER T. HOSLEY [2]	" "
Lieutenant GEORGE W. THOMPSON [1]	" "
Lieutenant JOSEPH WALLIS [2]	" "
Major GEORGE W. STACKHOUSE [1]	91st New York
Captain HENRY S. HULBERT [2]	" "
Lieutenant SYLVESTER B. SHEPARD	" "
Lieutenant VALOROUS RANDALL [2]	110th New York
Colonel ELISHA B. SMITH [2]	114th New York
Captain CHARLES E. TUCKER [2]	" "
Colonel EDWARD P. CHAPIN [1]	116th New York
Lieutenant DAVID JONES	" "
Lieutenant TIMOTHY J. LINAHAN [2]	" "
Colonel DAVID S. COWLES [1]	128th New York
Lieutenant CHARLES L. VAN SLYCK [1]	" "

[1] *In the Assault of May 27th.* [2] *In the Assault of June 14th.*
[3] *In the affair at Clinton, June 3d.*

Lieutenant NATHAN O. BENJAMIN [2]	131st New York
Lieutenant BENJAMIN F. DENTON [1]	133d New York
Lieutenant-Colonel THOMAS FOWLER	156th New York
Major JAMES H. BOGART [2]	162d New York
Lieutenant JOHN NEVILLE	" "
Lieutenant STEPHEN C. OAKLEY [1]	" "
Lieutenant-Colonel ABEL SMITH, Jr.[1]	165th New York
Lieutenant CHARLES R. CARVILLE [1]	" "
Major A. POWER GALLWAY	173d New York
Captain HENRY COCHEU [2]	" "
Lieutenant SAMUEL H. PODGER	" "
Lieutenant MORGAN SHEA [2]	" "
Colonel MICHAEL K. BRYAN [2]	175th New York
Captain HARMON N. MERRIMAN [1]	177th New York
Lieutenant JAMES WILLIAMSON [1]	" "
Lieutenant STEPHEN F. SPALDING [2]	8th Vermont
Colonel SIDNEY A. BEAN	4th Wisconsin
Captain LEVI R. BLAKE [2]	" "
Lieutenant EDWARD A. CLAPP [1]	" "
Lieutenant DANIEL B. MAXSON [3]	" "
Lieutenant GUSTAVUS WINTERMEYER [2]	" "
Lieutenant BENJAMIN WADSWORTH	10th U. S. Volunteers, Corps d'Afrique

COX'S (OR KOCH'S) PLANTATION.

July 13, 1863.

Captain DAVID W. TUTTLE	116th New York
Lieutenant DE VAN POSTLEY	174th New York

THE RED RIVER CAMPAIGN.

March 10–May 22, 1864.

Lieutenant LOUIS MEISSNER	13th Connecticut.
Lieutenant CHARLES C. GROW	30th Maine
Lieutenant REUBEN SEAVY	"
Lieutenant SUMNER N. STOUT	"
Captain JULIUS N. LATHROP	38th Massachusetts
Captain CHARLES R. COTTON	160th New York, April 9th
Captain WILLIAM J. VAN DEUSEN	" " " "
Lieutenant NICHOLAS MCDONOUGH	" " " "
Lieutenant LEWIS E. FITCH	161st New York, April 8th
Colonel LEWIS BENEDICT	162d New York, April 9th
Captain FRANK T. JOHNSON	" " " "
Lieutenant MADISON K. FINLEY	" " " "

[1] *In the Assault of May 27th.*   [2] *In the Assault of June 14th.*
[3] *In the affair of Clinton, June 3d.*

Lieutenant WILLIAM C. HAWS 162d New York, April 9th.
Lieutenant THEODORE A. SCUDDER "   "   "   "
Lieutenant-Colonel WILLIAM N. GREEN, Jr. 173d Infantry
Captain HENRY R. LEE 173d New York
Lieutenant ALFRED P. SWOYER 47th Pennsylvania, April 8th
Lieutenant James A. SANDERSON 1st United States Artillery

THE OPEQUON.

September 19, 1864.

Lieutenant-Colonel FRANK H. PECK 12th Connecticut
Lieutenant WILLIAM S. BULKLEY "   "
Lieutenant GEORGE W. STEADMAN "   "
Lieutenant WILLIAM S. MULLEN 11th Indiana
Captain SILAS A. WADSWORTH 18th Indiana
Captain DAVID J. DAVIS 22d Iowa
Captain BENJAMIN D. PARKS "   "
Lieutenant JAMES A. BOARTS "   "
Captain JOSEPH R. GOULD 24th Iowa
Lieutenant SYLVESTER S. DILLMAN "   "
Captain JOHN E. PALMER "   "
Captain SCOTT HOUSEWORTH "   "
Captain DANIEL M. PHILLIPS 12th Maine
Captain SAMUEL F. THOMPSON "   "
Lieutenant WILLIAM JACKMAN 14th Maine
Lieutenant AJALON GODWIN "   "
Major WILLIAM KNOWLTON 29th Maine
Lieutenant JASPER F. GLIDDEN 3d Massachusetts Cavalry.
Lieutenant JOHN F. POOLE "   "   "
Major EUSEBIUS S. CLARK 26th Massachusetts
Captain ENOS W. THAYER "   "
Lieutenant JOHN P. HALEY 30th Massachusetts
Colonel ALEXANDER GARDINER 14th New Hampshire
Captain WILLIAM H. CHAFFIN "   "   "
Captain WILLIAM A. FOSGATE "   "   "
Lieutenant ARTEMUS B. COLBURN "   "   "
Lieutenant JESSE A. FISK "   "   "
Lieutenant HENRY S. PAUL "   "   "
Lieutenant GEORGE H. STONE "   "   "
Lieutenant MOULTON S. WEBSTER "   "   "
Lieutenant-Colonel WILLOUGHBY BABCOCK 75th New York
Lieutenant EDWIN E. BREED 114th New York
Captain JACOB C. KLOCK 153d New York
Lieutenant HERMAN SMITH 159th New York
Captain Sir N. DEXTER 160th New York
Lieutenant B. FRANK MAXSON "   "   "

CEDAR CREEK.

October 19, 1864.

Captain JOHN P. LOWELL	12th Connecticut
Lieutenant GEORGE M. BENTON	" "
Lieutenant HORACE E. PHELPS	" "
Lieutenant-Colonel ALEXANDER J. KENNY	8th Indiana
Captain WILLIAM D. WATSON	" "
Lieutenant GEORGE W. QUAY	" "
Lieutenant-Colonel WILLIAM S. CHARLES	11th Indiana
Major JONATHAN H. WILLIAMS	18th Indiana
Lieutenant-Colonel JOHN Q. WILDS	24th Iowa
Captain JOHN W. RIEMENSCHNEIDER	28th Iowa
Lieutenant JOHN E. MORTON	1st Maine Battery
Lieutenant HENRY D. WATSON	12th Maine
Lieutenant-Colonel CHARLES S. BICKMORE	14th Maine
Lieutenant JOHN L. HOYT	29th Maine
Lieutenant LYMAN JAMES	3d Massachusetts Cavalry (dismounted)
Lieutenant ALBERT L. TILDEN	26th Massachusetts
Lieutenant GEORGE F. WHITCOMB	30th Massachusetts
Lieutenant WILLIAM F. CLARK, Jr.	" "
Major JOHN C. SMART	90th New York
Lieutenant THADDEUS C. FERRIS	" " "
Captain DANIEL C. KNOWLTON	114th New York
Lieutenant ISAAC BURCH	" " "
Lieutenant NORMAN M. LEWIS	" " "
Lieutenant WILLIAM D. THURBER	" " "
Lieutenant CHRISTOPHER LARKIN	156th New York
Lieutenant JOHANNES LEFEVER	" " "
Major ROBERT McD. HART	159th New York
Captain DUNCAN RICHMOND	" " "
Lieutenant JULIUS A. JONES	176th New York
Captain EDWIN G. MINNICH	47th Pennsylvania
Captain EDWARD HALL	8th Vermont
Lieutenant NATHAN C. CHENEY	" "
Lieutenant AARON K. COOPER	" "

NOTE.—Unfortunately, it has been found impossible to obtain a complete list of officers who fell in skirmishes or minor affairs.

PORT HUDSON FORLORN HOPE.

Officers and men who volunteered for the storming party under General Orders No. 49, Headquarters Department of the Gulf, June 15, 1863 [1]:

Colonel HENRY W. BIRGE, 13th Connecticut, Commanding.[2]

STAFF.

Captain DUNCAN S. WALKER, Assistant Adjutant-General.[3]
Acting-Master EDMOND C. WEEKS, U. S. Navy, A. D. C.[2]
Captain CHARLES L. NORTON, 25th Connecticut.[2]
Captain JOHN L. SWIFT, 3d Massachusetts Cavalry.[2]
First Lieutenant E. H. RUSSELL, 9th Pennsylvania Reserves, Acting Signal Officer.
Assistant-Surgeon GEORGE CLARY, 13th Connecticut.[2]
Lieutenant JULIUS H. TIEMANN, A. A. D. C., 159th New York.[2]

FIRST BATTALION.[4]

Lieutenant-Colonel JOHN B. VAN PETTEN, 160th New York.
Captain EDWARD P. HOLLISTER, 31st Massachusetts, Senior Major.
Captain SAMUEL D. HOVEY, 31st Massachusetts, Junior Major.
Captain ISAAC W. CASE, 22d Maine, Quartermaster.

---

[1] *The original roll of the storming party was made up in duplicate. After the siege, one copy was retained by General Birge, the other being turned in to the Adjutant-General's Office, Department of the Gulf, by Captain, afterward Brevet Brigadier-General Duncan S. Walker, Assistant Adjutant-General. The latter copy has not been found among the documents turned over to the War Department in 1865. All Birge's papers and records were captured by the Confederates and among them his copy of the roll was lost. In 1886, from one of his officers he obtained a book containing a third copy of the roll, described by him as "complete and perfect," and placed it in the hands of Captain Charles L. Norton, 25th Connecticut (Colonel 29th Connecticut), himself one of the stormers, by whom the volume was delivered to Colonel D. P. Muzzey, President, and Captain C. W. C. Rhoades, Secretary, of the Forlorn Hope Association. The list here printed is made up by collating with this roll the detached and obviously incomplete memoranda gathered into the XXVIth volume of the "Official Records." So many mistakes in names have been found in the certified copy of Birge's list as furnished to the author, that others are likely to exist among the names marked [¹], that could not be compared with the records. For example, it is found that Privates F. L. Scampmouse and Levi Scapmouse, Company C, 156th New York are the same man and, Seven Soepson, same regiment, is Sven Svenson.*

[2] *Not on the roll as printed in Official Records, vol. xxvi., part I., pp. 57-66.*

[3] *Not on Birge's duplicate roll.*

[4] *The names of the Battalion Field and Staff Officers appear again under their proper regiments.*

Captain WILLIAM SMITH, 2d Louisiana, A. D. C.
Lieutenant G. A. HARMOUNT, 12th Connecticut, Adjutant.
Surgeon DAVID H. ARMSTRONG, 160th New York.

SECOND BATTALION.[1]

Lieutenant-Colonel CHARLES S. BICKMORE, 14th Maine.
Major ALBION K. BOLAN, 14th Maine, Major.
Lieutenant I. FRANK HOBBS, 14th Maine, Adjutant.
Lieutenant EDWARD MARRENER, 174th New York, Quartermaster.

12TH CONNECTICUT.

	Company.		Company.
Captain LESTER E. BRALEY,	G	Sergeant ANDREW H. DAVIDSON,[3]	G
Lieutenant A. DWIGHT MCCALL,	G	Corporal JOHN T. GORDON,	G
" STANTON ALLYN,[2]	K	Private OLIVER C. ANDREWS,	G
" GEORGE A. HARMOUNT		" J. E. CHASE,[2]	G
(Adjutant),		" JAMES DUNN,	G
Private CHARLES J. CONSTANTINE,	A	" PATRICK FITZPATRICK,	G
Sergeant JOHN MULLEN,	B	" PATRICK FRANEY,	G
Private CHARLES DUBOISE,	B	" WILLIAM TOBIN,[2]	G
Corporal JOHN MOORE,	C	" JOSEPH W. WEEKS,[2]	G
Private GEORGE T. DICKSON,	C	Sergeant SOLOMON E. WHITING,[2]	H
" WILLOUGHBY HULL,	C	" JOHN W. PHELPS,	H
" WILLIAM PUTNAM,	C	Corporal JOSEPH W. CARTER,	H
" CHRISTOPHER SPIES,	C	" CHARLES E. SHERMAN,[3]	H
" GEORGE W. WATKINS,[3]	C	Private EDWIN CONVERSE,	H
" JOHN P. WOODWARD,	C	" HUGH DONNALLY,[2]	H
Sergeant ALEXANDER COHN,	D	" WARREN GAMMONS,	H
Corporal GEORGE SHAW,[2]	D	" JOSEPH GRAHAM,[2]	H
" JAMES ROBERTSON, Jr.,[2]	D	" MILES P. HIGLEY,[2]	H
Private L. P. FARRELL,[2]	D	" WILLIAM LENNING,	H
" GEORGE KOHLER,	D	" THOMAS MCCUE,[2]	H
" REUBEN MILES,	D	" MELVIN NICHOLS,	H
" FREDERICK C. PAYNE,	D	Corporal DANIEL B. LOOMIS,[3]	K
" WILLIAM P. SMITH,[3]	E	Private FRANCIS BEAUMONT,[2]	K
" EDWARD L. MILLERICK,[2]	E	" A. M. PERKINS,[2]	K
Sergeant CHARLES E. MCGLAFLIN,	G		

13TH CONNECTICUT.

	Company.		Company.
Captain APOLLOS COMSTOCK (commanding regiment),		Captain CHARLES J. FULLER,	D
		Lieutenant PERRY AVERILL,	B
" CHARLES D. BLINN,	C	" FRANK WELLS,	I
" HOMER B. SPRAGUE,	H	" CHARLES E. TIBBETS,	A
" DENISON H. FINLEY,	G	" WILLIAM F. NORMAN,	K

[1] The names of the Battalion Field and Staff Officers appear again under their proper regiments.
[2] Not on the roll as printed in Official Records, vol. xxvi., part I., pp. 57-66.
[3] Not on Birge's duplicate roll.

	Company.		Company.
Lieutenant Charles Daniels,	K	Private Morant J. Robertson,	B
" Charles H. Beaton,	E	" Sidney B. Ruggles,	B
" John C. Kinney,	A	" Felix Schreger,[1]	B
" Louis Meisner,	I	" Louis Schmeidt,	B
" Newton W. Perkins,	C	" Frederick L. Sturgis,	B
" Louis Beckwith,[1]	B	Sergeant Everett S. Dunbar,[1]	C
Corporal Francis J. Wolf,	A	" Charles H. Gaylord,[1]	C
" Christopher Fagan,	A	" John N. Lyman,	C
" Andrew Black,	A	" John Maddox,	C
Private William Bishop,	A	Corporal Lewis Hart,[1]	C
" Michael Cunningham,[1]	A	" Homer M. Welch,[1]	C
" Walter Eagan,	A	Private Willis Barnes,[1]	C
" John Fagan,	A	" Seymour Buckley,[1]	C
" Francis J. Gaffnay,	A	" Chauncey Griffin,	C
" James Gilbert,[1]	A	" Charles Hotchkiss,[1]	C
" Edward Lantry,	A	" Charles Mitchell,[1]	C
" John McGuire,	A	" John O'Dell,[1]	C
" Joseph Mack,	A	" Frederick W. Pindar,[1]	C
" John Martin,[1]	A	" Joseph H. Pratt,	C
" Henry Morton,	A	" George Roraback,[1]	C
" Loren D. Penfield,	A	" Mortimer H. Scott,	C
" John O'Keefe,[1]	A	" Joseph Taylor,	C
" John Quigley,[1]	A	" Daniel Thompson,	C
" Thomas Reilly,[1]	A	Sergeant John J. Squier,[1]	D
" Charles R. Rowell,[1]	A	" Ezra M. Hull,[1]	D
" John Smith,[1]	A	Corporal Edward Alton,	D
" Edward Stone,[1]	A	" William Fennimore,[1]	D
Sergeant George E. Fancher,	B	" Andrew Holford,[1]	D
" George H. Pratt,	B	Private Thomas B. Andrus,[1]	D
" Alonzo Wheeler,	B	" Antonio Astenhoffer,[1]	D
Corporal Francis E. Weed,	B	" Henry F. Bishop,[1]	D
" Roswell Taylor,	B	" Charles Bliss,[1]	D
" Isaac W. Bishop,	B	" John Crarey,[1]	D
Private George M. Balling,	B	" John Dillon,	D
" John J. Brown,	B	" John Fee,	D
" William B. Casey,	B	" Henry F. Fox,[1]	D
" Balthasar Emmerich,	B	" Gotleib Falkling,[1]	D
" Peter Gentien,	B	" Thomas Fitzpatrick,[1]	D
" Dennis Hegany,	B	" Joseph Gardner,	D
" William W. Jones,	B	" Newton Gaylor,[1]	D
" John Klein,	B	" Gaspar Heidsick,[1]	D
" Benjamin L. Mead,	B	" Louis Hettinger,[1]	D
" John Mohren,	B	" Julius Kamp,[1]	D
" Charles Nichols,	B	" Henry Kuhlmaner,[1]	D
" Victor Pinsaid,	B	" Henry Long,[1]	D
" George Prindle,	B	" George Losaw,[1]	D

[1] Not on the roll as printed in Official Records, vol. xxvi., part I., pp. 57-66.

	Company.		Company.
Private LUKE MCCABE,[1]	D	Sergeant JOHN W. BRADLEY,	G
" HENRY E. POLLEY,[1]	D	" FRANCIS HUXFORD,	G
" FREDERICK POUSH,[1]	D	Corporal MOSES GAY,	G
" HORACE B. STODDARD,[1]	D	" LOUIS FROTISH,	G
" WILLIAM H. TUCKER,[1]	D	" EDMUND BOGUE,	G
" MARTIN TYLER,[1]	D	" TIMOTHY ALLEN,	G
" LOUIS WALTERS,[1]	D	Private FRANK AUSTIN,[1]	G
" EDWARD WELDEN,	D	" GEORGE I. AUSTIN,	G
Sergeant NICHOLAS SCHUE,	E	" JOHN BRAND,	G
" RICHARD CROLEY,	E	" OCTAVE CERESSOLLE,	G
Corporal ROBERT C. BARRY,	E	" WILLIAM B. CRAWFORD,[1]	G
" LEONARD L. DUGAL,	E	" CHARLES CULVER,	G
Private JACOB BROWN,	E	" JAMES GAY,	G
" ADAM GERZE,[1]	E	" ALBERT HOPKINS,	G
" FREDERICK HANNS,	E	" JOHN HUNT,	G
" GEORGE W. HOWLAND,	E	" HENRY A. HURLBURT,	G
" MICHAEL MURPHY,	E	" ASAHEL INGRAHAM,	G
" CHARLES F. OEDEKOVEN,	E	" JEREMY T. JORDAN,	G
" FRITZ OEDEKOVEN,[1]	E	" MICHAEL KEARNEY,	G
" F. F. F. PFIEFFER,	E	" JOSEPH KEMPLE,	G
" ANDREW REAGAN,	E	" ALBERT LELEITNER,[1]	G
" FREDERICK SCHUH,	E	" WALTER MCGRATH,[1]	G
" JOSEPH VOGEL,[1]	E	" JOHN MCKEON,	G
" AUGUST WILSON,	E	" WILLIAM M. MAYNARD,	G
Sergeant EUGENE S. NASH,[1]	F	" DANIEL MOORE,	G
" JOHN T. REYNOLDS,[1]	F	" MORRIS NEWHOUSE,[1]	G
Corporal JAMES CASE,[1]	F	" TIMOTHY O'CONNELL,	G
Private JAMES BARRY,[1]	F	" WILLIAM H. REYNOLDS,[1]	G
" GEORGE BOGUE,[1]	F	" ELLIS B. ROBINSON,[1]	G
" DAVID H. BROWN,[1]	F	" HENRY ROBINSON,	G
" HENRY CLOUSINK,[1]	F	" JOHN RYAN,[1]	G
" JAMES COSGROVE,	F	" ANTON SCHLOSSER,	G
BYRON CROCKER,[1]	F	" MARTIN J. SHADEN,	G
" DAVID D. JAQUES,[1]	F	" MARTIN SHEER,	G
" ABEL JOHNSON,[1]	F	" CHARLES SIDDERS,	G
" PATRICK LEACH,	F	" EDWARD SKINNER,[1]	G
" PATRICK MARTIN,[1]	F	" JOHN SUARMAN,	G
" THOMAS R. MCCORMICK,[1]	F	" ANSON F. SUBER,[1]	G
" JAMES O'NEIL,[1]	F	" SEBREE W. TINKER,	G
" HENRY E. PHINNEY,	F	Sergeant WILLIAM H. HUNTLEY,	H
" THOMAS POWERS,[1]	F	" DENNIS DOYLE,	H
" ORRIN M. PRICE,[1]	F	" HERMAN W. BAILEY,	H
" THEODORE SECELLE,[1]	F	Corporal THOMAS HARRISON,[1]	H
" WILLIAM L. WEBB,[1]	F	Private PHILO ANDREWS,	H
Sergeant SAMUEL L. COOK,[1]	G	" NIRAM BLACKMAN,	H
" CHARLES B. HUTCHINGS,	G	" JOHN BLAKE,	H

[1] Not on the roll as printed in Official Records, vol. xxvi., part I., pp. 57-66.

	Company.		Company.
Private Frank Patterson,	H	Sergeant Charles E. Humphrey,	K
" George H. Twitchell,	H	Corporal Herman Saunders,	K
" William H. Smith,[1]	H	" Herbert C. Baldwin,	K
Sergeant John Duress,[1]	I	" John Nugent,	K
" Abner N. Sterry,	I	" Robert Hollinger,	K
" Samuel Taylor,	I	Private John Bennett,	K
" Engelbert Sauter,	I	" Benjamin E. Benson,	K
Corporal Francis W. Preston,[1]	I	" Frank C. Bristol,	K
" Joseph Franz,[1]	I	" William Call,[2]	K
" Garrett Herbert,[1]	I	" George Clancy,	K
Private William Albrecht,[1]	I	" William J. Cojer,	K
" Fritz Bowman,[1]	I	" Thomas Duffy,	K
" Ulrich Burgart,[1]	I	" Samuel Eaves,[1]	K
" Michael Burke,	I	" Edward Ellison,	K
" James Dillon,	I	" John Gall,[1]	K
" Patrick Hines,[1]	I	" Thomas Griffin,	K
" Thomas McGee,	I	" William Kraige [1, 3]	K
" Clifford C. Newberry,[1]	I	" Patrick Mahoney,	K
" Henry Reltrath,[1]	I	" Thomas Morris,	K
" Edward Smith,[1]	I	" Richard O'Donnell,	K
" Edward O. Thomas,[1]	I	" George C. Russell,	K
" Henry Whiteman,[1]	I	" Bernard Stanford,	K
Sergeant Miles J. Beecher,	K	" John Storey,	K
" George H. Winslow,	K	" Bartley Tiernon	K

25TH CONNECTICUT.

	Company.		Company.
Lieutenant Henry C. Ward		Private Eli Hull,[1]	B
(Adjutant).		" Samuel Schlesinger,	F
" Henry H. Goodell,	F	" John Williams,[1]	H
Sergeant-Major Charles F. Ulrich.			

1ST LOUISIANA.

	Company.		Company.
Captain J. R. Parsons,	I	Private Joseph Briggs,	I
Lieutenant C. A. Tracey,[2]	I	" Leonard Demarquis,	I
" J. T. Smith,[1]	I	" John Fahy,	I
Sergeant Michael H. Dunn,	I	" John Hunt,	I
" James York,[2]	I	" Henry Kathra,	I
" George McGraw,	I	" Alex. Kiah,[2]	I
Corporal Henry Carle,	I	" James Manahan,	I
" John Emperor,	I	" James McGuire,[1]	I
" Jos. A. Scovell,	I	" John Reas,	I
" John Lower,	I	" Joseph Reaman,[3]	I
Private Charles Baker,	I	" Jerry Rourke,	I
" Richard Balshaw,[2]	I	" James Smith,	I
" Patrick Brennan,	I		

[1] *Not on the roll as printed in Official Records, vol. xxvi., part I., pp. 57-66.*
[2] *Not on Birge's duplicate roll.*
[3] *Probably Krug, or Kramer.*

2D LOUISIANA.

	Company.		Company.
Captain WILLIAM SMITH,[2]	H	Private GEORGE TYLER,	F
Private LEWIS DIEMERT,	A	" EUGENE GALLAGHER,	G
" HENRY MAYO,	A	Sergeant THEODORE LEDERICK,	H
" FREDERICK A. MURNSON,	A	" BENJAMIN C. ROLLINS,[2]	H
Sergeant ALBERT SADUSKY,	B	Corporal JACOB STALL,[2]	H
Corporal JOHN HOFFMAN,	B	Private JOHN BRENNAN,	H
Private JAMES CLINTON,	B	" PATRICK DEVINE,[2]	H
" MICHAEL DUNN,[2]	B	" JOHN ELDRIDGE,[2]	H
" BARNEY MCCLOSKY,	B	" PATRICK GARRITY,[2]	H
" WILLIAM ROCHER,	B	" LOUIS HARRELL,	H
" JAMES SULLIVAN,	B	" JOHN HAYES,	H
Sergeant B. E. ROWLAND,[1]	C	" LOUIS ICKS,[2]	H
" ANDREW HARRIGON,	C	" JOHN LANE,	H
Private PATRICK BROWN,[1-2]	C	" THOMAS R. BLAKELY,[2]	I
" JAMES DONOVAN,	C	" LOUIS L. DREY,	I
" JOHN FRY,[2]	C	" JAMES E. MARINER,[2]	I
" WILLIAM HAYES,[1]	C	" FRANCIS MCGAHAY,[2]	I
" ADOLPH JOINFROID,[1]	C	" EDWIN RICE,[2]	I
" DANIEL THEALE,	C	Corporal OTTO FOUCHE,[2]	K
" WILLIAM WILKIE,	C	Private HENRY GORDON,[2]	K
" LEON PAUL,	D	" GEORGE SEYMORE,[2]	K
" JOSEPH DUPUY,	F	" PAUL E. TROSCLAIR,[2]	K
" WILLIAM GALLAGHER,	F		

1ST LOUISIANA NATIVE GUARDS.[2]

	Company.		Company.
Sergeant JOSEPH FRICK,	C	Private ROBERT LOTSUM,	G
" CHARLES DUGUÉ,	C	Corporal JULES FRITS,	H
" ERNEST LEGROSS,	C	Private JAQUES AUGUSTE,	H
Corporal ARTHUR MEYÉ,	C	" HENRY BRADFORD,	H
Private VALCOUR BROWN,	C	" JOSEPH CARTER,	H
" CAMILE CAZAINIER,	C	" ISIDORE CHARLES,	H
" EDMOND CHAMPANEL,	C	" EMILE CHATARD,	H
" EUGENE DEGRUY,	C	" FREDERICK DERINSBOURG,	H
" CLEMENT GALICE,	C	" FRANCIS FERNANDEZ,	H
" LOUIS LACRAIE,	C	" ARTHUR GUYOT,	H
" PIERRE MARTIEL,	C	" SAMUEL HALL,	H
" JOSEPH MOUSHAUD,	C	" JOHN HOWARD,	H
" ARMAND ROCHE,	C	" JOSEPH JACKSON,	H
" FRANCOIS SEVERIN,	C	" RICHARD JOHN,	H
" HENRY SMITH,	C	" JOE JOSEPH,	H
" J. BAPTISTE SMITH,	C	" AUGUSTE LEE,	H
" MARTIN WHITE,	C	" HENRY LEE,	H
" JOSEPH LEWIS,	G	" OSCAR POINTOISEAU,	H

[1] Not on the roll as printed in Official Records, vol. xxvi., part I., pp. 57-66.
[2] Not on Birge's duplicate roll.   [3] Not on muster roll.

	Company.			Company.
Private JOSEPH PATTERSON, Sr.,	H	Private	CHARLES BRANSON,	I
" JOSEPH PATTERSON, Jr.,	H	"	ALEXANDER JONES,	I
" PERRY RANDOLPH,	H	"	WILLIAM MCDOWELL,	I
" JAMES RICHARDS,	H	"	COLLIN PAGE,	I
" BENJAMIN STRING,	H	"	THOMAS REDWOOD,	I
" RALEMY WALSE,	H	"	WILLIAM WOOD,	I
Sergeant JOHN J. CAGE,	I	"	GEORGE BURKE,	K
" JOHN W. BERWEEKS,	I	"	ED. MADISON,	K
Corporal THOMAS ALEXANDER,	I	"	CHARLES SMITH,	K

3D LOUISIANA NATIVE GUARDS.[2]

	Company.			Company.
Private ABRAM FROST,	A	Private	W. HENRY,	E
" HENRY MARSHEL,	A	"	BENJAMIN JOHNSON,	E
Sergeant WADE HAMBLETON,	C	"	JOSEPH MILLER,	E
Corporal MASSALLA LOFRA,	C	"	THOMAS SIMMONS,	E
" WILLIAM MACK,	C	"	J. W. THOMAS,	E
" E. THOMINICK,	C	"	EDWARD BROWN,	H
Private DANIEL ANDERSON,	C	"	ISAAC GILLIS,	H
" —— BRACTON,	C	"	—— JOHNSON,	H
" WILLIAM DALLIS,	C	"	SILAS HUFF,	H
" JACK DORSON,	C	"	LEWIS PAULIN,	H
" WILLIAM FINICK,	C	"	JOHN ROSS,	H
" SOLOMON FLEMING,	C	"	J. SMITH,	H
" WILLIAM GREEN,	C	"	SILAS DICTON,	I
" GEORGE JOSEPH,	C	"	LOUDON MCDANIEL,	I
" VICTOR LEWIS,	C	"	JOHN TALLER,	I
" —— SAUNDERS,	C	"	ISAAC TWIGGS,	I
" —— TAYLOR,	C	"	GEORGE WASHINGTON,	I
" —— WHITE,	C	"	—— WILLIAMS,	I
Sergeant THOMAS JEFFERSON,	E			

12TH MAINE.

	Company.			Company.
Captain JOHN F. APPLETON,[1]	H	Private	EDGAR G. ADAMS,	E
Lieutenant DANIEL M. PHILLIPS,	H	"	OLIVER D. JEWETT,	E
" MARCELLUS L. STEARNS,	E	"	NATHAN W. KENDALL,	E
Private JOHN COOPER,	A	"	JAMES POWERS,	E
" ISAAC R. DOUGLASS,	A	Sergeant	WILLIAM M. BERRY,	H
" ALMON L. GILPATRICK,	A	"	JAMES W. SMITH,	I
" JOHN WELLER,	A	"	HENRY TYLER,[2]	H
Sergeant SEYMOUR A. FARRINGTON,	E	Private	FRANK E. ANDERSON,[2]	H
Corporal HENRY S. BERRY,	E			

13TH MAINE.

Lieutenant JOSEPH B. CARSON.[1]

[1] *Not on the roll as printed in Official Records, vol. xxvi., part I., pp. 57-66.*
[2] *Not on Birge's duplicate roll.*

14TH MAINE.

	Company.
Lieutenant-Colonel CHARLES S. BICKMORE.	
Major ALBION K. BOLAN.	
Captain GEORGE BLODGETT,	K
Lieutenant JOHN K. LAING,	F
" I. FRANK HOBBS,	G
" WARREN T. CROWELL,	K
" MERRILL H. ADAMS,	B
" WILLIAM H. GARDINER,	G
" CHARLES E. BLACKWELL,[2]	I
Sergeant-Major CHARLES W. THING.[2]	
Sergeant Jos. F. CLEMENT,	A
" GEORGE C. HAGERTY,	A
Corporal WILLIAM C. TOWNSEND,	A
" OTIS G. CROCKETT,	A
" ALVA EMERSON,	A
Private PETER BEAUMAN,	A
" WILSON BOWDEN,	A
" RICHARD J. COLBY,	A
" SETH P. COLBY,	A
" PETER MISHER,[2]	A
" IRVIN MORSE,	A
" EDWIN ORDWAY,	A
" ALBERT WEBSTER,[2]	A
Sergeant JOHN DOUGHERTY,	B
" JAMES SHEHAN,	B
Corporal PETER EMMERICH,[1]	B
Private JOHN DARBY,[1][3]	B
" BENJAMIN DOUGLASS, Jr.,	B
" JAMES ELDERS,	B
" GEORGE N. LARRABEE,	B
" JOHN DAILEY,	C
" SIMON BEATTIE,	E

	Company.
Sergeant F. H. BLACKMAN,[1]	F
" JOS. W. GRANT,	F
Corporal WILLIAM M. COBB,[1]	F
" WILLIAM F. JENKINS,	F
Private EDWARD BETHUM,	F
" WILLIAM E. MERRIFIELD,	F
" HORACE SAWYER,	F
Sergeant ARCHELAUS FULLER,	G
Corporal EDWARD BRADFORD,	G
Private SAMUEL CONNELLY,	G
" EZRA A. MERRILL,	G
Sergeant CALVIN S. GORDON,	H
Corporal LOUIS C. GORDON,[2]	H
Private JOHN CUNNINGHAM,	I
Sergeant C. PEMBROKE CARTER,	I
" SAMUEL T. LOGAN,	I
" JOHN S. SMITH,	I
" WILLIAM L. BUSHER,[1]	I
Corporal JOHN HAYES,	I
Private WILLIAM R. HAWKINS,[2]	I
" JOS. PREBLE,	I
" ALBERT B. MESERVY,	I
" BENJAMIN F. ROLESON,	I
Sergeant WILLIAM MULLER,	K
" ALEX. WILSON,	K
" BAZEL HOGUE,	K
Corporal JOHN MOORE,	K
" WILLIAM DARBY,	K
Private DANIEL CONNERS,	K
" BENJAMIN SANDON,[1]	K
" GEORGE WATERHOUSE,	K
" JULIUS WENDLANDT,	K
" CHARLES WILKERSON,	K
" ELLIOT WITHAM.	K

21ST MAINE.

	Company.
Captain JAMES L. HUNT,[2]	C
" SAMUEL W. CLARKE,	H
Private J. MINK,[2]	A
" OTIS SPRAGUE,[3]	A
" SEWELL SPRAGUE,[3]	A
" JOEL RICHARDSON,[2]	B

	Company.
Private ANDREW P. WATSON,[2]	B
" JOHN H. BROWN,	C
" JOHN E. HEATH,	C
" CHARLES T. LORD,	C
" GEORGE F. STACEY,	C
" WILLIAM N. TIBBETTS,	C

[1] Not on the roll as printed in Official Records, vol. xxvi., part I., pp. 57-66.
[2] Not on Birge's duplicate roll.
[3] Not on muster roll.

Company.		Company.	
Corporal GALEN A. CHAPMAN,	D	Corporal MINOT D. HEWETT,	G
" ALONZO L. FARROW,	D	Private LEANDER WOODCOCK,[2]	G
Private DAVID O. PRIEST,[2]	D	" FREDERIC GOUD,[2]	H
" DAVID B. COLE,[2]	E	" THOMAS WYMAN,[2]	H
" CHARLES S. CROWELL,[2]	E	" JOHN B. MORRILL,[2]	I
" MELVILLE MERRILL,[2]	E	" JAMES S. JEWELL,[2]	K
" WILLIAM DOUGLASS.[2]	F	" FRANK S. WADE,[2]	K
" GUSTAVUS HISCOCK,[2]	F		

22D MAINE.

Company.		Company.	
Captain ISAAC W. CASE,	H	Corporal D. S. CHADBOURNE,[1]	E
" HENRY L. WOOD,	E	Sergeant SAMUEL S. MASON,	F
Lieutenant GEORGE E. BROWN,	A	Private TIMOTHY N. ERWIN,	G
Private VAN BUREN CARLL,	B	" AMAZIAH W. WEBB,	K
" DANIEL MCPHETRES,	B		

24TH MAINE.

Company.		Company.	
Sergeant GEORGE E. TAYLOR,	H	Private JAMES HUGHES,	H

28TH MAINE.

Private JAMES N. MORROW.

3D MASSACHUSETTS CAVALRY.

Company.		Company.	
Colonel THOMAS E. CHICKERING,[2]		Private JAMES GALLAGHER,[2]	G
Captain JOHN L. SWIFT,[1]	C	" JOHN GRANVILLE,[1]	G
" FRANCIS E. BOYD,	H	" JAMES MCLAUGHLIN,[1]	G
Lieutenant WILLIAM T. HODGES,	C	Sergeant PATRICK S. CURRY,[1]	G
" HENRY S. ADAMS[2] (Adjutant).		Private SOLOMON HALL,[1]	G
" DAVID P. MUZZEY,	G	Sergeant WILLIAM WILDMAN,	H
" CHARLES W. C. RHOADS,	H	" JOHN KELLY,	H
Sergeant-Major WILLIAM S. STEVENS.		" GEORGE E. LONG,[1]	H
Private FERDINAND ROLLE,	A	Corporal WILLIAM S. CALDWELL,	H
Sergeant NATHAN G. SMITH,	C	" RANDALL F. HUNNEWELL,	H
" HORACE P. FLINT,	C	" WILLIAM P. PETHIE,	H
Corporal GEORGE D. COX,[1]	C	" CHARLES MILLER,	H
Private JOSEPH ELLIOTT,	C	" WILLIAM R. DAVIS,[2]	H
" EDWARD JOHNSON,	C	Private EDWIN T. EHRLACHER,	H
Corporal PATRICK DUNLAY,	G	" GROS GRANADINO,	H
Sergeant JASON SMITH,[1]	G	" ELI HAWKINS,	H
Private SIMON DALY,	G	" PATRICK J. MONKS,	H
" PETER DONAHUE,	G	" JOHN VELISCROSS,	H
		" GEORGE WILSON,	H

[1] Not on the roll as printed in Official Records, vol. xxvi., part I., pp. 57-66.
[2] Not on Birge's duplicate roll.

13TH MASSACHUSETTS BATTERY.

Private CESAR DUBOIS, | Private JOHN V. WARNER,[2]

26TH MASSACHUSETTS.
Lieutenant SETH BONNER,[2] Company F.

30TH MASSACHUSETTS.

	Company.			Company.
Captain EDWARD A. FISKE,	D	Corporal CHARLES D. MOORE,		D
Lieutenant THOMAS B. JOHNSTON,	H	Private JAMES BOYCE,		D
" NATHANIEL K. REED,	C	" WILLIAM KENNY,		D
" FERDINAND C. POREE,[2]	C	" HORACE F. DAVIS,		E
Sergeant W. H. H. RICHARDS,	B	Sergeant MURTY QUINLAN,		F
Corporal GEORGE E. COY,	B	" THOMAS A. WARREN,		F
" THOMAS COURTNEY,	B	Corporal MICHAEL MEALEY,		F
Private JAMES M. BROWN,	B	Private J. SULLIVAN,[1, 3]		F
" ANDREW COLE,	B	Sergeant JOHN LEARY,		G
" MARTIN HASSETT,	B	" WILLARD A. HUSSEY,		H
" GEORGE TOOWEY,	B	Private JOHN BATTLES,		H
Sergeant LUTHER H. MARSHALL,	C	" JOHN HIGGINS,		H
Private WLLIAM MCCUTCHEON,	C	" PAUL JESEMAUGHN,		H
" CHARLES B. RICHARDSON,	C	" WILLIAM F. KAVANAGH,		H
" GEORGE SUTHERLAND,	C	" JOHN WELCH,		H
Sergeant GEORGE H. MOULE,	D	" JOHN WILSON,		H
" JOHN E. RING,[2]	D	Sergeant SAMUEL RYAN,		I

31ST MASSACHUSETTS.

	Company.			Company.
Captain EDWARD P. HOLLISTER,	A	Private FRANK FITCH,		A
" SAMUEL D. HOVEY,	K	" WILLIAM THORINGTON,		A
Lieutenant LUTHER C. HOWELL		" PETER VALUN,		A
(Adjutant).		" ETHAN H. COWLES,		B
" JAMES M. STEWART,	A	" WILLIAM J. COLEMAN,		K
Private CHESTER BEVINS,	A	" MAURICE LEE,		K
" PATRICK CARNES,	A			

38TH MASSACHUSETTS.
Lieutenant FRANK N. SCOTT, Company D.

48TH MASSACHUSETTS.
Private MICHAEL ROACH, Company G.

---

[1] *Not on the roll as printed in Official Records, vol. xxvi., part I., pp. 57-66.*
[2] *Not on Birge's duplicate roll.*   [3] *Jeremiah, Co. B, James, I, or Michael, F?*

49TH MASSACHUSETTS.[2]

	Company.			Company.
Lieutenant EDSON F. DRESSER,	F	Private EDWIN N. HUBBARD,		D
Private JAMES W. BASSETT,	A	" FRANKLIN ALLEN,		H
" WILLIAM E. CLARK,	A	" GEORGE KNICKERBOCKER,		H
" WILLARD L. WATKINS,	A	Corporal JOHN KELLEY,		I
" GEORGE DOWLEY,	B	Private ZERA BARNUM,		I
" HENRY F. GRIFFIN,	B	" PHILANDER B. CHADWICK,		K
" CONRAD HEINS,	B	" THOMAS MALONEY,		K
Corporal THOMAS H. HUGHES,	D	" ALBERT F. THOMPSON,		K
Private PETER COME,	D			

50TH MASSACHUSETTS.

	Company.		Company.
Corporal E. S. TUBBS,	G	Private JAMES MILLER,	G

53D MASSACHUSETTS.

	Company.		Company.
Private PETER T. DOWNS,	G	Private PETER DYER,	H

6TH MICHIGAN.

	Company.		Company.
Private ROBERT ATWOOD,	A	Private JACOB URWILER,	E
" JOHN R. COWLES,	A	" ALFRED E. DAY,	F
" JAMES E. ROOT,	A	" GEORGE W. SPARLING,	F
Sergeant LESTER FOX,	C	Sergeant GEORGE H. HARRIS,	G
" ALBERT B. CHAPMAN,[2]	C	Corporal PETER A. MARTIN,[2]	G
Corporal WILLIAM A. PORTER,	C	" FRANCIS M. HURD,	G
Private WALTER B. HUNTER,	C	Private GEORGE W. DAILEY,[2]	G
" JOSEPH W. ROLPH,	C	" FREEMAN HADDEN,[2]	G
Corporal CHARLES ST. JOHN,	D	" JOHN W. MCBRIDE,[2]	G
Private PETER DORR,	D	" ROBERT PAYNE,[2]	G
" HENRY PLUMMER,[1]	D	" CHARLES E. PLUMMER,[2]	G
" TOBIAS PORTER,[2]	D	" ENOCH T. SIMPSON,[2]	G
Sergeant FREDERICK BUCK,	E	" OSBORN SWEENEY,[2]	G
" WILLIAM L. LEINRIE,	E	" THEODORE WEED,[2]	G
Corporal HARRY S. HOWARD,	E	Sergeant A. C. WHITCOMB,[2]	H
" WILLIAM KELLY,[2]	E	Private HENRY B. DOW,[2]	H
" HENRY RHODES,	E	" GEORGE A. BENET,[2]	I
Private JOHN AUSTIN,	E	Corporal LEVI A. LOGAN,[2]	K
" DANIEL FERO,	E	" JOHN H. WISNER,[2]	K
" WILLIAM HOGUE,[2]	E	Private SIMON P. BOYCE,[2]	K
" JAMES R. JOHNSON,	E	" DAVID H. SERVIS,[2]	K
" AUGUSTUS JONES,	E	" FRANCIS E. TODD,[2]	K
" WILLIAM RAPSHER,	E		

[1] Not on the roll as printed in Official Records, vol. xxvi., part I., pp. 57-66.
[2] Not on Birge's duplicate roll.

8TH NEW HAMPSHIRE.

	Company.		Company.
Captain JOS. J. LADD,[2]	D	Private JOHN RINEY,[2]	B
Lieutenant DANA W. KING,	A	Sergeant JOHN FERGUSON,[1]	I

16TH NEW HAMPSHIRE.

	Company.		Company.
Captain JOHN L. RICE,[2]	H	Corporal CLINTON BOHANNON,	C
Lieutenant EDGAR E. ADAMS,	F	Private ASA BURGESS,	C
" EDWARD J. O'DONNELL,	C	Corporal WILLIAM A. RAND,	K
Corporal DANIEL C. DACEY,	A	Private RUFUS L. JONES,	K
Private EDWARD J. WILEY,	B		

75TH NEW YORK.

	Company.		Company.
Private EDSON V. R. BLAKEMAN,	B	Private MARTIN NORTON,	I
" LEVI COPPERNOLL,	B	" JONAS L. PALMER,[1]	I
" LENOX KENT,	B	" CHARLES WRIGHT,[1]	I
" ETHAN BENNETT,[1]	I		

90TH NEW YORK.

	Company.		Company.
Captain HONORÉ DE LA PATURELLE,		Private JAMES PROCTOR,[2]	F
	E	Corporal WILLIAM DALLY,[1]	G
Sergeant HENRY M. CRYDENWISE,	A	Private TIMOTHY QUIRK,[1]	G
Private NICHOLAS SCHMILAN,[1]	A	" —— SERRILER,[1]	G
" ALBERT BARNES,[1]	B	" CHRISTOPHER AUTENREITH,	K
" GEORGE ROBINSON,[1]	B	" JOHN HERON,	K
Corporal JOHN NEIL,	F	" AMOS MAKER,	K
Private JOHN MCCORMICK,	F	" NELSON ROOT,	K
" MARTIN MCNAMARA,	F		

91ST NEW YORK.

	Company.		Company.
Private SAMUEL WEBSTER,	A	Private EDWIN DE FRATE,	C
Sergeant JAMES A. SHATTUCK,	B	Corporal CHARLES E. BOWLES,	E
Private JAMES T. MCCOLLUM,[2]	B	Private JOS. C. WALLACE,	E
Sergeant EDWARD R. CONE,	C	Corporal CHARLES KEARNEY,[1]	K
Corporal PLATT F. VINCENT,	C		

114TH NEW YORK.[1]

	Company.		Company.
Sergeant WILLIAM H. CALKINS,	I	Private HERBERT CHISLIN,	G
Corporal NATHAN SAMPSON,	G	" WARREN H. HOWARD,	G
" C. L. WIDGER,	I	" WILLIAM POTTER,	G

[1] Not on the roll as printed in Official Records, vol. xxvi., part I., pp. 57-66.
[2] Not on Birge's duplicate roll.

116TH NEW YORK.

	Company.			Company.
Corporal Frank Bentley,	A		Private Theodore Hansell,	E
Private Isaac Colvin,	A		" Thomas Maloney,	E
" Andrew Cook,	A		" Henry C. Miller,	E
" Daniel Covensparrow,	A		" Frederick Webber,	E
" Philip Linebits,	A		Corporal Joshua D. Baker,	F
" Jacob Bergtold,[2]	B		Private Jacob Demerly,	F
" Sylvester Glass,[2]	B		" Frederick Jost,	G
Corporal George W. Hammond,[2]	C		" William Martin,	G
Private Henry D. Daniel,	C		" Samuel Whitmore,	G
" Charles Fisher,	C		" Henry Trarer,[1]	H
" Frederick Hilderbrand,	C		" Jacob Tschole,	H
" Christian Grawi,[2]	D		" Jacob Zumstein,	H
" William W. McCumber,[2]	D		" Philip Mary,	I
" Cornelius Fitzpatrick,	E		Corporal Albert D. Prescot,	K
" James Gallagher,	E		Private Nicholas Fedick,	K

128TH NEW YORK.

	Company.			Company.
Captain Francis S. Keese,	C		Private Edward Delamater,	C
Sergeant Theodore W. Krafft,	A		" Peter Dyer,[1]	C
" Freeman Skinner,	A		" Albert P. Felts,	C
Corporal Milo P. Moore,	A		" Charles Murch,	C
Private Jos. M. Downing,	A		" Daniel Neenan,	C
" John N. Hague,	A		" George A. Norcutt,	C
" Jared Harrison,[1]	A		" John R. Schriver,	C
" Jos. C. Mosher,	A		" John L. Delamater,	D
" James Mosherman,	A		" William Platto,	D
" Freeman Ostrander,	A		" Charles P. Wilson,	D
Sergeant Charles W. McKown,	C		Corporal Charles Brower,	F
" Henry A. Brundage,	C		Sergeant C. M. Davidson,[1]	H
" John H. Hagar,	C		Private John A. Wamsley,[1]	H
Corporal Clement R. Dean,	C		" Charles F. Appleby,	I
" David H. Haunaburgh,	C		" Stephen H. Moore,	I
" Elijah D. Morgan,	C		Corporal Sylvester Brewer	K
" George F. Simmons,	C		Private Thomas Rice,	K
Private Albert Cole,	C		" William Van Bak,[1]	K
" George Cronk,	C			

131ST NEW YORK.

	Company.			Company.
Lieutenant Eugene H. Fales,	C		Lieutenant James E. McBeth,	K
" Eugene A. Hinchman,	H		Private William Burris,	B
" James O'Connor,	F		" Charles Cameron,[2]	B
" Louis F. Ellis,	I		" Nicholas Hansler,[2]	B

[1] Not on the roll as printed in Official Records, vol. xxvi., part I., pp. 57-66.
[2] Not on Birge's duplicate roll.

	Company.			Company.
Private GEORGE E. STANFORD,	B		Private RICHARD M. EDWARDS,	C
Sergeant ROBERT W. REID,	C		" THEODORE KELLEY,	C
Corporal JONAS CHESHIRE,	C		" CHARLES W. WEEKS,	C
" EDWARD NORTHUP,	C		" JACOB HOHN,	I
" ISAAC OGDEN,	C		" FERDINAND NESCH,	I
Private HENRY AYRES,	C			

133D NEW YORK.

	Company.			Company.
Captain JAMES K. FULLER,[2]	C		Private CYRUS TOOKER,	F
Lieutenant RICHARD W. BUTTLE,	D		Sergeant GEORGE GIEHL,	G
" HENRY O'CONNOR,	I		Private JOSEPH J. BURKE,	G
Private NICOLAS PITT,	B		" GEORGE SCHLEIFER,	G
" NELSON BEANE,	C		" JAMES BRENNAN,	I
" PATRICK BOYNE,	C		" JOHN H. DAWSON,	I
" JOSEPH FINN,	C		" JOHN H. GALE,	I
" PETER HUDSON,	C		Sergeant GEORGE HAMEL,	K
" JAMES G. KELLY,	C		Corporal WILLIAM STRATTON,[2]	K
Corporal JOHN EISEMANN,	D		Private PATRICK COSTELLO,	K
Private JOHN NEWMAN,[1]	D		" HENRY HODINGER,	K
" JOHN A. SHEPARD,[1]	D		" PHILIP READY,	K
" PATRICK CALLANAN,	E			

156TH NEW YORK.

	Company.			Company.
Private INNUS A. GRAVES,[1]	B		Private J. R. SLATER,[1]	C
" THOMAS HORTON,[1]	B		" JOHN STRIVINGER,[1]	C
" HENRY JONES,[1]	B		" WILLIAM THADDUCK,[1]	C
" PHILIP LEWIS,	B		Corporal RICHARD ELLMANDORPH,[1]	D
" BENJAMIN ROBERSON,[1]	B		" ARCHIBALD TERWILLIGER,[1]	E
" SIMON WASHBURN,[1]	B			
Sergeant C. G. EARLE,[1]	C		Sergeant JOHN D. FINK,	F
" DANIEL B. DEGS,[1]	C		" HIRAM S. BARROWS,[1]	F
" CLEMENT Y. CARLE,[1]	C		Corporal GEORGE BRADSHAW,[1]	F
Corporal J. B. BARLISON,[1]	C		Private JAMES R. LANE,[1]	F
Private STEPHEN R. ACKER,[1]	C		" EDWARD LITER,[1]	F
" MATHEW DIETS,[2]	C		" MICHAEL MCGORM,[1]	F
" STEPHEN ERNHOUT,[1]	C		" CHARLES L. MEGUIRE,[1]	F
" JOHN HERRINGER,[1]	C		Lieutenant EDWARD OLRENSHAW,[1]	H
" A. JARVIS HATER,[1]	C		Private JOHN MARVELL,[1]	H
" ABRAHAM KEYSER,[1]	C		Captain ORVILLE D. JEWETT,[1]	I
" ALEXANDER LOWN,[1]	C		Lieutenant JAMES J. RANDALL,[1]	I
" F. L. SCAMPMOUSE,[2]	C		" CHARLES W. KENNEDY,[1]	I
" A. C. SCHRIVER,[1]	C		Sergeant EDWARD STEERS,[1]	I
" W. SHADDUCK,[1]	C		" WILLIAM S. COSTILYOU,[1]	I
" A. G. SLATER,[1]	C			

[1] Not on the roll as printed in Official Records, vol. xxvi., part I., pp. 57-66.
[2] Not on Birge's duplicate roll.

	Company.		Company.
Sergeant THOMAS F. DONNELLY,[1]	I	Private CHARLES GAY	K
" THOMAS SAUNDERS,[1]	I	" AUGUST LEONARD,	K
Private JAMES BROUGHAM,[1]	I	" NEIL NEILSON,	K
" WELKIN MOOREHOUSE,[1]	I	" SAMUEL OUTERKIRK,	K
" JOHN PROVOST,[1]	I	" CHARLES PODRICK,[1]	K
" JAMES WATSON,[1]	I	" SVEN SVENSON,[1]	K
Sergeant CHARLES B. WESTON,	K	" CHARLES STUMP,	K
" HENRY ABBOTT,[2]	K	" AUGUSTUS SWENSON,[1]	K
Corporal IVAN NETTERBERG,	K	" JOSEPH VON MATT,	K
" ISAAC W. FULLAGER,	K	" THEODORE WEBSTER,[1]	K
Private SIMEON FRITTER,[1]	K	" ALEXANDER WEHL,[1]	K

159TH NEW YORK.

	Company.		Company.
Captain ROBERT McD. HART,	F	Private JOHN THORP,	E
Lieutenant ALFRED GREENLEAF, Jr.,	B	Sergeant GILBERT S. GULLEN,	F
" DUNCAN RICHMOND,	H	Private BARTHOLOMEW TOSER,	F
Private AMOS HARK,	B	Corporal E. HOLLENBACK,[1]	H
" GEORGE W. HATFIELD,	B	Private H. McILRAVY,[1]	H
" HUGH McKENNY,	B	" D. C. McNEIL,[1]	H
" JOHN TAYLOR,	B	" JAMES BRAZIER, 2d,	I
Sergeant MICHAEL HOGAN,	C	" GEORGE W. SCHOFIELD,	I
Private CHRISTIAN SCHNACK,	C	Sergeant THOMAS BERGEN,[1]	K
Sergeant JAMES T. PERKINS,	E		

160TH NEW YORK.

	Company.		Company.
Lieutenant-Colonel JOHN B. VAN PETTEN,		Sergeant J. SAHVEY,[1]	E
		Private MICHAEL HILL,	E
Assistant Surgeon DAVID H. ARMSTRONG.		" JOHN LONG,	E
		" JOHN O'LAHEY,[2]	E
Lieutenant WILLIAM J. VANDEUSEN,	A	Sergeant B. F. MAXSON,	G
		" ELON SPINK,	G
Lieutenant ROBERT R. SEELEY,	I	" SAMUEL KRIEGELSTEIN,	G
Private OSCAR CURTIS,[2]	B	" JACOB McDOWELL,	K
" A. A. HAMMER,	C	" MICHAEL HEWITT,[1]	K
" JOSEPH S. INSLEY,[2]	C	Private ARTHUR CLARKSON,	K
" HENRY F. McINTYRE,	C	" LEWIS KRAHER,	K
" GEORGE MATTHIES,	C	" JOHN RAINCE,	K

161ST NEW YORK.

	Company.		Company.
Major CHARLES STRAWN.[2]		Captain BENJAMIN T. VAN TUYL,	A
Lieutenant WILLIAM B. KINSEY (Adjutant).		Sergeant GEORGE E. ROSENKRANS,[1]	A
		Corporal CLARK EVANS,	A

[1] Not on the roll as printed in Official Records, vol. xxvi., part I., pp. 57-66.
[2] Not on Birge's duplicate roll.

	Company.			Company.
Private WILLIAM JOLLEY,	A	Private LUMAN PHILLEY,		D
" CORNELIUS OSTERHOUT,	A	" THOMAS A. SAWYER,		D
" JAMES ANDERSON,	B	" JOHN VAN DOUSEN,		D
Sergeant LEWIS E. FITCH,	C	" MADISON M. COLLIER,		E
Corporal MAHLON M. MURCUR,	C	Sergeant BASKIN FREEMAN,		F
Private EDGAR L. DEWITT,	C	Private CHARLES ROBINSON,		F
" HENRY W. MEAD,	C	Sergeant DE WITT C. AMEY,		H
" GEORGE OLIVER,	C	Corporal SAMUEL ROBINSON,		H
" CHARLES SPAULDING,	C	Private JOHN F. YOUNG,		H
Sergeant DENNIS LACY,	D	" JOHN REAS,[1]		I
" BRADFORD SANFORD,	D	Sergeant SILAS E. WARREN,		K
Private JAMES E. BORDEN,	D	Private CHARLES A. HERRICK,		K

162D NEW YORK.

	Company.			Company.
Captain WILLIAM P. HUXFORD,	G	Private PATRICK GINETY,		E
Lieutenant JOHN H. VAN WYCK,	G	" DANIEL GRAY,		E
" WILLIAM KENNEDY,	E	" LAWRENCE HALLEY,		E
" R. W. LEONARD		" GEORGE LARMORE,		E
(Adjutant).[1]		" JAMES MCCALL,		E
Sergeant JOHN MCCORMICK,	A	" MATHEW MULLEN,[1]		E
" THOMAS BARRY,[2]	A	" THOMAS PERRY,[1]		E
" JOHN E. BURKE,	B	" PATRICK SWEENY,		E
" HENRY LANDT,	C	Corporal GUSTAVE NORMANN,		F
" FREDERICK SHELLHASS,	C	Private JOHN G. THALMANN,		F
Private ANTON BLEISTEIN,	C	Sergeant GEORGE W. GIBSON,		G
" WILLIAM F. EISELE,	C	" EDMUND NOURSE,		G
" JOHN ENGEL,	C	Private WILLIAM FERGUSON,		G
" ALEX. HERRMAN,	C	" WILLIAM KEATING,		G
" LEO KALT,	C	Corporal EDWARD MURPHY,		I
" CONRAD SIEGLE,	C	" JOSEPH MARTINES,		I
Sergeant THEODORE CHURCHILL,	D	" MAXAMILLIAN MILLER,		I
" WILLIAM KELLEY,[1]	D	" DAVID HART,[1]		I
Corporal THOMAS MCCONNELL,	D	" GEORGE WELCH,[1]		I
Sergeant JAMES STACK,	E	Private JAMES BRADY,		K
" GEORGE W. KEILEY,	E	" PETER CHERRY,		K
Corporal JOHN MCLAUGHLIN,	E	" EUGENE DETRICH,		K
" GEORGE W. WAITE,	E	" JOHN FRAZER,		K
" JAMES BALL,	E	" JOS. GITEY,		K
" LORENZO SULLY,[1]	E	" FLEMING KNIPE,		K
Private THOMAS CLAREY,	E	" DOMINICK MCCONNELL,[1]		K
" PETER CORBETT,	E	" JOHN MCDONALD,		K
" THOMAS DUFF,	E	" LEWIS YOUNG,		K
" DANIEL W. DUNN,	E			

[1] Not on the roll as printed in Official Records, vol. xxvi., part I., pp. 57-66.
[2] Not on Birge's duplicate roll.

165TH NEW YORK.

	Company.			Company.
Captain Felix Agnus,	A	Private John H. Valk,		A
" Henry C. Inwood,	E	" Edward Vass,		A
Lieutenant Gustavus F. Linguist,	C	Drummer Michael Donohue,[1]		A
Sergeant Walter T. Hall,	A	Private Elisha E. Dennison,[1]		B
" William T. Sinclair,	A	" Patrick H. Matthews,		B
" John Fleming,	A	" John Cassidy,		C
" John W. Dickins,	A	" Robert Hobbey,		C
Corporal Richard Baker,	A	" Laurentz Lange,		C
" Josiah C. Dixon,	A	" John Laughtman,		C
" George E. Armstrong,	A	Corporal James F. Campbell,		D
Private James E. Barker,	A	Private Eugene Deflandre,[1]		D
" Peter Beaucamp,	A	" Henry Edward,[1]		D
" Samuel Davis,	A	" Henry R. Loomis,[1]		D
" Gustav Druckhammer,	A	" Thomas Belcher,		E
" Thomas Kerney,[1]	A	" John Feighery,		E
" David Lewis,	A	" Stephen Gillen,		E
" George McKinney,	A	" Edwin A. Shaw,		E
" George A. Metzel,	A	" William Vero,		E
" Elias H. Tucker,	A			

173D NEW YORK.

Private Alexander Hendrickson, Company C.

174TH NEW YORK.

	Company.			Company.
Lieutenant Edward Marrener,	I	Private Thomas Williams,		E
" Latham A. Fish,	E	" Thomas Fletcher,		G
" Eugene E. Ennson,	C	" Henry D. Lasher,		G
" Charles Emerson,[2]	I	" Charles N. Thompson,		G
Sergeant Samuel Wilson,[1]	A	Sergeant Charles Gardner,		H
" Morris Lancaster,	A	Private Thomas Carroll,		H
Corporal Louis Hageman,	A	" William Johnson,		H
Private William Cooper,	A	" Henry Jones,		H
" John Cullen,	A	" Cornelius Mohoney,		H
" John Maloney,	A	" Joseph Messmer,		I
Corporal George Anderson,	B	" Henry Pooler,		I
Sergeant John Gray,	C	" Richard Schottler,		I
Private John Kuhfuss,	C	Sergeant Charles Draner,		K
" Gustavus Heller,[1]	C	Private Frederick Bandka,		K
" George W. Jones,[1]	C	" William Heinrichs,		K
" William McElroy,[1]	C	" Edward Kuhlman,		K
" Ernst Schmidt,	C	" Julius Ladiges,		K
Sergeant John Kenney,	E	" Frederick Nilsen,		K
Corporal Joseph H. Murphy,	E			

[1] *Not on the roll as printed in Official Records, vol. xxvi., part I., pp. 57-66.*
[2] *Not on Birge's duplicate roll.*

175TH NEW YORK.

	Company.		Company.
Lieutenant Seigmund Sternberg,	I	Private Patrick Manering,	D
Sergeant Major Abraham Loeb,		Sergeant William O'Callaghan,	E
Private Frank Markham,	A	" James Hillis,[2]	E
Corporal Timothy Allen,	B	" James H. Callor,[1]	E
Private Otto Dornback,	C	Private John O'Conner,	E
" Richard O'Gorham,	C	Corporal Philip Daub,[2]	K

177TH NEW YORK.

	Company.		Company.
Sergeant John D. Brooks,	A	Private Eben Halley,	B
Corporal Percy B. S. Cole,	A	" David N. Kirk,	B
Private Seymour D. Carpenter,	A	" Charles M. Smith,	B
" John J. Gallup,	A	" Samuel H. Stevens, Jr.,	B
" Thomas J. Garvey,	A	" John Gorman,	C
" William Hemstreet,	A	" Moses De Coster,	D
" John Housen,	A	" Charles W. Lape,	E
" Barney Lavary,	A	Corporal Alonzo G. Ludden,	G
" Richard C. Main,	A	Private S. W. Meisden,[2]	G
" Adam Milliman,	A	" Elias Nashold,	G
" Henry von Lehman,	A	" Jeddiah Tompkins,	G
" Willard Loundsbery,[1]	A	" Russell W. Cooneys,	H
Corporal George A. McCormick,	B	" George Merinus,	I

8TH VERMONT.

Captain John L. Barstow,[1,2] Acting Assistant Adjutant-General.

	Company.		Company.
Private John Adams,[1]	C	Sergeant Byron J. Hurlburt,	F
" James K. Bennett,	C	Corporal Edward Saltus,[2]	F
" Francis C. Cushman,[1]	C	Private George N. Faneuf,	F
" T. E. Harriman,[1]	C	" David Larock, Jr.,	F
" Frank Lamarsh,[1]	C	" Abner Niles,	F
" Jovite Pinard,[1]	C	Corporal Abner N. Flint,	G
Sergeant George G. Hutchins,[1]	E	Private Seymour N. Coles,	G
Corporal N. H. Hibbard,[1]	E	" Lyman P. Luce,	G
" Benjamin F. Bowman,[1]	E	" Andrew B. Morgan,	H
Private Thomas F. Ferrin,[1]	E	" Patrick Bolan,	I
" Thomas Holland,[1]	E	" D. Martin,[1]	I

2D U. S ARTILLERY.

Private J. D. Hickley,[1] Company C.

[1] Not on the roll as printed in Official Records, vol. xxvi., part I., pp. 57–66.
[2] Not on Birge's duplicate roll.

4TH WISCONSIN.

	Company.		Company.
Lieutenant ISAAC N. EARL,	C	Private PATRICK PIGEON,[1]	A
Corporal L. C. BARTLETT,	C		

NOTE.—On the 28th of June, 1863, Birge reported to Headquarters, 2 battalions of stormers, of 8 companies each, present for duty—67 officers, 826 men, total 893. His duplicate roll, evidently of later date than June 28th and not later than July 7th, accounts for 10 companies with 71 officers and 865 men, total 936. The list here printed gives 1,230 names, probably representing 1,228 persons.

ARTICLES OF CAPITULATION[2]

Proposed between the commissioners on the part of the garrison of Port Hudson, La., and the forces of the United States before said place, July 8, 1863.

ARTICLE I. Maj.-Gen. F. Gardner surrenders to the United States forces under Major-General Banks the place of Port Hudson and its dependencies, with its garrison, armament, munitions, public funds, and material of war, in the condition, as nearly as may be, in which they were at the hour of cessation of hostilities, viz., 6 A.M., July 8, 1863.

ART. II. The surrender stipulated in Article I. is qualified by no condition, save that the officers and enlisted men composing the garrison shall receive the treatment due to prisoners of war, according to the usages of civilized warfare.

ART. III. All private property of officers and enlisted men shall be respected and left to their respective owners.

ART. IV. The position of Port Hudson shall be occupied to-morrow at 7 A.M. by the forces of the United States, and its garrison received as prisoners of war by such general officer of the United States service as may be designated by Major-General Banks, with the ordinary formalities of rendition. The Confederate troops will be drawn up in line, officers in their positions, the right of the line resting on the edge of the prairie south of the railroad depot, the left extending in the direction of the village of Port Hudson. The arms and colors will be piled conveniently, and will be received by the officers of the United States.

ART. V. The sick and wounded of the garrison will be cared for by the authorities of the United States, assisted, if desired by either party, by the medical officers of the garrison.

---

[1] *Not on Birge's duplicate roll.*
[2] *See ante p. 231 and Official Records, vol. xxvi., part I., pp. 52-54.*

NOTE ON EARLY'S STRENGTH.

BY BREVET BRIGADIER-GENERAL E. C. DAWES, U.S.V.

The return of the Army of Northern Virginia for October 31, 1864, gives the "present for duty" in the Second Army Corps commanded by General Early, in the infantry divisions of Ramseur (Early's old division), Rodes, Gordon, Wharton, Kershaw, and the artillery as.................... 12,516
The cavalry division of General Lomax, by its return of September
    10th, numbered for duty....................................... 3,605
The cavalry brigade of General Rosser [1] about.................... 1,300
The cavalry division of General Fitz Lee [2]....................... 1,600
The casualties of the army at Cedar Creek were 3,100
Total force engaged at battle of Cedar Creek...................... 22,121

Lomax's division probably lost 500 men in the different actions prior to Cedar Creek after its return of September 10th. To offset this no account is made of the "Valley Reserves" (men over and boys under conscript age) and "detailed men" (those subject to conscription who were permitted to remain at home to do necessary work), who joined the army after its defeat at Fisher's Hill. General Lee wrote General Early 27th September: "All the reserves in the Valley have been ordered to you." That the order was obeyed appears from the following extracts, from the diary of Mr. J. A. Waddell of Staunton, Virginia, printed in the "Annals of Augusta County, Va.," page 325 *et seq.*

"Saturday, September 24 [1864] : A dispatch from General Early this morning assured the people of Staunton that they were in no danger, that his army was safe and receiving reinforcements. He however ordered the detailed men to be called out. . . . October 15 : Nothing talked of except the recent order calling into service the detailed men. . . . The recent order takes millers from their grinding, but men sent from the army undertake in some cases to run the machinery. Farmers are ordered from their fields and barns and soldiers are detailed to thresh the wheat. All men engaged in making horseshoes are ordered off so that our cavalry and artillery horses will have to go barefooted."

The return of the Army of Northern Virginia for 30th November, 1864, confirms the figures given above. It shows "present for duty" in the infantry

---

[1] *Rosser's brigade belonged to Hampton's old division. This division, with Rosser's brigade, numbered for duty September 10, 1864, 2.942. On October 31st, without Rosser's brigade, 1,547. It is fair to assume the difference as Rosser's strength.*

[2] *Fitz Lee's division on return of August 31st numbered for duty 1,683; on 30th November, 1,524.*

division of Ramseur, Rodes, Gordon, Wharton, and Kershaw, and the Second Corps artillery.. 15,070
In the cavalry divisions of Fitz Lee and Lomax (2 brigades, Payne's and Rosser's, not reporting) 3,625
Add for Rosser's and Payne's brigades............................ 2,000
Total of Gen. Early's army, November 30th........................ 20,695

Kershaw had returned to Richmond, but the above figures include the organizations present at Cedar Creek.

CINCINNATI, August 24, 1890.

ALSO FROM LEONAUR
AVAILABLE IN SOFTCOVER OR HARDCOVER WITH DUST JACKET

CAMP-FIRE AND COTTON-FIELD by *Thomas W. Knox*—A New York Herald Correspondent's View of the American Civil War.

SERGEANT STILLWELL by *Leander Stillwell*—The Experiences of a Union Army Soldier of the 61st Illinois Infantry During the American Civil War.

STONEWALL'S CANNONEER by *Edward A. Moore*—Experiences with the Rockbridge Artillery, Confederate Army of Northern Virginia, During the American Civil War.

CONFEDERATE BLOCKADE RUNNER by *John Wilkinson*—The Personal Recollections of an Officer of the Confederate Navy.

THE SIXTH CORPS by *George Stevens*—The Army of the Potomac, Union Army, During the American Civil War.

THE RAILROAD RAIDERS by *William Pittenger*—An Ohio Volunteers Recollections of the Andrews Raid to Disrupt the Confederate Railroad in Georgia During the American Civil War.

CITIZEN SOLDIER by *John Beatty*—An Account of the American Civil War by a Union Infantry Officer of Ohio Volunteers Who Became a Brigadier General.

COX: PERSONAL RECOLLECTIONS OF THE CIVIL WAR--VOLUME 1 by *Jacob Dolson Cox*—West Virginia, Kanawha Valley, Gauley Bridge, Cotton Mountain, South Mountain, Antietam, the Morgan Raid & the East Tennessee Campaign.

COX: PERSONAL RECOLLECTIONS OF THE CIVIL WAR--VOLUME 2 by *Jacob Dolson Cox*—Siege of Knoxville, East Tennessee, Atlanta Campaign, the Nashville Campaign & the North Carolina Campaign.

THE RELUCTANT REBEL by *William G. Stevenson*—A young Kentuckian's experiences in the Confederate Infantry & Cavalry during the American Civil War.

KERSHAW'S BRIGADE VOLUME 1 by *D. Augustus Dickert*—Manassas, Seven Pines, Sharpsburg (Antietam), Fredricksburg, Chancellorsville, Gettysburg, Chickamauga, Chattanooga, Fort Sanders & Bean Station.

KERSHAW'S BRIGADE VOLUME 2 by *D. Augustus Dickert*—At the wilderness, Cold Harbour, Petersburg, The Shenandoah Valley and Cedar Creek.

HISTORY OF THE CAVALRY OF THE ARMY OF THE POTOMAC by *Charles D. Rhodes*—Including Pope's Army of Virginia and the Cavalry Operations in West Virginia During the American Civil War.

AVAILABLE ONLINE AT
www.leonaur.com
AND OTHER GOOD BOOK STORES

ALSO FROM LEONAUR
AVAILABLE IN SOFTCOVER OR HARDCOVER WITH DUST JACKET

CAPTAIN OF THE 95th (Rifles) *by Jonathan Leach*—An officer of Wellington's Sharpshooters during the Peninsular, South of France and Waterloo Campaigns of the Napoleonic Wars.

BUGLER AND OFFICER OF THE RIFLES *by William Green & Harry Smith* With the 95th (Rifles) during the Peninsular & Waterloo Campaigns of the Napoleonic Wars

BAYONETS, BUGLES AND BONNETS *by James 'Thomas' Todd*—Experiences of hard soldiering with the 71st Foot - the Highland Light Infantry - through many battles of the Napoleonic wars including the Peninsular & Waterloo Campaigns

THE ADVENTURES OF A LIGHT DRAGOON *by George Farmer & G.R. Gleig*—A cavalryman during the Peninsular & Waterloo Campaigns, in captivity & at the siege of Bhurtpore, India

THE COMPLEAT RIFLEMAN HARRIS *by Benjamin Harris as told to & transcribed by Captain Henry Curling*—The adventures of a soldier of the 95th (Rifles) during the Peninsular Campaign of the Napoleonic Wars

WITH WELLINGTON'S LIGHT CAVALRY *by William Tomkinson*—The Experiences of an officer of the 16th Light Dragoons in the Peninsular and Waterloo campaigns of the Napoleonic Wars.

SURTEES OF THE RIFLES *by William Surtees*—A Soldier of the 95th (Rifles) in the Peninsular campaign of the Napoleonic Wars.

ENSIGN BELL IN THE PENINSULAR WAR *by George Bell*—The Experiences of a young British Soldier of the 34th Regiment 'The Cumberland Gentlemen' in the Napoleonic wars.

WITH THE LIGHT DIVISION *by John H. Cooke*—The Experiences of an Officer of the 43rd Light Infantry in the Peninsula and South of France During the Napoleonic Wars

NAPOLEON'S IMPERIAL GUARD: FROM MARENGO TO WATERLOO *by J. T. Headley*—This is the story of Napoleon's Imperial Guard from the bearskin caps of the grenadiers to the flamboyance of their mounted chasseurs, their principal characters and the men who commanded them.

BATTLES & SIEGES OF THE PENINSULAR WAR *by W. H. Fitchett*—Corunna, Busaco, Albuera, Ciudad Rodrigo, Badajos, Salamanca, San Sebastian & Others

AVAILABLE ONLINE AT **www.leonaur.com**
AND OTHER GOOD BOOK STORES

ALSO FROM LEONAUR
AVAILABLE IN SOFTCOVER OR HARDCOVER WITH DUST JACKET

WELLINGTON AND THE PYRENEES CAMPAIGN VOLUME I: FROM VITORIA TO THE BIDASSOA by *F. C. Beatson*—The final phase of the campaign in the Iberian Peninsula.

WELLINGTON AND THE INVASION OF FRANCE VOLUME II: THE BIDASSOA TO THE BATTLE OF THE NIVELLE by *F. C. Beatson*—The second of Beatson's series on the fall of Revolutionary France published by Leonaur, the reader is once again taken into the centre of Wellington's strategic and tactical genius.

WELLINGTON AND THE FALL OF FRANCE VOLUME III: THE GAVES AND THE BATTLE OF ORTHEZ by *F. C. Beatson*—This final chapter of F. C. Beatson's brilliant trilogy shows the 'captain of the age' at his most inspired and makes all three books essential additions to any Peninsular War library.

NAVAL BATTLES OF THE NAPOLEONIC WARS by *W. H. Fitchett*—Cape St.Vincent, the Nile, Cadiz, Copenhagen, Trafalgar & Others

SERGEANT GUILLEMARD: THE MAN WHO SHOT NELSON? by *Robert Guillemard*—A Soldier of the Infantry of the French Army of Napoleon on Campaign Throughout Europe

WITH THE GUARDS ACROSS THE PYRENEES by *Robert Batty*—The Experiences of a British Officer of Wellington's Army During the Battles for the Fall of Napoleonic France, 1813.

A STAFF OFFICER IN THE PENINSULA by *E. W. Buckham*—An Officer of the British Staff Corps Cavalry During the Peninsula Campaign of the Napoleonic Wars

THE LEIPZIG CAMPAIGN: 1813—NAPOLEON AND THE "BATTLE OF THE NATIONS" by *F. N. Maude*—Colonel Maude's analysis of Napoleon's campaign of 1813.

BUGEAUD: A PACK WITH A BATON by *Thomas Robert Bugeaud*—The Early Campaigns of a Soldier of Napoleon's Army Who Would Become a Marshal of France.

TWO LEONAUR ORIGINALS

SERGEANT NICOL by *Daniel Nicol*—The Experiences of a Gordon Highlander During the Napoleonic Wars in Egypt, the Peninsula and France.

WATERLOO RECOLLECTIONS by *Frederick Llewellyn*—Rare First Hand Accounts, Letters, Reports and Retellings from the Campaign of 1815.

AVAILABLE ONLINE AT **www.leonaur.com**
AND OTHER GOOD BOOK STORES

ALSO FROM LEONAUR
AVAILABLE IN SOFTCOVER OR HARDCOVER WITH DUST JACKET

DOING OUR 'BIT' *by Ian Hay*—Two Classic Accounts of the Men of Kitchener's 'New Army' During the Great War including *The First 100,000* & *All In It*.

AN EYE IN THE STORM by *Arthur Ruhl*—An American War Correspondent's Experiences of the First World War from the Western Front to Gallipoli and Beyond.

STAND & FALL by *Joe Cassells*—A Soldier's Recollections of the 'Contemptible Little Army' and the Retreat from Mons to the Marne, 1914.

RIFLEMAN MACGILL'S WAR by *Patrick MacGill*—A Soldier of the London Irish During the Great War in Europe including *The Amateur Army, The Red Horizon* & *The Great Push*.

WITH THE GUNS by *C. A. Rose & Hugh Dalton*—Two First Hand Accounts of British Gunners at War in Europe During World War 1- Three Years in France with the Guns and With the British Guns in Italy.

EAGLES OVER THE TRENCHES by *James R. McConnell & William B. Perry*—Two First Hand Accounts of the American Escadrille at War in the Air During World War 1-Flying For France: With the American Escadrille at Verdun and Our Pilots in the Air.

THE BUSH WAR DOCTOR by *Robert V. Dolbey*—The Experiences of a British Army Doctor During the East African Campaign of the First World War.

THE 9TH—THE KING'S (LIVERPOOL REGIMENT) IN THE GREAT WAR 1914 - 1918 by *Enos H. G. Roberts*—Like many large cities, Liverpool raised a number of battalions in the Great War. Notable among them were the Pals, the Liverpool Irish and Scottish, but this book concerns the wartime history of the 9th Battalion – The Kings.

THE GAMBARDIER by *Mark Severn*—The experiences of a battery of Heavy artillery on the Western Front during the First World War.

FROM MESSINES TO THIRD YPRES by *Thomas Floyd*—A personal account of the First World War on the Western front by a 2/5th Lancashire Fusilier.

THE IRISH GUARDS IN THE GREAT WAR - VOLUME 1 by *Rudyard Kipling*—Edited and Compiled from Their Diaries and Papers Volume 1 The First Battalion.

THE IRISH GUARDS IN THE GREAT WAR - VOLUME 2 by *Rudyard Kipling*—Edited and Compiled from Their Diaries and Papers Volume 2 The Second Battalion.

AVAILABLE ONLINE AT **www.leonaur.com**
AND OTHER GOOD BOOK STORES

www.ingramcontent.com/pod-product-compliance
Lightning Source LLC
Chambersburg PA
CBHW021956160426
43197CB00007B/147